Eren Yıldırım Yetkin
Violence and Genocide in Kurdish Memory

In memory of my parents
Yıldız and Eşref

Qualitative Case Studies and Analyses of
Social Processes
Research on Biographies, Interactions
and Social Worlds

Volume 24

Edited by

Karin Bock
Jörg Dinkelaker
Werner Fiedler
Jörg Frommer
Werner Helsper
Rolf-Torsten Kramer
Heinz-Hermann Krüger
Heike Ohlbrecht
Anna Schnitzer
Fritz Schütze
Sandra Tiefel

Eren Yıldırım Yetkin

Violence and Genocide in Kurdish Memory

Exploring the Remembrance
of the Armenian Genocide
through Life Stories

Verlag Barbara Budrich
Opladen • Berlin • Toronto 2022

This book is based on the doctoral dissertation "Social and Individual Awareness Contexts of the Armenian Genocide in Eastern Anatolia as an Aspect of Collective Memory", submitted to the Faculty of Social Sciences, Institute of Sociology, of the Goethe University Frankfurt in 2020. The publication is financially supported by the Hans Boeckler Foundation.

Hans **Böckler** **Stiftung** ▬▬

Mitbestimmung · Forschung · Stipendien

A CIP catalogue record for this book is available from
Die Deutsche Bibliothek (The German Library)

© 2022   by Verlag Barbara Budrich GmbH, Opladen, Berlin & Toronto
www.budrich.eu

      ISBN   978-3-8474-2584-7 (Paperback)
      eISBN   978-3-8474-1742-2 (PDF)
      DOI   10.3224/84742584

Die Deutsche Bibliothek – CIP-Einheitsaufnahme
Ein Titeldatensatz für die Publikation ist bei der Deutschen Bibliothek erhältlich.

Verlag Barbara Budrich GmbH
Stauffenbergstr. 7. D-51379 Leverkusen Opladen, Germany

86 Delma Drive. Toronto, ON M8W 4P6 Canada
www.budrich.eu

Jacket illustration by Bettina Lehfeldt, Kleinmachnow, Germany – www.lehfeldtgraphic.de
Typesetting by Linda Kutzki, Berlin, Germany – www.textsalz.de

Contents

Glossary 7

Notes on Translations, Names, and Citations 9

Acknowledgement 11

1 Introduction 14

2 Research Design 26

3 Studying Memory. Approaches, Concepts, and Complexities 43

4 Armenian Genocide and the Story of Van 63

5 The Conflict of Recognition and Denial 100

6 Life Stories. Reconstructing Biographical Experiences
   and Memories 152

7 Violence and Genocide in Memory. A Comparative Discussion 220

8 Conclusion 267

References 271

Index 293

List of Illustrations

Figure 1: The exhibition Nar Niyetiyle 112

Figure 2: The exhibition hall hosting Bizzat Hallediniz 117

Figure 3: Exhibits from "Left Behind" 121

Figure 4: The city of Van from Mount Erek 126

Figure 5: The memorial monument of Zeve 128

Figure 6: A forsaken and ruined building in the city centre of Van 130

Glossary

Aga/Agha/Axa: The landowner in the Turkish as well as Kurdish countryside, who organise croppers for his fields. In the narratives, *aga* indicates a certain power relation (in the periphery).

Armenian Revolutionary Federation (ARF) or Dashnaktsutyun (in short, Dashnak): Founded in 1890, the ARF has been one of the first Armenian political parties. The party is still active in Armenia and the diaspora communities.

CUP (Committee of Union and Progress)/ITC (Ittihat ve Terakki Cemiyeti): Founded in 1889 by the contemporary Ottomanist and nationalist elites as a secret society, over the course of crises it evolved into a political party. After the revolution in 1908, the party came to power. The 1913 *coup d'etat* consolidated its power. Under the triumvirate of Enver Pasha, Talaat Pasha, and Cemal Pasha, the country was led to war and the deportations of Armenians and Assyrians, and extermination campaigns took place all over the country.

Devlet Güvenlik Mahmeleri (DGM)/State Security Courts: The State Security Courts were established by the junta government of 1980 coup in the early 1980s. Composed of two civilian judges and one military judge, these courts had jurisdiction over crimes against Turkey's territorial integrity and national unity. In 2004, they were finally abolished following a number of judgments of the European Court of Human Rights that found the presence of military judges in the trials against civilians to be a violation of the right to a fair trial under the European Convention on Human Rights.

Islamised Armenians: One of the key elements of the Armenian Genocide was the enforced marriage, adoption, and assimilation of the surviving Armenian children and women. This mechanism of political violence resulted in an unknown number of converted Armenians. The term "Islamised Armenian(s)" connotes the group setting of the action and its enforcement. It also implies the powerholder perspective, i.e. Islamisation as a step in the process of assimilating the remaining Armenian population and thus changing the figures.

Kaymakam/Kaimakam: The governor – civil servant – who is assigned by the central government for a district; district governor.

Mala/Mele/Molla: The patriarch and religious authority in a particular town or village.

Sancak/Sandjak: A district in the Ottoman administrative system.

Sequence: A paragraph of the oral account in text form, a part of a story segment.

Segment or *Story Segment*: A segment determines a certain story with a start and an end in the narration. It can subsume more than one sequence.

Sur/Suriçi: Historical downtown and central district of the city of Diyarbakır/ Diyarbekir/Amed, surrounded and fortified by the ancient city walls.

Susurluk accident: A seemingly simple car crash that took place on 3 November 1996 in the small town of Susurluk revealed the relations between the state apparatus, politicians, and far-right paramilitaries in Turkey. Three people were killed in the crash: secret service agent and far-right paramilitary Abdullah Çatlı, a senior police officer, and Çatlı's girlfriend. The only survivor of the accident was an MP from Siverek.

Vanetsi: A native or citizen of Van who was Armenian.

Vilayet: A province in Ottoman administrative system; involving several districts or sandjaks.

Notes on Translations, Names, and Citations

For this study, I considered literature in three languages: English, German, and Turkish. Furthermore, the biographical narrative interviews I conducted in Turkish make an essential proportion of the data this study reflects. In order to reduce the number of translations, in the early periods, I have decided to compose this work in English. For the genocide and memory studies have aroused in the tradition of British and US-American schools. It was a pragmatic decision. This choice, of course, led me to further challenges. For instance, I needed to practise the tricks of the trade in writing an English manuscript or translating the interviews – at least the ones for the case studies. As you can imagine having an experiential writing background in German for more than a decade was not an advantage. All interview translations are my own. Some of the literature I cited needed translation as well. I marked these with [translated by E. Y.]; in repetitive citations of such works I avoided repetitive markings about the translation.

Personal names of my interview partners (and the names that they mention in our recorded talk, for instance, their friends) were pseudonymised, as described in Chapter 1.2 Research Ethics. Instead of using codes, such as *V1* for an informant from Van, I renamed them like Azim or Merve so that reading the study would not be exhausting. Names of institutions and most of the town names were anonymised as well; in this case, I coded them. When I could be sure that the place name would not cause any harm, for instance because of its metropolitan size, like Istanbul or Van, I left these untouched. The same applies to the Diyarbakır district of Sur because of its size and the special present and past conditions.

In case of interview transcriptions, I have cited the given sequences and lines as follows: *sequence 1: 15* or *sequence 2; 4*. In the first example, the number after the colon refers to the line in the sequence; in the latter, the number after the semicolon refers to another sequence. Only for the three case studies that are presented in this manuscript, I added the references of sequence and line. In other cases, like the interviews of further informants, there are no sequential citations. In the historical chapter of this study, I also quoted some oral history accounts that were archived by the Zoryan Institute Toronto. I cited these as follows: *X. Y. – Zoryan Institute Oral History Archive, 19xx* (the year of audio-visual recording), *20:00* (minute and second).

I paid attention to not to alter or correct anything in the transcriptions. In this sense, the translation echoes the original recording. Furthermore, another sort of rhythm occupies the quotes from the interviews. Punctuation marks do not work to divide sentences or modify syntax. These fulfil another function as the list below portrays. One exception applies to the long quotes from the interviews in the flow text. At some points, these include "..." punctuation marking a later passage from the same or a subsequent sequence.

Mark-ups

,	short stopping, non-grammatical
.	one second silence
.. or ...	two or three seconds of silence
(4)	silence of x seconds
issue/non-issue	to correct themself
I: but what about disclaimer	simultaneous speech
P: Well	
iiiiih	vowel lengthening
(laugh), (cough), (sigh)	non-verbal activity
(noise: coffee machine) (music)	distracting object voice-over in the room
exactly	stress (ling.)
it is really important to tell	in a low(er) voice
the manner of the subject-	breaking off
well there is (some)	unclear, vague
( )	unclear with app. length
mean-while	stuttering, syllabify
[describe]	interviewer's note

Acknowledgement

Even though my name stands below the title of this book, this study could not be finished without the tremendous support, valuable comments and striking questions that my colleagues, friends, mentors, advisors, and of course my family provided. My advisor from the Goethe University Frankfurt, Lena Inowlocki, has been a source of ongoing support. Her insightful comments, critical advice, and encouraging words have lightened my path in realising this project. Her wise words and profound guidance motivated me constantly to think about my work, my words, and my perspective. She taught me the scholar's self-critical and reflective positioning to emerging knowledge. Without her encouragement, patience, and supporting presence, this study could not have achieved its final form.

In 2018, Kira Kosnick agreed to be the second advisor of my doctoral thesis. Even though she could not render her opinion on this project after submission because she assumed a post at another university, I am also very thankful for her readiness. Hopefully, our paths will cross again, and we can work together another time. At the beginning of 2020, I was able to witness the same scholar solidarity by Lars Meier from the Goethe University Frankfurt as he accepted to advise my project. His willingness to support me echoed as an incredible motivation in composing the last pages of my dissertation. This book, the final form of my study, reflects critical questions posed by both, Lena Inowlocki and Lars Meier. The same applies to the questions by the further members of my defence commission, Ursula Apitzsch, Helma Lutz, and Uta Ruppert, and of course the points raised by Fritz Schütze and Anna Schnitzer, the series' publishers at the Verlag Barbara Budrich. I am deeply thankful for all the scholarly critique and support in this process of writing the thesis and its revision for the book publication.

Additionally, I have had the chance to relish the support of a mentor, Yektan Türkyılmaz. His profound advice and detailed feedback on various drafts helped me orientate myself in the world of historiography and the Armenian Genocide studies. He also raised my interest in another world of narratives, the vinyl. Without our meetings in Berlin and hours-long talks on politics and arts, I would have lost my way in this lonely venture of writing a PhD thesis. Also, I want to thank Yetiş Akdemir for the very same reason, to hold my interest in different topics alive. His friendship has been an anchor in Berlin and in this process.

A number of other friends and colleagues, who I met thanks to the Frankfurt University affiliation or in other contexts, influenced this work in different ways, by being open to hear my hardships, giving insightful comments and posing critical questions. They include but are not limited to Alice von Bieberstein, Anastassia Pletoukhina, Esra Demir, Gwendolyn Gillerion, and Yudit Namer. I believe without the interview analysis meetings that I had with Anastassia Pletoukhina regularly, this study would have missed crucial points to consider. Without Yudit Namer's or Esra Demir's patience to listen to me about my setbacks, researching further could have become a tough question. And, of course, my courageous friend Serdar Korucu has given me thoughtful insights on the debates every now and then.

There are two distinguished institutions that I want to mention on these pages. Without the scholarship of the Hans Boeckler Foundation from 2015 to 2019, the thesis would not have been realised in its final form. The solidarity, the focal aspect and motivation of the trade unionist Boeckler foundation, facilitates the work of many brilliant minds in Germany, some of which I could meet at the seminars and projects organised by the foundation. I am thankful for the financial and ideal scholarship by the foundation and of course the financial support for this publication. There is a person who I want to thank especially in these terms, my advisor for the scholarship, Sabine Hess from the University of Göttingen. Her presence in the institutional context helped me to orientate. I hope our paths meet again in the future.

When my paper abstract was accepted for the XIX. ISA World Congress of Sociology in Toronto, I came to the idea of doing research in the oral history archive of The Zoryan Institute. George Shirinian and Greg Sarkissian provided an enormous support and enabled my access to the audio-visual recordings of the genocide survivors from Van and Bitlis. Thanks to their cooperation, the voice of the survivors echoes in this work.

With the in-depth comments on the text, and his readiness to discuss the features of this work, my brother Mutlu Yetkin has been a premise empowering me along my way. I hope to continue our constructive disputes due to which we both find ourselves faced by new questions. I am indebted to him for his invaluable support. And my beloved partner Hanna's support was so crucial without which I could have not come so far. It is uncontroversial that her patience, her understanding voice, and kind-hearted presence have lit my path and motivated me even under the most unclear circumstances. The weekends and holidays that I sacrificed for this work and that I could not spend with Hanna and our son Kaya have never been put into question. It was also Kaya's patience that endured my absence. I cannot forget their selfless backing.

Lastly, I want to thank the people who contributed to this study and whose names I cannot mention. The support my gatekeepers in Istanbul and Van gave me was crucial for every single step of this research. My gatekeepers not only arranged meetings, in their personal network they also declared their trust in me. They answered my most naïve questions. Their trust means a lot to me.

Furthermore, without the willingness of my interview partners in Istanbul and Van to tell their life stories, I could not have the capacity to carry out such a project. First and foremost, this is their work, too. I am also thankful to the ones who rejected to recount their biography, their most personal details. Every one of them, the persons who accepted to spend their precious time for my project and the ones who justly denied, reminded me of the boundaries of scholarship and introduced me to their perspectives. They deserve all my gratitude for their invaluable time and trust.

This study could have never been completed without the generosity of all these people. Yet, all mistakes in this book are, of course, my own.

1 Introduction

The vast majority of people in our modern societies leads a routinised everyday life. To this routine belongs, for instance, the practice of commuting to the workplace and coming back home. From 2006 to 2010, "my workplace" was the mountainous and remote areas in Turkey and it regularly took several hours for me to arrive to this "workplace". Covering such distances is common among people who assume a job in the "niche" sector of outdoor tourism. Another ordinary notion of this profession is that one particular region receives the focus and the given person travels there frequently. For me, it was the Mount Ararat and Van region. In the Armenian history, this province was the heart on the ancient high plateau. Prior to the genocidal events of 1915–16, more than 350 villages, towns, and monasteries inhabited by Armenians had been documented in the historical Ottoman Sandjak of Van (Kévorkian and Paboudjian 2012, 511–59).

Van lies on a plateau at an altitude of 1,700 meters, surrounded by goliath-like mountains and a lake that stretches to the horizons. A two-hour journey from Van to the north is required to reach the last town, Doğubeyazıt, before the gigantic volcano of Ararat. And this is the most frequently used way for a trip to the mountain. The road to Doğubeyazıt crosses the lakeside. Then the valley floor of Muradiye province follows, or with its old Armenian name Pergri, in Kurdish Bergri. Until the mid of the 2000s, a military checkpoint had fortified the entrance of the valley, signalling as if you were leaving something significant behind or entering an insecure territory, or, as regular, the domain of a certain powerholder. In those four years, I had been on this very road at least fifty times.

Thereafter, only a few minutes of driving, a ruined massive-stone building suddenly rises observing the basin from its rocky left shoulder. For the people who pass by and could see the building standing on a slope approximately two hundred meters higher than the regular road, the "forsaken" Armenian Arkelan Monastery (Kévorkian and Paboudjian 2012, 543) could imply different things. With its at least 700 years of history and maintaining its tower-like shape, this monastery represents, on the one hand, the Armenian past of the region. On the other, with its demolished façade and crumbling walls, the monastery points to the circumstances of the last 100 years. Being ruined by treasure hunters several times and left to vanish from the landscape in the long term are the key elements in describing the relation of this building with this time period.

Every single time I saw this monastery, I thought of stopping the bus, stepping out, and walking up on the slopes even though such Armenian remnants were widespread in the region. Thus, it could not have been a wonder to see such an architectural object although back then I had practically no idea about the Armenian history. Every now and then I read a newspaper article about Van or Armenians, but it was not pivotal to my life-world.

My interest in the recent past of this region started to arise parallel to my master's graduation in Germany in 2010–11. Until that period, the monastery had been a forgotten detail for me. Or so I thought. It had been, in fact, more a "passive memory" than a disregarded scene I had been encountering, i.e. a "reservoir for future active memories" (A. Assmann 2010, 140). Even, when I started to read up on the places I have visited in Turkey, for instance, churches whose ruination would be dated to the first half of the 20th century, this passive memory was, so to speak, not activated immediately. I rather focused on the well-known remnants, for instance, the Varak Monastery, and of course the political disputes and violence. Over the course of this retrospective investigation of recollections (cf. Davis 1959),[1] I stumbled on maps about the Armenian districts of Van. However, I could not locate the monastery's image in my mind on any map. So, this remembrance began to trigger further questions.

I did not know whether it was a church or a monastery; whether it was Armenian or Assyrian. Such a piece of information would have eventually led to identifying it. Nevertheless, I did not have it. Furthermore, back then, I carried out no talk, discussion, or any kind of interaction with any other member of the society concerning this particular building. So there was no narrative in my recollections about this monastery (cf. Brockmeier 2015; Halbwachs 1991; 2012), in my memory I "possessed" only a repeatedly captured image behind the windscreen. Nevertheless, the image in my mind was somehow not enough to match with other memories and find the exact location. That was, for instance, not the case for other "forsaken" properties because either I visited these during some hiking tours or I discovered them with my friends when we were opening new paths to hike. However, I never walked on the slopes where the monastery rises.

Without any pictures, historical or made in the recent past, I could only narrow down the possibilities to two: the Arkelan Monastery (and most probably its Surp Asdvadzadzin Church, The Church of Our Lady) or Surp Tateos Monastery in Köşg. These buildings had only been a few miles away from each other, according to Raymond H. Kévorkian and Paul B. Paboudjian (2012, 543 f). They were the only identified Armenian monasteries on the western side

---

[1]   This study is not an autoethnographic research, but rather very much inspired by how Fred Davis integrates his earlier professional experiences into the paper *The Cabdriver and His Fare: Facets of a Fleeting Relationship.*

of the road connecting Van to Doğubeyazıt via the provincial town Çaldıran,[2] and between the two Turkish military checkpoints: the first one, as mentioned, before you access the valley, and the other at the pass of Mount Tendürek. The second outpost on an altitude of 2,644 meters was notorious because of the numerous heavily armed military vehicles and the strict command chain attitude of the soldiers there. This place was guarded in tightened terms because, reportedly, at that particular mountain the Turkish military of republican times had the highest loss rate per km2 in the war against the Kurdish PKK. But what was the reason for such an outpost? Had the army foregrounded the security of its soldiers in that given locus? Or did the institutional memory provide the army with the justification for fortifying a mountainous terrain? In other words, what was the heavily armed checkpoint standing for, its symbolic effect or security policies?

At this outpost, you had to wait in line for an ID-check. And it was prohibited to step out of the vehicle without the authorisation of the military personnel. When someone received such an authorisation, it implied the officers would question that person. That place had an effect that you would start to think about the checkpoint before you arrived. It ruled not just a space in its spatial boundaries, but expanded even to the last checkpoint 60 kilometres before, involving the scene of the monastery.

Returning to the point with this particular Armenian remnant, an initiative based in Paris, *Collectif 2015 : reparation* (www.collectif2015.org), shed light on the dilemma with which I have been struggling. The *Collectif 2015* initiative, demanding monetary reparation and return of the expropriated immobile Armenian wealth from the Turkish government, which was confiscated during or in the aftermath of the extermination campaigns, digitalised a representative list of monumental Armenian properties. In most cases, these properties were left to their fate after the genocide. That transnational draft of the cultural remembrance in digital space helped me to clarify for which monastery I had been looking: it was the Husgan Orti Church of the Surp Istepannos Monastery (Saint Stephen Monastery) at Arkelan.[3]

---

[2]   Kévorkian and Paboudjian's distinguished study provides maps for every Ottoman *vilayet* and *sandjak,* displaying a vast amount of villages, towns, and monasteries where Armenians lived before the extermination campaigns. In their comprehensive study, you can compare the maps of Sandjak of Bayazid (today's Doğubeyazıt) – a part of the Vilayet of Erzurum (p. 461), and Sandjak of Van (p. 512), and come to the conclusion that there was no recorded Armenian monastery or whatsoever in the valley except these two.

[3]   On the following webpage of the initiative, you can find a detailed description of monastery's past and information about its complex. According to this webpage,

In addition to my "unreliable" memory which was "haunted by forgetting" (Huyssen 2000, 38), I did not have the exact lead for finding out the right church, except the right monastery complex. Indeed, my efforts required the organisational quality of "cultural memory" (J. Assmann 2013), which involves scripts and archives. However, except the webpage above and books, there is no such cultural memory with critical organisational quality in Turkey concerning the Armenian past. Furthermore, I believe even that sort of memory work – a (semi-)structured cultural memory in this field – would not have been enough to correspond to my recollections. For I had further experiences from these trips. I have needed to reconstruct my memory and generate a narrative, for instance, concerning the military outpost. Thus, my experience would stay in touch with my biography and the social world and help me in my meaning making efforts concerning those moments (Brockmeier 2015; Bruner 2004; Ochs and Capps 1996). In this regard, my narrative would also remain open for interaction with other personal memories and hence change.

The same mechanism applies to collective memories as well. Remaining in the same spatial area, such an extent from personal to collective memory would subsume various narratives generated in the Kurdish society of Van. There should exist numerous collective memories (Halbwachs 1991) in this particular region concerning the Armenian past, certain properties, and the conflict and war between the Turkish State and PKK, i.e. the political violence. These features locate in an interwoven space of recollections linked to other experienced events, images, and stories with their own temporal organisations. Thanks to the same narrative elements, the Kurdish "social time" emerges reconstructed (Sorokin and Merton 1937; cf. Nassehi 2008; Wallerstein 1988; 1998).

Collective memories would furthermore include the old city centre of Van which was entirely destroyed during the extermination campaigns targeting the Armenians. Perhaps, the short-term successful Armenian resistance *in situ* would be another event remembered. Moreover, the historiographic reconstruction of these events in the hands of the Turkish State or the Kurdish movement(s) should be counted as indicators for such memories as well since they have provided people with an interpretational template (for a detailed historical portrayal, please see Chapter 4 of the present study).

In addition, the critical examination of the Armenian past and the tendency to face past crimes, by some (socio-)political initiatives in the Turkish and

after years of demolishment in the hands of gravediggers and the devastating Van earthquake of 2011 whose epicentre was not far away, there survived only two architectural elements of the church. https://www.collectif2015.org/en/100Monuments/Le-Monastere-d-Arkelan-ou-de-Saint-Etienne-de-Pergri/

Kurdish societies of the country, lived a *belle époque* of liberalisation in the 2000s, following the revocation of state of emergency in Kurdish populated regions in Turkey, or North-Kurdistan, in 2002 and during the cease-fire. For instance, Kurdish municipalities started the renovation of Armenian and Assyrian churches in their area of administration – yet, not reaching the remnants that are away from urbanity. In those years, statements asking Armenians for "forgiveness" or accounts about "ancestors' ill decisions for participating in massacres" have become publicly discussed and widespread in general in Turkey and in particular in the Kurdish society – deriving from the fact that a very high proportion of the Armenians were living prior to the extermination campaigns approximately in today's North-Kurdistan or their historical homeland, West-Armenia.

Progressiveness was ruling the debates. Perhaps, it was clear for most people that a governmental acknowledgement of the genocide was unrealistic in the short term. However, the attempts to reconstruct the past (through memories or renovation campaigns) were now circulating in the social arena. And these were also pointing at the responsibility of the state. Concerning the other side of this coin, the Turkish State was still engaging in improving the denialist repertoire (Göçek 2016; Turan and Öztan 2018). Discovering new forums, reshaping old discourses, and motivating new actors were now the techniques of the negationist (institutional) agents in Turkey. Denying the genocide was not confined to the floors of diplomacy, academy, or official institutions anymore (for a discussion on these points, please see Chapter 5).

In these terms, I drafted two hypotheses about the Kurdish remembrance on the Armenian Genocide. The first has postulated that the recognition of the Armenian Genocide (and demanding such a step from the government) has been *a political tool* to deconstruct the nationalist structures. Additionally, it could be seen as an item for bonding the Kurdish collective identity, illustrating the progressive Kurds vis-à-vis the denialist Turkish State. This hypothesis was based on the very fact that (active) memory involves political motives and, at the same time, considering the present situation (A. Assmann 2010; J. Assmann 2013; Halbwachs 1991; Türkyılmaz 2011).

The second postulate has been a sort of opposite to the first. Deriving from the circulated stories, and for instance anecdotes shared by Kurdish politicians (cf. Dinç 2016), the other hypothesis has assumed a trajectory of facing the past crimes without the political intentions as described above. And indeed, it was, therefore, ignoring the socio-political quality of remembering. In this constellation with defined "extremes", this study has aimed to explore the memory constructions in the Kurdish society concerning the genocide and the Armenian past. In particular, it set the focus on the city and region of Van. In these terms, it looks into biographical narrative interviews (Schütze 1983) and the ethnographic data – field protocols, photographs, and visual material from exhibitions and denialist memorials. For the analysis of life stories would disclose amorph standings, fluid perspectives, numerous ways of argumentations, and hence deconstruct the face value of various discourses (Schütze 2008a; 2008b). Thus, the study unearths the life-worlds (Schütz and Luckmann 2003) in-between these two hypotheses.

In other words, this book is about the (narrative) zones of memory that emerge under circumstances of political violence in Kurdistan. Based on the ethnographic data, it also carefully investigates denialism in this specific case and, of course, recognition arguments. In doing so, the study seeks to accomplish the task of sketching the contested landscape of collective memories. Hence, this study presumes (collective) memory as reconstruction of (past) experiences and meaning-making efforts for the present.

By means of the analysis of life story narratives and further data, the book argues that the Armenian Genocide memories in the Kurdish society in Turkey function in multidirectional terms (Rothberg 2009). The narratives on the genocide, be they acquired from a family member or referring to collectively shared stories, link personal and social experiences of political violence to each other, or in Michael Rothberg's terms they "juxtapose two or more disturbing memories and disrupt everyday settings" (p. 14). Thus, the genocide memory assists the narrator in reconstructing the spacetime of their home region, even expanding it to the whole of Kurdistan. Personal and collective experiences of violence and injustice emerge at this juncture, connected to the Armenian past and remodifying each other in reciprocal terms. Based on the study's sample, I also propose a further possible quality of the Armenian Genocide memory: making the topic of political violence in the Kurdish space describable and discussable (cf. Bar-On 1999). But why do people use stories on Armenians to talk about the state violence and not any other narrative concerning Kurds, for instance, about the Dersim Genocide 1937–38 or Anfal Genocide under the Saddam Regime? What does the Armenian Genocide memory reconfigure in terms of socio-political frameworks in Kurdistan? How does narrating 1915 influence the temporal organisation of social time? The Armenian Genocide memory provides the narrator with a template to locate own biography – and community – in the widened history of the region. It generates a comparability of violent experiences and hence remodifies the victimhood categories (cf. Jeffery and Candea 2006; Türkyılmaz 2011). In this sense, 1915 occurs as a pivotal element to clarify the meaning of violence and injustice.

1.1 Access to the Field and Research Process

As indicated, this study is an empirical qualitative social study. In general, its data set consists of autobiographical narrative interviews that I gathered in two different cities: Van and Istanbul. Altogether, it subsumes 15 face-to-face recorded narrative interviews, five of them from Istanbul and ten from Van. Additionally, at the beginning of my research, I recorded two expert interviews. And after I called off my field research trips another interview via Skype.[4] But for the analytical discussion, I narrowed down the sampling to ten interviews, three of which you can find presented as case studies in this book. Seven further life stories emerge in the comparative discussion.

While I was engaged in my proposal in 2014, the political atmosphere in Kurdish cities in Turkey was bright and peaceful. A peace process between the Turkish government and the PKK was carried out. Scholars and journalists were undertaking their research almost without any obstacles. However, after the June elections 2015, the Turkish government retuned its political trajectory into repression and oppression. Curfews were declared, armed forces took the streets. This time, (provincial) downtowns were the central places of clashes. And non-combatant civilians were targeted as well. There was a difference in comparison to the war in the 1990s. The media landscape had been much more homogenous in those years. However, when the war was reignited in 2015, people living in the centres of curfew started to report what was happening, for instance, through social media. So, clear images of violence were circulating.

This change in the situation forced me to rethink my approach. Although I was deliberately planning to carry out a study in the periphery, I had to reorientate myself. I did not know if I would ever have a chance to reach my contacts who were living in the villages. Therefore, I aimed to seek interview partners from the city centre of Van instead of the provincial area. I also decided to add the city of Istanbul as a part of my study. The time I spent in Istanbul provided me with the chance to collect further ethnographic materials such as from the exhibitions launched about the Armenian past and set a comparative framework to discuss issues concerning remembrance. While I was elaborating the level of saturation after Grounded Theory (Glaser and Strauss 2009a) based on the interviews I already collected in December 2015 and the following spring in Istanbul and Van, a military coup was attempted in Turkey in July 2016. A new state of emergency was declared to rule under the AKP regime thereafter. The

---

[4]   There had also been further follow-up occasions of some exchange with other informants whom I interviewed during my field trips – some recorded with their permission
or written down in notes.

war in the state itself (or perhaps a better formulation, among its structures) became more and more public, for which there had already been some clues since 2013. So, the regime obtained the hand to justify its illegal, unethical, violent, and politically corrupt actions, such as replacing elected mayors of the Kurdish cities with its assigned trustees like governors and arrest local politicians. In her essay published in the edited book "40 Year 12 September", which looks into the societal dynamics and perception of the 12 September 1980 military coup and the post-coup junta regime, the former mayor of Diyarbakır Gülten Kışanak (2020, 139), who has been replaced with a trustee and arrested end of October 2016, points out that "[t]he government has seized the power of ruling with the 'trustee system' and set it further with the decree-law 674 (declared in the official gazette of the Turkish Republic on 1 September 2016) whenever it wants" [translated by E. Y.]. In fact, the government has legalised the trustees system extending its reign beyond the state of emergency. After further deliberation, I called off additional field trips because I could only see an increased proportion of rejections and of course possible risks and harm targeting my informants. In other words, my decision stood for working with 15 interviews in total.

In terms of analytical relevance, I sought my interview partners from a widely defined spectrum of politically active people. It includes, for instance, (active) members of the Kurdish left-wing parties, country wide the HDP and the BDP in Kurdistan, and people who are engaged in non-governmental and non-party organisations. It was crucial for the research that none of them would be an expert in the field of the Armenian Genocide studies. For such an expert position would then deteriorate the conditions of a possible life story narration, as Daniel Bertaux suggests (2018, 61). Furthermore, I wanted to concentrate on the biographies in the secondary zone with regard to the contemporary debates, so to speak. Due to its focus on a single region, the limited number of interviews, and most importantly the gender imbalance in the sample, perhaps a theoretical saturation of the theory extrapolating to the region and similar issues has not been achieved (cf. Corbin and Strauss 1990; Glaser and Strauss 2009a). However, the analysis of narrative interviews showcases another perspective on the public debates (cf. Bertaux 2018, 63). In these terms, I considered additional (empirical) material like special exhibitions, their catalogues, memorial places captured visually, and some archival materials like oral history accounts and witness reports, literary accounts, and, of course, other secondary literature.

In most cases, I reached the interview partners through gatekeepers – individuals and friends instead of institutional door openers or distributors which could have ignited a hierarchical framing (cf. Schütze 2008b, 3 f). The interviews were carried out in a place that the narrator chose and acknowledged as safe, either the personal office, home, or in a third party place such as a café.

Without a doubt and as it is always the case, this project developed further during field research and most importantly during the analyses. What I had expected concerning the regimes of collective and personal memory in Kurdistan and what was in store for me turned out to be totally different. Of course, I had some ideas. But these did not match people's realities.

1.2 Research Ethics

The question of research ethics subsumes several points such as the protection of informant's rights, prevention of possible risks and harm targeting informant privileges and even their health, voluntariness to participate, confidentiality, and of course anonymisation of data. In the process of preparing my PhD proposal, carrying out my field trips, and analysing the gathered data – including writing this manuscript, these issues have occurred continuously because the ethics question was not to be answered in generalised terms since I have been conducting a qualitative social research project – moreover, with a particular focus on autobiographies (cf. von Unger 2018; Siouti 2018). While preparing my field trips, for the orientation I have used the ethics codex of the German Society of Sociologists and Union of German Sociologists (DGS & BDS 2017).

As mentioned before, the reignited war in Kurdistan following the June election of 2015 has changed the circumstances tremendously. And the effects of this change have echoed in my project, not just concerning the narratives I collected but in my approach. Before the war erupted again, I had the chance to conduct interviews with two experts from the field. During this period, the atmosphere was entirely different, and I was thinking about including the analysis of these recordings into my research – and perhaps to gather further expert interviews. However, after the violence *in situ* and the repression of critical voices became the "norm" again, I cancelled the part with the experts because anonymising relevant sections was impossible. Even though I would have tried to work with such interviews in masked versions, having such a small community (working on the Armenian Genocide and Kurdish–Turkish conflict) that has been perhaps under the surveillance of state institutions posed equally high risks. The question was now how to deal with information from those interviewees who are not known publicly.

My field trip in Istanbul at the end of 2015 clarified the contours of my approach. During this trip, I could collect three biographical interviews. Before the interviews I gave a detailed explanation of my research, information regarding my position as researcher (being a PhD student, how I finance my research, my background, how come I do have an interest in this very topic, et cetera), and described the interview context: that I have only one preformed question to ask and further questions would find shape while they tell me their life story. With most of my informants, I spent some time prior to the interview situation so that we develop a mutual understanding and trust. For instance, in the case of Delal – in Istanbul, we met several times before we recorded an interview. Some other pre-interview-periods were shorter of course, for instance with the interview partners that I met in Van via gatekeepers. Several people rejected to participate in this study, some also after I described my research interest or my approach.

When I was in Turkey after I recorded the interviews, I sent them immediately to another encrypted email of mine, which I created only for this purpose and erased them from the recorder as well as my computer. First, after I finished my field research in Turkey, I downloaded these data and saved them in my desktop computer because I was going to revisit the field. When I thought that I had enough interviews to write my study, I started to use my laptop for my research project and erased that encrypted email. And of course, I never brought my laptop to Turkey when I visited the country for personal reasons. While planning this procedure, it became clear to me that I could not use any printed document which would deteriorate and risk my informant's conditions if something happens to me before I cross the border. This is why I did not use any informative research and confidential disclosure agreements that were to be signed by my interview partners and sealed with a name. I also explained why I do not have any printed agreements and offered my informants to send the anonymised interview transcription whenever they would want it.

Due to my research topic, encountering narratives on personal or family experiences of violence was not avoidable (von Unger 2018, 687). It even was essential to understand the life stories because when my interview partners had started to talk about the violent events that they lived through, it implied I was a confidant to them. Indeed, being a confidant and having the power of "possessing" these data has brought along challenges for the whole length of the research. How I could clarify that I would not abuse this power in analysing the interviews was the crucial question. Because I do focus on the attempts of meaning-making by my interview partners, I could have crossed the thin red line between the reconstruction of narratives and ascription of some (alleged) implicit constructions (pp. 685 f). To minimise this risk, I took part in interview analysis meetings, asked for different perspectives of people who are not active in the Kurdish and Armenian Genocide studies. On such occasions, I only provided excerpts of transcribed and anonymised interviews.

The study includes no (audio-)visual evidence such as photographs or links to videos and recordings of persons whom I interviewed in order to ensure the participants' anonymity. To guard the issues of anonymisation and confidentiality, I have changed and masked personal names, family names, places, towns, working places, and institutions. In the interviews, I let only a few town names uncloaked since they are metropolitan and highly populated cities, like Istanbul and Van, or since they are crucial to understanding the biographical project of the person. The original recordings were then encrypted and kept in an – again encrypted – USB disk. Except for two interviews that were transcribed by a confidant of mine under full confidentiality agreements, the data sets, recordings as well as transcriptions, have not been given to any third party.

1.3   Outline of the Study

This book contains eight chapters, including this introduction. Every single chapter, except the introduction, includes a part to conclude the points underscored on the previous pages. It occurs in Chapter 2 fused with research questions and in further parts as concluding remarks. Additionally, every subchapter of the comparative discussion, Chapter 7 Violence and Genocide in Memory, has a short summary so that the reader can easily follow the line of argument. A glossary on terminologies, for instance from Turkish, and notes on citations are to be found on the first pages following the table of contents.

Following these introductory words, I portray the research design where you can find a detailed description of the methodologies I used – ethnographical fieldwork and biographical narrative interviews. The theoretical chapter on memory issues follows this part on methodologies. In Chapter 3, you can find an analytical discussion concerning this trans- and interdisciplinary field. In the next chapter on historical research, I first sketch what the historiographical concepts concerning 1915 were, for instance, in the early republican era or during the junta regime in the early 1980s. Then I depict the situation in Van in 1915–16. Furthermore, this chapter involves ethnographic and sociological perspectives paving the way to the issues of remembering.

Chapter 5, The Conflict of Recognition and Denial, aims to shed light on discourses of different parties through reconstructing the "old" as well as current frames of denialism and recognition debates. It also tackles with theoretical concepts of denialism, developed by Stanley Cohen (2001), or discussions in this regard, for example, by Marc Nichanian (1998; 2011). In doing so, this chapter includes visual data such as photographs taken at exhibitions, urban space, and memory places in Istanbul and Van. Publications of Kurdish intellectuals on this very issue, the Armenian Genocide and Kurdish complicity, are further materials that are considered in this part.

The following chapter contains three case studies – the in-depth analysis of the biographical narrative interviews from Van and Istanbul. In their analysis, I have faced the significance of violent experiences and their place in biographical reconstruction. In order to capture the violence in a picture – that is repeatedly accentuated by all my informants, I have worked on these life stories splitting their analytical portrayal into two main parts: the biographical synopsis and the violence in narration.

In Chapter 7, this book takes the turn of a comparative discussion and looks into the memory (re-)constructions of violent events, the concepts of repression, and state political violence from the perspective of people affected. In these terms, the study takes narratives from the three case studies and further seven biographical interviews into consideration. This core chapter involves a discussion that synchronises theoretical compounds and narrative structures in developing theories of (collective) memory. Hence, this discussion chapter yields and renders several elements from the whole manuscript. It consists of three main layers that I view crucial to understand the Kurdish memory: the issue of being able to describe and discuss own experiences; the questions of narrative temporal organisations; and the contestation of memories.

Then the conclusion of this book follows, crystallising my key findings and arguments. Instead of portraying a complete summary of every chapter and their arguments, I intentionally kept this part as compact as possible to provide the readers with a simple orientation.

2 Research Design

From the beginning on, my plan was to gather the empirical data as fundamentals of theory to be built. Instead of working with a grand theory to verify the hypothesis, I aimed to use an abductive approach as Barney Glaser and Anselm Strauss (2009a) explain in their ground-breaking work, Discovery of Grounded Theory.[1] Hence, the study would become able to reveal missed or muted stories, highlight the ambiguities, and link between personal and collective memories.

In these terms, I regarded my researcher role as an "active sampler of theoretically relevant data" who should "continually analyse the data [concerning this particular phenomenon of remembrance] to see where the next theoretical question will take" me (p. 58). While carrying out the sampling and analysis processes, categories and properties different than in earlier studies have emerged, for instance about the nature of discussing the Kurdish experience in the last decades and its relatedness to the Armenian Genocide narratives. I have used these to generate and saturate theories "until it [became] clear which are core categories" (p. 71). In this sense, this study has been nourished in its every step by Glaser and Strauss' Grounded Theory approach to the empirical data and sociological thinking.

However, the tremendously and rapidly changed circumstances on-site, as described in the introduction, urged me to rethink and reconsider the research subject and possible approaches as well. The view in advance was not fitting for the new conditions anymore; for example, I had planned long-term stays or wanted to reach a sampling through data collection after having a core portrait of the previous one. Due to these new conditions, I had to conduct short-term field research trips, one in November 2015 to Istanbul – in order to experience the socio-political sphere at first hand – and another in spring 2016, which was carried out in Van and Istanbul. Nonetheless, the analysis of the first three

---

[1]   According to Glaser and Strauss, theoretical sampling is the reciprocal process in which the researcher (or the research team) conducts the analysis parallel to data gathering and develops the data collection based on the (maximal and minimal contrasting) analysis (2009, 45; for a thorough description by authors, please see: Chapter III). In this process the theory would be generated. The researcher hereby refigures the orientation or the study aim through "the emerging theory". The theory will be then based on a continuation of a comparison of cases (considering the social settings) (pp. 47 f) and further conceptualisation (sampling) until the theory is saturated (pp. 61 f). The process of theoretical sampling requires, in this sense, thinking of the steps ahead with regard to generating the theory as well as the data collection, or in Glaser and Strauss' words, the "theoretical sensitivity" (ibid., Chapter III).

interviews that I recorded in 2015 influenced the steps of theoretical sampling laying before me. After these trips, I have remained in contact with some of my interview partners. Through my gatekeepers, I even reached new people who were interested in my project. Under these terms, I worked with the theoretical sampling model of Grounded Theory as far as the field circumstances allowed.

To treat the multidimensional space of memory suitably, I have furthermore decided to continue my research with a multimethod approach: using ethnographic field research methods and the research concept of biographical interview. The methodology of biographical narrative interview helped me in exploring numerous facets of memory. For setting of narrative interviews provide the informant with a free space and the scholar with a data collection to be treated abductively. This open space gives the informant the chance to "differentiate, precise, and comment [their answers]" (Bertaux 2018, 39) [translated by E.Y.]. Remarks made by informants have the quality to clarify the boundaries of public discourses, memory frames and state of their actions.

Furthermore, biography as a phenomenon has its own temporal compartment parallel to the collective time as Bertaux (p. 90) points out "both time axes – historical and collective as well as the biographical time – function parallelly." And biography is bonded to other social entities (like family, class background, milieu, et cetera), not only through determinants but also through interactions, and their time conceptions (for an in-depth discussion on the time question concerning memory, please see: Brockmeier 2015). In this regard, I view biography as a project – the biographical project – with a vision of and for the future, nourished by the past experiences.[2]

Concerning the multidimensional nature of the field, I gathered further data during my field trips and put it in comparison to contextualize the setting. The materials from the field, for instance, stories that are not spoken during an interview but under different circumstances; discourses that are "dominant" in society; pictures, places, and objects that are important in the collective mind; and text materials such as from digital platforms and/or exhibitions are treated based on focused ethnography methodology (Knoblauch 2005; Wall 2015; cf. Woermann 2018). These data were carefully analysed based on the very ideas of Grounded Theory. These were used in Chapter 5 to reveal the dynamics of recognition and denial debates in the socio-political spectrum.

---

[2] The biography considers possible actions in various forms of social settings for the present and future. And indeed these actions are based on the experiences and the visions, so to speak. In this sense, the biographical approach discloses the multidimensional nature of social life (with the spectrum of possible actions taken or not-taken) and memory (with the spectrum of possible ways to reconstruct the experiences), as memory studies occupy it as well due to its trans- and interdisciplinary nature.

In sum, this chapter is assembled through three subchapters and contemporary discussions of two approaches that were fundamental to the sampling and analysis of the empirical material: focused ethnography and biography research. The subchapter on the biography research includes a brief portrayal of the steps that I followed. The concluding subchapter includes information about the research questions. Furthermore, it is about how the questions had to be and had been reformulated *en route*.

2.1 Focused Ethnography

In order to understand and interpret the biographical narratives, the study required an analytical portrayal of the context. Therefore, I decided to gather ethnographic data during my field trips in the early stages of my project. The field trips needed to aim at meeting possible autobiographers and, at the same time, to integrate images, stories, actions, and social scenes concerning the genocide memory from *in situ* into the research. The relation between the biographical projects and collective memories is, from my point of view, a reciprocal interplay. Thus, it required understanding these life stories in their given contexts and displaying the contemporary sociopolitical situation. In other words, the settings concerning the two research locations needed to be clarified and portrayed.

Inspired by sociologist Hubert Knoblauch's concept (2001; 2005), the focused ethnography, which he has further developed into what he calls video-interaction-analysis or videography (2004; Knoblauch and Schnettler 2012; sequential analysis of video data was also proposed, please see, Woermann 2018), I started to prepare my field visits. In a glimpse, Knoblauch pinpoints that the long-term ethnographic studies' struggle with time can be compensated through short-term field visits with an emphasis on data recording – audio, photographic, and audiovisual – and its subsequent intensive analysis. In these terms, I gathered visual and further textual data (such as from exhibitions) but not audiovisual material because I found it risky to have two huge data sets, biographies and videos – which could lead to a chaotic pile of materials. Furthermore, the confidentiality of participants could also come under risk.

Knoblauch (2005, 1) adds that the idea of focused ethnography, however, "should not be construed as an opposition" to conventional ethnography. He proposes the way of research: organising short-field trips and an intensive analytical work on gathered data. The core idea of focused ethnography concerns the intensive data analysis. From my point of view, it resembles narrative analysis (Schütze 1983; 2008a; 2008b).

Over the course of time, I have realised that focused ethnography – which is not a programmatic, systematic technique but rather a modifiable approach or suggestion – offers researchers working with autobiographies, a profound ground to triangulate approaches since it concentrates on recording the processes. It strives to look into the resemblance and differences of actions in the micro or focused field (Knoblauch 2005, 4; 6–8). Moreover, the researcher's role is questioned as well since the person comes to the research area with a possibly different role and disposition than the interviewee – also due to their background knowledge (2005, 3). Focused ethnography in this sense relies on the line of Schütz' social phenomenology (Knoblauch 2001; 2005; cf. Woermann 2018, 8), so does biography research.[3]

Hence, I have approached the field inspired by the above-mentioned terms of focused ethnography: gathering a diverse data collection in a short time and concentrating on its interpretation and analysis. For clarifying the context, I focused on the social setting concerning the Armenian Genocide – including debates revolving around its denial and recognition. In these terms, the field research included the visual data I gathered – exhibitions on the Armenian Genocide for instance. Furthermore, it aimed to collect particular images of the urban area, and document narratives concerning certain buildings. Through that I aimed to scrutinise the context – the socio-political setting in Turkey – and the sub-context – the Kurdish remembrance and perception of violence.

2.2 Biographical Research

Considering biographical materials, autobiographies of well-known persons, biographies written by third party authors and/or (family) memoires have a long tradition in literature studies as well as media and social sciences. The profound and pioneering work *The Polish Peasant in Europe and America* by William I. Thomas and Florian Znaniecki, published in five volumes from 1918 to 1920, has created a milestone in understanding the social dynamics of migration and migrant groups through an "upwards" lens on the one hand (cf. Rustin 2003). And on the other the above-mentioned study represents a starting point for the focus on biographical materials in social sciences. In spite

---

[3] Knoblauch (2005, 11) thus contemplates the researcher doing focused ethnography not as a participant observer but embodying a "field-observer role." Furthermore, he pins down that "focused ethnographies are studies of highly differentiated divisions of labour and a highly fragmented culture" (p. 12) that elaborate significant moments in one's or the collective's social life.

of the fact that the theoretical discussions regarding human interaction and its biographical meaning were carried out in the following years, for instance, by immigrant scholars from continental Europe in flight from Nazi perpetrators, like Alfred Schütz (cf. Schütz and Luckmann 2003) or Karl Mannheim (cf. Apitzsch 2003, 95 f); biography as a subject and focal point of social investigation has displayed its value first within the tradition of the Chicago School of sociology (Chamberlayne, Bornat, and Wengraf 2003b). The nourishment of those second generation discussions was based on contemporary social research traditions such as ethnomethodology, symbolic interactionism, and, of course, Anselm Strauss and Barney Glaser's Grounded Theory (Apitzsch and Inowlocki 2003).

In the bygone forty years, since the 1980s, biography has been taken into consideration more and more by scholars internationally, for example, Daniel Bertaux (2018; first published in French 1997) in France with the life story approach; Paul Thompson (2000) in the UK with the oral history approach; and by scholars in Germany such as Martin Kohli (1981) with his early thoughts on biographical emphasis in its social realm; or Fritz Schütze (1983) with his concept of autobiographical interview, which Gabriela Rosenthal (1995) further conceptualised. And it has always remained as an approach to question, discuss, reconstruct and understand the processes occurring in the society, communities, and institutions from the perspective of the participants and people affected: the acting subjectivities (cf. Apitzsch and Inowlocki 2003).[4]

The first and fundamental methodological notion of the biographical narrative interview is that the informant, the autobiographer has to be asked to tell their life story. It provides the autobiographer with an unframed and unrestricted setting. The whole interview context can be partitioned into three phases: the main narrative, the questions concerning this main part and the questioning of the arguments. Schütze (1983; 1984; 2008a; 2008b; cf. Apitzsch 2003) advocates that the main narrative – or in his words, the extempore narrative – of the autobiographer follows this elementary and only pre-structured question "to tell their life story". This part, according to him, marks the core material for further interview and analysis as a sovereign part. With the end of the main narrative, or with the first coda, the researcher starts posing questions to fill in the gaps. First questions are related to the narrator's experiences – the

---

[4]   The enrichment in and growing attention to the qualitative methods short before the collapse of Soviet Union (has) also affected the biography research. This international acknowledgment found its institutional representation first through the ad-hoc group established in International Sociological Association in the early 1980s and then with its Research Committee under the same roof (ibid.).

narrative units – expressed in the main part. Following this step, descriptions and arguments made by the informant will be considered and questioned by the researcher (Schütze 2008b, 11). It is indeed important not to argue with the narrator, which is against the nature of this very methodology. In this sense, the questions to be posed are based on the delivered narration, are inscribed by the interviewer whilst the narrator talks, and reformulated to disclose further information in this regard. Instead of "why" questions, the research asks whether the narrator could tell in more detail about the time they experienced the given situation. Thus, the biographical interview method gives the informants the chance to express themselves freely and without being judged. It also gives the researcher the chance to theorise the particular social condition through the participants' eyes.

But what is the goal of such an approach? What does it bring us when people find a free space to reconstruct their experiences? Prue Chamberlayne, Joanna Bornat, and Tom Wengraf (2003a, 3) frame the biographical methods as "engaging with personal accounts meant valuing and finding ways of eliciting and analysing the spoken and written words of people who, earlier, had been seen as marginal to history making or to sociological explanation ..." Similarly, Ursula Apitzsch and Lena Inowlocki (2003, 55) point at the focus of the biographical methods on margins as "not presupposing social normality" and the significant point of understanding the social processes through biographies "during times of social transformation and in moments and times of crisis." With regard to the question of what biography research aims to investigate, Michael Rustin (2003, 49) puts it that "ethnography and biography explore process, rather than merely structure" through accepting individuals' agencies which he calls "biographical point of view" (p. 46).

Based on these points, we can say that biography is to be approached with a sense of process-analysis in an abductive way. Biographies show their embeddedness and entanglements in social and socio-political organisations – such as institutions and family – and developments and changes – such as unemployment, sickness, catastrophe, war, or insurgency. These show individuals' actions in dominant socio-political settings. In this sense, the life story of an individual appears as an active part of collective trajectories shedding light onto "number of cases and, furthermore, how sociological theory can emerge from the analysis of individual cases"(Apitzsch and Inowlocki 2003, 55). In these terms, the focus on intergenerational relations (Bertaux and Thompson 2005; Rosenthal 1997) or one's educational course (von Felden 2008) have also been research subjects.

In Schütze's terms, the "autobiographical recollection" is an act of retrospective reconstruction by the informant (or autobiographer) in "shaping her or his own biographical identity: but the task of the meaningful ordering of pieces of biography originally evolves from life historical experiences" (2008a, 9 f). The criticisms vis-à-vis biographical methods made in the past targeted the relation of researcher to informant's reconstruction, namely that a recollection would include falsely marked veins of storytelling such as lies or finely tuned narratives due to the current position(ing) of the informant; or that an account built and provided by the autobiographer cannot reflect the social phenomena because of its collective patterns (Apitzsch 2003, 98 f). Nevertheless, the reconstruction of several accounts which is performed by the scholar has been the core point of the whole concept since the early years of this very research tradition. Schütze (2008b, 15) points out that "the verbal representations and interpretations of the interaction partners and biography incumbents" should be considered in-depth and not to be taken "at face value". Bertaux (2018, 85), in these terms, argues that the job of the researcher is keeping distance from "two extreme positions", one that claims everything that is told by the informant is right, and the other insisting everything is false.

We should remember that the personal memory pops up during an autobiographical interview not in a chronological order but as parts of puzzle(s). In reconstructing this ensemble of narratives, the researcher takes the social space and trajectories into account (Apitzsch 2003, 98 ff). The approach aims not only to "solve" the whole puzzle of one (or several) person(s), but also to understand the sociological case within the radius of actions thoroughly. Reconstructing several accounts, bringing the resemblance and differences of those into discussion and enabling typologies (for example, of trajectories) for critical reflection that represent a social state or mode are parts of this process (Apitzsch 2003; Bertaux 2018; Rustin 2003; Schütze 1981; 1983; 2008b; 2008a; Wengraf 2003).

In these terms, the researcher's life-world is much more significant and critical than the autobiographers' positioning of themselves. The lack of critical self-review would lead to a non-critical case reconstruction. A reflective approach means, on the one hand, a continuous questioning of researcher's standing vis-à-vis and in relation to the empirical cases. It involves the critical consideration of their efforts on the other. A self-review would enable the person to reconstruct the social case – through disassembling the so-called face values.

However, it does not imply that the self of the researcher has to be avoided in the study. Contrarily, it does pin down pulling this self under reflective terms into the research as a substantial part of it, as Tom Wengraf (2003, 143) puts it "We cannot evade our specific inheritances and our training, and they are valuable cultural capital when properly used, but we can avoid giving them a false ontological inevitability which blocks any critical self-review." This should cover (or accompany) the analysis as well as the data gathering steps of the study.[5] One of the options to reach this critical self-review, apart from individual moments of thinking, are interview analysis panels and specific groups established only to discuss such interviews gathered by peers, as it was the case for this present study (Bertaux 2018, 96; Wengraf 2003, 145). Such groups established in order to analyse interviews or even only some segments make it possible to experience different angles of interpretation. For various backgrounds in the group would influence the interpretation process and make the researcher or the project team aware of potential biases.

2.2.1 Biographical Narrative Interviews: Overview of some Terms

Subsequent to field research, the recorded interview is to be entirely transcribed and anonymised (Bertaux suggests, for instance, transcribing the first three or four interviews: 2018, 83). The transcribed interview can be then considered as a text data. Before the analysis, the text should be segmented.

The first step of the analysis involves the structural description: the story units will be interpreted by means of indicators, narration forms, and language markers. The main objective is to reconstruct these units within the biographical project and to analyse person's interaction to the social setting(s) in different occasions and time periods. In this phase, the researcher further develops the sensibility that started to emerge whilst hearing and reading the interview several times. Following the structural description, the suprasegmental elements are to be taken into consideration. These can be content-based or narrational linkages. Through the interpretation of such elements, the biography is reconstructed in its own complexity as a sociological subject. This part of the analysis and reconstruction is called the analytical abstraction. A further aim of the analytical abstraction is to pull out possible indicators for the theory building from the segments and locate these into the (relational) context of biography and society. The last analytical stage is then the comparison of such indicators. But what are the elements to be studied, reflected and interpreted in such a text material? What features, that are to be found in the interview, help the researcher to reconstruct the biography? What is the relation between content and language mechanisms?

The narrative mode of the interview provides the informant, as said before, with a space to "shape own biographical identity"(Schütze 2008a, 9). It is

---

[5]   Similar to Wengraf, Strauss and Corbin speak of the individual experience of the researcher as an important element of the procedure (1990, 43). From their point of view, it is crucial to develop a certain sensitivity.

important to keep in my mind that the life story of an informant would not be told in a "linear and coherent" way (Bertaux 2018, 88), so shaping it in a diachronic way is the target of the reconstruction (or the researcher's job). Concerning this feature of providing the free space, Schütze first defines the life story as a narrative "gestalt" that is fashioned through one's own experiences in segmental and sequential form. He points to four process structures that he has discovered to be "the most important ordering principles" in biographies (2008a, 11 f; 1981; 1983; 1984, 92–98). In a nutshell, these are: a) biographical action schemes; b) trajectories (of suffering); c) institutional expectation patterns; and d) creative metamorphoses of biographical identity.

Under the biographical action scheme, the person takes initiative to change, shape, design, and/or influence their own life course. Under the second term, the trajectories of suffering, the events taking place in the primary or secondary zone of the individual's social attendance (Schütz and Luckmann 2003, 80) do grasp their life or the given situation with tongs so that the person cannot overcome the suffering, only counters it, acts up and starts to be alienated from own identity in a cumulative process (cf. Riemann and Schütze 1991; Schütze 1981, 88–103; 1995).

Schütze (2008a, 11) explains the third process structure as follows, "Institutional expectation patterns, in which persons are following up institutionally shaped and normatively defined courses of life" which includes career ideas as well as family modes. The creative metamorphoses pattern, contrary to the latter two processes, is a flourishment of an inner development of the autobiographer that was/is discovered by the same (Riemann 1987, 29).[6]

According to Schütze, the biographical recollection would be built up through "sequential combinations" of such process structures. In this sense, a biographical narrative interview as a text data should be analysed, as the first step of the reconstruction, through employing a segmental, sequential disassembling of the text (2008a, 12). In other words, the text structure (or the transcript) is to be partitioned from one story to another story considering if the one or other sequence represents a narrative, descriptive, or argumentative scheme (Schütze 1983; 2008a, 15; cf. Ochs and Capps 1996).[7]

These three language forms utilised in narrations differentiate themselves from each other (cf. Schütz and Luckmann 2003, 286–304).[8] While the nar-

---

[6]   In his study on psychiatry patients and their biographical identity formations, Gerhard Riemann sees these four process structures as "important guides" for reconstruction.

[7]   In their article, from another point of departure, Elinor Ochs and Lisa Capps (p. 20) point out: "While differing in complexity and circumstance, narratives transform life's journeys into sequences of events and evoke shifting and enduring perspectives on experience."

[8]   To exemplify such forms, I assume remembering the motives of action moments would

rative sections convey incumbent biographical concepts – the (somehow) rendered past experiences, the descriptive sections of the narration, according to Schütze, consist of explanations of social setting(s) and "unknown phenomenon". And when an interpretation is required, it occurs in arguments built on the informant's perspective (Schütze 2008a, 57 f). Again Schütze points out that goal of both forms – description and argumentation – is to clarify the subject matter for the interviewer and elucidate the possible vagueness in the self-presentation. The argumentative passages of a story involve features of biographical identity of the informant due to its interpretative nature (2008a, 59 f; cf. 1983, 286).

Continuing with the steps of the analysis, the fundamental aspect in partitioning the text data is the determination of the language activities such as forms of narration, discourse markers, speech acts, verbal and non-verbal reactions, and conjunctions and formulations pointing to temporal and causal changes in one's biography. The informant might utilise these in order to fade-in or fade-out another story, change the topic, mute certain experiences, or prepare an argument. Concerning the aforementioned biographical process structures, the narrator would employ language markers, such as "and then I thought" (Schütze 2008a, 26f; 1981; 1984). Parallel to the consideration of language-based forms and codes used by the narrator, the researcher elaborates the content.

Concerning the descriptive and argumentative forms, Schütze (1983; 2008a; 2008b) reports that these find place mostly at coda or in pre-coda moments to end the interview with a self-theoretical assumption. He (2008b, 42) then adds

be helpful that Alfred Schütz highlights as "in order to" and "because (of)" junctures. He distinguishes these two motives due to their temporal patterns that build the causality order. "In order to" builds the causal chain with a perspective to present and future, and the latter – "because (of)" conjunction – is to be found in the biographical sedimentation. Schütz illustrates his point about the interpretations behind human actions with the example of a man who goes to his room to sleep and notices a shadow which seems to be a snake (p. 288). In order to prevent a possible danger instead of ignoring it and disregarding that moment of interpretation the man finds a stick because he is frightened of snakes (pp. 296-99). In a post-narration of this situation (in our case an interview), this man's interpretation would be told first perhaps in a form of narrative that he was going to sleep, et cetera. Nevertheless, when he would also see the need of explaining what his interpretation was at the moment in that very room that led to his action with a stick, he would describe his motives using one of these two junctures. The argumentative form would be then employed just like descriptions to clarify his action motives at this very moment, perhaps, entangled to his past experiences. In sum, the narrative form of storytelling would lead and/or include possible descriptive and argumentative patterns. And both of these forms would be utilised to clarify the setting and biographical position that reflect each other reciprocally.

that self-theorisations are like double-edged swords, they can be central as well as intervene in the biographical storytelling. Of course these argumentations do not necessarily occur at the end of the main narrative, for instance, when the informant wants to comment on a specific trajectory, they would break the narrative flow for a brief moment (Schütze 1984, 98). An argument around coda would be employed to summarize certain biographical processes, like the trajectory of suffering in relation to the biographical complexity (p. 103) – the balancing of biographical account at juncture of the informant's interpretation (p. 107). In this sense, Schütze underscores the argumentative motive of remarking the crisis and biographical curves for the individual that echoes in one's life even afterwards (p. 103).

Reflecting Schütze's point, Bartmann and Kunze (2008) point out that argumentative passages can appear as metaphorical descriptions, like in Iranian films, in which prohibited images, ideas, and actions are reconstructed through metaphors. They set in their paper three further argumentative forms: the argumentation with the aim to lead the narration to a biographical narrative unit; the argumentation that subsumes substantial life historical elements and their reconstruction in post period; and the argumentation that follows the autobiographical narrative unit to, for example, underline self-positioning (pp. 185–90). Furthermore, since argumentations represent core – and perhaps raw – self-theoretical reconstructions of past experiences, these can be the modes of displaying the "nonexplicit [biographical] narratives" (p. 180). These are also "highly reflexive" biographical moments instead of "deficits" (like the intervention of self-theoretical actions in Schütze's terms), according to Sylke Bartmann and Katharina Kunze (p. 190).

2.2.2 Data Collection

Prior to Interview

The interview preparation contained three main steps: a) the preparation of the open stimulus question and the preparation of the explanation of the study and the personal research interest for the possible informants; b) finding interview partners/informants/autobiographers and/or possible gatekeepers and contacting them via different channels such as key persons (siblings, family, friends, et cetera) prior to field research; and c) approaching interview partners, explaining the research, research perspective and its objectives in common codes instead of using an abstract research language. All of these steps should contain an openness on the part of the researcher vis-à-vis partners, which means that the researcher would not cover any specific interest. The last patterns also include specific technical information to be given such as how long an autobiographical interview takes, what the informant expects, and that the confidentiality of the narrator will be assured and protected through anonymisation. At this first step, it becomes clear if the possible informant wants to take part or if they reject providing the research with their life story. Due to the conditions in Van and its surrounding area, for instance, I often encountered people who rejected to be narrators. I also made mistakes such as utilising a complex research language while expressing my interest, which led to rejections.

Interview Situation

As aforementioned, my informants chose the place for the interview, some of them were conducted in a café, some in their flats, or office. Every interview could be recorded thanks to my informants' agreement. I was able to keep in touch with three of my informants after our first meeting. Unfortunately, no follow up interview – with recording – could take place. Most of the interviews took approximately 90 to 120 minutes, with a main narrative of 30 to 45 minutes in most cases. Yet, I have also collected some interviews with a duration of one hour in total or one of them around three hours. Moreover, one of the interview partners did not provide any biographical information and talked instead about history and current conditions ruling in the Kurdish society.[9]

The first round of questions I posed after the autonomously structured main narration was based on my notes that I took whilst they were providing their main narrative. The aim was to extend my knowledge for the reconstruction of the relevant situation. Following the first round of questions, I pointed at their descriptions or arguments concerning different topics they highlighted. However, it is important to specify that this sort of "chronological flow" of questioning was not always the case. Questions, for instance, related to their arguments also followed some of the questions concerning biographical narrative units in order to reach a proper understanding.

After every interview, I returned to the step of finding my next narrator who would "fit" into my research project in terms of viewpoints, contrasts and resemblances. The questions I asked myself concerned, for instance, the age, gender, and political background. In this regard, I had the chance to receive the help of my gatekeepers of course. Nonetheless after my field research in Van,

---

[9] Perhaps, the reason why this informant did not give any biographical information or disregarded my aim was my lack of experience or the conditions that made this meeting possible. "The conditions" indicate here my gatekeepers who respect informant's works about the Kurdish society and history. Meeting a public figure also kept my mind and perhaps influenced my approach to this particular person. And, therefore, it caused this sort of outcome. I revisit this occasion further in Chapter 5.3 Contemporary Situation in Van.

I realised I could not conduct any interviews with the women there. Unfortunately, the hope of getting back to Van anytime soon (for another attempt) did not come into question anymore. In this sense, the sample – especially from Van – is not gender-balanced.

2.2.3 Analysis

To begin with, the interviews were transcribed and certain parts were masked such as the names or certain towns where the informant lived. In order to secure the anonymity of the informant, some story segments that could result in the evident identification of the person were deleted from the text too. For the transcription I also used my field notes and notes from the interview situation in order to take into consideration non-verbal activities for instance.

The first step of the analysis is differentiating segments of the narration or how Schütze calls it the text sort differentiation (2008b, 17 f). After that, the analysis consists of the reconstruction, interpretation, and sociological theory building through the comparative discussion of several interviews. Under these very terms, the interview was then treated as an autobiographical text material a) within its certain context; b) following the question of how the interaction parties – the researcher and autobiographer – viewed the interview situation; c) looking after and marking the communicative schemes such as narration, description, and arguments; and d) elaborating the "direction of" the textualization and the material itself (ibid.). In other words, what the material tells us during its editing procedure.

With the third sub-step, marking the non-narrative sequences, the next part of the analysis starts: the structural description. At this step, I partitioned the text material thoroughly into sequences based on the stories told. Every story has a beginning and an end in different forms. Due to this fact, the text has to be differentiated into its sorts and the narrative, descriptive, and argumentative units have to be marked. These units tell us thanks to their very nature how the experience is processed and reconstructed. This is also why the transcription would be partitioned into its various segments.

Structural Description

The core of the analysis consists in the structural description. Until this stage of my work, I have transcribed the autobiographical material, handled its composition as a whole and then differentiated into story units. Then the analysis starts with the interpretation of language and content. First, language mechanisms such as indicators, discourse markers, pauses, fade-in and fade-out moments, revisions by the autobiographer, self-questioning moments, and background constructions are significant to be dealt with (Riemann 1987, 55 f; Schütze 1984; 2008b). I then interpreted the sequences line by line in order to understand the way of storytelling, the framework the storyteller employs and, of course, what phenomena are more important or less important for the informant. Such language codes and forms show us the categories that are built by the informant. With the help of these categories, the researcher is responsible for sketching the typologies of personal and social processes. The abstraction of these categories would finally lead to sociological theories.

Of course, at this very point of the analysis the content of what the autobiographer tells plays a major role. Under these terms, I have always considered the given social context of the interview. When they talked to me about the violence they encountered in their childhood, I needed the background knowledge to understand the biographical processes. For instance, how the operations of counterguerrilla in the 1990s are portrayed or how specific historical information concerning the Armenians of the very hometown is used in storytelling were questions related to the background knowledge. The comparative interpretation and discussion of autobiographer's personal memory starts at this point, which is the comparison of different stories or sequences in one single interview. In other words, the question was how the very content was implied or explicitly provided. Language mechanisms could play a role at this level as well. Whether one tuned into or muted a narration and why they did it were the points that followed. Furthermore, this procedure made me familiar with the informants' life stories before jumping into theoretical discussions.

Analytical Abstraction

Following the profound analysis through the structural description method, I took the text material into consideration in its entire complexity. At this step of the interpretation and reconstruction, which is a sort-of-conclusion for one biographical storytelling case, the research examines "the reconstruction of the linkage, concatenation, embeddedness and domination competition, overlap intertwining of the various structural processes of biography" (Schütze 2008b, 24). Riemann (1987, 59) defines two steps for the analytical abstraction, first to sketch the biographical holism through "supra-segmental markers" and then to focus on the autobiographical argumentations, the self-theoretical segments. Similar to Riemann, Schütze (2008b, 40; cf. 1983) directs us to three steps: first to consider the supra-segmental narrative units; then to discuss and reconstruct the trajectories and dominant process mechanisms (cf. Riemann and Schütze 1991) and notions of metamorphosis; and finally to elaborate the argumentative reactions of the person to their own biographical processes.

Under these terms, the researcher composes an analytical description or portrayal of the biography including the "most important specific and universal features and process mechanisms of the life history" (Schütze 2008b, 43) and "[generalising] grid structure of categories" (p. 45). The same interpretation process is then repeated for every autobiographical interview and only at the very end of the analysis are they compared with each other in order to reconstruct a theoretical model.

Based on these analytical steps, I wrote the analytical abstraction splitting them into two parts: *the biographical synopsis* and *the elements of violence in narration*. First, I reconstructed the biography within its diachronic nature, for instance regarding the person's experiences with the household first, then the school and professional occupation. The biographical synopsis involves, in this sense, the portrayal of the life story in its social setting. Later, I focused on violence since the narrators employed such compartments in order to tell their life stories, in the main narrative as well as afterwards. In these terms, I have discussed the arguments and descriptions of the informant. Furthermore, argumentative passages – apart from their dominance in some interviews or main narrative parts – often involved similar storytelling patterns to what Bartmann and Kunze (2008) proposed: the argumentation leading to a biographical narrative unit; following the biographical narrative unit; or involving life historical elements and their reconstruction in post period. In consequence, these had to be carefully studied as links to narrative units and stories.

It is important to remark that such arguments were not discussed in terms of whether they were correct or not, but rather in terms of what their meaning for the biography and its transmission under the given current circumstances could be. In this manner, whether a socially dominant narrative, for instance stories of coexistence, that one can hear in similar ways in different places concerning the Armenian Genocide, were true is not the question of this study, but rather what this experience means for the informant's present. Or questioning how they replace the subjectivity in their stories – for instance, seeing people as generalised victims without agency – was a vital point in the reconstruction of biographies. Due to that, arguments in my informants' stories constituted key elements in reconstructing the narrator's self and locating the self in the social setting.

Comparative Analysis

Schütze (2008b, 47) suggests two general approaches to run a comparative discussion: either to compare cases and "contrast maximally" for "explor[ing] and map[ing] a new field" or the line of cases to "contrast minimally" in order disclose the socially embedded "process mechanisms". Both can be carried out in a parallel fashion in every case. What Schütze proposes is indeed developing of a trajectory of thought based on Grounded Theory and its involvement in maximizing and minimizing the differences across comparative groups toward generating theories (Glaser and Strauss 2009a, 45–58).

2.3 Research Questions

The primary questions that this study poses for the discussion based on the comparative analysis of empirical data, the autobiographical interviews and ethnographic materials, had to be reconsidered due to the rapid changes in Turkey. When I was planning and drafting this research project, it was the years 2013 and 2014, when a cease-fire between the government and PKK was in effect in the whole country and a possible peace was thought to be close enough. Furthermore, that time period (has) also opened a space for critical discussions concerning the Armenian past. The civil society actors, firstly in the Kurdish society, have launched genocide debates and discussions about Kurdish complicities in it. Such circumstances motivated researchers and journalists to conduct their projects in the region. Due to this fact, I have outlined questions considering different angles of the Kurdish collective memory.

In the beginning, my focal interest was examining the collective memory in the periphery of Van and finding answers or further conflict areas in response to the question: *How are the genocidal past, the experience of violence and years of nationalistic denial represented within the political and cultural framework of the region?* The term "framework" contains numerous actors, various abstract and concrete aspects, and collectivity features. Furthermore, my main intention after this core research question was to gather and analyse intergenerational data in a comparative sense. Yet, the situation *in situ* became challenging for this idea.

Because of the war that reignited after the elections in June 2015, the second and embedded research question emerged to take the place of the first one: *What are the reflections of the past in a form of collective and/or individual remembrance?* Instead of questioning identity formations directly, I sought to display forms of individual memories and their relation to the collective memory regimes. Nonetheless, the identity question is a fundamental aspect, one that should not be overlooked or ignored in biography research, since the narrator conveys a reconstruction of own biographical identity. In this sense, we can see the reconstructions of individual experiences as particular features of one's identity formation. And the life story narration makes them surface.

Based on Grounded Theory (Glaser and Strauss 2009b), I have regarded the life stories – of course with the help of further materials – as a source to generate theories of collective notions. In these terms, the following question has replaced the first and the latter ones: How are the genocidal past and the (individual) experience of violence reflected in personal and collective memories as well as in narrating the Self, family past, and political sphere?

In these terms, the study first concentrated on reflecting and analysing the individual and, in relation to that, collective memories, and the act of storytelling itself. The act of storytelling provides us with different aspects regarding the features of memory in a collective and personal sense.

As mentioned before, the war disqualified the chance to carry out an intergenerational discussion based on narratives of two or three generations from the same family. It had two main reasons: first because I was urged to carry out short field trips which were not appropriate for such an intergenerational concentration; and secondly because trust came to be a hard deal under such heated circumstances. Most of my interview partners were reached through my gatekeepers. In these terms, the third research question discarded itself: *How do people in the periphery begin to talk about the traumata of the Armenian Genocide – as grandchildren of victims, non-victims, or victimisers?* Nevertheless, the main target of this question – discussing what lies behind and conceptualising triggers, has remained during the whole process and has preserved a certain reflexivity in the analysis of gathered autobiographies. The focus on narrative triggers (and beyond, for instance an experience of an event) echoed in the following research question: How do people talk about the violence and/ or the Armenian Genocide in their narration? Formulating the question above in this open and maybe naïve way made me further consider the component of triggers. The biographical experiences narrated in interviews have widened the spectrum of the "trigger" concept.

3 Studying Memory. Approaches, Concepts, and Complexities

In the case of this book, there were two primary issues in discussing theories. Both flourish from the very nature of memory studies. The first question has been: how can one summarize such theories since the studies inquiring into the aspects of remembering and various data of memory are rooted in different disciplines – cultural studies, sociology, political studies, psychology, ethnomusicology, film studies, and history? The vast palette that involves questions on memory issues is to be considered transdisciplinary. Social scientist Jeffrey Olick (2009, 249) asks in this context if "memory studies, social or otherwise, [is] a field" based on his early inquiry with Joyce Robbins (Olick and Robbins 1998). Of course, scholar's perspective that is shaped in their specific field has influences in the given discussion, contextualisation efforts as well as findings. I have been deliberately thinking the present study had to look into theory from the vantage point of narrations, echoing the pioneers' works in experimental psychology (for instance, Bartlett 1995), sociology (for instance, Halbwachs 1991; 2012), literature (for instance, Bakhtin 1981), and so forth. So the diverse nature of the field – if there were a homogenous field in social sciences at all – was the first point to consider in the process of my analysis (cf. Erll 2011).[1]

The further issue was being possibly trapped by – in American psychologist Kenneth Gergen's (1994) words – the "dualistic epistemology" and splitting the concept into individual and collective memory. Although it has been "clear" to me for years that this chapter had to be based on these two main core constructions – individual and collective, building such compounds seemed to me not saturating after spending such an intense time interpreting life stories. However, I could not find the right path to contextualize.

Social scientist and psychologist Jens Brockmeier's (2015) masterpiece *Beyond the Archive* gave me the inspiration to deal with this puzzle: the narrative. Memory is a theme conceptualised and reconceptualised through interactions (cf. Prager 1998, 60).[2] And the narrative is one of the essential tools in these interactions. It binds the social context to the personal realities and the other way around, "[a]t any point in time, our sense of entities, including

---

[1]   Alongside the disciplinary variations, Astrid Erll differentiates the national compounds of debates on memory as well, highlighting, for instance, the "rigorous definition" of the cultural memory by Aleida and Jan Assmann in Germany or the Birmingham school tradition in the UK.

[2]   Sociologist and psychoanalyst Jeffrey Prager (p. 60) calls this interactionist nature the "intersubjectiveness of memory".

ourselves, is an outcome of our subjective involvement in the world. Narrative mediates this involvement" (Ochs and Capps 1996, 21). It does, of course, not mean that collective and personal memories were to be seen as the same. Nevertheless, they also should not be viewed as entirely different phenomena in strict ways (cf. Rothberg 2009, 15).[3] There is a fundamental connection between those two premises, may it be (or come out through) language, commemoration events, counter-stories, or the media (Huyssen 2000; Misztal 2010; Ryan 2011). The point is the reconstruction of experience.

In these terms, I have organised this chapter in two main parts: 3.1 Conceptualising Memory and 3.2 Contested Memories. This chapter continues without splitting the theoretical discussion(s) into personal and collective bases, keeping the question in mind how scholars working on issues of memory (have) argued when it comes to the interaction and narrative's performative power. In the first subchapter, I question the place of (human and narrative) interaction in studies. Is memory put under collective terms or considered through the looking glass of individuality? Is the interaction somehow linked to the process of memory reconstruction and how? Thus, I come to the point of highlighting the narrative quality. The narrative is the outcome of the individual and collective interpretational schemes that render conceptions of time and place in a setting of (endless) interactions. They are the key members of our memories. Additionally, in a short subchapter I discuss the question of how violence is considered in our interpretational frameworks after the violent events or in the next generations.

The second subchapter is about the contested memories. I present contestation as a standard feature in the memory landscape instead of putting it in the margins. Hence the study's argument is, stemming from the essentiality of interaction in producing a narrative and reconstructing past events in here and now, that contested memories belong to the very nature of any memory formation.

3.1   Conceptualising Memory

In his profound work *Das kulturelle Gedächtnis / Cultural Memory and Early Civilizations*, Jan Assmann (2013, 20 f) presents the term "cultural memory" as the fourth option alongside a) mimetic memory, that is in his terms based

---

[3]   In the introduction of his distinguished study *Multidirectional Memory*, Michael Rothberg (p. 15) points out, based on Halbwachs' discussions, "all memories are simultaneously individual and collective."

on the everyday routines; b) the memory of materials; and c) communicative memory, that is based on the system(s) of language and non-verbal communication and stems from social interaction. Assmann's cultural memory subsumes all these three forms. Furthermore, it creates a space for materials, interactions, and their new possible linkages, transforms them into scripts, and transfers the meaning and knowledge into social compounds. Assmann (pp. 52 ff) calls cultural memory a phenomenon looking "for fixed anchors in the past" having carriers/transmitters embodied in institutions or individuals – as he calls for instance bards whom I see in both shapes as an institution and at the same time an individual. Notwithstanding, he distinguishes communicative memory from cultural memory, underlining the absence of institution in the first. However, when we consider family for example as one of the most common and widespread institutions in our society, the question occurs inevitably: how should a family member tell a story from the past – with or without an anchor in the personal past – viewed in Assmann's framework? To what extent can we distinguish the communicative, institutional, social, or of course individual aspects from each other?[4]

In his pioneering work *Das kollektive Gedächtnis / La mémoire collective* that has become one of the fundaments of studies on collective memory, Durkheimian sociologist Maurice Halbwachs (1991) outlines this particular phenomenon in an interwoven space with parties such as individuals, groups, and institutions engaging simultaneously. He argues – in historian Patrick Hutton's words (2000, 537) – that the "collective memory evokes the presence of the past" in a continuous social reconfiguration. The reconstruction of an experience or event in different social settings in Halbwachs' terms points out an inevitable bounding between group and individual memories in fact – even if he differentiates these two agents on the same pages (the collective and the person) (cf. Olick 1999; for an in-depth discussion on Durkheim and memory: Misztal 2003; Bartlett also underscores briefly the nuance of Durkheim's sociology in Halbwachs' theory building please see: Bartlett 1995, 294 f). Olick and Robbins (1998, 109) highlight in their initial inquiry that "for Halbwachs ... memory is a matter of how minds work together in society."

---

[4] How Assmann treats the myths and their function would be an interesting point to keep in mind. He differentiates two possible working principals of myths: one concluding the present in positive ways; and the other settling in nostalgias of the past and problematising gaps in the present social world. Both, however, influence the group orientation which Assmann calls *Mythomotorik* (pp. 78–80). Both can be employed simultaneously in correlated forms even though they contest each other. So following question occurs: what is the relation of past with history and memory considering the perspective which claims that myths provide an orientation for the collective?

Halbwachs struggles with the heterogeneity which is embodied in his work as "collective memories" (in plural). In this regard, he points at various subjective perspectives, that derive from social settings. Due to this configuration, he sees memory (this diverse liquid world) as an antagonist to history, and makes history a rigid component. Assmann (2013, 43, footnote 24; cf. Lorenz 2014) yet points out that Halbwachs was opposing the "positivist term of history" and the historiography of his time which is to be seen today critically by historians themselves.[5] So, then how can we put history into the framework of memory? To where does Halbwachs' "memories" description lead us? What is the relation of memory to history? With an alternative contextualisation: what is the relation of individuals to institutions in writing and speaking about the past?

Halbwachs' concept (1991, 31 f) epitomises the fundament that "every individual memory is a 'perspective' looking upon the collective memory." And this perspective relays different elements when the patterns change, like when the person comes in contact "with other milieus". "The relation to different collective milieus" determines the perspective and how we remember. Although the perspectival changes he describes are mostly based on nations and national narratives, he comes back to integrative conceptualisation of "collective memories" (pp. 35–44; 71 f). We can and must indeed expand this national framing of Halbwachs so that the term would involve different groups and (even) individuals' reconstruction of the past. In his other inspirational work *Les cadres sociaux de la mémoire / On Collective Memory*, he (2012, 121) emphasises that without "framework" – or [its] various patterns – there is no memory.[6]

His understanding of a group is predicated on non-abstract or semi-abstract spaces (1991, 108 f). In the very same lines of *La mémoire collective*, Halbwachs yet sort-of disintegrates his term of collective memories from the national frames and speaks of interpretation patterns that are "fused" into each other. For him, memory is an issue of reconstruction nourishing our relation(s) with or perspectives unto the collective.

---

[5] Assmann's footnote reminds us remarks of several critical scholars on historiography, like Foucault, Agamben, and Hobsbawm. Historian Chris Lorenz, for instance, points at the "temporal simultaneity and coexistence of past, present and future" (p. 46) of the progressive time conceptions disregarding a linear flow. He also questions that putting history and memory in polarity. For instance, he argues that there is a need for a new form of questioning of time conceptions since the past moments stay in the present and build a temporal ambiguity (p. 57).

[6] On the previous pages, Halbwachs constructs his theory beyond the boundaries of national narratives and continues developing it through discussing family and religious group settings.

In quasi contrast to the Halbwachsian concept, British psychologist Frederic Charles Bartlett (1995, 296) addresses the "memory *in* the group, and not ... *of* the group" (author's emphasis). He points out that Halbwachs highlights elements of social-group frameworks influencing the remembering. In his words, "it [the group] provides either the stimulus or the conditions under which individuals belonging to the group recall the past" (p. 294). He is not deterministic in his discussion, but he views critically the determinism of somehow crystallising the memory *of* the collective.

Bartlett continues his critique of memory *in* the group underscoring two features: first that there is always oppositional view in the group; and "certain persistent human tendencies" would bring sort-of domination to "certain features" (cf. Wertsch 2004, 23).[7] Contemplating the interaction in the social context, Bartlett (p. 298) further argues that the path should start with questioning the individual, and then leading it to the "properties both of behaviour and of experience" as outcomes of collectives. In his view, the interaction between people and collectively produced social elements (and the interaction of different temporal constructions) play the most influential role in the memory regimes *in* the group. In short, he discusses memory not as "accurate and true representations of past events and experiences" but as designs "to fulfil a social function" (Brockmeier 2015, 57).

In her empirical work *Personal trajectories, collective memories*, Constance de Saint-Laurent (2017) enquires into the individuals' relation to history and collective understandings of historical moments. She proposes working on this subject with the concept of trajectory that would reflect the dynamic pattern of memory and changings in personal interpretation in time. She defines collective memory, paraphrasing her, as dialogical action in a culturally mediated realm contemplating self, signs, and others' stories (pp. 265 ff). In discussing the trajectories in their social frameworks, she (p. 268) underscores the need to shed light on "which resources, information, values and representations are available to [people] and what importance they may give to them." In this respect, the interaction stands as the basic module in making, changing and transferring the memory. The term interaction involves not just the relation between and among people but furthermore the interplay between socially and politically (re-)constructed features such as historiography or other elements like memorials, public speeches, and movies.

---

[7]   As a brief remark on the first point which Bartlett highlights, social scientist and anthropologist James V. Wertsch (p. 23) speaks of "complementary" form of "the distributed version of collective memory." How group members glance at or remember a past event differs, yet these also "exist in a coordinated system of complementary pieces." His argument stands as an antagonist to the descriptions of homogenised collective memory.

The dynamic pattern of memory has been a significant point of discussion among scholars. For instance, Astrid Erll (2011, 12) proposes the concept of travelling memories as follows "that *all* cultural memory *must* 'travel', be kept in motion, in order to 'stay alive', to have an impact both on individual minds and social formations." In doing so, she underscores the "transculturality of memory" which, according to Erll, is not a new phenomenon but can be traced back to the ancient times. She "conceive[s] 'transcultural memory' as an approach which is based on the insight that memory fundamentally means movement: traffic between individual and collective levels of remembering, circulation among social, medial, and semantic dimensions" (p. 15). According to her, the transcultural state of memory disregards strict frames, like "site-bound" and "nation-bound" premises (ibid.), as well as the container-like descriptions of memory.

With a particular focus on narrative, Kenneth Gergen (1994, 95) reminds us that biographical memory is to be read in its given social context that "suppl[ies] a wide variety of memorial devices." Considering especially textual accounts, he pinpoints five "rules of narrative" that organise the story (pp. 91 ff).[8] In these five rules, the individual (or the phenomenon which we call personal memory) never stands alone, but instead finds itself in a broad network with a variety of interconnections, be it causal, social, or temporal. The person who produces the narrative, the memory of an event or the experience is driven by further orientations or motives (p. 82). Thus the processing towards the narrative outcome is run through a "circuit" of several different questions in interval of individual, group, society, time, and so on. In this sense, he points out the embeddedness of narrative in a social setting (cf. Prager 1998). As Jeffrey Prager (1998, 167; cf. Zittoun 2017) puts it, based on his experience as a therapist, "we find autobiography anything but autonomous; it is more properly sociobiography."[9]

---

[8]   First of all, the story requires an anchor for (re)construction which Gergen calls *valued endpoint*; then *related events* are to be selected and organised around this endpoint; a *temporal ordering* gives shape to the flow of events – at this juncture, he reminds of the non-linear time constructions of Proust and Joyce; in order to direct to the endpoint or answer how this endpoint would be possible, the *causal linkages* between events will be put down; and *demarcation signs* for raising questions or "tantalizing doubt" would be added at the end.

[9]   In this scope, Tania Zittoun speaks of "semiotic loops" that are formed in the process of meaning-making when we "move" in temporal sense between our experiences, the past, and present as well as possible or wished future scenarios. She argues that memory on a personal level "demands certain semiotic loops" considering the construction of the past and present as well as "interactions with others". At the same time, collective remembering "can be in contrast conceived as remembering something about a

In another study on the (collective) memory (Wertsch 2008), we encounter two distinct theorisations of narrative conduct: One specified by the singular individual experiences, and the other generating frameworks, making comparison possible and soiling a fundament for reconstruction. While the first operates through fixed anchors and frames episodes of a lifetime, the latter, the "schematic narrative templates" (ibid.), facilitates an organisation of (past) experiences. In this regard, Bresco de Luna (2017) highlights the term prolepsis, borrowing it from literary theory and summarizes it as follows "bringing the future into the present ... is a narrative mechanism for guiding the reader, since subsequent events in the plot acquire meaning and directionality vis-à-vis a future scenario already presented." (p. 283) De Luna proposes to rethink our longstanding "traditional linear concept of time" when it comes to the collective memory regimes (p. 282). Hence, he (p. 283) underscores a pragmatic approach – "whereby collective memory is understood as a socio-culturally situated activity aimed at giving meaning to the past in order to meet present demands and attain different future goals" (similarly cf. Prager 1998, 91). In other words, how we reconstruct past events depends on our interpretation of the present conditions and imaginations of the future. What we should also look after in the memory is the elements of forthcoming and possible events (cf. Ochs and Capps 1996).[10]

Within this context, De Luna (2017, 286 f) sees (group) narratives vital for conceptualising time scopes. These narratives or their patterns would then be utilised as prolepsis notions in the reconstruction of the past (cf. de Saint-Laurent et al. 2017).[11] Additionally, Wertsch (2008, 124) emphasises that the "schematic narrative templates" are not universally singular but outcomes of social knowledge productions so that every single one varies from the others. Similarly, we can and should read the prolepsis structures. These patterns vary. De Luna (2017, 289) underlines that this is only "one of a range of possible ways imagining and articulating the past, the present, and the future vis-à-vis different political projects."

configuration of events in the past, which affected many lives in an interrelated manner, and collectively designated as such" (p. 297). This semiotic process, also reminding of de Saint-Laurent's trajectory of memory concept, is open for interplays and modifications in making the loops.

[10] Ochs and Capps, for instance, describe their point in these terms as follows: "Narratives situate narrators, protagonists, and listener/readers at the nexus of morally organized, past, present, and possible experiences" (p. 22).

[11] For instance, the study which is cross-referred (de Saint Laurent et al. 2017) explores the collective memory as a political tool in post-truth times. It emphasises that this phenomenon is used emblematically for visions of the present and future by referring to the past.

Comparably, US-American psychologist Jerome Bruner (2004) starts his inquiry on autobiographical memory defining narrative as the most significant temporal pave instead of any other – mostly linear – understanding. He (p. 692) argues that the interpretation of past experiences should be seen as part of the biographies as well, or in his words "narrative imitates life, life imitates narrative." Taking the context-dependence – social, historical, and linguistic aspects – into consideration, our ways of interpretation can alter in various forms. And therefore, the narratives too. Bruner's argument "a life as led is inseparable from a life as told" (p. 708) points out not only the attempts in reconstructing the past but also the state of now and an envisioned future. To sum-up preliminarily, when we talk about memory we in fact refer to interpretational structures that are based on interactions of temporal and social settings. These moreover function to narrate on the past, present and/or future, "[t]he narrated past matters because of its relation to the present and the future. Interlocutors tell personal narratives about the past primarily to understand and cope with their current concerns" (Ochs and Capps 1996, 25).

In his thoroughly run critical study on memory issues, social scientist Jens Brockmeier sets his focus on the autobiographical process and the narrative – viewing it as "the language of existential meaning-making" (2015, 51). He (p. 61) describes the possible approach to the memory structures as "understand[ing] practices of remembering as embedded or embodied … in environments, Umwelts, eco-niches, media ecologies, meaning contexts of everyday life, and historical Lebenswelten (life-worlds) of action and interaction." He discusses all these "conventions" contextualising memory debates throughout neuroscientific research, literature, cultural, and social studies. From his point of view, the language that he considers in Wittgenstein's terms and calls "the hub of humans' semiotic universe" operates significantly in all these frames. Alongside other studies, Brockmeier (p. 125) reminds us of Austin's (1972) speech act theory,[12] which discloses the performativity of language, as follows: "there is no basic divide between narrative as representation and narrative as action and social interactions… Stories are strategic interventions into ongoing activities." At this point, Wittgenstein's remark on language dwells in his conceptualisation that language cannot be seen as a divided subject from its social context (cf. Halbwachs 1991, 31; 2012, 368).[13]

[12] I would also add John R. Searle's further works on this very concept, such as *Speech Acts* or *Making the social world: the structure of human civilization.*

[13] Halbwachs points out that our interpretations (or memories) are directly bonded to the collectivities (or milieus as he expresses). When our relation to the collective changes, so our memories would be affected by this change. Furthermore, in the social entity, language rules the reconstructive level for and of our memories.

In the autobiographical process of memory, time (or in other words, temporal comprehension) plays an important role. According to Brockmeier (2015, see especially Chapter 8), the classical chronological linearisation of time starting from Aristoteles and reaching to Newton has started to be critically grasped with the rise of modern evaluation of time.[14] Through the lens of narrative, he (pp. 272 f) argues our "ideas and concepts of time" cannot be located to or around fixed anchors, neither are they "universally given entities, nor epistemological preconditions of experience." In his reference, we deal with "cultural and historical constructions, created by human beings" that are employed for meaning-making processes of our societal life (cf. Sorokin and Merton 1937; Wallerstein 1988; 1998).

We can see this complex territory involving time, space, social interaction, and personal interpretation, in a way, as a realm of heterogenous contestations. The tool of language affects our autobiographical localisation in particular temporalities. How Brockmeier (2015, 273 f) maintains, we deal with the narrative structures, "our most advanced ways to shape complex temporal experiences, including remembering." Alongside the meaning-making and positioning to produced knowledge, we build "temporal scenarios" when we tell stories. In other words, the narrative that helps us to localise ourselves in time, meaning, and new layers of interpretation, does not concur with the linear time structures when we employ relativities flourished from individual settings. What we deal with is much more complicated than a linear temporal building. For instance, Halbwachs (1991, 71 ff) values the relativity due to the individuals and multiple group settings when he underlines the plurality of collective memory(ies) and rejects the idea of "a" universal memory. Even though from time to time he comes back to rigid or semi-rigid formations of time and space (p. 150), he pinpoints numerous potential individual encounters.

In sum, what Brockmeier pulls into the discussion is that all these notions challenge the classical idea that sees the memory as a vast archive or storage with rigid boundaries and semi-perfect organisation. He portrays a much more dynamic and liquid phenomenon that is continuously configurated by various social subjects in different social settings with numerous purposes and motives. This conceptualisation corresponds to his description of narrative and argument on our time understanding. In his terms, "the word memory is like the word time: there is no place, no spatiotemporal field, no *res extensa* that it can capture, although it has the flavour of it" (2015, 307).[15]

---

[14]   In this respect, Brockmeier treats not just the relativity theory of Einstein but also approaches of Proust, Eisenstein, Benjamin, or Woolf, and of further figures (p. 261).

[15]   We can loop back Brockmeier's point of view to another part from his study to

3.1.1 Violence in Processing

Every single event in our experiential repertoire and emotions that allow the interpretation of those events play a unique role in the reconstructive scheme. Based on the previous arguments we can easily say, these also help us to locate ourselves in the present situation. The term events, in this case, involves not just significant, spectacular, or tragic incidents, such as weddings, Olympiads and championships, or violent (armed) attacks but further social-microcosms like a barbeque party, a theatre visit, a police inquiry into a traffic jam, or a lecture. And how we felt ourselves at these moments (angry, depressed, shocked, mentally pummeled, gorgeous, happy, et cetera) helps us to frame these events. These emotions give us a sort of stimulus for the way of our treatment in interpreting the past. Even our attitudes in face-to-face interactions – in Goffman's terms (1990), our performance(s) – would bring further angles into the debate. How we process the past is a question about our efforts in reconstructing past events and their possible connections to each other and the present.

In their study on the remembrance of descendants of perpetrators of the Holocaust, social scientist Harald Welzer and his team (Welzer, Moller, and Tschuggnall 2002) have focused on the communicative memory in the family structures and the cognitive knowledge that is transmitted. They discuss the shaping of memory throughout generations instead of what is not told. They have found out that children and grandchildren reconstructed the stories their (grand)-parents articulated through (or adding) positive patterns. For instance, a story of a bystander obtained layers of resistance; or in the narration, a victimiser grandparent has become an actor of opposition. Over time, the first original narration of the person who took part in the event was reconfigured by the descendants. The authors (please see Chapter 2 of their monography) called it the "cumulative heroization".[16]

According to Welzer and his team (p. 53), this particular phenomenon takes place under the influence of two major factors: the loyalty to the family

---

understand the relation between narrative, autobiographical process and the social setting, "narrative experience is experience interpreted... Autobiographical memories cannot be understood independently from their interpretation" (p. 114).

[16] The results of the longitude quantitative study MEMO, short for Multidimensional Remembrance Monitor, conducted by the scholars of the Institute for interdisciplinary Conflict and Violence Research (IKG) at the Bielefeld University, show us that there have been widespread patterns comparable to the concept "cumulative heroization" in Germany. These interpretations mainly occur if it is about the involvement of ordinary people in genocidal crimes. Study reports to be found at: https://www.stiftung-evz.de/handlungsfelder/auseinandersetzung-mit-der-geschichte/memo-studie.html

memory; and the (critical) cognitive awareness about the national socialist terror which arose in the post-war Germany – differentiating Nazis and Germans (pp. 78 ff). Concerning this second point, the team adds the effects of media such as movies, books, and (documentary) series on this very subject (for a comparative study considering Welzer and his team's point please see: Zittoun 2017). Under these circumstances, the grandparents' memories were reshaped to fit into frames of social or descendants' acceptance. So the violence was rendered not only in the individual reconstruction of one person who was affected – here the grandparent – but concomitantly the family members participated in this course of being affected by those mentioned factors. In this case, time in society is a major player. The new reconstruction had to tackle the "old" or "native" forms of narratives in order to concur with the current social needs.

In sort-of-contrast to the latter study, psychologist Dan Bar-On (1993, 279; cf. 1999, 218) speaks of "double walls" in his work on the narrative of victimisation in families: one distributed by the victimiser/perpetrator parent to safeguard own emotions; and the other wall generated by their descendant with the same purpose. Nevertheless, the walls are no rigid and robust entities that could not be overcome, or whose "disappearance" would not make any change (cf. Bar-On 1999, 168). On the very same pages, Bar-On reminds us of the social context in Germany in the 1980s (concerning the descendants of perpetrators who felt alone in their struggle of facing victimisers in the family). The person had to tackle the gaps in parent's stories to unfold the reality (cf. Smart 2011).[17] Moreover, Bar-On (1993, 281) adds that the interviews had motivated the informants to investigate their family past. Perhaps, the power installation that the walls obscured did become clear to Bar-On's interviewees. Instead of Welzer's "cumulative heroisation", we see in Bar-On's research the conflict with the past of the closest family member and the challenge to disclose untold stories and niches. There is also a profound resemblance in both studies, I suggest: the social context as a factor impacts the next possible moves of narrators – of victimisers themselves and their descendants.

At this point, I would like to loop back the discussion to the notion of memory's relation with social settings. In his case study on misremembering, Jeffrey Prager (1998, 80 f) argues "viewing memory as the intersection between cultural *explanada* and mental experience allows us to explore the intersection of the material reality of the external world with the inner world of the mind." Hence he (pp. 89–94) views memory in a role of mediating selves

---

[17]   At this juncture to keep in mind, secrets "can defend an individual against other family members, or it can empower some members against the interests of weaker members" (Smart 2011, 540).

in the web of social and cultural settings and temporal frameworks – which sounds similar to Brockmeier's emphasis on meaning-making. Prager (p. 215) calls it the *social embeddedness* of memory. Regarding this notion, memory is required to be elaborated as *"representation* of the past and not a *return* to the past itself" that blossoms over time and "current interests of the interpreter". Seeing the individual in their social context, he finds the narrative crucial to render the traumatic memory. For Prager, it is "a form of externalization" when the traumatic experience would be mastered and transformed into a component of life story (p. 134). Sketching the narrative, nourished from the present self, would also help to overcome the misremembering of traumatic memory, he argues (pp. 218 f).[18]

In another study, Bar-On (1999) – concerning the social context – points out the power of ideology and its impact on societal patterns and discursive composition. At this juncture, he uses the terms "pure" and "impure" ideologies. While the pure ideologies delegitimise the questioning of facthood, action, and gaps in stories and stem from silencing – which overlaps in some cases with the totalitarian regimes, the impure structure hosts spaces for further inquiries of the subject matter. He notes that, for instance, impure ideological social contexts can also involve pure ideological compounds. Or vice versa, a pure ideology can allow niches for further questioning (pp. 128 ff).[19] Bar-On (p. 137) also writes down that "there are very few examples in history of pure ideological systems which coped with their reality by completely excluding pragmatic and realistic considerations. Those which did, did not survive for long." So the "pragmatic and realistic" approaches can also be observed in – even most of – the pure ideologies.

---

[18]   Prager describes in his case study how Ms A recalled a childhood abuse by her father and projected it to the therapeutic setting involving her and Prager. Thanks to the dialogical framework of the sessions, she transforms this recollection into a narrative.

[19]   Social anthropologist Paul Connerton, in his widely discussed paper "Seven types of forgetting" (2008), describes the processes of forgetting and highlights the possible agents of forgetting. The spectrum concerning this phenomenon includes, for instance, oppressive forms as well as forgotten past for the sake of newly generated social identity after mass violence. Without connoting any positive or negative interpretations – perhaps, with an exception concerning state handed erasure, Connerton works on these thoroughly. He points out that the entire modern production system works as the agents of the planned obsolescence – the act of forgetting based on consume. Instead of going through every single one of these types, I would like to emphasise that these forms can be read in conjunction with Bar-On's latter points as well. An impure ideological setting would host Connerton's forgetting as an annulment. Having the relief to forget after archiving the information or the structural amnesia as a sort of family or community practice concurs with Bar-On's above articulated suggestion.

Continuing with Bar-On's points, he (pp. 71 f) highlights *indescribable* features whose existence "can hardly [be] acknowledge[d]" due to traumatic experiences and social settings: "The indescribable had to do more with what has been left out of one's own conceptualization, rather than what was included and discussed within it." Those experiences would not find a free space in inter-action like dialogues easily. He (p. 130; 155) pinpoints that silenced facts have contact with the collective discourse and memory. He (p. 152) sees these as structures that are "thereby placed outside the reach of our discourse" becom-ing "undiscussable". Exemplifying from his case studies, he articulates that one would be trapped "between two realities", between the lived and silenced ones and the socially discussable ones (p. 160), under the circumstances of, for instance, pure ideological settings. Nourished from his thesis of generated and developed structures of silenced facts, he recognises the possible transforma-tion of individual indescribable features into the undiscussable patterns in such social environments, even throughout generations (p. 199).

Not just in the phenomenon of undiscussability but in indescribable experi-ences as well, we face the impacts of social conditions. In other words, none of both is a – roughly speaking – strictly individual situation concerning violent experiences. These require intersubjective loops in their developmental phases of becoming indescribable or undiscussable. These emerge throughout differ-ent configurations in society involving various figures, not just a state forma-tion and victims but also bystanders, for example. The violence therefore, we can argue, can expand its effect widely in social space involving further actors, and in temporal meaning such as when these happen in times of post-violence, impacting the lives of next generations (cf. Hirsch 2012).

Affected by her grandmother's attitudes concerning food and impacted by its memory after decades when she read about Holodomor, Maria Tumarkin (2013, 318) proposes to look into the possible forms of memory embodiment. On the same page, she says, "*Deep* encoding is a process, by which people's memories were preserved, communicated and transmitted inter-generationally through their attitudes to food, knowledge, neighbours, authority and other people." The intergenerational transmission of memory can have various shapes. How the violence is processed, whether or not the one has faced own experiences, or what social conditions were ruling that hindered or motivated the person to treat such a traumatic issue are the questions that affect the way of description. The articulation of violence (being able to describe) does not need necessarily words. At times, (non-verbal) attitudes substitute the words, according to Tumarkin.

3.2 Contested Memories

When it comes to the collective perception of past events such as political violence, war, natural and industrial disasters, and the lack of humanitarian support in such cases, or of happy moments like celebrations, we perhaps face first a dominant narrative that appears to be singular in its field. That seems to be "true" or to be taken at its face value. However, historical truth involves perspectives as well, such as investigating different archival materials before coming to a conclusion. Furthermore, the face value assessment degrades itself in this very process of comparative work and interpretation. Without a doubt, the dominant narrative is a crucial party in meaning-making concerning the past. Nonetheless, it is only one of the parties of this discussion.

Katharine Hodgkin and Susannah Radstone (2012, 1) start their edited volume *Contested Pasts: The Politics of Memory* with a brief theoretical outline on the term and point out "contests over the meaning of the past are also contests over the meaning of the present and over ways of taking the past forward." The temporal hint applies to the notion of contestation as well. And *per se* the story that is dominant in the social setting plays on the same ground where the contesting narratives locate. It is the same social setting.

One of the pioneers of memory discussions, Alessandro Portelli (1988, 46) speaks, for instance, of *uchronia* as the "nowhen event ... offering glimpses of favoured alternatives." He (p. 50) views the *uchronic* stories' quality "as one possible narrative expression of the refusal of the existing order of reality." Thus, meaning-making itself comes to be an area occupied by debates and fights, based on Portelli's definition. In the same work on Italian communists' remembrance, he discloses the shapes of time constructions in narratives and how these are very much entangled in pictures of the past and intend some identity forms for possible future visions. He (pp. 52) then adds "while uchronia claims that history has gone wrong (has been *made* to go wrong), the common-sense view of history amounts to claiming that history *cannot* go wrong ..." Portelli in fact, with his discussion on *uchronia*, outlines how widespread the space of contestation could be, I suggest. Although he focuses only on the narratives of Italian communists who disagree with the party leadership narrative – a sub-group of a political group that locates in the vast political spectrum of Italian society in the 1980s, Portelli from my point of view portrays the nature of contestation. So the following question occurs: What does a nowhen event, a *uchronia*, tell us concerning the social setting?

What is the role of a dominant narrative in such a setting? Or how does such a meaning-making-action affect the individual? Paul Connerton (2008, 63–66) describes, for instance, the social dynamics of forgetting for the formation of a new identity or planned obsolescence based on informational and material consumption. While repression performed by a government to protect and stabilise a narrative on the past would maybe irritate people and inevitably push them to think on the margins, other dominant forms would not necessarily have the same countereffect (cf. Passerini 2012). Alternatively, while some social groups would go along with a dominant narrative, others would not. And these people who would be dissatisfied with the story told by the normative group would seek alternative stories. A majority vis-à-vis minority constellation of narrative fights yet is not necessary or not the only way to treat the concept of contested memories, I argue.

Most of the fruitful debates on the term contestation that took place in memory studies are based on empirical studies. For instance, based on the oral history accounts collected in the 1960s, Anne Heimo and Ulla-Maija Peltonen (2012) explore how the Finnish Civil War of 1918 was recalled and how the political positions were, so to speak, cemented concerning historical truth-finding after more than 40 years. While the party in proximity to the Reds of the civil war insisted on coming to terms with past, empowered by their narratives, the opposite party – people who identified themselves in the circle of Whites – stressed a future path out of forgetting the past – and again circulating their own narrative compositions.

With an explorative genealogical perspective, the authors found out that the development and transfer of memory occurred first of all through communicative schemes in social settings. In other words, the narrative of the Reds came to be part of oral communication in the family, at the workplace, or on social occasions only for Reds. Besides, the same applied to the Whites as well (p. 48). So there was a lack of interaction between these two parties. Meanwhile, the Whites could refer to official historiography, which the victorious Whites generated (p. 53). In such settings, the narratives found new shapes. Heimo and Peltonen also point out that with the 1990s the Finnish civil war has not been recounted anymore in such a contextualisation of antagonist parties of Reds and Whites. It has, however, become reorganised employing "non-locals", foreigners and foreign forces like "Germans" or "Swedish speakers" as culprits of the violence. The new fashioned has underscored the victimhood of all Finnish "we"; and idealised the pre-war conditions (ibid.). Currently, they articulate unity for the present and future, according to the authors. Their study shows a contestation between social states that are to be observed in narratives. At the same time, it (indirectly) revisits the question of how different the time motives could be employed – as shown the Whites first standing for the future, Reds for facing the past, and after the 1990s a coalition has claimed the present emphasising even tales from pre-war time.

Contradictive and contested memory regimes are mostly portrayed in antagonist frameworks, like two distinct peoples and their fighting memories (for instance, Karrouche 2018)[20] or a fight between state and people's narrative (for instance, Menin 2018).[21] Further examples with similar frameworks can, of course, be given that resemble the subject of Heimo and Peltonen's paper (please see, Farzana 2017; Pelt 2017; Roberts 2013; Sivac-Bryant 2016).[22]

The contested frameworks such as settings of people's narrative versus official narrative can be discussed indeed as a notion of "mnemonic resistance" that starts with marginalised agents telling their stories and reconstructing the field vis-à-vis dominant collective (cf. Mignolo 2009; 2011; 2012; 2013).[23] In her article, Lorraine Ryan (2011, 165 f) speaks of a reciprocal change in memory of the individual and the collective through constant negotiations and defines it in terms of "processual nature". The framework of contestation, which the present book proposes, concurs with Ryan's conceptual design. A contestation needs different parties – at least two of them. Hence, the typical construction

[20]   Karrouche's paper explores the Berber memory in Morocco and the diaspora, focusing on the violence and how it "provides individuals, groups and generations with a sense of destiny and identity" (p. 224). Hence, visions concerning now and a future are produced, in their very context against the Moroccan State official narrative.

[21]   Laura Menin, for instance, looks into the social framework of memory in Morocco in case of forced disappearances under King Hassan II and how some family narratives of the victims who were disappeared by the state forces raised public interest in the 1990s. The contestation Menin portrays appears between official and family narratives. Hence, the families were reinforced to participate in or organise demonstrations and, at the same time, reconstruct their stories in literary forms. Nevertheless, they still had to wait for some improvements even after the establishment of reconciliation commissions. Being an active agent in the struggle, as Menin articulates, was perhaps nourished by the past but motivated by the present.

[22]   Jo Roberts, for instance, investigates Jewish Israeli and Israeli Arab memories on Israeli Independence Day and Nakba narratives that were consolidated in the same country. Or in exploring the home town stories and expulsion of Greek Orthodox Christians from Cilicia region with the establishment of the Turkish Republic, Mogens Pelt describes one of the parties in the contested memory regime of this very context: the narrative of Christian victims standing opposite to the Turkish nationalist historiography. Nevertheless, in this context, they recall good relations with their Muslim neighbours. Sebina Sivac-Bryant explores the story of the returnees to Kozarac, a small region in Bosnia, after the war and their struggle with the social setting in the multi-ethnic collective *in situ*. It was a struggle with the agentless victimhood narrative that they encountered and tackled through their actions. Kazi Fahmida Farzana scrutinises different dominant narratives constructed by three agencies about Rohingya expulsion and violence in Myanmar: the UNHCR, Myanmar, and Bangladeshi governments. She then compares these with the narratives of refugees.

[23]   This point resembles the notion of, what Walter Mignolo calls, "epistemic disobedience", the act of resistance to knowledge production through endorsing the generation of subaltern knowledge.

of antagonist parties in forms of "we" and "the others" pops up more regularly than some "marginal" forms of contested memories, I agree. However, the question should be if this sort-of-regularity could outplay other possibilities in our assumptions.

In her study, Sarah H. Awad (2017) tackles the political symbols in Cairo after the military coup, and sheds light on the three major memory formations in the urban area: one distributed by the army; other reconstructed by the activists; the last utilised by the Muslim Brotherhood. She concludes that the official power dominated the transmission of the past, yet other storytellers would eventually create pockets through different methods, like the art. In this context, Jarula MI Wegner (2018) takes a progressive step and considers the counternarrative (cf. Foucault 1984, especially Part II) of the Black and Jewish alliance in American rap music. Wegner (2018, 7) underlines the transcultural alliance in this music scene in the USA that finds common ground in reminding past violence – Holocaust and slavery – and stressing the "Never again!". This sort of narrative alliances (Nijhawan, Winland, and Wüstenberg 2018)[24] between affected groups shall be discussed under the lens of anachronisms of course (cf. Rothberg 2009). Wegner (2018, 4) also points out that "any memory may be contested by countless counter-memories." It implies the diversity as well as interwovenness of the narratives.

Anachronism – the projection of present issues onto historical notions – is a compelling narrative tool. The 18th century philosopher and historian Giambattista Vico considers anachronism as a byproduct of false historiographic reading which does not concur with the "chronological canon." He (1948, 251) distinguishes four types of anachronism: a) erasing the truth about a period and introducing it "uneventful"; b) filling a period with events that is actually "empty of facts", literally the vice versa approach; c) "uniting times which should be divided"; and d) "dividing times which should be united"[25] again the contrary approach to the former one (Rothberg 2009, 136 f).[26] As a brief

---

[24] The citizenship would be perhaps another fundamental for such alliances. It functions in Canadian case for the first nations and marginalised immigrant communities.

[25] These last two anachronist templates are the most common ones in the Kurdish narratives I gathered. They remodify temporal organisations. I discuss the anachronisms and analogies in the next chapters in-depth, revisiting the publications and political speeches of Kurdish intellectuals in Chapter 5 and continuing it in the following chapter through the case studies as well as in the comparative analysis of the narratives further, in Chapter 7.

[26] Rothberg refers to another translation which seems to be easier to follow. However, I, unfortunately, could not find that edition. Therefore, I have cross-read and cross-referred the cited Vico publication and the quotation in Rothberg's monography, which also reminded me of Vico's conceptualisation.

remark, from my point of view Vico's concepts can be clustered under two main categories, the more-content-based (the first two) and the more-temporal-dimension-based ones (the last two) – yet without strict boundaries to each other – but in an interwoven space. According to Rothberg (see Chapter 5 of his study), such anachronist reading efforts of the past would mainly be considered "errors" from a historicist perspective, yet thanks to their binding power they have another effect on the approaches of storytelling – and thus on collective memory, as he shows in his analysis of the literary works on the Holocaust and colonial past(s). In his conceptual comparison of the multidirectional memory with the Freudian screen memory, he points out that "the multidirectional memory … frequently juxtaposes two or more disturbing memories and disrupts everyday setting" (p. 14). This quote also gives us a hint of how Rothberg sees anachronistic arguments.

How anachronism affects the discussion on contestation is, from my point of view, that we can reconfigure our understanding of the "players" (or items) in the contested area of memories. They do not need to compete with each other (cf. Rothberg 2009). They can develop linkages with each other as well when, for instance, the temporal boundaries become eroded due to anachronist templates. In her article on Rwanda and Great Lakes region Andrea Purdeková (2018, 3) differentiates between two memory regimes: the *contestatory* (negatively effective) and *consolidatory* (positively effective). She uses the term "contestation" loaded with a negative connotation, as it can urge new conflicts. She (p. 11) refers to the post-genocide Rwandan memory as an example of consolidation that honours the citizens with a new social and socio-political umbrella. However, I argue that we should rethink the role of contestations. These can also lead the way to consolidation. Based on the points I have raised and referred to, for example, possible alliances can come through.

While acknowledging the power of contestation in urging new conflicts, what this book proposes is to consider contestation a type of negotiation, not necessarily as a part of the contentious setting that is entangled to the idea of competition. The negotiation of narratives defines and transforms the space and time constructions. Hence, the nature of memory consists of contestation. The contestation provides space for various collective memories. This interaction is more an epistemic question than a question of practices such as what issues it would bring up. It is much more about the nature of memory itself. My argument resembles Rothberg's description of memory's multidirectional patterns, "as subject to ongoing negotiation, cross-referencing, and borrowing; as productive and not privative" (2009, 3). His suggestion that we have to stop considering memory as "a zero-sum game" (ibid.; p. 21) and as a "one-way street" (p. 6) that emerges due to competition, but to start thinking on the links of various elements in collective memory, is inspiring in discussing the term contestation.

Inspired by Andreas Huyssen's (2000, 33 f) point that the "binary fram-ing" in arguments of "lieux versus milieux" should be "pushed in different direction", I argue that the contestation of memories should be reconsidered as well. Counter-memories and -narratives are to be pulled into a discussion not as necessary antagonist forms generated to compete but as a preface of a possible consolidation of remembrance. We cannot think about a non-contested memory. Contestation in memories is a discussion of destabilizing and/or sta-bilizing the setting. When no one contests a narrative with their own, then it would mean there is the high possibility of silence and total acceptance – like in a radical pure regime in Bar-On's terms. In short, contestation is one of the possible forms of interaction of memories. It is there, in every social and polit-ical context, with or without any dominant and hegemonic narrative, happening between various remembrance regimes.

3.3 Concluding Remarks

The connection of personal memory to the collective notions is reciprocal. What I – based on theoretical studies – scrutinise is how the development and consolidation of a memory regime occurs. This discussion piggybacks the presumption that memories are open for change; they are fluid *par excel-lence*, travelling as Erll (2011) argues, and multidirectional as Rothberg (2009) points out. I suggest that the following questions pop up: What elements play a crucial role in the transition of collective memory? When we accept that the reconstruction of experience (the narrative) is used in the process of mean-ing-making of the past and present – and even for the envisioned future, how should we consider the time question? Should we categorise the content of memories depending on the, for instance, historiographical truth (cf. Danziger 2008, Chapter 7)? Do memories tell us more than their content, for instance, could they provide us some clues concerning the present social setting?

Knowing that I cannot give all the answers to those questions – perhaps, I can deliberately multiply the questions – I have outlined the discussions that are conducted by scholars working on the concepts of collective and personal memory. Herewith I have focused on two significant aspects that interest my research fundamentally: the narrative (as an outcome of interactions) and the temporality. While the narrative is the elementary form transmitted through, for instance, the medium of language, the time issue appears as the forming character of the story. Hence, the nature of the narrative is conditioned by the question of time. In such a context, the question about the truth of the narrative content comes to be located in hindsight, I suggest. We, perhaps, first need to drive from the motives of the narration to understand a) the circumstances that produce the given narrative and b) the relation of the individual and collective perception of past in social terms but not in terms of historical truth-finding. In doing so, we need to reconfigure and pose our questions considering individual experiences the narrator made, their family biography, and of course the current socio-political context. Thus, we also (re-)determine our point of departure in discussing memory issues; instead of past events we set the focus on the present situation.

Since (collective) memories emerge in a space of interactions, one of the possible contact forms of these is contestation. Instead of strict boundaries and destructive confrontations between memory regimes, we witness negotiation and harmonisation of narratives as well as their reconfigurations, due alliances and consolidation. And in most cases, there are more than two participant parties producing, distributing, and stressing their narratives. This interaction, or contestation, serves as one of the possible premises for memory's multidirectional nature (Rothberg 2009), I suggest.

4 Armenian Genocide and the Story of Van

The following pages portray the historical events of 1914–17 as well as the time following the mass extermination campaigns. Due to my research objectives, I particularly focus on the events in Van from May to August 1915. The fundamental discussion characteristics of this part dwell on the phenomena of locality, participant parties, motives of perpetration and bystanding, and the impacts, outcomes, or results of (re-)actions related to violence. In this respect, I conduct an ethnographic and sociological evaluation of histories. I aim to outline the heterogeneity and complexity in the historiography of the Armenian Genocide and to clarify the historical references of my discussion on remembrance. Hence, I tackle the question of genocidal violence through the following concepts: a) actors and protagonists such as victims, victimisers, bystanders, institutions, et cetera – echoing Holocaust scholar Raul Hilberg's (1992) heuristics; b) motives and (possible) triggers – individual or group-based; c) politics of governance – which indeed can be listed under motives; d) the locality in terms of socio-political making.

In this regard, I have organised this historical part in five subchapters. It starts with a brief overview of the years 1915–17, including some remarks on the political atmosphere of prior years. This subchapter also reflects the main historiographical approaches in Armenian Genocide studies. Then it continues with the subchapter on Van, the Armenian resistance organised in the city and its successional local Armenian government that lasted for two months. The subsequent subchapter on societies in the post-extermination period deals with the issue of contextualisation efforts, that emerged in affected societies and political authorities in various ways. The focal point of this part is illustrating the circumstances and subjectivities in the aftermath. It is followed by a short bibliographical discussion concentrated on the social scientific studies treating the topic genocide. At the end, this chapter is concluded with a short summary.

Herewith I briefly argue that the focus on regional aspects and (subaltern) narratives would portray the violent events and their retrospective interpretation efforts in different manner than an enquiry about the central government actions. A further argument is that regional histories (with the help of eye witness accounts), and utilising different historiographic approaches in juxtaposition, would unearth the cumulative trajectories of such social processes.[1]

---

[1]   Here I do not use the term "cumulative" in historian Donald Bloxham's (2005) way of interpretation of events. Bloxham puts the happenings in a context of growing radicalisation, or steps of radicalisation that we know from Holocaust research. The

Hence, I see the genocide phenomenon as a socio-political process that is designed and influenced through the partaking of various actors. It includes trajectories of violence – making this process evolve cumulatively. The effects of such trajectories would be observed in the post-extermination era, for instance, in figurations of collectivities. Nevertheless, as the genocidal process itself is an "imbroglio", the narratives after mass violence would be considered with their fragmented quality.

4.1   A brief Introduction to the Context

The Armenian Genocide had various actors. The palette of actorship included different colours and tones and possible (conglomeratic) mixtures that meant chances to step-in, step-out, change, or improve roles. Hilberg (ibid.) discusses this issue, in the context of the Holocaust, in more (strictly) constructed categories, yet, he also underscores the interchangeable role of (some) participants in the process of mass violence. With regard to other examples, political violence contains not only a destruction but also the idea of a "rebirth" and "refounding" moment. Alongside the ideological structures that may propagate such a vision, it is also to be traced in the perpetrators' approach in decision-making as well as in the aftermath context.

Concerning the actors, this feature highlights that a perpetrator or a bystander can make profit from the extermination campaigns even after the violence has stopped or the force of atrocities has decreased somehow. Alternatively, the bystander can become a perpetrator who participated in looting. In his book about the perpetrators in Aintab in 1915, historian and genocide scholar Ümit Kurt (2018, 76) notes down that this sort of profit was perceived by the perpetrator not as "theft or plunder" but as a "reward for their actions in annihilation of maleficent and traitorous elements" [translated by E.Y.]. The confiscation and plunder of Armenian wealth should be read in its contemporary "ideological and rationalised" terms instead of interpreting it as "greed", further adds Kurt (cf. Gölbaşı 2017).[2]

cumulation, in my view, determines more a social process. Every single decision that was made by the governor, local actors (perpetrator or victim), or the central administration, for instance, created diverse pockets for further possible actions and positionings. In this respect, the violence was improved in cumulative sense – without regard to radicalisation templates. It was not decided and orchestrated single-handedly, although the state hierarchy was pivotal to mass violence.

[2]   In the conclusion of his work on the Hamidian massacres 1894–96, historian Edip Gölbaşı emphasises a notable critique on the actorship conceptions blossoming out of

Even in the case of helpers, we can see this feature. A helper of one group could join in the mob against other groups, like in a story from the anti-non-Muslim pogrom of 6–7 September 1955 in Istanbul when the Muslim protector of one family participated in the plunder of another household (Güven 2005, 25). In his recent study, historian Uğur Ümit Üngör (2020, 13) points at one of such transformative possibilities in relation between paramilitary and state structures: "What can begin as a rebel group, can transform into an informal militia, and become regimented and formalized within a state's security sector." Perhaps, the hardest transition of actorship would apply to victims and victim groups because they need clear cuts like the end of the orgy of violence, mob, lynching, or a revolution-like-impact.[3]

In the case of the Armenian Genocide, the victim groups tried to survive and to this purpose people utilised several approaches, including conversion (Akçam 2014; Yılmaz 2015; for oral history accounts: Altınay and Çetin 2009; Ritter and Sivaslian 2013). Alongside individual or group-based participation, the institutions of the Ottoman State were the operating figures beyond doubt, not only because of their orchestrating power but also because of their members' involvement in the killings, plunder, and even in the long-lasting expropriation of properties.[4]

how people read historical events, which in my point of view is a significant point for the further discussion alongside this chapter: "The legendary claims and rumors to the effect that the Sultan issued a *ferman* (decree) permitting the killing and looting of his Armenian subjects easily found willing ears among Muslim masses, especially among Kurdish tribes. Leaving aside such allegations, myths, and conspiracy theories, it is important to note that in my cases, the perpetrators believed violence against the Armenians was desired and would not be punished by the government authorities. As historical and contemporary cases proved, a sense of impunity and official support on the part of aggressors is an important aspect of ethnic-religious riots across time and countries" (p. 60).

3 A revolutionary change involves the meaning of apprehending the ruling order and transforming those conditions in favour of victims. Some (short-term) examples were to be seen during the genocide, for instance the actions of Armenian governorate in Van in the aftermath of resistance against Ottoman army and militias.

4 Again Kurt's study (2018) shows the spectrum of institutional involvement and its embodiment in perpetrators. He portrays the biographies of three distinct protagonists: Ali Cenani, a local powerholder of Aintab, CUP member and MP of Aleppo and later of Aintab, who even served as a minister of the Kemalist regime; Ahmet Faik Erner, a member of the Ottoman armed forces who orchestrated systematic deportations of Armenians in Aintab from August 1915 onwards; and Mehmet Yasin Sani Kutluğ, who served in the Ottoman Army and was responsible for the deportations from Aintab to the Syrian deserts, and who was mandated as MP in the Kemalist period. Erner was not just an army officer, he was entangled in *teşkilat-ı mahsusa*, the secret service of CUP as well (p. 121).

With regard to the importance of region, locality, and periphery-versus-centre phenomenon, we cannot ignore various entanglements of the Ottoman government, i.e. the CUP triumvirate (for a similar discussion about land issues and Ottoman centralism in the late 19th century, please see: Astourian 2011; and concerning massacres in Hamidian era: 2018). For instance, the Young Turk administration issued different governmental decrees concerning the conversion of Armenians. Conversion was strictly prohibited then with the decree of 1 July 1915. The July decree underlines the deportation of the ones who converted after this date (Akçam 2014, 123–29). In his book on forced assimilation, historian Taner Akçam (ibid.) outlines the CUP's web in the local authorities in carrying out the extermination. The CUP carefully considered the local circumstances. For instance, the prohibition of conversion did not affect those who were already deported and had survived the death marches, like in case of the camps in Syria (p. 116). The prohibition imposed on conversion was cancelled on 4 November 1915, being in force for four months. Within the same decree, the Armenian religious practice in the camps was restricted as well (pp. 170 f).[5] Based on such policies, we can read the efforts of the central Ottoman government for tuning the violence locally.

The mobilisation, starting on 3 August, helped the CUP to decrease the physical power of the Armenian society. Moreover, labour battalions established in the army based on the decree of the Ministry of War in February 1915 (Suny 2015, 244) – through disarming non-Muslim soldiers – had been an instrument in order to gather the "interior enemy" before killings. Nevertheless, this policy was performed not simultaneously in every battalion of the Ottoman army (cf. A-Do 2017, 49; Akçam 2014, 174). In his thorough study, historian Raymond Kévorkian (2015, 345 f) gives the example of an Interior Ministry brochure in this regard and points at the designed propaganda based on the disarming of Armenians. On the same pages, he also underlines the huge numbers of mobilised Armenian soldiers from Van, Bitlis, and their sequential disarmament.[6] But he also underscores that disarming and labouring these soldiers did not mean *per se* including them into labour battalions. It was

---

[5]   Another example of local tuning appears in the telegram of 1 July 1915. Akçam (p. 164) reports that the Armenians who were deported to the Ottoman-Russian borderlands and the Cilicia region, which would become the Turkish–Syrian borderland, were only allowed to speak Turkish. This decree reconciles with the endeavours to govern the deportation destinations and deportees as well as the principle of locality.

[6]   According to Kévorkian, two-thirds of the 36,000 soldiers in that region were Armenians. This details disconcerts the teleological readings and perceptions concerning the Armenian relations with their Ottoman state. Similar anecdotes come up in A-Do's report Van 1915 to which I refer extensive in the coming pages.

a tool of ruling the circumstances in the army structure. In these terms, locality does not only apply in geographic means but also in (abstract) institutional spaces. Nonetheless, this diversity of decrees and laws does not mean that the genocide was carried out totally by the local cadres. On the contrary, it depicts a systematic extermination process of Armenian presence that concerned the regional conditions thoroughly.

How the systematic mass murder was performed brings up the question of whom to recruit and how to motivate possible participants. While the CUP was the head of orchestration, the local authorities held the power to (re-)master the decisions of the Sublime Porte considering local circumstances (cf. Akçam 2007; Kurt 2018; Türkyılmaz 2011; Üngör 2011, 55–100). This is also why we see in every region different local actors – civilians, civil servants, or power-holding families – with their various motives affecting the trajectory of violence cumulatively. Considering the control of ongoing violence, both the central power (or the orchestrator of the extermination) and local powerholders were required to build a collaborative pact, suggests Ümit Kurt (2018, 165 f). The trajectory of violence could only work through such a mutual understanding of the fact that they need each other – which could, of course, transform in time.

The fact of ordinary people's participation brings us to the point where we start the questioning of motives. The then motivating factor, offer or profit, had a wide range from material benefits like properties, labour force of enslaved children, or women in forced marriages, to metaphysical illusions like promises of paradise, enmities as well as the chauvinist state protectionism of civil servants. Nevertheless, the term "enmity" does not imply a homogenic hate toward Armenians even if its sort-of-reconstruction became a part of stab-in-the-back propaganda, utilising, for example, the *Sarıkamış* defeat of the Ottoman army in winter 1915, the Van resistance, or the Armenian resistance to conscription in April 1915 in Zeitun, Cilicia (cf. A-Do 2017, 60; Astourian 1990, 113 f; Foss 2016; Kieser 2007, 372; 392). It was much more a framework nourished by local circumstances such as resentment against particular Christian families or a framework with actors such as neighbours with profit orientation – keeping Kurt's (2018, 76) point on rationalisation in mind.

From a group-based viewpoint, the Armenians had been targeted with systematic political violence in those years. Yet, Armenians were not the only group affected by such acts and events even if they formed the vast majority of victims and the decisions that were made during and after the extermination campaigns to prevent the possible revival of the Armenian life. The first deportations of Armenian civilians started in February and March 1915 in Cilicia (Akçam 2007, 153; Kévorkian 2015) while massacres performed by irregulars were taking place in Armenian villages in the Van province (A-Do 2017).

Meanwhile the governor of Van, Jevdet Bey, raided Assyrian villages across the Persian border. The Syriac Christians (Assyrians, Nestorians, and Cheldanians), Pontic-Greeks, and the Yazidis had also been murdered, deported, forcibly assimilated, and their heritage was wiped out from their ancient homelands (Akçam 2012; Bjørnlund 2008; Gaunt 2011; Shirinian 2017).[7]

Beyond that, the pogroms, expulsion, and massacres started in June 1914 targeting the Greek Orthodox of Phocaea and surrounding Agais region, resulting in a mass immigration to the Greek mainland which, as far as scholars suggest, was the goal of the ruling CUP authority (Kieser 2007, 345; cf. Akçam 2012; Bjørnlund 2008). Historian Taner Akçam suggests a continuum between the early expulsion regulations targeting Greeks and the extermination of Armenians (2012; Der Matossian 2015). These acts against the Greek Orthodox communities were carried out with the aim to be used as an instrument of fear and achieving an ethnically cleansed area – next to the coastal border – for the resettlement of Muslim refugees from the Balkan regions who fled because of the war and the rising new state powers like Bulgaria and Greece in those lands (Suny 2015, 212 f). This element – the loss of Balkan wars and its consequences – is indeed very much connected to the motives of state institutions and the question of governance. Yet, it is also important not to fortify the genocide within this particular setting of war. In other words, the war was not the reason for the upcoming extermination, but offered a sort of premise. In his profound work, anthropologist Yektan Türkyılmaz (2011, especially Chapter 2) portrays the conditions in post-Balkan-war Ottoman Empire concerning the peace attempts between Turkish and Armenian protagonists. He (p. 114) points out, to conclude his interpretation, that "the time period between the end of the Balkan Wars and World War I was not a prelude to the Armenian Genocide or to the overall catastrophe in the region."

There were different phases. For instance, the Hamidian massacres of 1894–96 and the Adana massacre of 1909, following which inspectors from international authorities and the Sublime Porte were sent with the task of composing reports on these events. Both events targeted the Armenians. While the inspectors in 1896 were assigned to find out how the Muslim community was affected, the commission visiting Adana after the massacres of 1909, which had cost tens of thousands of souls, tried to shed light on the facts

---

[7]　In case of genocidal violence against non-combatant Assyrians, David Gaunt shows what role the Ottoman local authorities played even though "there was much less central government propaganda identifying the Assyrians as traitors" (p. 249) and how the Sublime Porte took action in this process. Beyond that, Jevdet's violent campaigns across the borders remind us of the seductive effect of teleological readings, I suggest.

and experiences (Yesayan 2014; Şekeryan 2015).[8] The latter was formed by the CUP and ARF in cooperation. Yusuf Kemal (Tengirşenk) Bey reported from Adana "I am of the opinion that the great majority truly believed that their government, their lives and their religion were under threat" (recited from Akçam 2007, 35). Nonetheless, Der Matossian (2016, 253–66) reports of various collaborative forces – ordinary people, seasonal labourers, and the same group that actively organised the counter-revolution in Constantinople in the very same days; and, of course, CUP officials' participation in the events and unwillingness to expose the perpetrators afterwards (cf. Astourian 2018, 90–94).

The Adana Massacre marked a sort-of-consolidation of CUP-ARF cooperation whose flourishing moment is to be dated back to the 1907 Dashnak congress (Der Matossian 2016, 41). This coalition continued until 1914. In this period, ARF further sought the reform in Armenian provinces and the returning of the wealth that had been appropriated, for instance, in the Hamidian era (p. 224). Akçam (2007, 64) points out "an extra-territorial cooperation" in which the CUP was "support[ing] [ARF] against the czar in Russia" and Ottoman Armenians "collect[ing] money for legal assistance to Armenians imprisoned in Russia." This partnership remained approximately – and in official terms – until the ARF general assembly rejected the CUP's requests of espionage and of building militias in favour of the Ottoman Empire on Russian territory via utilising Dashnaks there (Suny 2015, 223). Yet, Türkyılmaz (2011, 157–67) illustrates the complexity of the negotiations carried out at this meeting in Erzurum and points out that, first of all, the Dashnaks did not give any answer to the proposal of the CUP delegates. Furthermore, he suggests that that proposal was a political game which was introduced by the same emissaries as a sort-of-next-step of the CUP-ARF cooperation. In addition, this cooperation had developed in earlier years through blocking the way of other Armenian parties opposing the Ottoman government (pp. 138–57). Furthermore, CUP's proposal was an act meant to clarify possible political manoeuvres. As with the consequences of the Balkan wars, Türkyılmaz (p. 166) argues that "...the Erzurum meeting did not mark the beginning of the end." We can say that the cooperation of both parties should have kept in

---

[8] The Armenian novelist and intellectual from Constantinople, Zabel Yesayan is a well-known woman figure of the Armenian 20th century. Her widely known book *In the Ruins* is composed of her witness accounts from her visit to Adana and Cilicia immediate to the massacres. Being able to escape the deportations from Istanbul on 24 April 1915, she fled first to Bulgaria and her journey ended in the new homeland of Soviet Armenia. As a victim of the Stalinist purges, she probably died in Siberia in the 1940s.

check some of the motives for violence on the highest political level, at least for a while. However, the question is whether the society could have perceived this change and to what extent.

Historian Hans Lukas Kieser (2007, 339) emphasises the significant role of ethno-religious nationalism in the deterioration of the social bond of people(s) that rapidly influenced the conditions at a time the war was imminent and substantiated the upcoming violence. However, the chauvinist waves – even under Social Darwinist terms of the CUP – can never be the single reason for genocidal brutality or a singular motive for participation, I argue. For the notion of institutional control loses its importance in a case of an uncontrolled lynching mob, as Hilberg (2017, 44–53) sheds light on the example of the 1938 November Pogrom in Nazi Germany and how Goebbels was disqualified and considered by other Nazi perpetrators as a player "dangerous" for the totalitarian state power. In the eyes of an orchestrating government, enmity has to be supported, protected, and most importantly controlled and regulated by the institutions and laws (cf. ibid.). The consequences of a pure uncontrolled arson triggered by resentment is hard to be measured even for such ruling powers. It cannot fit into a framework of state power anymore, and therefore genocidal violence requires further motives for a "balance".

4.1.1 History of Histories

The historiography of the Armenian Genocide can be partitioned into three main trends of approaches: the premeditation argument and focus on ideological background; problematising the financial aspects of this mass violence; and interpreting the numbers such as the population census. However, before these historiographic approaches there were the accounts of eye witnesses and survivors that marked the early period of the enquiry. Perhaps, the main goal was not an investigation or leaving a sort of legal or scientific document to the next generations. The early period of genocide scholarship regarding the extermination campaigns from 1915 onwards was a mixture of engagements rather than a professional occupation (cf. Cheterian 2015, 91; Der Matossian 2015, 144 ff). It was carried out by the survivors as witness accounts (for instance, Andonian 2010; Balakian 2010) or literary works (Oshagan 2014; and for an in-depth discussion of treating such pieces, please see Nichanian 2011); some third party reports of missionaries (Lepsius 2011; Ussher 1917), embassies (Morgenthau 2012), or of companions of Czarist army or Armenian legions under czarist rule, such as the ethnographic account of A-Do (2017) on Van/ Vaspurakan; and reports written by foreign country institutions like the British blue book (Bryce and Toynbee 2009). Concerning the survivor narratives, Marc Nichanian (2011, 38) stresses that a witness account or a literary formulation of victim experiences "should not be read as a record [in legal terms] but as text" [translated by E.Y.].[9]

Perhaps, the only exception to this list was the Ottoman civil servant Naim Bey's telegram collection (because of his position during the events) that was obtained and published by the Armenian intellectual Aram Andonian who survived the deportations (2018; for a historical discussion on these documents please see, Akçam 2016).[10]

Following this early wave composed by the first-hand narratives, the scholarship developed primarily on the pillars of the *premeditation argument* and scrutinising the possible *ideological premise* that had led to the massacres. The pioneering scholars who worked on and through this postulate have methodically claimed that the conflict between Turks and Armenians in the Ottoman Empire that should be predated to the *Tanzimat* reforms of 1839, the reform edicts of 1856 declaring equal rights to all Ottoman citizens independent of their religion and ethnicity, or the 1878 Berlin Congress. They further argued that the early conflicts and massacres, like the Hamidian massacres of 1894–96 and Adana Massacre 1909, are to be considered as the first steps of a violent process which ended up with the decision-making and orchestration of the genocide (Dabag 2002; Dadrian 1999; 2003; 2004; 2004; Hovannisian 1992; Melson 1996; Ternon 2012; cf. Cheterian 2015, 115 with regard to the critiques on Dadrian's works). This argument has also involved the feature of ideologies in its tight-knit historicised reasoning and stressed that the early form of Islamism, nationalism, racism, Turanism, and social Darwinism (especially among Ottoman ruling class) paved the way to extermination. And the war gave the

---

[9]   In their extensive on the financial side of the genocide, Uğur Ümit Üngör and Mehmet Polatel (2013) also set a focus on the legal conundrum of wealth transfer. According to them (p. 8) "[t]here is a direct continuity between the expropriation of Armenians, and post-genocide Armenian efforts to document the crime." And alongside the point that Nichanian questions, the emphasis by Üngör and Polatel reveals parts of the foggy terrain of early scholarship, texts, and accounts in the early years after the extermination campaigns.

[10] This collection launched a huge discussion in which different parties partook, even in the early period. The claims made by denialists include arguments such as the Ottoman interior ministry letterhead was not authentic in these documents; the cypher used in these telegrams did not match the common cypher of those years, based on the existing (and accessible) Ottoman archival documents; and there is no record of any civil servant named Naim Bey in the Ottoman archives. In this way, the denialist party of the debates has argued that the telegrams were a hoax. In the recent years, with the genocide scholar Taner Akçam's latest publications on those documents, the focus shifted back to these telegrams, reignited the discussions and, in fact, turned the way of discussion back to the archival lens in the genocide debates. This last point concerning the emphasis on the archives is studied further in the next chapter on recognition and denial.

Ottoman rulers the chance to close up this history. Beyond that, the notion of radicalisation under the circumstances of war was a part of this argument. A later approach focusing on the ideologies treated the radicalisation phenomenon concerning the dimension of war circumstances and disassembling it from the premeditation argument (cf. Bloxham 2005). For historian Donald Bloxham, the radicalisation towards the imminent massacres and orchestration of extermination was cumulative in nature and should be built up in the boundaries of war period.

When we consider this above mentioned thesis on the ideological premises then we find out that reciting Koran before the massacres as well as explicit time frames e.g. organised violence following Friday prayers – implying the time and a gathering of the mass – were reported by the witnesses (Akçam 2007, 34). Nevertheless, the Jihad declaration of the Ottoman sultanate was, in this context, of auxiliary importance for stimulating local participation (cf. Akçam 2007; 2014; Kieser 2007, 441).

Moreover, according to Akçam (2014, 122), the Muslim witnesses – imams among others – in Ordu, a small town on the Black Sea coast, asked the authorities for pardoning their Armenian neighbours from upcoming deportation.[11] Such brief and simple examples provide us the pieces of the heterogeneity of actions during the extermination campaigns. At least because of the fluid circumstances, the assumption of a homogenous total war concept had to be reconsidered thoroughly (cf. Aktar 2007).[12]

One of the outcomes of the Ottomans' approach to the problems was the establishment of the Hamidiye Regiments in 1891. Recruiting (mostly) the Kurdish aghas and their tribes on the side of Ottoman authority was seen as a possible solution for expanding the Ottoman rule to eastern regions (Gölbaşı 2015; Klein 2014). It was, in fact, a modernist idea for the Ottoman State in order to stabilise the governance, whilst producing new (Kurdish) actors under administrative protection. Furthermore, sultan's planned action of founding these regiments and recruiting Kurdish landowners had goals such as silencing Armenian parties and their demands as well as binding the Kurds to the

---

[11]   A recent article published in the newspaper AGOS points to conversion of Armenians in Ordu and how the state institutions of the early Turkish Republic observed them closely (Gül 2021, in press). Even after the forced conversion and adoptions, the survivors and their children were perceived as possible threat.

[12]   Sociologist and historian Ayhan Aktar underlines in his article on the Istanbul parliament discussions in 1918–19 that "[t]hese governors and local administrators opposed the deportation orders both directly and by delaying them. Other individuals and groups refused to implement the orders for religious, humanitarian, ideological, or cultural reasons" (p. 264).

Ottoman State (that could not have been achieved through tax and military service). In these terms, governing a region was one of the key factors of the generated mass violence, creating further victims and their persecutors. Historian Edip Gölbaşı (2015, 171) points out that these regiments and their actions were under the control of the sultanate. Afterwards, while Kurdish intellectuals in Constantinople following the revolution of 1908 were discussing new chances for Kurdish–Armenian relations, proto-nationalist Kurdish uprisings took place, for example, in Bitlis (Bozarslan 2015, 472 f; cf. Cora 2015, 131).[13] Based on these examples, questioning the public participation in the genocidal events and different forms of coalitions forming out of violence and taking further narratives into consideration as well come to be more significant, I suggest (cf. Gerlach 2010; cf. Türkyılmaz 2011; 2015b).[14]

The governance of such regions was a huge question mark hanging in the air. It meant, for some Armenian protagonists, the protection of their own community and independence or, even, a federal statute like in Hentchak's party programme (another Armenian political movement) and for some, working together with the CUP for the sake of reforms like in Dashnak perception. In favour of such reforms, Dashnaks worked with the CUP cadres together. In this contentious context, however, different parties played their roles to remain in the game. As Türkyılmaz (2011, 27) emphasises "as of July 1914, many outcomes were still possible. The eventual catastrophe was only one of those possibilities, and indeed perhaps the least foreseeable."

The circumstances of the relation among Armenians (local power), Kurds (local power), and Turks (supraregional institutional authority and local power) is noteworthy to highlight in order to understand the socio-political situation. However, the agencies (had) developed on a fluid ground affected by (changing) local circumstances. With a particular focus on Van and the surrounding

---

[13] Nonetheless, it would be incorrect to say that Armenians and/or Kurds in those years could be seen as homogenous groups. Yaşar Tolga Cora points at various social and local circumstances and classes among Armenians and Kurds. Hence, he highlights the need of a proper differentiation between Armenians living, for instance, in Istanbul and ones living in Bitlis under the rule of a Kurdish landowner. The same also applies to the Kurdish society.

[14] In his comparative study *Extremely Violent Societies* on mass violence in different contexts, from the Indonesian Genocide of 1965–66 to the political scope of famine in Bangladesh and Greece's occupation by Germans, historian Christian Gerlach brings the social texture of genocidal violence into the discussion. One of his main arguments is "that the bulk of modern mass violence occurs in the context of socioeconomic change that transforms a traditional countryside into a surplus-generating sphere of a national, imperial, or world economy, which serves industrial capital accumulation and thereby also affects the urban sphere" (pp. 288 f).

area, we can trace the escalation or, as a matter of fact, the normalisation of political violence on a regional level prior to the genocide.

In the region, prior to the systematic extermination campaigns, the conflict between Armenians and Kurds carried on and killings occurred – in the 19th as well as early 20th centuries in which the various Armenian and Kurdish actorships were formed and reformed. Following the Kurdish rebellions in this region, scholar Ronald Grigor Suny (2015, 193) says, "large armies were deployed and twelve Kurdish leaders were executed in Bitlis" and adds "about the same time government regulars joined together with five hundred Dashnak fighters to suppress the Kurdish Gravi tribe located between Van and Başkale." Even though the Armenians were not the targets of state violence and persecution, ARF took as a cooperative of the Ottoman government an important actorship in the midst of this conflict. In this context, Kurds as well as Armenians were persecuted by each other and by the Ottoman authorities.[15]

Akçam (2007, 37) argues that the massacres before the genocide were "local in nature" and were steps of achieving the systemic nature of 1914–15. In spite of this systematisation in the state structure, a sort-of-learning-by-doing, the escalation argument does not totally serve to explain the genocidal process. Türkyılmaz (2011, 15) calls it *the escalation bias* and describes as follows:

> … a tendency to focus on the factors that led to genocide over those that militated against it. Whatever pertains to peace of the possibility of de-escalation, in other words, is often downplayed, ignored or left unnoticed in the historical discourses produced around the genocide, sometimes including that of scholars.

Beyond the premeditation argument, *concentrating on the financial side* of the genocide has become a particular approach in the scholarship. Thanks to recent studies, scholars working on late Ottoman and early Republican period have become increasingly familiar with the ensemble of laws and measures

---

[15] Bitlis uprising of Kurds and the collaboration of ARF with the CUP raises the question whether the Ottoman administration had not enough power in the Armenian/Kurdish periphery even in 1914 and needed specific local cooperation to solve such problems. Similar help was required to exterminate the Armenians a year later, this time by the Kurdish tribes. In his recent comparative study on paramilitary groups, their violent actions and connections to the state formations, historian Uğur Ümit Üngör (2020, 68) points out that "[t]he Ottoman Empire never pacified all of its territory to the same degree." And in order to reach out mountainous regions such as the provinces of Bitlis or Van and monopolise the state power in process, Sublime Porte made deals with local power holders.

regulating plundered wealth among the "stakeholders" of the Muslim society (Akçam and Kurt 2012; Çetinoğlu 2006; Morack 2017; Onaran 2013; Üngör and Polatel 2013).[16] The Ottoman government also used the confiscated property to cover the military expenses, in reorganising posts for armed forces, concerning the costs of deportations, and state needs during the campaigns (Akçam 2007, 209 f). The dispossession and confiscation of Armenian properties had continued under the Kemalist Ankara government as well (cf. Kurt 2018, 161 ff).[17] In this respect, Bloxham (2005) points out that the Turkish middle/upper class arose thanks to the dispossession. In terms of economics, the genocide can be read as a foundational moment, which historians Uğur Ümit Üngör and Mehmet Polatel (2013, 168) put as "[e]conomic destruction served and precipitated economic construction." Nonetheless, it would be wrong to illustrate a single path; or "the expropriation process cannot be pressed into a straitjacket of a single policy or law" (p. 165).[18]

Perhaps, we can predate the organisational background (or patterns) of such a massive regulation of plundering to the boycotts of Austrian and Bulgarian goods in 1908 and the following boycott of (Ottoman) Greeks in 1910 (Çetinkaya 2015; cf. Üngör and Polatel 2013) – even to the plunder of Armenian wealth at the 1894–96 massacres (Astourian 2018). The boycott actions were first initiated by social actors and then by the CUP, redefining the national identity. Yet, such boycott measures "did not hurt Armenian businesses

---

[16] Researchers working on wealth transfer in the late Ottoman periods and early Turkish republic consider different readings, some even teleological ones. While some like Çetinoğlu have underscored a (semi-)linear continuity of capital homogenisation from late 19th century up until to the mid 20th century, some scholars have looked into short term practices and policies, and how these were transferred to the successor regime(s), such as in the book by Akçam and Kurt. For a contextualisation of such debates in the Armenian Genocide studies, please see (especially the introduction) Üngör and Polatel's study *Confiscation and Destruction*.

[17] Historian Ümit Kurt provides a glimpse on the regulation of wealth transfer in his study on Aintab.

[18] Continuing from this point made by Üngör and Polatel, I would like to frame the terminology question concerning wealth transfer. They reflect their choice for "dispossession" problematizing the palette of terms picked to describe that very process. It includes expropriation, dispossession, confiscation, plunder, theft, and so on. They underscore that "this debate is interminable because it is unterminable" (p. 5) since we need several contact points to the legal field and social sciences as well as the sociopolitical reality during the mass violence. Üngör and Polatel have decided to use "confiscation", for instance, instead of juristic euphemisms generated and circulated by Ottoman officials – like the "abandoned properties" (*emval-ı metruke*) (f). In this book, I have used different vocabularies to accurately portray the various ways of plunder and reflect on the diversity of violence.

in eastern Anatolia. [It] only affected smaller Armenian communities residing in the European territories and those Anatolian towns where significant Greek populations lived", says Türkyılmaz (2011, 52). In spite of this fact, I would suggest, in these instances we can trace the notion of plunder in resentment and identity figuration, remembering the point Kurt (2018, 76) underscores in unfolding the idea of profit: it was a reward for the actions exercised by the perpetrators.

Furthermore, the land and property issue built the foundations of this bureaucratic ensemble for regulating such procedures. It was linked, on the one hand, to the seizures of the 33 year-long era under Abdülhamid II and, on the other, to the claims of Armenian parties, as respondents and affected actors – that were to be seen in the Ottoman public on legalised basis from the 1908 Young Turk revolution onwards (Der Matossian 2016). The property question, targeting the confiscations under the Hamidian regime, was prior to the revolution a fundamental topic of the Armenian parties organised in the diaspora. Yet, with the regime change, for instance, ARF sought cooperation with CUP to solve this problem (Türkyılmaz 2011). Even after the Adana Massacre of 1909, Dashnaks continued this cooperation (Der Matossian 2016, 266; Türkyılmaz 2015a, 333), as mentioned before. These tell us that there was a clear presence of socio-political and interethnic conflicts in the Ottoman society and an awareness of past events.

After the extermination campaigns of 1915–16 – in smaller proportions following the 1894–96 and 1909 massacres as well, the spectrum of properties that had belonged to the victims indicated a huge collection of objects, from furniture, manuscripts, or jewellery to estates, and even children. The adoption of Armenian children was synchronised for the assimilation of those children – as one of the instruments for the annihilation of the Armenian existence. These children were the carriers of wealth transfer as well (Akçam 2014; Sarafian 2001). In most cases, they became forced labourers. The extermination of Armenians gave rise to economic crises in Anatolia. And children who had been enforced to labour were meant to be a coverage for the losses of the war (Akçam 2014).

One of the most common way of perpetration, that formed a continuity, was the abduction and Islamisation of Armenian women and children. The form of integration into families varied from sexual assaults, forced marriages and to creating hard labour conditions (Akçam 2014; Hartmann 2017). The Islamisation as a method to expand the communal power was already performed during the massacres in late 19th century and included even the mass conversion of male Christians and the transformation of churches into Muslim properties, as Akçam (2014, 103 f) mentions.

The feature of conversion in case of the Armenian Genocide can and perhaps should be (cross-)read through the lens of another approach: focusing on *the census and figures* in interpreting the events. The pioneering works in this debate focused on the Ottoman population demographics and the government "regulations" with regard to their nationalist future visions (Akçam 2014; Dündar 2013). In case of conversion, while the victims' fundamental motivation relied on a survival reflex, governance through changing the demographics was one of the focal points for the decision-makers, suggests this approach (ibid.). Local participants were on the other hand inspired through sexual fetishism, state fetishism, and plunder, i.e. material fetishism (cf. Aydınkaya 2015).

The idea of governance aimed to decrease the remaining number of the minority population between 5% to 10% – keeping the objective of further assimilation in reserve (Akçam 2014; Dündar 2013). This goal had to be achieved through deportations and Islamisation. It welcomed the active participation of local families as new actors and used orphanages for the assimilation of Armenian children (Akçam 2014). Meanwhile, actions of local victimisers were protected and promoted through laws and decrees that underlined the wealth transfer powered through adoptions and marriages (2014, 203; Akçam and Kurt 2012). In the eyes of the CUP, the annihilation of a community and the "reconstruction" of Armenian collectivity had to be realised for the sake of the state power in those regions (Akçam 2014, 184 f). The help of local "ordinary people" was mobilised with this purpose.

The Armenian question, moreover, received the first official international attention with the Congress of Berlin in 1878 (Akçam 2007, 22 f). It had even become a theme of international enquiries, such as with the London protocol of 1877. With the conference declaration the Armenian question had become a concern of the European powers in official terms (Adanır 2015, 39–43; Akçam 2007, 26; Astourian 2018, 73; Der Matossian 2016, 34 f; Dündar 2015, 113 ff) even if the worries of the Armenian Council were not taken into consideration by the attending parties. Fuat Dündar (2015, 116 f) underscores the "[focus] on quantities" in the reform proposals and plans of the congress 1878. These aimed to designate the numbers of Armenians living in eastern regions. Yet, it was a hard deal because the parties involved – such as the Sublime Porte, the British Empire, and the Armenian Patriarchate – provided different numbers based on different approaches and motives.

Conflicts existing in the region continued with ups and downs and peaked with the massacres of Hamidian Cavalries. These started with the pretext of Sasun resistance of 1894, which was distributed as a rebellion, and ended around 1896 resulting in hundreds of thousands of deaths in the internationally known *Vilayet-i Sitte* – the six regions (Der Matossian 2016, 38 f), not to mention the forced conversion, and displacement. Even the reform plans drafted and signed in different periods from the Congress of Berlin onwards could not have been a solution anymore because the demographics had changed drastically – to keep in mind, there was no international law or a juridical definition of crimes against humanity. From the viewpoint of Great Powers and Ottomans, governance was the key issue to solve these problems. And for a stabilised governance they required the numbers. However, the numbers were open for change.

The concrete focus on numbers in historiography aims primarily to critically reflect the work that has been provided by the parties involved from the late 19th century on. Reading such statistics in an analytical contextualisation of events would help us to understand the motives and the core argument of this approach. Next, I would like to portray the situation in Van and try to underpin the niches that do or do not concur to these major argumentative frameworks.

4.2   Van

According to the numbers Hovhannes Ter Martirosian (from here on A-Do) presented in his comprehensive report on events in Van/Vaspurakan – the resistance, occupation, war, and extermination – that he published first in 1917 in Yerevan, Armenia, which was translated into English by historian Ara Sarafian in 2017, 121,377 Armenians were living in the province, and from that 3,000 *Vanetsis* in the city centre and 20,000 in Aykesdan, the gardens (A-Do 2017).[19] A-Do was an Eastern-Armenian born intellectual who published various manuscripts concerning the Armenian society, its history and emerging conflicts in the region. He visited the province of Van in 1915–16 and reported that the city of Van had resided in two separate areas: the old city centre beneath the Van citadel and the gardens, Aykesdan, located in North-East and East of the old city. Thanks to the increased prosperity in Van, people had moved to Aykesdan that "was surrounded by vineyards, gardens and orchards" instead of walls (p. 135).

The old city was co-inhabited by 1,000 and Aykesdan by 17,000 Muslims (p. 135). These numbers originated from Armenian church's population census of 1914 that scaled the number of Muslims in the same region at, approximately, 30,000. The Ottoman official records from the very same year shows the Armenian population at 67,792 and Muslims around 180,000 providing a contrary image (Dündar 2013). Remembering the points mentioned above and as historian Fuat Dündar postulates in his comprehensive work, the population

---

[19]   The pages of this study on the history of Van defense are predominantly based on the report by A-Do and physician Clarence D. Ussher's first person account published in 1917. Anthropologist Yektan Türkyılmaz' (2011) profound work "Rethinking Genocide: Violence and Victimhood in Eastern Anatolia, 1913–1915" made me acquainted with A-Do and Ussher's accounts as well as understand the situation in Van. Türkyılmaz' manuscript (especially Chapter 5) offers a much detailed portrayal of the events in Van.

census came to be a political apparatus used by Ottoman State structure as well as different communities in order to claim the governmental authority or, on the contrary, the regional autonomy. Again according to Dündar, while the Armenian Church was proclaiming a population of two million Armenians living within the borders of the empire, the Sublime Porte was disregarding this account issuing its own demographic census. Nonetheless, Van was the only province and city with its Armenian majority in the empire, until the province included the Sandjak of Hakkari with its Muslim Majority in 1888 (Hewsen 2016, 43 f; Ter Minassıan 2016, 201).

Apart from the population demographics, the ancient city of Van/Vaspurakan, that had already witnessed the Hamidian massacres and a resistance of Vanetsis in 1894–96, followed by a further massacre targeting civilians (Hovannisian 2016, 10), subsumed international missions and consulate buildings in its pockets. It also witnessed the founding moments of the first Armenian political party: the liberal Armenakan in 1885 (Der Matossian 2016, 36). This liberal group would later establish the Ramkavar party and run for MP seats in the national assembly against the candidates of ARF-CUP alliance in Van, following the 1908 revolution (p. 182). The political dispute among the Armenian parties had its roots in the Armenian National Assembly that was based on the 19th century Ottoman reforms (p. 137). ARF was already standing at gunpoint of critiques because of its cooperation with the CUP when the political turbulences of post-revolution were in effect (cf. p. 42).

Although trade in the 19th century created a new middle class in Van and prosperity rose in the Armenian community, the periphery of the province was still struggling with poverty and did not receive the same attention like its centre. Similarly, while the centre of Van was facing the new army command centres and bureaucracy since the Hamidian era – as follow-up measures of massacres in the late 19th century, the governance in the periphery was handed to the local powerholders (cf. Hewsen 2016; Ter Minassıan 2016).[20]

4.2.1 Towards the Van Resistance

The Vanetsis were affected by all the measures issued by the Sublime Porte, including the mobilisation and war tax (*tekyalif-i harbiye*), that aimed to create resources for the Ottoman Army. The commissions, mainly membered by civil

---

[20] The difference was also to be seen in the literacy rates in which the country side of Van was to be placed way down with its illiterate population in comparison to its centre. This asymmetry applied to the Muslim – Turkish and Kurdish – inhabitants of the rural side as well. (Ter Minassıan 2016: 213)

servants like *kaimakam*, were established on a local level in order to collect and control the war tax to be paid by every household. These official collectors were set "free" in their decision making. After all, it impacted the minorities at a horrendous level (cf. A-Do 2017, 42 f). This state-regulated robbery demanded, alongside money, movable wealth like grain, cattle, or textile. In other words, the decisions made by local authorities were off-the-grid – in terms of a structured bureaucracy vis-à-vis the desires of local officials, mainly motivated by the idea of Ottoman State victory and its continuity.

The mobilisation meant the forced recruitment of all men between 20 and 45. American physician Ussher who was stationed in Van (1917, 217) points out that "very many Armenians enlisted willingly, glad of a chance to demonstrate their equality with the Turks, and these became brave and efficient soldiers." The ones who could not pay the exemption tax to be excused from military service had to attend it. Due to the settled war tax, the so-called exemption tax became out of question for many. In such a conflict-loaded situation, Aram Manukyan, the ARF representative of Vanetsis who would become the governor following the resistance, mediated between the Ottoman authorities and Armenian young men, who rejected to be drafted, in favour of their conscription, as A-Do (2017, 45) narrates:

"This is not a good sign and we have to do something about it," he [Aram] thought. He then invited 300 young men to meet him and led them in a procession from Aykesdan to the governor, accompanied by a fanfare of drums and pipes. The governor thanked Aram for his exemplary conduct. All of the young men were registered and the incident was forgotten.

It took place in the beginning of mobilisation, around August 1914. Even if the labour battalions were not fashioned with the ministerial decree at that time, the Armenian soldiers were transferred to places far away from their homes without any training and/or stationed for unarmed background duties (A-Do 2017, 49; Ussher 1917, 217).

Meanwhile, the Ottoman authorities were pardoning prisoners and building up irregular militias, including the former prisoners, for the upcoming war against the Russians (A-Do 2017, 50 f; 64 f). With their participation in the violent acts, the militias became the new actors on local level. We can assume the motives provided to them were rooted into their pardons.

In few months, even weeks after the aforementioned mobilisation the first expulsions and massacres started in the towns and villages bordered to Iran, such as on 3 October 1914 in Satmants/Saray – prior to the war declaration against Russia – where all the Armenians were displaced and it resulted with death of 12 children (pp. 74 f). Further violent events targeting Christian civilians had followed after the czarist army occupied positions in the Ottoman borderlands from November 1914 forwards. Because of the war and the Russian occupation, the Ottoman battalions stationed in Van started to disarm their Armenian recruits, which would mark the beginning of labour battalions in the region and persecution of these soldiers (A-Do 2017, 62 f; Ussher 1917, 218).

From December 1914 onwards, similar violent acts committed by gendarmes and irregular militias took place in several places of the province of Van. Nonetheless, most of these had to face voluntary Armenian defence units. Over the course of time – especially after the revolution, the ARF politicised and organised people of such peripheral towns, such as Alchavaz/Adilcevaz, and armed small groups with the support of CUP after 1909. Nevertheless, the resistance in such places was to be organised on a local level by the initiative of small groups instead of ARF assemblies, so these did not spread to other villages or towns.[21]

Furthermore, the measures against Assyrians reached a new level even before the declaration of war, as it was with the Armenians. The Sunni Muslim population across the Persian border was motivated by Ottoman propaganda against Christians. Irregular units under the command of Jevdet, *mutassarif* (governor) of provincial town Bashkale attacked the Assyrians living across the border and the deportation order of Nestorians in Hakkari arrived at the local authorities, after these imperial subjects rejected to join the Ottoman Army. This was even pursued after the withdrawal of the czarist army (Gaunt 2011; cf. Ussher 1917, 226).

After the military campaigns in Iran, Jevdet was appointed to the governorship of Van in February 1915. He arrived in the city with his troops and irregular forces in March 1915 (Ter Minassıan 2016, 208) and was welcomed with a reception in Kurubash village. ARF representatives Aram and Vramian Efendi were among the participants, with the intention to show good will after the resistance of Armenian units in the country side (A-Do 2017, 93). Jevdet immediately had a meeting with these ARF politician (pp. 91 ff). According to A-Do, Vramian then assured his compatriots that "he had calmed the governor down" (p. 93).

---

[21]   Nevertheless, the resistance movements of course affected surrounding areas through rumours and news. It implies the significance of locality from the perspective of victims. Beyond that, A-Do reveals that Kurds and Armenians in various towns found a common ground, surviving the violence of war via helping each other: "We will defend you if the government oppresses you, and you will protect us if the Russians occupy our lands." (p. 52) This remark on survival strategies underpins options of local awareness on the question of what the war would lead to.

On 11 April, the news reached Van that six teachers including an ARF member had been arrested in Tagh, Shadakh, which triggered an Armenian resistance *in situ*. The Armenian council of Van agreed with Jevdet's suggestion to send an Armenian representative delegation, decided to provide 400 Armenian recruits – doctor Ussher working in the American mission in Van talks about 4,000 men (1917, 235 f) – and calm people in Tagh as well as in Van. High-tension was ruling in the city (A-Do 2017, 94 f). On 16 April, a delegation of eight people, four ARF, one government representative and three gendarme officers, started its journey to Tagh. The ARF representatives of the mission were murdered by irregular Circassian militias in the house of a Kurdish agha in Hirj, when they were resting for the night (A-Do 2017, ff; Ussher 1917, 237).

As Ussher (p. 237) mentions, the next morning "Jevdet summoned four leaders of Dashnakists [ARF], Vramian M.P.; Terzibashian, Jidatchian, and Aram. The last-named for various reasons was not able to present himself." A-Do (2017, 96) stresses concerning this particular moment that when Vramian went to Jevdet, he left a note warning Aram not to attend the governor's invitation. This marked Aram's survival and thus the start of his leading role at the resistance of Van. Again A-Do (ibid.) reports the reaction of Vanetsis to the incidents in Hirj and Vramian's disappearance:

"Iskhan and his three comrades have been treacherously killed at Hirj!" and "Vramian has been deceived by Jevdet and has disappeared!" These two pieces of shocking news spread like lightning across Van … "Treachery!" they exclaimed, as they took to arms. They were not unprepared. They had spent months planning for the unexpected and began to mobilise. Communications ceased between the city and Aykesdan. The markets were closed, relations between the government and Armenians were severed, and Armenians in outlying areas moved to more central Armenian quarters in the city. The young people began their preparations to resist.

One of the witnesses and survivors, Aghasi Ivazian, who as a child was involved in the resistance as a supplier for the Armenian militias, reports from separate defences in the city and Aykesdan as well (*Aghasi Ivazian – Zoryan Institute Oral History Archive* 1987, 20:00). On 17 April 1915, the morning when Jevdet Bey summoned four Armenian representatives, Ussher visited him too and witnessed that he ordered the colonel of his irregular units – what the governor called "Butcher Battalion" – "to wipe out [Armenians]" in Shadakh (Ussher 1917, 237 f). The next thing that Ussher encountered was: he was asked by the gendarme for stationing "fifty soldiers with cannon and supplies for ten days in our [American] mission compound", which he refused (ibid. ff). With the help of Jevdet's plans and acts, the sides in this tense conflict became clarified.

4.2.2 Resistance of Van and Mass Destruction of the City

Although 24 April 1915 is the acknowledged start and the commemoration day of the Armenian Genocide, on which Armenian intellectuals and politicians in Constantinople were detained and persecuted per the decree of the CUP-government, political violence had already started, as explained on previous pages. The organised mass and political violence was developing in a process from December 1914 onwards.[22]

In this scope, the resistance of the local Armenians in the city of Van started on 20 April and lasted for 27 days, until it ended with the retreat of the Ottoman regular forces. The Ottoman governor of the Van province and Enver Pasha's brother-in-law, Jevdet Bey, was the leading figure of these massacres and remained at the top of the local orchestration. However, the resistance dismantled and disentangled the cumulative process in a way. It overturned the organisation of political violence and changed the conditions thoroughly.

According to American Ambassador in Constantinople Henry Morgenthau (2012, 299), "the whole Armenian fighting force consisted of only 1500 men; they had only 300 rifles and a most inadequate supply of ammunition, while Jevdet had an army [of] 5000 men, completely equipped and supplied." In her study, historian Anahide Ter Minassian (2016, 254) points to a setting of 10–12,000 armed subjects under the leading command of Jevdet (6,000 troops and again around 6,000 Kurdish and Circassian irregulars) and on the opposite side 1053 Armenians under the leadership of Aram. Yet, the battalions of resistance were fashioned by all three Armenian parties Ramgavar, Hinchak, and Dashnak (pp. 250 f). These units included volunteers from newly coming refugees from the countryside as well as Assyrians (ibid.; A-Do 2017).

This clear unification of parties and non-party member civilians, such as business men, clerics, craftsmen, and landowners, resulted in a profoundly coordinated resistance. It required, of course, arms and armed forces to protect the civilians and fronts in the Armenian quarters of the city and Aykesdan. The resistance had to arrange different commissions, among others justice and

---

[22] Aspects similar to other regions were present in the province of Van even though the resistance was marked by other features. Concerning this pattern, political violence against own minorities – and of course their resistance – on the Armenian High Plateau can be predated even to the end of 1914 because of the massacres in Hazara (north of the city of Van), the massacre in the eastern provincial town of Satmants, or the resistance in Pelou and Atanan in Van (A-Do 2017, 74 f; 82 ff). This process improved in a cumulative setting subsuming all the participant parties, including state officials like Jevdet, ARF members like Aram, and local Armenian units and civilians, while making them actors.

health commissions, for gathering food, medical supply, possible goods for families, and ammunition. Furthermore, the armed forces were split into police and resistance groups in seven sectors (A-Do 2017, 135–226).[23]

Meanwhile the contact or negotiations with the Ottoman governorship was done through Italian and American missions in Aykesdan and the city. However, the inner-circulation of information was restricted. Aykesdan and the city, carried out two different resistance movements and were not able to communicate each other until the withdrawal of the Ottoman forces on 16 May 1915.

What did governor Jevdet have under his control against the organised resistance? And what did he do in order to oppress these armed resistance units? It was not just the armed Ottoman and irregular forces that he utilised. He used the same communication channels, Italian and American missions, in order to lure the Armenian leaders into disarming their units as well as to persuade these missions to accept stationing governmental troops with the pretext of protecting the mission employees and buildings. When the alleged protection was not accepted, these missions including the American hospital came to be at gunpoint and bombarded by the Ottoman troops, especially when Jevdet launched his withdrawal (Ussher 1917, 277 f; 280).

Furthermore, Jevdet continued the lootings and massacres in a more radical way in the surrounding area. Although the irregular units faced Armenian defence in certain places like Hayots Tzor, the civilians fled to nearby towns and particularly to Varak monastery (A-Do 2017, 120–26). During the resistance of Varak Monastery – at the same time, the resistance in Van and Aykesdan were ignited (p. 133), Ottoman troops withdrew on a short notice, despite their progress, "leaving the road to the city open" (ibid. f). Hence the evacuation of the monastery started and thousands of Armenian refugees entered the city, "all Armenian forces were now concentrated in Van" (p. 134). Historian Raymond Kévorkian (2015, 456) argues that the decision of Ottoman withdrawal from Varak and the opening of a way for evacuation seem to be a military tactic.

---

[23] One of the such groups, which was responsible for gunpowder production, manufactured even a cannon that, however, was not effective enough to destroy the walls of Ottoman garrisons – the Hadji Bekir barracks had been then destroyed by the resistance units though (cf. Ussher 1917, p. 282; Richard Ashton – *Zoryan Institute Oral History Archive*, 47:30). However, the cannon achieved the point of creating a legend in the stories of Van resistance. Thus, as A-Do reports "It was the fate of the owner of the forge, Tokmadji Garibjanian, to become Aykesdan's Krupp" (pp. 211 f). However, a quick look into the contemporary cannons and howitzers with a critical eye would raise the question if the Vanetsi forge could command the metallurgical and industrial expertise to produce a working cannon under circumstances of a siege. Probably, its morale-boosting effect was its primary purpose.

For the increasing number of people would trigger the struggle with limited resources and would eventually cause famine in Van.

Beyond the massacres in the surrounding provincial side performed by government troops and Kurdish militias against Armenians and clashes in Van, Jevdet was occupied with the state ruling in Tagh, Shadak (Türkyılmaz 2011, 277). The Ottoman forces were struggling with an unbreakable resistance of the local Armenians there and Jevdet was commanding the *kaimakam* of Shadak using telegrams (A-Do 2017, 227–48). This, however, ended with the victory of the resistance and with the *kaimakam*'s retreat on 23 May 1915 (Türkyılmaz 2011, 265).[24]

The Ottoman cannon attacks did not distinguish between civilian, neutral, or combatant targets. These also continued on 16 May 1915 when the Ottoman forces started to evacuate the Muslim neighbourhoods. Whilst disengaging the siege, the Ottoman forces were bombarding the city to make the Armenians stop chasing after. With the cease, resistance units entered the Turkish quarters looking for Armenian households in these neighbourhoods, trying to find out the fate of their inhabitants, as well as any hiding Ottoman forces (Ussher 1917, 282 ff). A-Do describes this moment as follows: "May 17 was a day of revenge, foolishness, and great excitement... The Armenian fighters were burning Turkish homes without sparing anything" (2017, 222). He continues that a group of units from Aykesdan entered the city after 27 days of siege and raised the flag at the Van fortress as a symbol of victory. He then on the same page adds, "Afterwards came the plunder and arson, and those two words became the motto of Armenians in Van on May 17. It was the eruption of a long-accumulated need for revenge. For two days they burnt down Turkish quarters ..." Nevertheless, he also argues that this event was the consequence of the acts of "barbaric Turkish government". Türkyilmaz (2011, 283–86) provides in his study further Armenian accounts criticising the first ever actions of the Armenian governorship of Van towards plundering Muslim properties and governmental buildings. Even some Armenian shops became targets of *talan* (plunder) and "a number of Armenian residents of the city rushed to join the *talan in the countryside*" after the Russian troops arrived the city (ibid. f).

---

[24] Furthermore, Ussher (p. 257) mentions that some Kurds from Bitlis who were fighting on Jevdet's side were "promised large rewards ... and had been assured by their sheiks that they were invulnerable." This again brings us to the point of motives. However, such a motive cannot be generalised for everyone in these territories since, for instance, Armenians of the southern provincial town Moks were protected by a powerful Kurdish landowner, an *agha*. And that the civilian Kurds helped civilian Armenians was repeatedly reported in Van (pp. 265 ff).

When the Armenian volunteer units of the czarist army entered Aykesdan on 18 May and the city on 19 May 1915, and then the General Nikolaey of the Russian Army on the very same day, they were embraced by an unexpected state and celebrations (ibid. f). According to Morgenthau (2012, 299), the regular troops of Russian Army encountered more than 50,000 dead bodies on their march to Van and cremated them. What they probably expected was simply traces of massacres. The only place to be inhabited after the clashes was Aykesdan. The old city centre was in ruins and was not to be rebuild again (Ussher 1917, 288). However, Vanetsis succeeded with their resistance.

A self-determined provisional government in the region, under the military entity of the czarist army and the governorship of Aram, had followed the armed resistance and remained in power for two months. The Russian army requested that the new government be entirely made up of local Armenians (A-Do 2017, 268). In its two-month life span, the provisional government was engaged with establishing administrational and juridical units, financial committees as well as security forces, municipal authorities and a budget (pp. 270–83). Some of those institutions, including the secret police and tax collectors, were adapted indistinguishably from the Ottoman system. In doing that, the governorship excluded Muslims from the system. The additional human power was received from Yazidis and Assyrians who fought on their side against the same enemy, the Ottomans. Nonetheless, the governmental cadre under Aram's control was formed predominantly by the ARF members (Türkyılmaz 2011, 290). In these terms, the Yazidis and Assyrians were also excluded from the governorship, they were seen just as human-power for the next battles (cf. p. 304). Now it was time to reconstruct. The reconstruction meant excluding, oppressing and in some cases killing Kurds since they fought together with Ottoman troops and could build a major society in the region (pp. 310–14).

Nevertheless, the time of the Armenian sovereignty in Van was also filled with internal conflicts and tensions between Vanetsis and Armenian volunteers of the czarist army (pp. 290–93). Another point of dispute between Aram's government and czarist army officials was about the Kurdish question – after the Russian General allowed the resettlement of Kurds and emphasised protection by Van administration (pp. 316–22). Moreover, Ussher (1917, 284–88) mentions that the Armenian refugees were leaving the American medical mission's premise – and later the German orphanage too – and it was now hosting nearly thousand Muslim refugees (p. 291). Thus, these civilians had to overcome epidemics (p. 295). Doctor Ussher's daughter, Eleanor Baker-Ussher who was born and lived with her family from 1908/09 to 1915 in Van mentions that workers of the compound became ill as well, including her mother who died of typhus on 14 July 1915 (*Eleanor Baker-Ussher – Zoryan Institute Oral History Archive* 1983, 52:00–53:00).

The Vanetsis were not involved in military campaigns towards Bitlis and Muş despite the czarist volunteers' wishful thinking. For the reconstruction of Aykesdan had been conducted and it was more significant for the people of the town (*Eleanor Baker-Ussher – Zoryan Institute Oral History Archive* 1983; Türkyılmaz 2011, 293 ff). Militias under governor's command were involved in looting and the oppression of Armenian civilians in the city and countryside. These acts were followed by corruption claims against Aram's administration, especially after the issued tax regulations. Türkyılmaz (p. 297) adds that "officials in the new administration quite quickly gained an image as corrupt, despotic and self-absorbed."

The Russian Army, yet, started to leave the city and the province on 10 August 1915. The regional Armenian government existed for 70 days. The czarist army was gathering and starting the resettlement of Armenian local population as well, although the local Armenian authorities were rejecting the idea and declaring their will to stay and fight against the upcoming Ottoman attack. The reasons why Russian Army withdrew vary. First of all, the army could not expand the occupation to the west, Muş and Bitlis, and when Vanetsis were asked to join new campaigns, their reply was to stay in Van and rebuild the city first. Hence, the czarists wanted to hold position, but the only way to achieve it was occupying further lands, and the Vanetsis were not interested in such "adventures". Moreover, there were rumours circulating in the city that the Ottoman Army was approaching. They disturbed the citizens (A-Do 2017, 288). In fact, Jevdet's units were approaching but not as fast as the rumours.

During the march to the Russian borders, the convoy was attacked several times by irregular forces. Hence the retreat with the civilians resulted in thousands of deaths. And 260.000 people from the plains of Van, Erzurum, and Bitlis, who survived the burning sun, Turkish and Kurdish irregulars' raids, lack of water and hunger landed in the refugee camps prepared close to Echmiadzin, Armenian region under Russian control (A-Do 2017; Ussher 1917, 311–14). In these camps, the epidemics grew fast and caused death due to horrible medical circumstances , even "natives of Echmiadzin died [too] because of the sanitary conditions" (*Aghasi Ivazian – Zoryan Institute Oral History Archive* 1987, 32:15). Doctor Ussher was one of few medical personnel in the camps, who also fled Van with his family and witnessed the conditions. Afterwards, he stayed in Yerevan until his return to the USA in 1923. He told his daughter "I've reached the point, where I simply could not open my front door and find another dead body on my step. So I just quit standing" (*Eleanor Baker-Ussher – Zoryan Institute Oral History Archive* 1983, 01:02:20).

The consequence of this withdrawal was that the town fell in the hands of Ottoman Governor Jevdet and his battalions. However, the city changed hands repeatedly after that moment (Kévorkian 2015, 469). This flow repeated itself, until the Ottoman army occupied the city finally. These massive army campaigns were destructive to the town and Aykesdan, apart from the arsons and plunder of local participants. Additionally, another survivor reports of a Russian bombardment campaign subsequently to the evacuation (*Richard Ashton – Zoryan Institute Oral History Archive* 1986, 48:30). These caused a total demolition of the urban area for which we can borrow the term urbicide (cf. Coward 2008).[25]

As mentioned above, what Aram, the Armenian governor of the autonomous region, first decided was the plunder and arson of the Muslim properties and households that were left by their owners when they fled with the Ottoman army. The city was completely destroyed first through the actions of the Ottoman army and militias, in particular during their withdrawal, then through the war situation triggered by the armed resistance, and the plunder by Armenian militias which was followed by the *talan*, repeated assaults and invasions organised by the Ottoman authorities. In this context, it can be postulated that the violent process in Van differentiated itself from the situation in other cities and regions, as Türkyılmaz (2011) underscores. Moreover, he (p. 22) highlights that the actions of short-lived Armenian governorship in Van "challenge[s] the binary of victim/perpetrator and exhibits the intricacies of Van Armenian victimisation ... that have rendered the experience of Armenian governorship tangential or marginal to simplistic yet canonical victim-perpetrator frameworks."

4.2.3 Post-1915 Van and Violence Afterwards

From the Ottoman withdrawal and Armenian governorship onwards, Van witnessed the total destruction of urban space and became an area to sketch performances of rebuilding attempts. Furthermore, Van became a subject of the denialist politics of the Turkish Republic due to the armed struggle and its success, like the theme of the Adana Massacres of 1909 (Der Matossian 2016, 253 f). During the extermination campaigns as well as later for example in the 1980s, when denialism was institutionalised throughout different (academic) milieus (cf. Göçek 2016; Turan and Öztan 2018; Türkyılmaz 2011, 24), we see this history of Van as a tool of legitimation of political violence performed by the Ottoman State. On the other side of the coin, Van defence came to be one of the core heroic subjects of Armenian storytelling concerning the genocide (Türkyılmaz

---

[25] The nuance that Martin Coward crystallises in his profound work on the concept of urbicide occurs to be that he pinpoints the destruction of chosen buildings that gained in importance for the certain "others" identity formation over the course of time. In case of Van, this term can also be employed since the whole city had represented a certain social fabric with a significant share of Vanetsis. Türkyilmaz' arguments on urbicide of Van open an important perspective on this issue.

2011, 274). This destroyed spatiality, open for rebuilding efforts from both sides, provided again these two parties with a space for their own narrative.

Today, the city of Van rises on the very place of the former gardens, the Aykesdan, containing still a few buildings from that time in the old city centre as well as orchards. Yet, after the declaration of the Turkish Republic the city of Van had to face violence again, for instance during the Kurdish resistance on the Ararat plain 1925–1930. The city experienced a massive politicisation and immigration of displaced people. The Turkish army carried out subsequently another massacre at Zilan river area in 1930 which is located in the north of the province and the survivors reached predominantly neighbouring villages or moved into centres. Beyond that, the killings of 33 unarmed Kurds who smuggled goods crossing the Iranian border in 1943, which was carried out by the General Mustafa Muğlalı of the Turkish Third Army, found a significant place in the storytelling of the Kurdish and Turkish left-wing movements, thanks to the poem *33 Bullets* by Ahmed Arif. In other words, almost 30 years after the extermination campaigns and Jevdet's raids across the Persian border, the state's violence monopoly was demonstrated once again: this time against Kurds.

Another remark about this post-massacre period belong to the survivor Aghasi Ivazian. According to him, his aunt went back to Van "every time when Van was taken" and in the end "they couldn't retreat and stayed there in Van until 1923, when Soviet and Turkish governments exchanged population" (*Aghasi Ivazian – Zoryan Institute Oral History Archive* 1987, 54:30). We also can assume that the aunt was not the only Armenian in the city after the war. In this regard, the city had witnessed the violence against – in terms of expulsion of – Armenians for the very last time in 1923. However, except Ivazian's account I could not find any further document about civilian Vanetsis who returned and stayed under Turkish command.

Another volatile regulation of the Turkish State is still effective: the remapping or Turkification of the place and village names. While the local inhabitants do not use these "tailored" names, the bureaucracy enforces their usage. It caused, for instance, logistical problems in the organisation of humanitarian help after the Van earthquake in 2011, as one of my outside informants told me. Meanwhile, the violence – as well as its memory – is still there, in connection with the coup d'état in 1980, the torture centres of the war in the 1990s and the displaced people who left their hometowns after bombings as you can see in my case studies as well (cf. Mahçupyan et al. 2008; Türkiye'de Göç ve Yerinden Olmuş Nüfus Araştırması 2006).[26]

---

[26]   According to the TESEV report 2008 by Mahçupyan et al., "950.000 to 1.200.000 persons" became a subject of forced migration "during the armed conflict that occurred

4.3 Naming the Context in (Post-)Violence and Struggle for those Left Behind

Suny (2015, 341) reports of that the making of politics was sharply formed by the perception and visions bound to Sevres Treaty 1920 in both parties, which appointed a partition of Ottoman lands between Armenians, Greeks, Kurds, and the Entente powers, yet which has never been effective. While it motivated Armenians, "for Turks Sevres [is] a nightmare" (ibid.). Without a doubt that Sevres has (had) an effect in the Turkish politics and making of politics since the first republican generations, at least on the discursive field. Yet, Türkyıl-maz' point on *escalation bias* should be kept in mind as well, in reading the early republican period (2011).

Sevres treaty became first a tool or parameter for international and national politics. In Turkey it was further used in denialist frameworks. The denialistic structures after the genocide have demonstrated their power in international area so rapidly that, for example, MGM studios cancelled its movie project of Franz Werfel's *The Forty Day of Musa Dagh* (Suny 2015, 347). However, the same book became one of the most read manuscripts among the Jews of the Warsaw Ghetto under the Nazi terror regime (Ihrig 2016). In these terms, the genocidal violence in Anatolia from 1915 onwards has been an international political theme that contained various actors and approaches contextualising the issue from their own perspective. Furthermore, international relief

in the Eastern and South-eastern regions of Turkey between 1984 and 1999" (p. 8). The statistical data authors refer to is provided in the following report published 2006 by the Hacettepe University Institute of Population Studies (p. 61). The latter contextualizes in its introduction the situation as domestic migration in a fifty years scope, "… population movements can especially be observed from underdeveloped territories into the developed areas. Replacements due to terror and security reasons, large scale development projects and natural disasters in Eastern and South-Eastern Anatolia have been appended to this fifty yearlong migration phenomenon. Particularly with the intensified terror between 1985–1996, some of the people living in the region were replaced mandatorily or voluntarily" (p. 1) [translated by E.Y.]. Even though the report acknowledges that one million people were "replaced", in its jargon, the researchers do not question the reasons and employ a language trivialising the state violence. Although the majority of 70 qualitative interviews were conducted in Kurdish (p. 12), the word Kurd occurs nowhere in the report – but emblematically defined as "people who can speak Kurdish" (ibid.). The conclusion furthermore includes policy recommendations emphasising such as subventions and infrastructure projects to make people possible to return (pp. 110 ff). This tendency continues in the following subchapter on the "integration of people who do not want to return" (pp. 112 f). How this report approaches the political conflict, state violence, and the Kurdish demands – through masking the reality – is unfortunately paradigmatic.

campaigns took place for the Armenian survivors organised by the survivors and helpers from foreign structures that worked *in situ* during the massacres, as Eleanor Baker-Ussher points out that her father Doctor Ussher remained active in gathering monetary help (*Eleanor Baker-Ussher – Zoryan Institute Oral History Archive* 1983, 01:03).

It is important to mark that the issue was not about naming the context as a genocide in these early years. Neither the Turkish denialist State, nor the Armenian survivors were after clarifying the issues of naming first of all. What the Turkish State distributed was the denialism of violence, belittling the events, and generating a stab-in-the-back legend (cf. Göçek 2016; Turan and Öztan 2018) even though in 1919 the post-war Ottoman government of Istanbul tried and criminally charged some of the perpetrator officials defining their actions as war crimes, massacre(s), and atrocities (cf. Dadrian and Akçam 2008). On the other side, the Armenians were fighting for a possible return to their ancient homeland and survival in their future homelands. Possible returnees had to face the fact that their journey subsumed further problems such as the question of appropriated (forsaken) properties, travel ban, visa issues, and, later, forfeit of citizenship (Akçam and Kurt 2012). For the ones who remained within the borders of the Turkish Republic the equality question was on its way to be faced (Suciyan 2016). Beyond that, Kurds became target of violent acts by Turkish army and officials in various ways. Türkyılmaz (2011, 336) points out:

Starting in the 1920s, however [despite their heterogenous actorship palette in the genocide as victimiser, bystanders, helpers, et cetera] the Kurdish nationalist discourse took shape as a simple binary narrative: the oppressed Kurds vs. the oppressor (Turkish) state. In the same period Kurdish and Armenian political leaders in the diaspora began to articulate a shared victim position at the hands of the Turk. Between 1924–1938, brewing Kurdish insurgency and brutal state repression – which in the case of Dersim (1935–38) was genocidal – further reinforced the dichotomous (Turkish State vs. Kurd) victim narrative.

Türkyılmaz sees in the discussions a "fruitful" premise for victimhood narratives that were employed by all the parties: Turkish government, Armenians, and Kurds. So, the discursive battle was now to be shaped through victimhood stories and constructions.

In a brief sketch, survivors of massacres against Christian minorities of the Ottoman Empire, among them Armenians, started to return to their homelands after the war. The Istanbul government, the successor Ottoman government, reported in 1919 and 1920 more than 200,000 returnees (Akçam and Kurt 2012, 78). Most of these people were living in the regions under *Entente* protection, for example in the French mandate of Antep, Maraş, or Adana, and had to leave when the Ankara government became successful in the political game over the Istanbul administration. The Ankara government under Mustafa Kemal's leadership was in a formation process in those years. It employed politics and policies fashioned by the CUP – alongside the reintegration of CUP politicians and genocidaires like Şükrü Kaya who became the Minister of the Interior for twelve years from 1927 onwards. For instance, the forsaken properties law, that was issued by the CUP government during the deportations, was changed for the sake of the future Turkish Republic (pp. 98 f); then with the Treaty of Lausanne 1923 – which acclaimed the international recognition of the Ankara government – the Armenians who were living in Turkey were given the right to regain their wealth, but not the Armenians living in other countries. However, these claims were set in a grey zone from which only the leading power had profited (pp. 107 ff; 125). Moreover, due to the Lausanne treaty the Ottoman citizens who were living in foreign countries (the survivors) had to apply to the Ankara government in order to keep their citizenships or would lose it, yet maintaining their properties (p. 127). Similar to those, the Ankara regime enjoined the ones coming from foreign countries (the survivors) from entering the borders of the Republic of Turkey with the regulation of 1 July 1924 (*Seyr-ü Sefer Talimatnamesi*) and restricted the travel of non-Muslim minorities of the country (p. 209). Under these conditions, Armenians who tried to return to the ancient homeland faced further difficulties.

Hence, defining the violence had to wait the end of other struggles. For the surviving Armenians, the question of naming first emerged after fifty years, when in 1965 the Soviet Union allowed Armenians to commemorate (Türkyılmaz 2011, 338) and diaspora communities, first of all in Lebanon and France, organised huge demonstrations for the recognition of the genocide (for an enquiry about the echoes in newspapers in Turkey, please see Korucu and Nalci 2014).

The cumulative process of the genocide, which was broader than the killings and deportation through, for example, wealth plunder and forced assimilation, continued in the post-war years – as rooted in the strategies of the new Turkish State (Akçam and Kurt 2012; Akçam 2014). How the Armenian forced adoptees and child labourers in Muslim families viewed the situation is, of course, a question. It came to be an issue for international powers (cf. Akçam 2014, 240) and was treated during the negotiation with the Istanbul government as well (pp. 221–27). In other words, the genocide was discussed by different parties as an international question – similar to the period that peaked with the Berlin Congress 1878 and the 1894–96 massacres (cf. Akçam 2007; Dündar 2013; Türkyılmaz 2011). Under these rapidly changing circumstances, the actors of the genocide were developing new positions and strategies. In those years, we see the early proxies of the question: defining the events.

4.3.1 Subjectivities

How the participants in the violent events would be defined – and in some ways categorised – is a further point regarding the contextualisation implemented by different perspectives. We see the first generalisations and subject descriptions when the issue started gaining international attention. When in the late 19th century the Ottomans tried to convince international powers to consider Kurds in reform discussions, the suggestion was declined "because they [foreign powers] believed the Kurds to be 'primitive'" (Akçam 2007, 27). Such attempts had remained and further embodied the arguments during the negotiations. When the Hamidian massacres took place, these arguments were still effective. However, they faded out after these massacres, until the discussions began again with the 1908 revolution (pp. 29–32).

Historian Hamit Bozarslan (2015, 473–77) summarizes the positions that were dominant among the Kurds in the same years, that (have) even bridged to the post-extermination period, as follows: the Istanbul based intellectual and Kurdish nationalist idealism "that was not effective except Istanbul based student groups and … [prominent Kurdish figures]"; Dersim Kurds' helper disposition to the Armenians during the genocide which was viewed by the CUP protagonists as no less than a treason (a figure from this context, Kurdish intellectual Nuri Dersimi, would then propose a generalised Kurdish helper identity promoting the thesis of "mutual killings" and discarding the victimisation of Armenians in his writings; see the Ch. 6.4.); and the Kurdish active participation in the killings. In this regard, and based on (or inspired by) historian Miroslav Hroch's (1993) conceptual questioning, historian Janet Klein (2015) discusses the Kurdish proto-nationalism in the Ottoman post-revolution period 1908–09. She points out that these early national "movement(s)" were not *a priori* separatist but stick to the Ottomanist ideas. Notwithstanding they had to run several struggles – especially about the issue of dispossessed Armenian lands by the Kurdish aghas in the Hamidian era. Similar to Bozarslan, Klein (p. 292) argues that the Ottoman Empire was not in threat by the "educated Kurds in Istanbul."

Not only in the international sphere but also in the country and in the communities, the definition of "others" was a part of the discussion with regard to the self and positioning:

Kurds represented as homogenous entity, stand as one yardstick against which the ideal subjectivities were to be measured … when discussing Kurds and Armenian simultaneously, the standpoints of each group have been treated as unitary categories, partly because the method of analysing relations between two entities inadvertently forces generalizations … Most prominent of those premises has been the general categorization of Armenians as victims and Kurds as victimisers. (Derderian 2016, 7 f)

Contemporary intellectuals integrated binaries in their discussions, so while the Armenians received the categorical definition of civilised, Kurds were displayed as barbarians, irregulars, and criminals (p. 6). Similar templates are to be seen in A-Do's report as well. Kurds appear in this report within the following forms and adjectives: "Kurdish looters" (A-Do 2017, 212), "Kurdish mob" (ibid. f), or "[Kurds] were in a frenzied mood" (p. 122). The same construction differentiates clearly the Kurds and the Ottoman army as well. While the Kurds are described as bystanders or victimisers and perpetrators with terms like tribes, brutal Hamidiye Regiments/Cavalries, militias, religious fanatics, mob, irregulars (*başıbozuk, çete*), and plunderer; the army, Ottoman State, or soldiers occupy the perpetrator role as Turks, the head of massacres, slave holders, bloodthirsty persecutor, or murderers – like Jevdet the great murderer or Jevdet "was a perfect Asiatic in his negative traits" (p. 93).

In this regard, the mercenary fighting for the Prussian Army Rafael de Nogales who was stationed at the Ottoman fronts pictures the governor Jevdet in his published chronicle differently. He calls (1925, 54) him "one of the most energetic powerholder of the empire" or "a tiger in human shape." His comments on Jevdet reminds us of the importance of affiliation and personal position in the given context. His illustration of this particular perpetrator stems from these very aspects.

At this very point, I find Ter Minassian's note (2016, 209) in her article about the life in Van before the genocide very significant. She points out that the urban Kurd was open for assimilation and blamed rural Kurdish landowners for having a propensity for violence. In this regard, the ARF-politician Garo Sasuni (1992, 163 f) argues that a high proportion of ordinary Kurds – not the rural landowners or urban middle class – was armed by the Ottomans and participated in the genocide for profit. Hence, the Kurds gained the identity of victimiser subjects.

Furthermore, in my research in Oral History Archive of the Zoryan Institute, in most of twelve audio-visual records I viewed, I encountered an (organised) victimiser image that was embodied by terms like Turks, army, soldiers, or gendarme. In these accounts, the persecution at the hands of the Kurds appears during the deportations and marches. A survivor from Aykesdan, Aghasi Ivazian, mentions "on the marches we were harassed by Kurdish irregulars, especially during crossing Pergrin valley, the bridge there, steep area, the gorge, Kurds opened fire to us and people" (*Aghasi Ivazian – Zoryan Institute Oral History Archive* 1987, 16:40–17:20).

In Burcin Gercek's oral history study which includes interviews with descendants of (Kurdish) rescuers (2016), the helper subjectivity carries patterns such as just, nature loving and a protecting personality, hope for coexistence and fear of being abused by Kurds and Turks during the protection of Armenians or afterwards, especially in Van, by Russians or Armenians. Similar to the interviews I conducted, the storytelling regarding these helper figures from Van contain inevitable binaries such as rescuer versus profiteer Kurd (cf. 2016, 207–15).

Political scientist Adnan Çelik and journalist Namık Kemal Dinç (2015) point out that the Kurdish society employs various definitions and descriptions of the genocide based on the regional and subjective aspects. Hence, the Kurdish society experienced a shift in the perception of this past violence and participation of their own grandfathers. To be specific, it was a change from justifying the violence to its condemnation in the family. The figurations have been changed through this new adaptation as well, whose impacts are still to be noticed in the Kurdish politics and public.[27]

In survivor, witness as well as descendant narratives – including the Kurdish stories, we encounter a specific stratification of perpetratorship which mirrors the decision-making group – the orchestrator(s), for instance, the governor – and further perpetrators – the participants, for instance, ordinary people. In doing so, these narratives echo the social dynamics of mass violence, its control, coordination, and the groups involved. Nevertheless, perhaps because of being-affected of the genocide or of the violence and injustice, the biographical memories do not differentiate particular groupings and persons mostly. The group-memberships or such labels occur to be the codes in order to describe the events and participating subjects – yet, without their subjectivities.

4.4   1915 alongside Historiography

In the bygone decades, the collective and cultural memory has increasingly become a topic among scholars and in activist networks in Turkey. Not only the Turkish society but also the remembrance regimes of the Armenian, Jewish, or Greek-Orthodox communities and of the Kurdish society have drawn the attention of researchers conducting oral history and/or ethnographic approaches

---

[27]   How an individual or collective act is defined depends on how the person or social formation is described. My attempt to discuss this very issue will continue in the next chapter(s) concerning recent debates in the Kurdish politics and society and, of course, throughout the case studies.

(e.g. Altınay and Çetin 2009; Bali 2016; Kaymak 2017; Özyürek 2006; Türker 2015). Furthermore, public discussions that have already been launched – for example, on violence of junta regime after 1980 or 1938 Dersim Genocide – started to be shaped through such ethnographic perspectives in addition to the contribution of historical studies. Apart from the debates on denialism and recognition scale, "new" layers of the issue have reached the public interest.

Alongside these subjects, the Armenian Genocide as a theme – predominantly the narratives of the proselytes' grandchildren (starting with Çetin 2004; Altınay and Çetin 2009; Ritter and Sivaslian 2013) – and the way of remembering this past in the (Kurdish) society (Biner 2010; Çelik and Dinç 2015; Neyzi, Kharatyan-Arak'elyan, and Simonyan 2010) have generated a sort of new area to investigate through which the country's past and the Turkish official historiography have been brought into critical discussion. Grandchildren's stories, of course, include various layers and aspects to reflect this very past. That triggered further dynamics in the historical studies, such as the memory that is connected to the place, i.e. wealth plunder and appropriation; and Islamised family members – which were in most cases grandmothers, i.e. violence performed on women and children. Moreover, the feature of speaking out the truth came to be the case. These dissidents and Islamised ones in the families silenced their stories for generations. Having someone in the family who forcibly converted meant (probably) having a perpetrator as family member as well.

Meanwhile, novels treating these subjects have been published in Turkish as well as in Kurdish. Although the most prominent authors of the country like Yaşar Kemal have already pinched this issue in their books earlier, Armenian remains from the genocide – objects, buildings as well as people and stories – came to be a topic for the new generation artists and novelists after the 2000s, thanks to family history accounts. In the scholarship, those are followed with a rising interest by studies focusing on the Turkish and Kurdish literature echoing the genocide and the issues around it (Çelik and Öpengin 2016; Galip 2016; 2018) – that I treat under the subject of next chapter in detail.

At this point, I want to underscore the inevitable and tremendous effect of such studies in social sciences and accounts of family members on victimisation and perpetration: the rising critical voice vis-à-vis official historiography on Turkey's past. The rule number one, so to speak, for publishing a well-appreciated and acknowledged historical study was the research in the state archives of Turkey. Not conducting such a research or in other words focusing "only" on oral history accounts as well as archives of other institutions and foreign powers', such as British, German, or American archives, was out of question for the historians' perception of history and for scholars who work on historical topics. We can call it a sort of archive fetishism. This includes, on the one hand, the ignorance of alternative data and, on the other, it employs a non-critical glance into state archival materials (cf. Gölbaşı 2017).[28] Stressing that official archival documents have an objective perspective is very difficult since the state/government as an institutional corpus carries out an actorship in violent and/or non-violent events. Therefore, the state (including its archives) has to be regarded, considered, and scrutinised within its own complexity.

One of the most known recent discussions about this feature, with regard to the Armenian Genocide, took place when social scientist Ayhan Aktar published the memoir of Ottoman Army Captain Sarkis Torossian in Turkish (Torossian 2012), who fought in the Gallipoli and Palestine campaigns during the First World War. Even scholars and historians who work(ed) on the Armenian Genocide and on denialism positioned themselves against family accounts and pointed to the state archives (following editorial sheds light on this very debate: Somay 2015; cf. Akçam 2014, 49–75). I faced this very same feature – regarding the understanding of the historical studies and the archival work fetishism – during my field research on the artistic works and exhibitions that I treat in the next chapter on denialism and recognition of the Armenian Genocide. In these terms, the question should be asked whether or not we consider the subjective positions and dispositions of actors that took part in the genocidal events and (re-)making of post-extermination conditions carefully through acknowledging their agencies.

4.5 Concluding Remarks

Continuing the discussion concerning the social science studies and historiography in Turkey, the field of the Armenian Genocide studies has subsumed various approaches. They have emerged not only through scholarship but also influenced by public political interest. As pointed out in this chapter, the political violence from 1915 onwards involves different facets to consider, scrutinise, and review in order to reconstruct this past. The very same pattern, in fact, applies to the bibliography of non-historiographical researches on the Armenian Genocide and violence in Turkey.

---

[28] The Ottoman official discourse on the Hamidian massacres would be an interesting example on the subject position in the archival materials, as Edip Gölbaşı puts forward: "In a nutshell, the official contention advanced by the Ottoman authorities was that the mass violence was simply the reaction of Muslim masses to the acts of provocation and aggression on the part of Armenians closely connected with revolutionary, 'seditious' committees" (p. 36).

Over the course of time, the focus relied on the ideological interplay in the Ottoman nationalism as the reason for genocidal violence – that was, without a doubt, pioneering in the field. Türkyılmaz calls this sort of approach "ideological determinism" (2011, 17). This focus has left its place to the methods reading the events in their multidimensionality, such as including appropriation of the so-called forsaken wealth and forced labour in the families. They point at the participatory motives in the society, for instance, or concentrate on the second phase of the extermination, which targeted the surviving Armenians in the concentration camps in Syrian desert (Kévorkian 2011; Mouradian 2018). Beyond the similarities of the violence in different places, the differences based on location gain(ed) importance in the historiography of the genocide. The question of partaking-motives has looked into groupings other than state elites since then. For variations concerning actorship, subjectivities, and perhaps resentment shaped the flow of events. Alternative actions of persons could show the cumulative processing of the genocidal events as well as various decision-making moments instead of a monolithic structure (cf. Üngör 2011).[29]

In other words, the history of the Armenian Genocide and its aftermath offers us a rich palette of approaches in order to explain the events, violence, and memory. Even only one example like Van includes different facets: the denial of violence that was performed on people and place, i.e. urbicide; actorship from resistance to refuge and perpetration; (nationalist) reconstruction of events for the sake of domestic and international politics; features regarding the centre and periphery of the city; and its reconstruction for the memorialisation.

I would like to summarize this chapter with a personal experience that in my opinion bridges the past to present – or this chapter to the next. In my years working in the region as a guide, it was a part of the common knowledge concerning the basics of group permits: Armenians are prohibited to climb Mount Ararat. Since the beginning of the 1990s, every person who wanted to climb Mount Ararat has required a corresponding military permit which was normally only a bureaucratic step for tourist groups. However, for Armenians this bureaucratic step has been a massive obstacle because their applications have never been considered or denied easily. Moreover, it is not a regular practice for other mountains in Turkey. The outposts of gendarmerie and military special forces in Doğubeyazıt, Ağrı, that are the

---

[29]   In his thorough study, Uğur Ümit Üngör deals with the history of homogenization in Diyarbekir region, including the time of the Armenian Genocide and the epoch of single party regime until 1950, questioning various parties joining and benefiting from this process.

authorised institutions for the permission have been denying to allow Armenians and their descendants, in practice, without regard to their citizenship, to enter the mountain region. This notion in my opinion includes several facets that are aforementioned, including the continuity in the legal framework. We can approach to this aspect through questioning the parties (or the actorship issue), problematising the permit regulations – considering localities and motives – or the politics that are being made through denying the access of Armenians to the territory.

5 The Conflict of Recognition and Denial

In this chapter, I explore impacts and shapes of denialism, or in historian Talin Suciyan's (2016, 73) terms the *denialist habitus,* that is on the one hand embodied in official practices and laws, and on the other in oppressive socio-economic practices like wealth tax in the first half of the 1940s. According to Suciyan, this (has) created over the course of time a discursive differentiation between Armenians in Turkey and the ones living in diaspora since the genocide, describing the former as "good Armenians" and the latter as "enemies". The denialist habitus was, moreover, nourished by its own product: the public silence in the Armenian and non-Armenian society (cf. 2016, 65). The burning topic back then for the Armenians in Turkey was not the recognition of the genocide but equal rights for all. This struggle was carried out by Armenian public figures. The discussions hosted a vast heterogeneity of Armenian positions as Suciyan (p. 125) remarks: "Armenian present was struggling against the eradication, although the reaction was by no means monolithic." This notion is in my opinion significant in order to approach and understand the debates around 2014–2016 as well. For resemblances were to be seen in texts that are published and public spaces that created pockets for (re)presentations.

Discourses and in particular the process of knowledge production itself – rather than the produced knowledge – are the focal points of this chapter. In these terms, this chapter does not aim to check the correctness of the denialist claims – or of revisionists, negationists' claims (cf. Hovannisian 1998a, 203 f; Ternon, Yves 1998, 237 f; Wetzel 2003, 28) – given the information regarding the Armenian Genocide, in other words, via cognitive knowledge (Cohen 2001, 9; Ch. 2). Instead, I pose questions such as how denialism functions and reorganises itself over the course of time. Thus, concomitant with the process of denialist knowledge production, I underpin the motives of participation and actorships, in fact bystander position(s) emerging in the denialist scene. Hence, I treat denialism as a process, more than a category (Göçek 2016; Turan and Öztan 2018), that adapts to changing circumstances of society and state formation.

Furthermore, I put forward some examples of counter-memory attempts that emerged under the ruling denialist power in Turkey, how the trajectory of trivialisation occurs in Van and how it is reflected in the Kurdish society throughout (critical) recognition debates. This chapter argues that the (non)-transformation always includes heterogeneities in which biographical and/or counter-memories do not correspond to or reconcile with dominant (national) narratives. This very situation brings about new challenges for the national narratives. In fact, the challenge has always been there. I argue that we need to discuss the contested memory spaces when we talk about any dominant narrative since, for instance, biographical memories constantly show a disobedience in recording and reconfiguring such stories or because public discourse is in an ongoing change.

First, I revisit the theories of denialism and denialism of the Armenian Genocide and then construct the focal point of my discussion concerning contemporary political debates through events that took place especially in Istanbul, Turkey. Following, I focus on the so-called *Just Memory* discourse that was distributed by the Turkish Foreign Office in the 2000s which I see as an approach of contemporary trivialization. In order to focus on current denialist habitus, I only briefly contextualize the history of denialism in Turkey, for example, (early) Turkish Republic's positioning itself in the discussion which also ended up with denying this foundational violence (Göçek 2016, 353).

The state of denialism in the Turkish case is a question of memory regime(s) in which, for instance, developing (or attempts to develop) a quasi-historiography becomes a priority instead of critically reflecting upon stories and narratives. Thereupon the Turkish Foreign Ministry exhibition *Nar Niyeti-yle*, launched in April 2016, lays in this framework – perhaps, the only material form utilising the *Just Memory* template, apart from foreign policies. I then present some other exhibition approaches that represented counter narratives. I consider these regarding their concepts, including questions concerning ways of storytelling. Hence, I ask what space they sought to create and to what extent these approaches could include critical stories that corrode boundaries of denialism.

The following pages concern the situation in Van. Under the subchapter 5.3 Contemporary Situation in Van, I discuss examples such as a monument reproducing official denialism via using local stories and ethnographic observations from my field research protocols. Afterwards, I introduce the recognition debates in contemporary Kurdish politics and society in order to bridge the situation to the biographies I gathered. These, in this juncture, influence and are influenced by the social context – in reciprocal sense. So I treat every subject separately and disclose the trivialization realms and recognition debates throughout examples from the field.[1]

---

[1]   As you have noticed already, I underscore repeatedly the phenomenon of denialism. It sounds like it may be an oxymoron to the title of this chapter: The Conflict of Recognition and Denial. Yet, in my opinion there is a brief explanation that deconstructs (takes apart and builds up again) this paradoxical terminology-usage. The recognition debates and/or arguments appeared to be either in international affairs, for example in foreign policy discussions concerning third parties' recognition like the German Bundestag or Swiss courts, or in the area dominated by the non-state/civil society actors in

5.1 On denialism (of the Armenian Genocide)

As Vaclav Havel's greengrocer hanged the poster bearing the slogan "Workers of the world, unite!" to express his need to lead a peaceful life free of conflicts, Havel (2018, 22; cf. Cohen 2001, 259) argues, he becomes "a player in the game" where he accepts "prescribed *ritual*[s]." Thus, through his contribution, the greengrocer could become a part of the whole picture, or in Havel's word "panorama" which is shaped by the participation of others and a familiar notion for everyone. In the sixth part of his essay, Havel (p. 31) adds "the greengrocer and the office worker have both adapted to the conditions in which they live, but in doing so, they help to create those conditions."[2]

In his comprehensive work *States of Denial*, Stanley Cohen (2001, 103–16) discusses the official denialism under three umbrella frames. Firstly, he starts with describing *literal denial* whence type of argumentation relies on total rejection of the assertion or claim. Literal denialism approaches the arguments offensively, that the accounts would not be reliable which, however, Cohen (p. 104) distinguishes from strategies of blaming the claimants as "terrorists", "racists", or "conspirators". He (p. 112) describes such strategies "counter-offensive". Meanwhile an *interpretative denial*, Cohen's second framework, stresses that the story can be read totally different (sometimes through the interlines) so it would portray another picture. It emphasises that the wheel of interpretation is dependent on who conducts it and how. In this manner, the interpretative denial contains euphemisms and language games (pp. 107 ff). He then concludes with *implicatory denialism*, or the justification of persecution. This can appear hand-in-hand with arguments of "necessary actions", "under such historical conditions" and polishing the "we" construction (pp. 110 f). Cohen also points out partial recognition of the problems when the sorts of denialism cannot function anymore (p. 113).

Turkey – NGOs, initiatives as well as political movements in a spectrum from liberal and left-wing to Kurdish parties. Since in my study I do not consider international politics of recognition, I also do not carry out a discussion regarding such third parties either. Yet, I do show some strategies and discourses manufactured by the Turkish Foreign Office as examples to contextualize the realm of denialism in the country. What (has) happened in Turkey – despite the state distributed denialist habitus – is the focal point here. Thus, I present these as counter memories claiming a space in a world of denialist narratives. These trajectories of recognition transform the narrative world into a contested memory space.

[2]   Stanley Cohen's work, *States of Denial*, inspired me to read Havel's essay again and consider the social dynamics of denying the truth. It also means that Cohen's approach to Havel's work has been a premise for me to reread the structure of denialism.

The question of how one can start denying past atrocities needs to spawn the following question as well: whether one can take (or acquire) a denialist or revisionist standing in a pattern of "naïvety" (cf. 'innocent denial' in Charny 2000). Even if it makes the issue much more complicated, we cannot ignore the reaction of the collective against the silence breaker, for which Eviatar Zerubavel (2006, 76) points out that they (the silence breaker) would be stigmatised as traitor by the then-former fellows. This implies at its core that people make decisions, which lead people to think about the facts, motives, (individual or collective) targets, perhaps, from a pragmatic perspective or a fanatical one. These decisions are shaped in one's life-world, milieu, and through habitus. Furthermore, this feature shows that the issue is not about the categories but processes – and of course trajectories. In this sense, the essentialist arguments regarding denialism, that it is up to culture, ethnicity, religion, or collective identification clusters, cannot describe the whole issue because it overlooks or ignores the political construction behind it (as following studies underscore: Göçek 2016; Turan and Öztan 2018; Türkyılmaz 2015b).

As Cohen (2001, 148) articulates "We must repeat the question of how much the ordinary Germans knew during the Nazi Years", we also have to question what the ordinary Germans knew about Shoah in the post-war period. Or adapting this very question into our case: what does the society in Turkey as well as in the diaspora know about the very political feature of (state) denialism. I suggest, by disassembling the term denialism we reach the following notion: euphemisms. Euphemism appears in justification, belittling, and silencing (Hovannisian 1998b; Zerubavel 2006). At first it is not the whole complex of official denialism that touches the ordinary peoples' life. In many cases, this is followed by or to be found in acknowledged (and hailed) victimiser narratives; ignoring survivor accounts; and perhaps violence in a pattern of continuity. Hence, this issue brings us back to the notion of awareness (cf. Glaser and Strauss 1965) regarding the violence, forgetting, and memorialization processes (cf. Charny 2000; Zerubavel 2006). Moreover, in terms of the genocide, while the Turkish State's denialist spheres have employed institutionalisation strategies, social involvement in denialism has become a significant question regarding the public awareness (Göçek 2016, 436; Hovannisian 1998a, 202; Suciyan 2016; Turan and Öztan 2018 Ch. 5). And of course it was challenged by the civil engagement in counter-memory production.

In his monograph, Miguez Macho (2016) exemplifies and describes the invented historiographical canon regarding the Spanish civil war, Franco-Era, and post-Franco denialism. Macho (p. 85) summarizes this canonical framework of storytelling under three points as follows: "All violence stems from the war and its context"; "Territories that are not fought over or are not war fronts do not exist"; and "Francoism is an anti-democratic and traditionalist ideology, but has no genocidal component". In addition to Miguez Macho's argument of canon of denialism, Hovannisian's comprehensive study on the denial of the Armenian Genocide and the Holocaust (1998a) embraces characteristics of such attempts. In this sense, the denialist canon concerning the genocide which has been drafted, reshaped, and (re-)produced by professional historians and state agencies – diplomatic missions and/or bureaucrats (Göçek 2016 Ch. 4; Hovannisian 1998a; Turan and Öztan 2018 Ch. 5) – includes arguments such as so-called wartime circumstances and/or "only deportations"; "extremists' job" (for a comparable case please see Rwandan Genocide denialism in Kimenyi 2001); a sort of stab in the back legend and/or provocation thesis (cf. Miguez Macho 2016, 71 f; in case of the Adana massacres 1909 please see, Suny 2015, 173); and the so-called enemy propaganda including "in aftermath exaggerated numbers by deportees". At a further stage one can encounter allegations based on enmity and racism such as "it is a lie invented by Armenians, Jews, the West..."; expressed differently, the "other" or the victim group – and an alleged international complicity – would be blamed.

Beyond that, the pseudo-scientific denialist studies adapt quantitative view-points and usually engage with "casualty figures", that in fact led to another discussion among denialist standings after journalist Murat Bardakçı's (first feuilleton, then monograph) publication of Talaat Pasha's notebook that included the figures of almost 925,000 Armenian deportees (see Bardakçı 2008; cf. Sarafian, Ara 2011). Different denialist positions were contoured over the course of time, as for instance the Military Museum in Harbiye, Istanbul, host(ed) the "Hall of Armenian Issue with Documents" presenting figures of 300,000 deportees rooted in the 1980s' institutionalisation (Turan and Öztan 2018, 347–50). These quantitative viewpoints also point out a quasi-compa-rability of the extermination campaigns. The core idea of "comparability" is also to be observed in other cases, for example Ernst Nolte's "comparative trivialization" (Hovannisian 1998a, 227) that started the *Historikerstreit*, or in the Rwandan case too (cf. Kimenyi 2001). Moreover, such professional historians and state institutions using this canon propagated pseudo-forensic "try-outs" for a time period through "revealing mass graves of Turks/Muslims murdered by Armenian gangs" (cf. Turan and Öztan 2018). It became a famous subject for Turkish mass media and was treated with festival-like attention. On the one hand, it reminds us of the Holocaust denialist Leuchter report, but on the other it gives hints regarding the Freudian projection in terms of the Armenian Genocide.

Sociologists Ömer Turan and Güven Gürkan Öztan underscore in their comprehensive work the relation between the Turkish "state mind" in Fou-cauldian terms and the denialism of the Armenian Genocide. They further discuss the effects of the distributed "collective Turkish victimhood" (2018,

402 f) in the construction and continuity of denialist habitus and underpin that this sort of projection discards and discriminates minorities from the "contract of Turkishness", which they discuss through the theorisation by sociologist Barış Ünlü (2014; 2018).[3] A brief quote from sociologist Fatma Müge Göçek's monography on denialism would summarize the points that are highlighted, I believe. She reports that concerning the ASALA assassinations Turkish journalists have argued "that, historically, the Turks had always been victims and the Armenians perpetrators, thereby effectively dismissing responsibility for past violence once again" (2016, 463). Thus, the argument would then (re-)generate hate speech, racism and xenophobia through the emblems "we" versus "others".

Moreover, the Armenian Genocide is frequently utilised by the governments of Turkey to make international politics (Chorbajian 2016; Göçek 2016; Hovannisian 1998a). Again, Turan and Öztan (2018) point out that the state mind utilised every niche from interior politics to legal apparatus and foreign office strategies to confront the recognition claims of Armenians – and of foreign powers – starting even during the genocidal violence. Nonetheless, politics of the Turkish Foreign Office has reached the perception of "being over the governments", e.g. "it follows only the national cause". Thus, a similar instrumentalisation of past violence can be observed in a broader scope of national and international politics of Turkey, for example within the Dersim Genocide debates started by the then-prime minister Erdogan himself in 2011 or with the Observer Membership of IHRA (Dost-Niyego and Aytürk 2016; Seni 2016).[4] As Şeni points out Turkey's "memorial policies", events, and production of, for instance, documentary films concerning the Holocaust give a sort of message to the international public that Turkey cannot be a successor of perpetrators of a genocide (2016; cf. Bali 2017; Turan and Öztan 2018). This approach to Holocaust commemoration obviously can be defined as instrumentalisation for a political win. Of course in the case of the Armenian Genocide, it is distributed in connection to the "collective victimhood" thesis. And with the rise of AKP power it employed the discourse of a "non-violent Muslim past" or "non-genocidal Muslimhood" (Turan and Öztan 2018, 384), accompanied by the political determination "ancestor's clean hands".

---

[3]   Sociologist Barış Ünlü claims, inspired by Black and post-colonial studies, that the sort of national or socio-political contract binds only the ones who accept certain religious, ethnic and political (national) boundaries. Yet, in my point of view his conceptualisation involves some gaps when one employs an intersectional perspective.

[4]   IHRA: International Holocaust Remembrance Alliance, the former International Task Force for International Cooperation on Holocaust Education, Remembrance, and Research (ITF).

At this point, it is important to mention that professional historians' or pseudo-scientists' denialism is replaced by – regarding the public attention – the social events and the collective involvement of ordinary Turks. Nevertheless, the denialist project(ion) of professionals and institutions is conducted alongside. In other words, the latent denialism or "the unwillingness to critically reflect" (Göçek 2016, 143) in the society has surfaced as a tool of denialist politics (primarily in foreign policy). With regard to the aforementioned canon, foreign office strategies, and social involvement, Cohen's description (2001, 103) seems to be adequate: "Sometimes, these appear in a visible sequence: if one strategy does not work, the next is tried... But these forms seldom run in sequence: more often they appear simultaneously, even within the same one-page press release."

5.1.1 The brief chronology of the Armenian Genocide Denialism

Denialism, not just in our case, is an evolving subject. When we look into the past of denialist historiography and the political denialist actions, we clearly see that the first years after the mass extermination campaigns (approximately 1916–22) hosted a wide spectrum of patterns from denying the violence (not the genocide because the term was not in circulation), to "not contradict[ing] the fact that massacres occurred" (Türkyılmaz 2015b; cf. Akçam 2007), even to the trials with criminal prosecution of some perpetrators (cf. Dadrian and Akçam 2008). Basically the simplest reason for such a division was the creation of the Republic of Turkey and the two existent governments in the country, one in Istanbul and another in Ankara, but both as successors of the Ottoman CUP. Nevertheless, this successors role was later suspiciously denied by the Ankara government. In those years, the genocide was also a theme for international affairs, perhaps, due to the question of Armenian refugees or the war and post-war circumstances. Türkyılmaz (2015b) points out that "the international public interest in the massacres" faded away with the establishment of Turkey and Soviet Armenia. And the Ankara government changed its course to trying to keep the extermination as a "non-question … to leave everything about the Armenians, their history and the massacres to oblivion." In Suciyan's study (2016; cf. Akçam and Kurt 2012), we see however that laws were regulated and executed to repress Armenians in the country and to prohibit the entrance into Turkey of those who were deported and survived or of those who left their homeland afterwards.

The Turkish official account on 1915 had then found its proto-fundaments in the 1950s with Turkish politician Esat Uras' denialist works (Turan and Öztan 2018, 186–99). After the first demonstrations in 1965 in diaspora and Soviet Armenia that used the term genocide for the very first time, Turkey started to take an offensive and proactive role in denying what had happened generating its own narrative. These arguments were designed primarily for international diplomatic campaigns and narrative building in academic sense defining Armenians as perpetrators and Turks as the victims. Following the military coup of 1980 and the armed ASALA attacks against several Turkish targets in the 1970s and 1980s, Turkey's actions in this regard would then involve utilising right-radical Turkish militants in foreign countries (Türkyıl-maz 2015b). Furthermore, the military junta continued the institutionalisation of denialism treating the subject with its own propagandist narrative in school books and academic circles (Turan and Öztan 2018, Ch. 5).

When symbolic years like 2005, the 90th anniversary of the massacres, approached, it raised the public and denialist interest repeatedly. Perhaps, it was the aftereffect of the experience of 1965. Yet, in the 2000s, Turkey witnessed a heterogeneous repertoire about the Armenian past and further protagonists such as Hrant Dink, an Armenian journalist based in Istanbul and founder of the Armenian paper AGOS. His murder in January 2007 "clarified" another issue in the public mind which is closely connected to denialism: the silence of governmental institutions concerning the right-wing violence and impunity.

5.2   The contemporary Situation in the "West"

Beyond the denialist attempts and established system, in recent years more and more intellectuals in Turkey have begun raising their voice for recognition. In this manner, genocide commemorations have started taking place first of all in historical and central Taksim Square Istanbul, public events and conferences have been organised and the subject Armenian Genocide recognition has come to be a part of even mainstream media discussion for several years from the late 2000s onward. A petition campaign had been launched asking for forgiveness. These, bottom line, (have) proclaimed reconciliation. Marc Nichanian (2011) has thoroughly thought out critiques at this point. He first underlines these two features, forgiveness and reconciliation (or peace), are two different acts building up their own time forms. While forgiveness is about the power of witness – if there is still a witness after extermination and historiographic cropping of accounts for the truth as Nichanian underscores in his essay, reconciliation indicates a political question that is to be performed through and under the power of jurisprudence (p. 162) even though it means eroding the truth (p. 198). In this respect, he (p. 123) pinpoints this prevailing question: Has the possible forgiver the power to forgive? Or in other words, is the person even a subject?

Keeping Nichanian's points in mind, I would like to tackle briefly the question of how such initiatives (have) appeared after decades of denialist hegemony. There, of course, are several reasons. First of all, scholars from Turkey or with a background from Turkey but living in other countries started facing the question of the past genocidal crimes. Furthermore, debates triggered and launched by the Istanbul Armenian newspaper AGOS and its editor-in-chief Hrant Dink, who was murdered by right-extremists in collaboration with state agents on 19 January 2007, transferred to the public the discussions that were first started by the scholars in the field. The core difference of Dink and AGOS' articles to the critical position of Armenian journalists in the early republican period was the latter's main struggle for equal rights for minority groups in Turkey (Suciyan 2016). Dink also struggled for equality, but he believed that a profound equality was only to be established when people would openly talk about the past (cf. Göçek 2016, 419). At this juncture, Dink's assassination made the public opinion on rights of expression emerge which could be observed at his funeral. It is important to underpin, I suggest, that attending Dink's funeral or the annual commemoration could not be considered automatically as the recognition of genocidal crimes in the country's past. It relied on the right of expression first of all. And following that, the very existence of bystander and victimiser disposition of state agents was the point that was problematised through attending the commemoration.

Even though the AKP government utilised democratisation policies and recognition debates, it has possibly never aimed to recognise the genocide which usually should include reparations, resystematising citizenship laws for survivor families and/or returning the confiscated properties to the descendants, in other words working the jurisprudence in fair ways (cf. Turan and Öztan 2018, Ch. 6). While such EU-proximal policies were declared to be in an ongoing process, conferences targeting such subjects were prohibited (*Agos* 2019),[5] people who spoke out their opinion or published research on the genocide were

---

[5]   The most recent example occurred while I was editing these pages. Hrant Dink Foundation, which was founded after Dink's assassination, has been engaged in organising conferences targeting free academic discussions on different regions and cities and their pasts. The last one in 2019 had to take place in Kayseri aiming the disclosure of the city's past in academic ways. Yet, first the organisation was prohibited by the local governorship of Kayseri. Subsequently, the foundation decided to relocate the conference to its own conference halls in Istanbul. The day prior to the conference, the foundation was informed that the Şişli district governorship (*kaymakamlık*), where the foundation's office resides, banned the organisation of the conference. In reverse conclusion, the foundation organised a food festival in its office building centred on the dumplings called *mantı* which is associated intrinsically with the city of Kayseri. So, the foundation endowed another example of bypassing.

sued based on Turkish Penal Code Article nr. 301 – insulting Turkishness, the Turkish nation and government – and the exhibition "Hall of Armenian Issue with Documents" distributing "Armenian cruelty thesis" was launched in 2006 in the Army Museum in Harbiye, Istanbul (Turan and Öztan 2018, 347–50). Yet meanwhile a fine-tuning in denialism had started that would "flourish" a "new" discourse with regard to the Armenian past.

5.2.1 Just Memory. A novel approach?

As former Foreign Minister of Turkey Ahmet Davutoğlu (2014) published his article *Turkish-Armenian Relations in the Process of De-Ottomanization or 'Dehistoricization': Is a 'Just Memory' Possible?* in the *Turkish Policy Quarterly*, an Istanbul-based policy journal, he was already conducting (official) practices based on this discourse in his international affair campaigns, as he mentions in the abstract of the article, for instance through the so-called protocol diplomacy with the Armenian government starting in 2008, which was unilaterally cancelled by the Armenian side in 2018 after experiencing that the Turkish government did not proceed further. Davutoğlu's article starts with criticism of national(ist) movements in the Ottoman Empire and their results within the scope of nation-building processes that he, however, defines as dividing the historical perceptions of and denying the past coexistence. He, moreover, extends his criticism to the identity questions of the autonomy-yielding movements, reconstructs their perspectives in a dichotomous framework of "We [the movements]" and "Ottomans". Yet, he claims that this binary was nourished by such movements and not by the Ottomans without considering Ottoman state policies – or plausibly ignoring them. He then concludes his argument or hypothesis that nation-buildings caused wrong interpretations of the past and a misuse of such narratives through stressing a quasi-continuity of national consciousness and – Davutoğlu employs this term – "alienation" from the reality of the "good past" (p. 24). Several times he refers implicitly to and then also cites Benedict Anderson's concept of imagined communities. Nevertheless, he conceptualises his entire work on an (imagined) idealised Ottoman past and the confrontations of nationalists based on the idea of modernity. At this juncture, he adds, the nationalist outbreaks used to work in "small feudal regions in Europe" for unification but resulted with the devastation of an Ottoman paradise, so to speak (p. 25).

After this introduction, Davutoğlu describes the past coexistence on the following three pages with positive historical accounts e.g. the establishment of the Armenian Patriarchate in Constantinople with the order of Mehmed II in 1461 or the first Turkish novel which was written by an Armenian, Hovsep Vartanyan. Nonetheless, he also points to intra-community conflicts within the Armenian society. The historical narrative occupies more than 1/3 of the whole essay.

For Davutoğlu, the Armenian Genocide is a topic that appears under memory discussions but memory as a part of the past. He calls the contemporary approaches concerning the year 1915 one-sided, and automatically unjust, whereas he allegedly presents a "multi-dimensional memory". For him the "one-sided" reading of history benefits a sector that feeds off the *status quo*. One of the amiss points in his article is how he treats Hrant Dink's assassination. From the republican period, he could only give the example of Hrant Dink's murder (which he calls "Hrant Dink'in vefatı") (Ozinian 2014, in press)[6] and the unexpectedly high number of participants at his funeral ceremony. However, he disregards that being at the funeral was a reaction to the Turkish State's criminalisation of Hrant Dink from 2004 onwards. In that year, Dink published an article about Sabiha Gökçen, who was the first female fighter pilot of the world, Atatürk's adoptive child and an Armenian orphan as Dink shed light on.

Nevertheless, Davutoğlu titled his concept *Just Memory* with the emphasis lying on "memory", not on "just", I argue. Since Davutoğlu tackles the question of how people need to reconstruct the past, i.e. remembrance, he focuses on a construction of the past centred on an idealised coexistence, in using the patterns of incorrect understanding of Ottoman policies like *Millet* system – without describing its strict hierarchisation of non-Muslims beneath the Muslim rulers. Thus, he "unearths" a century with polished storytelling while skipping the republican era, focusing on 1915 through the lens of the relationship between the Armenians and foreign powers as well as concentrating the narrative on the negotiations between Turkey and Armenia in 2009. Suciyan (2016) speaks of the republican period's anti-Armenian construct of "evil diaspora Armenians" which shows up as a continuation of Ottoman "fifth-column" allegations on Armenians. In this regard, continuing Nichanian's question "who is in charge of the 'truth of the facts'? Historians or tribunals?" (1998, 250), the following question appears: Who is ultimately in charge of the narratives and the memory?

It of course depends on each scholar's interpretation, but questions emerge inevitably. For instance, what does Davutoğlu's narrative tell us with such a long, shiny, and sunny Ottoman construct? What does he target by framing his article's historical part on the concept of imagined communities since he has also been a high ranking politician? Just a reminder, he reconstructs imagined

---

[6]   In Turkish, Davutoğlu calls the assassination "Dink's passing away" and in the English version "Dink's death".

Ottoman Christian communities and locates them under the European "other". Of course, one can pose the question whether *Just Memory* can be interpreted as a partial acknowledgement (cf. Cohen 2001, 113). I strongly suggest that this concept simply reproduces the old denialist and revisionist arguments: collaboration with enemy powers, some sort of coexistence under the fair Ottoman rule, and the nationalists' faults in dealing with the issue – shortly, through a biased generalising Ottoman-Armenian voices and struggles for equality and ignoring the power relations in the country. This time, nationalists from both sides, Turkish and Armenian, are at gunpoint. Perhaps, this is the new component in this approach. However, Davutoğlu does not borrow the dominant narrative of "being victims of the same tragedy" – or in words of Turan and Öztan (2018), the "Turkish collective victimhood" – that was distributed for instance in the exhibition *Nar Niyetiyle* (for a comparable discourse in case of Spanish civil war: cf. Míguez Macho 2016, 82).

In his book *Tell your Life Story*, Dan Bar-On presents his projects with German-Jewish and Israeli-Palestinian dialogue groups and discusses the issues around common understanding and collective memory building. In these terms, he (2006, 202) theorises the feature of a "good enough story" which is a story told in a group session and embraced by most of the group members with interest, eagerness, or maybe anger. In these terms, I assume that Davutoğlu tries to narrate a "good enough story" in the political domain by reorganising the memory to achieve a political benefit in the international area. All in all it seems to be a 21st century type reorganisation (or rerendering) of well-established denialist typologies.

5.2.2 On the field with events

From 7 April to 29 April 2016, the Turkish Ministry of Foreign Affairs financed and organised a short-term bilingual (English and Turkish) special exhibition entitled *Nar Niyetiyle: Türk – Ermeni İlişkilerinde Unutmanın Değil, Hatırlamanın Zamanı* in the *Tophane-i Amire* exhibition hall of the Mimar Sinan Fine Arts University which had once been a Ottoman canon casting arsenal. The main narrative of the exhibition was displayed at the entrance on three wide screens that constituted two gateways leading to the main exhibition hall through which the visitor had to pass. In other words, the visitor had no choice about how to approach the narrative.

A similar (but more disturbing) approach was employed by the Holocaust Museum in Dallas, Texas, at the beginning of the 1990s, when visitors had to enter the exhibition rooms through an authentic waggon that was used by the Germans in the Nazi era for the deportations to the east, the ghettos, and the concentration and extermination camps (Kuhls 1994). The museum then opened another gate "only for the survivors" after its design was criticised for reenacting the trauma suffered by Holocaust survivors once more while visiting the museum (ibid.). Yet this new gate was not open for all. Through such a comparison, we can assume that emotional bonding was the focal point of both exhibition concepts. And in the case of *Nar Niyetiyle* exhibition, it adopted the Turkish State's approach to the genocide and its recognition arguing that "it is the only path that can rule in our realm", so to speak. In other words, it resembled an authority for the visiting conditions of the exhibit.

Figure 1: The exhibition Nar Niyetiyle (Source: own illustration)
It "welcomes" the visitors by showing them the only possible path into the narrative.

While Davutoğlu's *Just Memory* concept and Erdogan's condolence messages from 2014 were presented on the middle screen along with a series of visuals depicting the mundane life of the Armenian community in the past that changed via pendulum effects that Türkyılmaz (2016 in press) defines as a "hypnotising pendulum", the screen on the left side showed the exhibition poster containing a picture of Ararat from the north-east side (the side of the Armenian State). And the right screen displayed two small girls plating pigtails and a poem stressing brotherhood with pomegranate metaphors.

The curators conceptualised and implemented the exhibition in a circular fashion with panels containing information about the Armenian–Turkish relationship, starting from the 11th century until the so-called 2009 protocol politics. In the middle of this circle, a constellation using the *Calumeno postcards*, titled "Armenians 100 years ago in Turkey with the postcards", awaited visitors. This compact ensemble was supported by interactive displays about these postcards, yet within a euphemistic framework (cf. ibid.).

According to the dominant narrative of the exhibition, "positive" stories had prominence, better displays, and a bigger size so that the so-called coexistence could be featured. On the one side, visitors could encounter several panels about Armenian handcraft and Armenian minds under the Ottoman rule. After these, a chronological fashion of storytelling perpetuated the exhibition's narrative focusing on, for instance, the Ottoman reforms and the Armenian political movements. The conflicts that resulted in bloodshed and their Armenian victims were belittled. And in contrast, the Ottoman politics and policies were presented as tools to establish security and save souls. Cover-ups and euphemisms occupied the whole storytelling. For example, information concerning the events of 1915 was featured on a single panel showing (from top to bottom) the metaphorical triangle of a description of the *Sevk ve İskan Kanunu* (known as *Tehcir*/Deportation Law as well) of 27 May 1915; information about Armenian nation state building; and a portrait of Talaat Pasha – the orchestrator of the extermination campaigns, yet in the exhibitive portrayal this notion was covered. In addition to the classical denialist manifests, for example the discourse that the rebellions were the reason for the deportation (in the exhibit's language: relocation), this panel approached the aftermath in three paragraphs starting with: "The relocation process and the developments in the subsequent years of war have led to the shrinking of the Armenian community" and ended with "…, civil servants and their families were murdered by terrorists in retaliation during the events of 1915."[7] The circle of panels did not only contain information about the so-called millennial coexistence, but it also stood away from various exhibition concepts that, for instance, would pose new challenging questions or would bring about the recent development in scholars' debates like the *Wehrmacht* exhibition from the Mid-1990s in Germany. The huge number of exhibitive approaches awaiting visitors avoided the chance to follow a clear path of storytelling, drawing attention to the designs instead of the narrative (Türkyılmaz 2016).[8]

In her interview with AGOS, curator Güzin Erkan describes her team's intention to exhibit "the contribution of Armenian people in this society", of course "without concentrating explicitly on those four years" – in other words, fading out the extermination campaigns (Diler 2016 in press). However, such idealisations skip the contradictions and ambiguities in the Ottoman society.

[7]   From the author's own visual archive of the exhibition.
[8]   Beyond the distributed positive stories, this exhibition also included a quote by Hrant Dink. In this context, Hrant Dink and his speeches (and, again, his murder) were instrumentalised by this reconstructed trivialization. Making Hrant Dink a content, a figure and even a category of memory without shedding light on the racist assassination, I argue, is a new form of whitewashing targeting, this time, the impunity.

Thus, the phenomenon of idealisation automatically refuses the ambiguity in its own arguments. Beyond that, since the genocide was called the "1915 events" and handled in a holistic way, it offers no room for personal accounts of victims or perpetrators. This interpretative denial (cf. Cohen 2001), like others, uses a euphemistic approach to tell people a story. Yet, its arteries lead to the classical denialist arguments and old modes of story-telling. With the genocide scholar Colin Tatz' assumption (2003, xv), the past is indeed a made-up foreign country, yet, I suppose, in this case memory occupies the place that was once occupied by the past.

5.2.3 Brief Excursion to Social Media and Political Engagement

Despite the rising *Just Memory* concept in those years, digital media has been hosting old-school classical denialism in its very pockets.[9] The multilingual platform *factcheckarmenia* with its twitter accounts, launched in March 2015 and still active in 2019, has perhaps been one of the first social media-based fact-checking platform in Turkey (cf. O'Connor 2019, 9–13).[10] Even though the website involves professionally handled video-spots on 1915 blaming the victims, distributing conspiracy theories making the complex stories simple for its followers – for instance through remanufacturing stab-in-the-back-legends targeting Armenians, it is unclear who the founders, sponsors, or editors are. Therefore, *factcheckarmenia* probably falls into the category of astroturfing: an acting non-profit organisation with sponsorships of big companies or governmental institutions in order to campaign in total closure due to the rules of

---

[9]   The digitalisation of denialism is indeed a theme of another comprehensive study, yet, I want to bring up some elements in order to create a comparative framework.

[10] Clustering current memory dynamics into three differentiated landscapes – folk memory, commemorative memory and mediatised memory, Paul O'Connor points out that the digitalised forms of memory transfer help us in the process of meaning-making, yet in newly emerged structures and through different approaches than the earlier established ones. He calls these the "mediatised memories" and describes its foundation as follows: "In a mediatised society, localised bodies of collective memory are assimilated to a storehouse of images, symbols, characters and narratives which is increasingly global in character. This comprises the raw material out of which a global memory-scape is composed and recomposed through ongoing processes of communication and mediation. However, only a tiny proportion of what is potentially accessible to memory actually gets remembered" (p. 10). Moreover, the element of entertainment is a socially-integrative part of this form. Perhaps, we also need to ask whether or not the denialist website resembles the mediatised memory of O'Connor, in its relation to social premises and in terms of the question of what the website's storytelling aims to evoke, rather than the discourse it utilises.

anonymous sponsorship. Thus, it instrumentalises the label of being a grass-roots organisation, running however big-budget campaign ads recruiting some so-called experts onto its own side.

In the same years, Turkish diaspora communities in different countries, like in the USA and Germany, were organised and mobilised for rallies like on 25 April 2015 or for *Dostluk ve Barış Buluşması* / *Meeting of Friendship and Peace* on 1 June 2016, the day of Armenian resolution talks at the Bundestag. Similar to digital platforms, the denialist narratives that were transmitted were reproductions of discourses from the late Ottoman and early republican peri-ods. Furthermore, the costs for those organisations – again despite its required budget for the stage, for instance – were covered as well. The people at the front were, however, from the well-known non-profit (and some grassroots) organisations. The slogans were based on emotional bounding layers such as "We did not commit genocide, we only defended our fatherland." Furthermore, these slogans were accompanied by Turkish flags, Atatürk posters, grey wolf symbols – Turkish right-wing extremists – and Islamist shouts – as Tanıl Bora (2003) describes the three patterns of Turkish right wing.

Both developments offered the opportunity to take part in Turkey's denialist cause via acting or enlightening others. One should point out the similarity of these with the policy of Turkish Foreign Office from the 1980s and 1990s, that appeared under the administrative role of Turkish diplomat Kamuran Gürün as creating a historiography, making the Turkish State's thesis "reconcilable" with the international public through events in Western countries (cf. Turan and Öztan 2018, Ch. 5; Ch. 6).

Yet, in current occasions the denialist arguments were defended by non-governmental and civil society organisations instead of a department of the Turkish Foreign Office turning up in a conference (Turan and Öztan 2018, 250; Ben Aharon 2015). In this respect, the Turkish "State mind's" denialism, in Turan and Öztan's description, was sort of successful in dividing the weight of discourse and task sharing. I do not argue that these organisations were assigned by the official institutions since we do not have any documents or clear evidence, however, they have attended actively to generate and spread the discourse and accept(ed) to assign themselves in protecting the policy and state-aligned historiography.

Back to Havel's greengrocer: He took part in generating the social envi-ronment, or again in Havel's words "creat(ing) those conditions" (2018, 31), though maybe it was not his aim to support an act of development. On the one hand, the poster was about self-determination and the perception of the condition(s), if not-hanging could cause trouble. However, the question of how close the greengrocer was to the other participants emerges at the very beginning. Zerubavel (2006, 54) points out: "Just as significant is the effect of social proximity among those standing around the elephant. Formal relations and the social environments that foster them [talking more openly] (such as bureaucracy), on the other hand, are more likely to discourage openness and thereby promote silence." In our case, the atmosphere that developed through the events against the recognition of the genocide encouraged many more to talk instead of remaining silent. However, it occurred on the other direction.

Regarding the realities, Miguez Macho (2016, 82) says "Denying the fact is not only a pathological behaviour at the individual level, but invents a new reality in social memory." In fact, in this diaspora case, there are several collective memory layers, one is, perhaps, similar to *Just Memory*, but another is the old denialist layer. And there are several elephants in the room. One of which is rooted in the denial of the Armenian Genocide which was maybe overlooked but has always been there. As the multi-layered social memory was evoked through such events, the old discourses came out. Yet, not all the elephants are sought in this regard, e.g. the denialism is publicly not outspoken.

5.2.4 The "Depo(t)" for counter memories

As mentioned before, the 2000s in Turkey witnessed discussions, events, initiatives that regarded the topic of the genocide on the Armenians. In this very time period, a contested memory space has emerged subsuming various trivialisation – using digital media or protests – as well as recognition approaches. One of the centres that has hosted several critical and reflective exhibitions and events is *Depo*, in Tophane district in Istanbul. It announced the period 2015–16 to be dedicated to exhibitions of national and international artists who expose narratives on the Armenian past and present as well as the question of memorialisation concerning the commemoration of 100 years since the genocide. In this exhibition schedule, I could see different works related to 1915, for instance the exhibitions in April–May 2016, while *Nar Niyetiyle* was displayed only a hundred meters away from this site at the *Tophane-i Amire* hall. In this subchapter, I am focusing on two of these regarding the discussions around counter-memories and exhibition concepts.

The exhibition *Bizzat Hallediniz* [Please deal inpropriapersona, translated by E.Y.], conceptualised and designed by the Istanbul-based NGOs *Babil* and *Tarih Vakfı* (History Foundation), was concentrated on the years 1915–18 and on the question of what happened to the Armenians through exposing some telegrams – mostly sent by Talaat Pasha to the regional governors or state agents – that were shared with the public for the first time, so the curator team claimed. According to the team, the exhibition was based on a comprehensive archival research that considered at first approximately five thousand telegrams filed in the Ottoman Archives of the Prime Ministry's State Archive and then used 400 pieces out of this number for the exhibition (Estukyan 2015 in press). Again according to the curators, they cooperated with a team of 20 historians and experts working on the topic rising their concept on four pillars-like focal themes: a) the colossal control of relocation, i.e. deportation politics; b) the plunder of Armenian wealth; c) forced assimilation of widows and orphans; and d) the time scope of the genocide – starting from 1914 and redeemed in 1918. Regarding the first point, the curators designed the exhibition hall in the fashion of a deportation map (ibid.). Since the focus was laid on the acquirement of cognitive knowledge on deportations, it quasi employed an aim to cognitively emotionalise or empathise with the past.

Figure 2: The exhibition hall hosting Bizzat Halalediniz (Source: own illustration)
It was designed through the 400 Ottoman telegraphs issued by the Sublime Porte or local state organs like governors or kaimakam. Yet, the visitors were left alone with this huge pile of paper due to the lack of given orientation.

In this respect, the main material of the exhibition – apart from the represented conversation between Talaat Pasha and Ottoman-Armenian MP Krikor Zohrab – was the state issued telegrams and their transliterations. These were the official records of the deportation orders, issued, and sent by Talaat. The originality that is to be sought in an exhibition was based only on the newly disclosed materials. The first impression it made was that with such a source like telegrams the curator team aimed to show the massive organisation and planning of the genocidal events and to claim that these actions were controlled by the Ottoman elites on the ground and by the Sublime Porte. Yet, the way of exhibiting the materials was very low-cost: A4-print-copies (not facsimiles) were hanged with adhesive tape on desks and on the walls of the hall, which is similar to some of the exhibition concepts of former concentration camp memorial sites in Germany in the 1980s (cf. Brink 1989, 40).

Through the selected objects and the way of exposing details over the past, the aesthetic impact on visitors was out of the question. Perhaps, due to the fact that they were the first, the curator team overlooked or ignored the aesthetic question and adopted the perspective of quasi classical historians to their work, that is based – at least in Turkey – on a strict archival lens. Nichanian (2011, 80 f) calls it the "modern reign of archive" that even sets rules for the memory of the witness. Yet, walls fully occupied in a linear framing of telegram copies without (or less than required) comments, remarks, inspiring questions, or even explanations gave the irritating impression of being in an unorganised archive. The only provided orientation consisted of the place names on the ground and the brief biographies of the governors or state agents who signed and/ or received telegrams sent by Talaat Pasha, hanged on the pillars of the hall. In other words, the expected impact of an exhibition to recall the knowledge collected earlier in other contexts was not existent in the room. The visitors barely had a chance to bridge own experiences to the displayed materials. In a manner of speaking, the exhibition fashion was asking its visitors to deal with the given information *in persona*.

In the exhibition catalogue of *Bizzat Hallediniz*, historian Ohannes Kılıçdağı, who was one of the project advisers, comes in for criticism on the archive fetishism of historiographical research perception that is dominant:

In our historiography and popular [current] history mentality, state documents we find in the official archives are more respected [valuable] than other inscriptive and nuncupative resources. A PhD without 'taking' a document out of archive would not be appreciated, [or] it would be considered inadequate, which is a reflection of this mentality ... Of course, state archives are very significant sources. First of all, it is almost impossible to find such a quantity of documents anywhere else. Yet, archival materials issued by state agents do not make them categorically the representation of truth. State as well as its agents are groups of (vested) interest. Furthermore, there are conflicts [and controversies] appearing among different levels and civil servants ... The essential point is a critical and comparative reading of [such] documents. (Babil Der 2015, 21) [translated by E.Y.]

Since the main resource of the exhibition, telegrams, was displayed *en masse*, his critique, I suppose, does concern the project concept, too. Portraying a singular resource to visitors – even after its critical interpretation – does not discard the fact that the official archival materials should emerge as the only source to underline the genocidal process. In other words, using the same component, the material spectrum that is stressed by the state official historiography as the only way to understand the past is a sort of acceptance of the terms emphasised by the same in advance – or in Foucauldian terms, the production pattern of subjugated knowledge. Ambiguity was the nutrition core of the project; the archive was approached by the team critically, yet meanwhile it was recognised as the only source for the concept. To sum up, the exhibition *Bizzat Hallediniz* was based not only on the official Ottoman documents but also on a parallel pattern of the historiography-understanding that is dominant in Turkey (cf. Hegasy 2019).[11] Indeed, the concept provided a critical approach in interpreting the data, yet it did not create spaces to link the knowledge and emotions of visitors to the exhibition in a reflective way. Furthermore, *Bizzat Hallediniz* embodied one of the approaches of critical scholars and historians working on the genocide, which did use the same weapon, the archives, against the denialist sphere, I argue.

In the coming weeks, following the aforementioned programme, *Depo* hosted further exhibitions. A few months later, in spring 2016, another exhibition came to be a subject of my research: *Left Over*.[12] It focused on the forsaken

---

[11] The archive which is underscored here is the place structured by the state, the official power, not the one which is established thanks to the trajectories of "archival activism" that Sonja Hegasy investigates in her article. The nature of this sort of archive, ensembled by private persons and/or initiatives in order to shed light on injustice and violence by the state, opposes the first one and "claim[s] to break up the monopoly of the state's historical production" (p. 249).

[12] It is described in the exhibition page as well as its postcard flyer why the project team decided to name their work *Left Over* as follows: "'Left over, left behind' even though they do not sound appealing, these are the most accurate terms which can be used to describe the last remnants on the Armenian plateau today, 100 years after the genocide. The exhibition consists of documentation of buildings left behind by Armenians, whose culture has been turned into a ghost in their own land after a century, as well as interviews conducted over a course of two years with hundreds of people in 27 provinces located on the exile route in order to better reflect the psychology, thoughts, concerns, and memories of those left behind. The exhibition tries to express what has happened since 1915 through the remaining bits of memories, the recollections of neighbours, 'savers', perpetuators and hiders. The project team followed the route of the exile looking for traces of Armenians in the cities they visited. Some of these traces, treasure maps, myths, ornate keys of Armenian homes sold over at vintage shops, saved family trees, et cetera, will also be displayed." In order to present the

elements of Armenians – ruins, left behind craftsmanship and people – on the route of deportation after 100 years. The project team (without a curator), with Aris Nalcı, an Armenian Journalist from Istanbul, as the project manager, exhibited authentic hand-drawn maps to certain topographies – inhabited by Armenians prior to the extermination campaigns – and to alleged Armenian treasures; family trees; objects like church keys the team encountered during field trips that are loaded with myths on Armenians; photographs of properties; video reportages with survivors' grandchildren living in small Anatolian towns revealing their struggle; and accompanied by music composed for the exhibition. Hence, various materials could be found in this short-term exhibition in order to draw visitors' attention. It contextualized the present situation of the Armenian High Plateau and the (past) existence of Armenians – in the collective and individual awareness of local people, for instance through the myths on hidden Armenian treasures. The exhibition – due to giving new faces and illustrations – individualised the story based on the interlocutors' accounts (cf. Köhr 2012, 134–50). In comparison to *Bizzat Hallediniz*, the exhibition employed an ethnographic approach in collecting the materials. This aspect applies to its fashion as well. It provided visitors with different initial points to bridge their biographical or collective experiences; stories told by family members or friends; and their cognitive knowledge through the geographical visualisation of deportation route as well as disclosing its narrative.

Moreover, one of the central points of the exhibition arose around the question of treasure hunters, the gravediggers. It displayed their maps so that it habitually portrayed the connection of the people to the past. The exhibition contained, for instance, pictures of recently built governmental social housings (TOKI) constructed near church ruins and questioned the transformation of treasure hunting (grave-digging) and ruining the memory.

Not only the design but also the objective of *Left Over* was different than *Bizzat Hallediniz*. It created an opportunity for engaging with and tackling the present and past of the country instead of opening a new chapter of historiographical knowledge production flourished from archives. Apart from the design, approach, and aim, the language which was in use in both exhibitions differentiated the concepts. While *Left Over* was using the term genocide, a method to bypass this was adopted by *Bizzat Hallediniz*. The focal point of it was *per definitionem* the deportations of Armenians during the genocide and it was displayed as *"tehcir"* (in quotation marks). While *Bizzat Hallediniz*

research material accurately, I stay with the exhibition title agreeing project team's point "even though they do not sound appealing". (https://www.depoistanbul.net/en/event/exhibition-left-over/; last accessed 22.05.2021) employed the Ottoman transliterations and the historian jargon which was dominant in the hall, *Left Over* considered different sociolects (for example, treasure hunters') and dialects of various regions.

In sum, recognition debates involve various actors and possible conflict zones too. There is no homogeneity, that of course cannot be expected. While the representation of non-governmental activities and initiatives became public in the last decades, a considerable amount of scholar works published in foreign languages were translated into Turkish and studies conducted in Turkey reached a memorable size. Even in those two examples given on these pages, *Bizzat Halledinz* and *Left Over,* the conflicts among approaches are clear to observe. Thus, these two exhibitions represent not only their work in the background – the preparation and design – but also the two lines of the same "party". It contours the dissimilarities of actors in the very same field clearly.

Figure 3: Exhibits from "Left Behind" (Source: own illustration)
Narratives of last members of the Armenian community in periphery and places that are "left behind". These found a place for their story through photographs, drawn family trees and video interviews – Katja Köhr describes such approaches as "bearing witness" out of the experience of Holocaust museums' exhibitions (Köhr 2012: 150–161).

Indeed, that sort of heterogeneity, including ambiguities and contradictions for example in definitions, applies to the denialist sphere as well. It can be seen even in the two given examples, the exhibition *Nar Niyetiyle* and the platform *factcheckarmenia*. The first was carrying out the same denialist arguments in conceptualising them in a sort of reconsidered trivialisation framework – with a different tone and language, while the digital platform was more tolerant in borrowing the classical denialist code. Yet, both employed arguments such as emphasising the inherited security arguments, continuing the thesis of collective victimhood of Turks, underscoring tolerance as a character of the Turkish nation and/or stressing ASALA activities – and in some cases linking it to PKK (Aksel 2012, 257–67).[13] The examples pictured in this subchapter show us the continuity of debates regarding recognition and negation in heterogeneity and ambiguities, or discussions taking place in both "parties" – since approximately the beginning of the 2000s. Furthermore, these illustrate the relation between debates and foreign affairs since the target group(s) of negationist events was the international public (cf. Turan and Öztan 2018, 324).

In this respect, further questions inevitably arise: Was/Is there a genuine conflict or fragmentation of perceptions among official denialism, its representation and civil society? Or, were only some foreign affairs strategies and social memory production policies probed and therefore different frameworks emerged to be seen (in the case of denialist spheres)?

5.3   Contemporary Situation in Van

My field research in spring 2016 began with me encountering a beautiful tulip on my very first day. This species was Tulipa sylvestris, the wild tulip. A botanist colleague led me to this tulip in a tea garden in downtown. He told me that this species is a native one in the alpine regions of France and Italy and is mostly cultivated in Holland but in Istanbul as well. However, there are no records of its existence in the Van region or on the Iranian borderlands. In spite of that, this species grows naturally every year in these tea gardens, close to tree roots, with two to three weeks of lifespan. They cannot live longer mainly because of the customer traffic.

My colleague's argument about the possible reason why this very species grows there was that before the genocide the gardens of the city, Aykesdan, mostly belonged to the Christians of the town and were located in the space

---

[13]   In his article, Kevork Aksel critically depicts the nationalist journey of how the Turkish discourse on "Armenian" changed over the years from "ASALA terror" rhetoric of the 1970s to an alleged causal connection of PKK with Armenians of the 1990s. Aksel discusses, especially in the cited pages and based on examples from (mainstream) media and Turkish State agents, what the elements of that rhetoric construction are.

corresponding to the current downtown of Van. Probably these spots belonged to Armenian or Assyrian merchants who were in the tulip business, he continued. This background reconstruction for the tulip embodied only one side of the coin. When we asked the owner of the tea garden whether he knew the story of the tulips, he told us that the Urartus had planted these tulips, and that they had been growing there since then. The Urartu empire was an ancient civilization which ruled the region from the 8th until the 6th century BC. This is an interesting narrative because there are stories or attempts in bounding the Urartu past to the Kurdish past and (modern) identity in order to argue that Kurdistan has an ancient history.

I encountered one of such narratives during an interview with an informant whom I asked for their biography, yet the person told me the history of Kurds starting thousands of years before. He was a recognised Kurdish elder who worked on the very past of his nation and the region he came from. My stimulus question in order to trigger his autobiographical narration, however, ended up with an hour(s)-long national documentary. The narrative that came to words was an attempt to outline the Kurdish history with ancient aspects in order to display to me the field in which I was moving and doing my research. Moreover, it was also what he wanted to share with me. It showed me the boundaries between national stories and biographies. Even if I tried to point at some biographical aspects for reasons related to my field research, he carried out personal narrative in such a contextualisation.

At first, I was of course disappointed with our meeting. However, after a while I realised that he in fact reminded me of my outsider position in working on the Kurdish and Armenian past. The stories concerning the Kurdish past and identity are foreign to me. They are not a part of my political identity construction just like the tulip whose existence I was not aware of. In this regard, I want to point out again, like in my introduction to the study regarding my person and approach to the field as a scholar, that following my years of professional work in the Van region my interpretation of Van is an outcome of my subjective position that has been shaped in time based on the developments in the country, in the region, and, of course, due to my individual experiences and readings. Thus, this tulip and the meeting with the Kurdish elder reminded me of the complexity of working on memory in general in North-Kurdistan/Western-Armenia and in particular in Van. It also clarified the possible personal perspectives, requested reflections about questions of collective and individual memory concerning political violence, that I was only facing as an outsider.

In this subchapter, I summarize issues I encountered during my stay in Van in order to sketch the situation in which I conducted my research and collected autobiographical narratives. In these terms, this subchapter involves points about the socio-political state of Van in Spring 2016 – under the circumstances of reignited war; state-fostered denialist memory regimes; as well as invented traditions (Hobsbawm and Ranger 2012); and stories circulating in the society of Van. It presents a discussion through ethnographic observations and rereading of my field protocols. Yet, it is also rooted into my five years of professional work as a guide – summoning my experiences from this time period (cf. Davis 1959).[14]

5.3.1 The War as the Context

Since some attempts occurred in Van at the beginning of the so-called protocol diplomacy with the Armenian government, such as the permission to hold an annual religious service at the renovated Holy Cross Aghtamar Church in Autumn 2010, the province of Van has witnessed a lot and the atmosphere has changed extremely. Of course, that permission subsumed controversial points: that, for instance, it was a permission given by a secular state for using a church. In addition, the permit was only provided for annual events and the Aghtamar island was decorated with Turkish flags as if the visitors needed to be reminded where they still were. Yet, civil society was captured by a sort of hope or positive feelings for the future of Turkey, that was indeed influenced by the ongoing development in the country's relations with the European Union or afterwards by the so-called peace process with the Kurdish movement that officially started in 2013, until it ended with the war in the cities in the summer of 2015. Impacts of such turning points were to be observed and traced in various provincial towns of Van. Some villages in the province that host Armenian churches or monasteries started, even earlier than the Aghtamar church regulations, renovating these Armenian properties or at least aiming to raise the awareness of people visiting their villages, such as the ancient Varagavank monastery in the Yedi Kilise village. In this respect, the Aghtamar ceremony was only the surface that could be seen easily because of the state intervention.

The downtown of Van, that lies more or less in the same area as the former gardens of the city and that consists of two major political districts, Tuşba and İpekyolu, hosts circa half a million inhabitants, a number which has increased in the last years due to the reignited war, the clashes and curfews in neighbouring provinces. During my stay, one of the main social subjects was the arrival

---

[14] While writing this subchapter I was strongly inspired by the outstanding approach of sociologist Fred Davis in his profound article "The Cabdriver and his Fare" for which he used his individual experiences and knowledge of six months of cab-driving in the city of Chicago in his research that he took up after four years.

of displaced people from Gever/Yüksekova of Hakkari province because of the massive destruction of its downtown after weeks of curfews. However, Gever was not alone in witnessing emigration because of the displacement of its inhabitants towards Van; it was followed for instance by Şirnex and even people from Cizre were arriving to their new temporary or perhaps permanent residence. In this sense, Van became a centre for displaced people from other parts of the region. At first, it sounds like Van was welcoming everyone without any hesitation or problem. However, when I talked to people from downtown, some criticism was to be heard among them regarding the attitude of other locals vis-à-vis newcomers. For instance, rental rates increased immediately; or newcomers were discriminated against in finding accommodation or jobs in Van's poor job market. The critiques against such attitudes subsumed a reminder as well that people from Gever were the first to help Van after the devastating earthquake of 2011.[15]

As mentioned, the war taking place in different towns of Kurdistan brought the question of housing for displaced people. At the same time, the clear presence of police and special forces could be observed in the centres as well as the country side even if the clashes were concentrated in only some neighbourhoods, for instance in the case of Van in Xacort/Hacıbekir. The heavily armed special forces, the mid-armoured vehicles or police panzers patrolled on the streets. Yet, everyday life carried on. In this respect, the presence meant a "coexistence" of state armed forces and its vulgar mental violence that was "reconciled" by the people of Van, perhaps, due to the past experiences such as the brutal war of the 1990s or the state of emergency that ruled the region from the 1980s until 30 November 2002. In the 2000s, the city of Van witnessed some sort of flourishing moments, firstly in tourism but later in industry as well. The number of direct domestic flights to Van increased and people of Van experienced the rise of a new middle class and mobility, which, in fact, ignored the ongoing violence in the periphery.

Furthermore, Van also represents a (strong) conservative line among Kurdish towns. AKP came out the ballots in the last three regional elections from 2004 to 2014 with at least 39%. When I visited the city in spring 2016, it was occupied with preparations for the *Kutlu Doğum Haftası*, Prophet Mohammad's

---

[15] At this point, it is important to underscore that Van had still not completed recovering the wounds of the earthquake, when the displaced people arrived in town. The public housing department TOKI may have built new accommodation possibilities for the earthquake victims, yet the destruction of downtown was still to be noticed. The rest of heavily damaged buildings were not disposed and damaged houses in the centre were still inhabited. The news about people who still were living in tents or prefabricated houses after almost five years were circulating in public news agencies.

Birth Week, with posters inviting people to several events. With regard to that, the public space was surrounded by different state agents, police forces, and religious-cultural events that simultaneously aimed to gather people in various neighbourhoods, such as through public recitation.

During my stay I encountered stories on two violent incidents that did not fall to the mass media's attention. A Kurdish teenager, who was allegedly a YDG-H member, was killed during an operation of the special forces on a football field in Xacort. At another tragedy which happened in Ertemetan/Edremit shortly before my trip, witnesses found the dead bodies of a dozen youngsters on an empty field. Due to a statement of the armed forces, these twelve people, who were called "terrorists" in the statement, were killed during a clash (Milliyet 2016). Yet, based on witness testimonies, some media organs – close to the Kurdish movement – pointed out that there was no clash but rather a house raid led by the special forces that ended with the killings. There was a muted public reaction in favour of a legal investigation of the cases, yet further steps were not taken or did not find public interest.

Figure 4: The city of Van from Mount Erek (Source: own illustration)
Approximately from an altitude of 2500 meters. The city grew to the east and on the northern shore of the lake covering the premises of former Aykesdan.

With the coup attempt in July 2016 and the following declaration of a state of emergency/exception, the AKP government and state forces increased the level of violence in Kurdish cities, including Van. The state of emergency provided the central government with new legal ways and opportunities for consolidating the state power in the region. For instance, trustees appointed by decree laws, in most cases governors or district *kaymakams*, were assigned to the mayor positions replacing the elected ones from the HDP. This applied to some districts of Van as well. Hundreds of employees of the municipalities were dismissed, several activists and politicians, like the mayor of Van (*Agos* 2016), were detained, taken into custody, and criminally charged. Several non-governmental organisations were shut down by means of the same decree laws (*T24* 2016). And of course impunity accompanied all of these developments in its rigid position.

5.3.2 Denialism as the Context: Memorial Site of Zeve

The state structure's approach aims to deny the genocide and, at the same time, to reorganise the history of the Kurdish people. In a place like Van which was changed by means of mass violence and urbicide (cf. Coward 2008), there are some state interventions in the sense of historiography and the (institutionalised) culture of remembrance and denialism (cf. Suciyan 2016; Turan and Öztan 2018). In this respect, the Yüzüncü Yıl University of Van and its history department organised a conference named *From Çanakkale [Gallipoli] to Zeve on the Path of History* which hosted denialist arguments in April 2016. At the same event, the conference participants as well as school students that are prepared by the Department of Education visited the denialist memorial site in Zeve, Van (*Van Sesi Gazetesi* 2016a; 2016b).

The Zeve Martyrdom Memorial Site was built by the governorship of Van during the enthusiastic search for mass graves of Muslims who were allegedly murdered by Armenian militias. The mass grave unearthing activities came to be an act of collecting "evidence" for the Turkish victimhood thesis in the 1990s. Alongside Zeve (*Van Sesi Gazetesi* 2014), state institutions and local governorships conducted similar events in which other social "stakeholders" such as universities and the media took part. Turan and Öztan (2018, 282) point at the symposium *Van in recent History* organised by the same university, which took place parallel to the mass grave excavation in Zeve. Hence, the Turkish victimhood thesis gathered participants and "stakeholders" not only on discourse level but also on an active organisational layer.

The memorial site is dedicated, according to the information board, to the "2,500 heroic Turkish sons who were murdered by the Armenian militias bloodthirstily in … villages in May 1915." Even though this information board stresses that it happened in May 1915, the governor of Van annually organises an event on 24 April, the international commemoration day of the Armenian Genocide, according to reports by my gatekeepers and contact persons. Officers working at the state departments in Van, soldiers and members of police forces located in the city and province participate or have to participate in this event, also reported by my contact persons. However, this memorial site is located approximately 25 kilometres away from downtown and there is no public transportation to the site. Therefore, the governorship arranges bus rides for civil servants.

Besides the commemoration activities, the text on this information board includes aspects of the remapping and renaming issue in Kurdistan and an ethnic redefinition of Kurds in a top-down attempt of the Turkish State. Although the majority of, if not all, of these villages were/are Kurdish (or Armenian), in this very text they carry Turkish names and the Kurds became Turkish sons. At this point, the state denialism concerning the modern-political Kurdish identity and revisionist claims on the genocide are structured and distributed together hand-in-hand.

 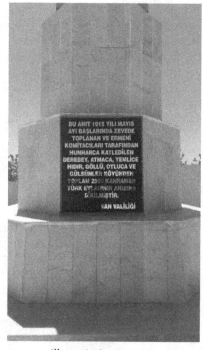

Figure 5: The memorial monument of Zeve (Source: own illustration)
The obelisk rises far away from the city centre of Van or any other provincial town and village stressing the controversial victimhood of Turks. As a matter of fact, the old nationalist design of the site allows the victimhood narrative to meet a national glory story, since it is supported by two other boards on the left and right side of the obelisk presenting the names of fallen soldiers from Van during the First World War, the War of Independence (İstiklal Savaşı) and in the republican period, i.e. the war against PKK.

Furthermore, the topography where Zeve resides does not host any other publicly known spot, village, or similar site. It is far away from other signs of inhabitation. Hence, it does not have any connection to the people, but arises as a secluded memorial on a separate road as if it had needed to be put away from public attention or ritualised in a protected space. In comparison to the exhibitions – like in the case of the Army Museum in Istanbul – and to public events taking place in western cities, the memorial site in Van makes the impression of having been abandoned for 364 days of the year and visited and considered only one day, in other words, when it is needed to attack the memory. Thus, the denialism is represented in a "sheltered" zone.

5.3.3 Collective Memory of the Armenian Past, Genocide, and Violence in Van

In 2010 and 2012, Van witnessed a grassroots initiative in the media, a multilingual newspaper, then a journal: Van Times. Local Journalist Aziz Aykaç who died in April 2011 first launched a campaign for "Welcoming Armenians to Van" and then published his new newspaper, Van Times. This periodical contained articles in Turkish, Persian, Kurdish, and English – and included Armenian in editorship of AGOS later on. He aimed to reach an audience at the religious service to be held at Aghtamar Church in 2010 (*Tert.Am* 2010). After Aykaç passed away, Istanbul-based journalist Aris Nalcı, who had already been cooperating with Aykaç, bore the responsibility to continue this initiative. Yet, it took some time for the newspaper to be published again because of financial difficulties and, of course, because of the Van earthquake in 2011. Following a crowdfunding campaign, the renewed Van Times (in a magazine format) was published in Autumn 2012. It included different articles in Turkish, Kurdish, Armenian, and English treating historical and socio-political questions as well as cultural (personal) accounts regarding the region and its past. On almost 50 pages, it provides a brief first picture of Van to its readers. However, the magazine finished its journey with only one volume. Questions such as whether it did not attract the interest of a large public in Van or in other cities of Turkey or whether the financial aspects overcame the initiative's existence remain open. Yet, the attempt to launch a new (multilingual) space for Van and for the collective memory concerning the Armenian past was witnessed only for a short period of time.

Apart from the cultural agency of Van Times, stories on the Armenian Genocide appear in the public discourse in a wide range, from pointing out the contemporary individual and collective identity questions and family biographies to the political issues regarding the Kurdish movement and recognition debates within it. At first, after my arrival for the field research, I experienced a semi-open awareness of people (cf. Glaser and Strauss 1965) on the town's past that did know the former Armenian existence, yet overlooked or was not familiar with the organised resistance of Vanetsis.

Figure 6: A forsaken and ruined building in the city centre of Van (Source: own illustration)

It must have been a torture place of paramilitaries and state agents in the 1990s and is located in the centre of downtown. It is not renovated, sold to a private person or disposed by the government, and yet it reminds people of this very past.

One of the most articulated narratives that I encountered in Van – alongside the nationalistic storytelling, for example, "Kurds remained while other nations vanished" or that "Kurds have an ancient history in the region" – emphasised the utilisation of Kurds by the landowners' (aghas') authority and by the Ottoman power-holders through a quasi-religious-nationalism or Jihad Declaration. It underscored a sort of metaphysical motivation, for instance Ottoman imams had announced that participating in the killings of Christians would allow people to make their way to paradise. Moreover, pointing out whose ancestors were from an Islamised Armenian family and who were Persian and so on was a part of such storytelling. Of course, it was accompanied in some accounts by the fact of having Islamised grandparents, which was generally not publicly acknowledged but rumoured regarding "others".[16]

---

[16]   Important to notice was that most of the people living in Van were not originally from the city, they moved downtown from various neighbouring provincial towns

Even if the city rose far from the ruins of the old city centre, the former downtown was surrounded with wires in order to keep the area clear of pedestrians. Yet, every single time I visited the castle and the old city centre of Van as a guide or in 2016 for research purposes, the ruins hosted families, children and young people who wanted to enjoy the sunny days. However, it does not mean that there was an emerging connection to the town's past. At least it was not the case from what I could observe. As aforementioned, it was clear for most of the inhabitants that the old downtown was to be associated with the Armenians, but in conversations – or in theoretical terms, in the collective memory – it did not occupy a noteworthy place. Rather the memory of the violence performed against Kurds in the 1980s and 1990s was active and alive. Maybe it was not a subject of everyday conversation. Nonetheless, for people of Van – first of all the ones close to the movement – the torture sites in the city centre strongly occupied this memory; I assume, primarily because people or their family members were affected by the paramilitary war exercised by the Turkish State in the 1990s. The collective memory on war established a dominance influencing a sort of blockade on the Armenian Genocide memory – at least, this was my first assumption. Yet, this blockage seems to be much more complex than the proto-hypothesis itself (cf. Van Ooijen and Raaijmakers 2012).[17]

The fact that a significant proportion of the Van inhabitants have migration and displacement experience in their family or individual background, which also is represented by my interview partners, plays a significant role in their stories. In fact, the stories were concentrated on the Kurdish experience of violence and repression, yet the Armenian past of one's hometown was active, too, more than any narration related to the downtown of Van. Concerning this aspect, I argue that the collective memory of Van represents contradictive and contested aspects in itself in a different way than in Istanbul or a western town of Turkey. What the person has experienced; what was told by the family regarding Kurdish and Armenian past of the particular hometown contain many personal layers; and these were in some way transferred and fused with(in) the

– including from the other side of the Lake Van like Hizan, Bitlis. Some made their way after experiencing displacement and some for raising economic chances in this centre. Yet, they carried their stories concerning their own family background and village's or town's past.

[17] With their research on the post-war and postcolonial Dutch memory, van Ooijen and Raaijmakers challenge the common assumption that the collective memory on the WWII in the Netherlands blocks the memory of Dutch-Indies' decolonization. Utilising a "multidirectional" perspective, based on Rothberg's concept, they argue that instead of "overshadowing" we surely can talk about a premise for postcolonial memory that is fashioned by the war memories.

city of Van. In respect to the fact that Van was completely destroyed and rearose from its ruins due to replacements following the genocide and World War I, the city contains memories of different spots and peripheries regarding the Armenian past as well since the replacement and migration did not end with the end of World War I or the clarification of the borders with the Armenian state in 1920–21 with the Gümrü and Kars treaties. The replacement is an ongoing phenomenon that is closely linked to political violence that one can trace back in personal accounts or whose hints one can encounter just by walking around in the city.

5.4 Recognition Debate(s) among Kurds in Turkey

Following theoretical discussions on issues of memory and the scope of scholar discussions around the questions of coming to terms with the past in (Kurdish) society and politics – treated briefly under subchapter 4.4 1915 alongside Historiography, in this subchapter I focus on the structure of socio-political debates in the present Kurdish society in Turkey (cf. Galip 2016, 458).[18] Kurds living in Turkey (have) showed an (pro)-active standing concerning the debates on the Armenian Genocide in recent years. That position includes a broad spectrum of activities beginning with restoration of sacral buildings by the Kurdish governed municipalities, integrating Armenian and Aramaic languages for public services to organising commemoration events, and public declarations on recognition of the genocide. Yet again, Kurds in Turkey live under conditions of violence that, according to arguments made by the movement and by some scholars, occur in a quasi linear continuum that is to be "backdated to 1915".

Moreover, in this subchapter you will find clear connection points to the reconstructions conducted by scholars that were discussed in previous parts. In these terms, I reorganise the debates, that were carried out in the last decades, in a retrospective sense and sketch a (multi-layered) line from political to social contextualisation – based on some studies conducted in recent years – before I concentrate on the biographical case studies of my research. In other words, I outline the current socio-political context regarding the genocide debates in the Kurdish society in order to clarify the framework in which I met my interview partners.

---

[18]   Apart from the fact that the Kurdish society lives in four regions of four different countries and in addition in the diaspora like in Germany or Sweden because of the displacement of the 1990s as well as so-called *Gastarbeiter* migration of the 1960s and 1970s, I discuss only the situation in Turkey.

How should we read and interpret Kurdish politicians' standing or organisations' disposition vis-à-vis the genocide when we want to discuss the social
and collective memory of the Kurdish society? Or let us ask the question in
a different way. What are the reciprocal terms and dissimilarities between
the Kurdish society and Kurdish politics regarding the Armenian Genocide?
In simple words, how do politics affect the Kurdish society concerning the
recognition and/or negation of the genocide? Or what else plays a role in the
formation of collective and individual memory regimes – in relation to this
socio-political subject? Of course, no single study can reply to these questions
in a nutshell, nor can one claim a rigid correct answer. What I do in these lines
is to give a glimpse of the discussions, to underline nuances, and question the
phenomena I encountered during my research.

5.4.1 Actors and Political Positions

In the introduction of his review of the Kurdish History magazine's 18th issue
1915 ve Kürtler / 1915 and Kurds, historian Emre Can Dağlıoğlu (2016)
glances over the debates regarding Kurds' role during the massacres:

> While some historians and journalists like Yusuf Halaçoğlu, Erhan
> Afyoncu and Murat Bardakçı who position themselves at the various
> pockets of the state narrative and point at Kurds as the main perpetrators
> of the massacres, the standing in Kurdish politics that is mandated by
> Ahmet Türk – and which in my opinion has a significant representational
> base – the story "Kurds are instrumentalised" becomes widespread ...
> On the one hand, we would get stuck in the answer "Kurds are perpe-
> trators" concerning the question "What role did Kurds play during the
> genocide?" when we try to think beyond the crimes and responsibility
> of individuals, families, tribes, or powerholders. On the other, we listen
> to the stories about that extrapolated Kurdish identity "how they do face
> this crime, apologise and that they bear a saviour identity." [translated
> by E.Y.]

Dağlıoğlu summarizes the discussions among various parties concerning
the involvement of Kurds in the extermination campaigns. It also provides a
summary of the scholarly debates held in the magazine's issue. In respect to
Dağlıoğlu's concluding part, I assume there is a concomitant relation between
scholarship and (socio)-political work when it comes to the recognition and
denial of the Kurdish involvement. At times, this occurs in the form of the utili-
sation/instrumentalisation thesis underlining the power relations of the Turkish
State, Kurdish powerholders/landowners, and ordinary Kurdish citizens; or it

accuses Kurds of perpetration as an alleged homogeneous victimiser group; and/or pinpoints the Kurdish side of the question with coming to terms with the past. This sort-of-correlation can also be seen in assumptions drawing a linear continuum from the 1894–96 Hamidian massacres to the Armenian Genocide 1915–17 (cf. Gölbaşı 2017).[19]

Both political and scholarly arguments nourish each other since, I argue, both try to establish a space under the hegemony of the Turkish State's denialist realm. Furthermore, based on Dağlıoğlu's portrayal, these debates and the interaction between politics and social sciences tremendously point at the controversial contours of rather undiscussed issues such as the bystanders of the genocide and what this violence meant to the society after the extermination campaigns regarding regional and national affiliations. In other words, the questions that are not precisely named are: how should we discuss bystanders; and the effects of this bystanding role on the era after massacres and deportations.

Perhaps, Fırat Aydınkaya's words (interview with AGOS, please see Balancar 2015) would help us to find answers to these questions. In his interview about Kurds and the recognition of the genocide, he firstly underlines that Kurds were not involved in any decision making of the genocide – or in his words in "theoretical parts". It is of ominous importance to capture the violent events that we call genocide in process-related cumulative terms as facilitating possibilities of active and semi-active participation instead of one-man or one-party dictating every single move – even the "theory". This nuance applies to other genocides as well that there was no single decision-making moment, but every locality in its very time contributed to the puzzle extermination (for some examples on local dynamics please see, Bartov 2018; Kurt 2018; Redlich 2002; Üngör 2011). The argument based on a misinterpreted Wannsee Conference disregards in its nature the details or at least overlooks the nuances of mass violence.

Aydınkaya (Balancar 2015) then recaps various perspectives concerning the role of the Kurdish society during the massacres. I believe, his words need to be quoted in long:

---

[19] Historian Edip Gölbaşı (p. 33) starts his article on the Ottoman official narrative of the Hamidian massacres with the following reminder regarding the possible obstacles of certain concentrations: "Overshadowed by the wartime genocide of the Ottoman Armenians, the mass killings of 1895–1897 have also been viewed in a retrospective and teleological fashion, as a rehearsal for and prelude to 1915, with little or no consideration for the specific historical context of each event."

First, there is this denialist tendency including Talaat Pasha and the former president of the Turkish History Association (TTK) Yusuf Halaçoğlu trying to disclaim their sins. In sum, they accused others and circulated the discourse that "we planned the deportations humane and sterile until Kurds took part. They sabotaged and exercised the genocide." Another claim is the "killing in mutual figures" which is pioneered by the Kurdish intellectual Nuri Dersimi. Dersimi found himself in a softer denialist sphere telling "Armenians were the ones who started it, Kurds only responded." Even though this perspective is an exception, it still is dominant in conservative Kurdish circles. The third claim is "We were instrumentalised ... utilised ... deceived.. because of our illiteracy." The founders and supporters of this thesis try to transfer the responsibility on the shoulders of some tribes... This thesis wants to show us two points. First, it is not the whole society that participated in this issue. Secondly, it is a defence mechanism in order to ignore the question through "utilisation, being deceived". Even though this thesis was so common among the Kurdish intellectuals of the 1930s, it was reproduced in the 1970s in a modern jargon. Since the 1970s, the Kurdish intellectuals who got educated by modern ideologies have told a fellow sufferer the story of Armenians describing the Kurdish role in the genocide under ambiguous feudality discourses. The fourth approach that I also advocate is that alongside the Kurdish tribes there was a considerable number of ordinary Kurds in an important scale to the whole population who took part in the genocide. And it was a proactive role. Some of the Kurdish tribes had already been trained for that, even since the 1890s. Which means these tribes did not pop up suddenly in 1915. It is a process that started with the Hamidian regiments in the 1890s. [translated by E.Y.]

Aydınkaya starts his portrayal of the Kurdish participation question with the Turkish State agents' denialist arguments that he sets in a continuity of 100 years. Such trivialising arguments transfer the perpetration on Kurdish responsibility, he argues. But more significantly the Turkish powerholders were the ones in a power to illustrate such actions. When the decision-maker in power relation makes a minority group, here Kurds, responsible of (every) violent action, it indicates that a top-down process of making "we" and "the others" emerge. While the "we" occupies non-violence or "purity" of language, time, and state of laws (cf. Nichanian 2011), the "other" parcels the premise of massive violence. Aydınkaya, in fact, points out a binary context in post-colonial terms that is employed in such arguments of the Turkish denialism.

What Aydınkaya picks up next is the argument of "killing in mutual size/ numbers on both sides [Kurds and Armenians]." In this context, he sets the example of Kurdish intellectual Nuri Dersimi. Born in 1893 in the Hozat, Sandjak of Dersim, he visited Hamidian schools in the region and later moved to capitol under CUP rule in 1911, where he studied veterinary, was politically socialised and became active in the Kurdish initiatives. He was an intellectual witness of the late Ottoman era and its violent decline with a certain distance and bearing the periphery and centre on his shoulders a notable actor in it. Witnessing the pre-genocide life of Armenians and Kurds, organising people in the political sphere in Constantinople, becoming a witness of massacres on Armenians during his military service, and of course having an actorship in the movement that ignited the Koçgiri uprising in 1921, which was cruelly slain by the Ankara Government army and further paramilitary units, are only a few of the noteworthy moments changing the course in Dersimi's life trajectory. In the end, his decision to live in exile, which he made in the days of the first Turkish military offensive of the Dersim Genocide 1937–38, brought him to Syria at the end, where he lived until 1973 (cf. Dersimi 2014; Kieser 1997). According to historian Hans-Lukas Kieser, the history of both peoples, Armenians and Kurds, were bond in the eyes of Dersimi. In his memoir books, he records a helper status to Dersim Kurds during the extermination campaigns against their Armenian neighbours and generalises it for all Kurds while he holds the leading CUP cadre responsible for killings (cf. ibid.). In his autobiographical memoir, Dersimi wants to show his existence, fight, life, and past. It is the first layer of his reconstruction. The second layer occurs to be the late Ottoman and early Turkish republican context where the violence ruled the decline of imperial rule and paved the foundations of the republican era. In his narrative, he puts his life puzzle in its midst and depicts his individuality with the premise of early Kurdish movements within the colliding and crushing Ottoman and republican life-worlds. Seeking clarification to these fused layers and labyrinth-like worlds come to be the goal of his memoir. Perhaps, this is where the most challenges confront his efforts of reconstructing past experiences (cf. Dersimi 2014). In the whole manuscript, the exiled political figure notes down the exact names and dates of the hotels where he stayed but struggles to describe the Armenian question in its very own dynamics. Hence, he presents Armenians as the brother nation that did not protect the moral values as Kurds did.

In detail, Dersimi (2014, 80–84) advocates that millions of Kurds were also murdered by Armenians in the same years, yet, this fact had been missed. He points out two notions as reasons, a) the protagonists in the Armenian diaspora blaming Kurds for the murders, and initially but implicitly with/for their alleged power in their hosting countries; and b) the powerholder's (Ottoman state's) conspiracy against Kurds, portraying them as perpetrators from the start. Beyond these, in his memoir he highlights three further aspects related to the Kurdish–Armenian life that constitute three significant narrative frame-works for this study: the peaceful coexistence of Kurds and their Christian neighbours prior to extermination campaigns; the causal contextualisation of the genocide based on escalation, or how Türkyilmaz defines the *escalation bias*, "a tendency to focus on the factors that led the genocide over those that worked against it" (2011, 332); and at last, predating the genocide to the Ottoman policies about the Kurds in the late 19th century – such as relating Hamidiye Regiments to the landowners today. *Just Memory* employs a simi-lar manner – regarding the quantity and form of the killings – as I discussed before. Calling the genocidal violence as a war – since a mutual size of killings implies a war setting – simplifies and even belittles the event that took place. Moreover, it only functions through an argumentation of who triggered or who started it – or let's say finding a usual suspect, without considering the scale of victimisation or its organisation.

Hovsep Hayreni (cf. 2015, 149–57) quotes meeting minutes with Abdullah Öcalan in prison from 23 June 2006. In sum, Öcalan argues that the Armeni-ans stood side-by-side with the foreign powers and became, therefore, targets of genocidal violence of the Ottoman State. He also suggests that Kurds had no other choice than collaborating with the Ottomans because, if not, Arme-nians would have invaded cities of today's Kurdistan. What Öcalan speaks of is pre-conditions of so-called mutual killings. He speculatively describes historical events and, in fact, justifies them looking at the results. In journal-ist Cengiz Kapmaz's book capturing Öcalans first ten years of imprisonment from 1999 forward, the reader encounters a leader figure negotiating with the state counterpart for a possible peace pointing at joint Kurdish–Turkish history where both peoples fought together against the occupiers after the World War (Kapmaz 2011, 184 f). Öcalan criticises the denialism of or ignorance on this mutual past (ibid.; p. 174) and declares "a cultural nationalism" in Atatürk's political moves concerning the name of the republic and his citizenship under-standing (p. 300). Nevertheless, we also see that he also looks for an "other" conspirator, like a certain Israeli lobby, backing leaders of South-Kurdistan in Iraq to establish an "Armenian-like-Kurdistan" (p. 380). Without disregarding his negotiating position under terms of solitary confinement in the first years of his imprisonment, this sort of explanation matches the contemporary grand nar-rative of history, further developed especially under AKP governments – where the coexistence and fights shoulder to shoulder are praised. In prison notes from 2013 to 2015 prepared in manuscript form by Öcalan himself – based on the meeting minutes with the HDP politicians during the so-called peace pro-cess, we encounter a reconceptualisation of the mass violence against Ottoman Armenians that occurs to be embedded in escalating dynamics of politics (Öcalan 2016). On the one hand, he acknowledges the genocide, emphasises the possibility of a future democratic coexistence, and condemns nationalism on all sides, including Dashnaks (p. 51). On specific points concerning the genocide and Armenian past, capitalism comes up as the source of the problems on the other (p. 224; 265 f). He claims that "[t]he genocide started in the second half of the 18th century and continued in 1914" where "Armenians became the servants of capitalist modernity... There is a need to make the connection of that genocide event to capitalism. Russians, English, and French played a role as well; not all the Turks can be made responsible. We need to discuss these issues well. We are not against Armenian citizenship. Explain it well" (pp. 265 f) [translated by E.Y.].[20] In short, he frames the genocidal violence in international scope and capitalism – predating escalations also.

The instrumentalisation thesis that Aydınkaya problematises as the third argument involves a strong victimhood narrative. Hence, the victimisation ran in the hands of state agents as well as oppressors of their own kin, the landowners. In this sense, it is a sort of counter-reflection of state agents blaming the Kurds. Or it is an answer that fights and simultaneously reconciles with such a denialist argument. It says that the CUP government or contemporary Turkish State utilised the Kurdish aghas and they deceived their own people. With regard to the Kurdish political struggle in Turkey, the modern Kurdish identity developed new discourses in order to clarify the frames of this affiliation. It has intensely opposed the structure of the brutal landowner in the Kurdish society and thus created the we-group independent from aghas and the oppressors' politics, e.g. the Turkish State policies (cf. Bruinessen 1992). In these terms, the victimisation was multi-layered. First of all, it was performed by armed forces of the state and then by landowners. And when, as I suggest, this affiliation framework was to be translated for the genocide discussions, it presented the same victimisers' ensemble with the instrumentalised Kurdish people. This narrative underscores the victimhood of ordinary Kurds in a multi-layered context rather than the persecution of the genocide victims.

In his study on genocidal violence and its pre-conditions, Yektan Türkyılmaz (2011, 335) points out that the idea of a Kurdish nation "was only a nascent form in a handful of elite political imaginations" and continues "[this] renders 'victimhood work' focal to the construction of Kurdish national identity, which like the Armenian and Turkish versions also entailed a collective self-image of

---

[20] A critical reconstruction of Öcalan's positionings concerning such themes in his prison time as a significant negotiator, but also before that, based on minutes and his writings lacks undoubtedly. These paragraphs in this chapter can only provide a glimpse of a huge discussion. An extensive biographical reconstruction would help us understand the ideological premises of his political positioning, effects of imprisonment, and his understanding of history only better – which, unfortunately, this research cannot provide.

unique victimhood at its centre." He adds that the "victimhood narratives" are "contextual" and mostly utilised for political stakes. With regard to Türkyıl-maz' points, the instrumentalisation thesis and the victimhood narrative illustrate neither the victims of extermination campaigns, nor the ordinary Kurds' victimisation in this context – even if it utilises this victimhood.

When Aydınkaya opposes this thesis of constellation of the ordinary citizens and powerful aghas, he pinpoints a continuum of landowners since the Hamidiye Regiments that, as I argued while discussing Dağlıoğlu's words, flourished in the very contact of political and scholar attempts. Nevertheless, it also involves a quasi-instrumentalisation, if we accept the Hamidiye Regiments as tools in the hands of aghas that were ordered and supported by the Ottoman Sublime Porte. In other words, the question is whether the linear continuum argument should be discussed as a different facet of the same instrumentalisation concept. What does this analogy tell us concerning the state of recognition and denial of the Armenian Genocide, violence, and impunity in the region?

Almost every single time I dug in the realm of Armenian Genocide debates within the current Kurdish movement, politics and society, I have encountered the instrumentalisation thesis. Either it was conceptualised within the claims of continuity of violence, for instance from 19th century Hamidiye to 20th century village guard system and the landowners' brutality, or it was marginalising the perpetration and the perpetrator. This marginalised violent actor is not acknowledged as part of society. In these terms, the marginalised one, the violent one becomes "the other" within the society and, therefore, blockades a critical facing moment. Historian and political scientist Hamit Bozarslan, based on contemporary discussions, points out an awareness within the Kurdish society, yet "the existing documents show this consciousness was not enough for a critical reflection of the Kurdish participation in the massacres by Kurdish leaders" (2015, 477) [translated by E.Y.].

Beyond that, both the instrumentalisation and the marginalised Kurdish perpetrators emerge as patterns of the same rhetoric and discursive construction. And this has in fact generated a sort of dominant narrative for Kurds – or knots for collective references, perhaps, because it was used by politics repeatedly and appeared to be a variety, a counter narrative to the state negationism. Among the four positions in the Kurdish society and politics that Aydınkaya describes, the instrumentalisation thesis came to be a part of the history of Kurdishness as well. The instrumentalisation argument was employed many times by different Kurdish protagonists who relocate their position in the Kurdish left-wing spectrum (2015; Balancar 2015). And without a doubt it regenerates a political identity form. Nevertheless, other ways of genocide-storytelling struggle to suit or transform this identity and are represented in different structures.

Aydınkaya's argument concerning this point reconciles with Türkyılmaz' description and problematisation of Kurdish victimhood (2011). It shows that victimisation narrative touching one's own group is a part of political agenda for identity formation.

Thus, in terms of instrumentalisation, this dominant narrative underscores the alleged binding power of Islam and the Jihad declaration of the Ottoman State so that Kurds could be utilised in the name of Islam. This thesis seeks to highlight perpetration of some landowners in the hands of a higher power – the religious aspect – and powerholder – Ottoman elites. Yet, it leaves the question of bystanders and civil participation in violence unvisited, while the victims of the genocide remain unconsidered. Furthermore, it historicises the past through the Kurdish movement's perspectives via constructing the ordinary Kurd again (cf. Aydınkaya 2015, 26).

In her article on Kurdish novels and the Armenian Genocide, scholar Özlem Belçim Galip (2016, 463–68) summarizes as an introduction to her main theme the attitude of Kurdish organisations, political and intellectual figures in the public vis-à-vis genocide recognition, drawing the line from the 1982 statement of PKK's official newspaper *Serxwebun*, "[t]hey [the Young Turks] attempted to suppress the right to self-determination with violence and did not even shrink from committing a barbaric genocide against the Armenians" (recited from Galip, 465) to the efforts of (regional) Kurdish politicians in the 2000s and 2010s, "2008 Ahmet Türk ... acknowledged Kurds' role in the Armenian Genocide, saying: 'Kurds contributed to the loss of this [cultural] richness. We are ashamed when we look at our Armenian and Assyrian brothers" (pp. 466 f). For instance, the mayor of Van or Diyarbakır stood for revealing the Armenian life and past in their towns, through opening Armenian language courses or conducting church restorations (2016, 467; Gültekin 2016, in press).[21] Of course these pro-active engagements embodied progressiveness in comparison to the Turkish State's denialism and rightfully urged the Turkish administration for the recognition of the genocide. Yet, particularly the political declarations and speeches Galip gives as examples include the very aspects discussed before, such as Kurdish landowners' perpetration and the utilised ancestors.

A clear example of reproduction of the instrumentalisation thesis would be the prominent Kurdish politician Ahmet Türk's statement at the panel discussion that took place in Sweden in December 2014 (*Agos* 2014; cf. Galip 2016, 466 f). Türk underlined in his statement that the Kurdish people had been

---

[21]   The very same church that was renovated by the municipality in Diyarbakır was expropriated with a degree issued on 25 March 2016 in an Official Journal. That is unfortunately not the only case.

"instrumentalised in the name of Islam" and added his wish "to be forgiven by Assyrian and Armenian people and Yazidi brothers". It was enclosed in a sort of emotional or dialog-based reconciliation.[22]

Journalist Namık Kemal Dinç's interview book *Onlar Gittiler Biz Barışı Yitirdik / They left, and we lost the peace* involves [translated by E.Y.] personal accounts of several prominent Kurdish figures. His work (2016) subsumes various positions and perspectives in defining the past and its connections to portray the situation in Kurdistan. Yet titling the manuscript after a composition proximal to the instrumentalisation thesis reproduces that dominant narrative overtly.

Dinç's question repertoire for his interviews concentrates on the memory of Armenian past in the region; the relation between Armenians and Kurds; and the issue of coming to terms with the violent past from the interviewees' perspectives. While Dinç aims to collect regional remembering regimes, for example the vocabulary to determine the genocidal violence – how it is or was called in the interviewees' social environment, he also looks into individual and family accounts thanks to the questions that he specially tailored for every person. In this sense, he outlines the standing of politically known protagonists. Yet, this draft is described overall as the perception of a Kurdish collective. Perhaps, the way in which he prepared his questionnaires influences the answers. But these questions frame the state of Kurdish society and politics regarding the recognition and collective memory in a picture where the continuity of violence tops the argumentation parallel to the past coexistence thesis. For instance, the Kurdish involvement in the massacres is described within the instrumentalisation thesis, e.g. in the name of Islam, by most of the interviewees. What further underscored is the violence against Kurds starting in the first decade following the extermination campaigns, referring for instance to Sheikh Said Rebellion 1925 and Turkish State's brutal operations against that (p. 91 – from the interview with the former mayor of Diyarbakır Osman Baydemir). Due to this point, the Armenian past is associated with Kurdish modern history – awareness of the victimised and subalterns so to speak (p. 86 – from the interview with Şeyhmus Diken). And last but not least, the inclusive system in Northern Syrian Kurdish Cantons that ensures the non-Muslim

---

[22] Nichanian (2011, 183) reminds us of Antigone's story who was imprisoned in her tomb because of standing against reconciliation (*Versöhnung*) that erupts the witness. Relying on Hegel's interpretation he points out that peace is seen as the key to make the *Gemeinwesen* of Thebai to survive. At this juncture, another question appears to be thought about: considering Nichanian's points and Hegel discussion, whether the Kurdish public and politics seek the peace to avoid further conflict full of consequences with the objective to make the *politea* survive even if it means to forget.

minorities' political participation is pinpointed as a future perspective for the region (p. 67 – from Ahmet Türk's answer to the Assyrian property questions). These prominent protagonists find another common ground when they consider the events and discussions in the Kurdish society insufficient regarding the Armenian Genocide (memory).

Perhaps it is a rough way to put it, but, in my view, the general outcome of Dinç's work is that it highlights the sort of the proxy state of the Armenian Genocide memory in remembering and reconstructing own experiences with violence performed by powerholders – or better said, its multidirectional nature (cf. Rothberg 2009). In the interviews, they appear as landowners, village guards, and as the Turkish State. Most of the remarks made by these important public figures tell the story of Kurds starting in 1915. In this respect, the mass killings of Armenians pop up as a proxy for the Kurdish story telling of the repression they lived in.

In this context, I use the terms "story" and "storytelling" in sense of social process(ing). The reconstruction needs stimulators or starting points loaded with contingencies. Hence, this storytelling borrows markings such as arguments of instrumentalisation, past coexistence, or the so-called peaceful episode in order to explain and in fact reconstruct one's own past. With regard to this notion, the Armenian Genocide appears to be not only an element of a narrative but a triggering feature of the storytelling itself.

5.4.2 Reflections in the Kurdish Society or Scholarship

In her article on the genocide's place in Kurdish novels, Galip argues that the left-wing oriented Kurdish movement – from 1978 forward – has given intellectuals an opportunity to face the past violent crimes and these "influenced the Kurdish literature highly". Based on her analysis of five Kurdish novels, she (2016, 479 f) continues:

> Novelists address the Armenian Genocide both directly and indirectly, often emphasizing the theme of solidarity between Kurds and Armenians. Their novels constitute storehouses of individual and collective memory; moreover, they help create "collective memory" and "social history" that associate Kurds and other communities within a shared geography. Here history is …, rather a set of applied memories: collected, persevered, transmitted, and thus *constructed* or even *"invented"*… Kurdish novels can reflect a certain didacticism as they proffer a history that counter the hegemonic Turkish version. (author's emphasis)

Furthermore, Galip problematises the narration of the idealisation of Armenian–Kurdish relations in the past and the instrumentalisation thesis (pp. 472–79). Beyond that, she adds that the protagonists of these novels are themselves victims of the Turkish State and Kurdish powerholders/landowners (p. 475). Thus, when we look at protagonists who break the silence in these writings, they are Islamised Armenians in most cases – the so-called proselytes. They are not just the transmitters of the facts out of their past, they are also pictured as the carriers of the memory and the sorrow.

As with Galip's study, Çelik and Öpengin's article (2016) focuses on Kurdish literature and the genocide memory in it. The authors underline the place of Islamised Armenians in Kurdish literature; pinpoint the idealised coexistence through *kirve* relations (that I consider on the next pages) – and call it "nostalgia of lost cohabitation" (pp. 9 f); and question the participation in violence of the Kurdish protagonists that appear either as utilised or in demonic portrayals. Mirroring Galip's analysis, the authors highlight the victimhood association between Kurds and Armenians, for instance through the usage of the Kurdish proverb "*em siv in hun ji pasiv in*" / "we are the dinner, you are the supper" in novels (p. 7). This quasi connection of two persecutions appears as an analogy of the genocide period and the 1990s – the brutal (paramilitary) war in Kurdish towns. In their analysis, Çelik and Öpengin draw our attention to the hegemony of state denialism, the authors' family narratives and their political engagement in the movement for understanding this social memory (p. 13). They then conclude with the remark(s) that these works "*refigure* the very collective memory they are born into" (ibid.; emphasis in original). In these terms, they underscore a supposed continuity of violence by associating two victimhoods.

Comparably, anthropologist Zerrin Özlem Biner (2010) discloses the circumstances reigning in the three different communities of Mardin: Kurdish, Arab, and Syriac Christians. The hegemonic discourse (or state denialism) is to be noticed in her interview situations as well as in the communities knowing the way to bypass it. For instance, an elder Arab she interviewed remarks that the Arab community was not "ignorant and subversive in dealing with authority… the real natives of Mardin—the Arabs and Syriac Christians—never subverted or challenged the Turkish state's sovereignty. It was the Kurds who created problems" (p. 77). This statement is the sort-of-embodiment of Türkyılmaz's *escalation bias* in public discourse, only continuing it with a shift on Kurds after the annihilation of Armenians – arguing that the historical escalation to be placed on Armenian position(s) and the present escalation on Kurdish ones. It also underlines a sort of continuity of bypass-methods against state oppression.

Meanwhile, Biner encountered the significance of family in facing this past and in allowing individuals to position themselves; a process in which the theme of Islamised Armenians play the role of a carrier of memory and sorrow again (p. 75; 79). And at this very point, the individual position, which has to be based on own experiences of victimisation, persecution and/or perpetration, appears in connection with family and surrounded by the dominant narrative(s). One of her gate keepers, for instance, invited her to their home to talk with the father of the household, an old Kurdish landowner, Osman Bey, who was born prior to the genocide or has some personal relation to this violent past. At this meeting, children and grandchildren exercised pressure to make this old man talk which resulted in an argument and Biner's withdrawal, "… while Osman Bey's eldest son took over conducting the interview, asking his father over and over again in both Turkish and Kurdish, 'Dad, Dad, do you remember? Tell us what happened to the children of the Christians during *ferman.*' Osman Bey refused to break his silence" (p. 79; emphasis in original). In this sense, I find Çelik and Öpengin's (2016) assumption very precise that positioning vis-à-vis the genocidal events is carried out under the hegemony of state denialism and its historiography as well as its generated socio-cultural memory and silencing the truth. In other words, remembering Armenians can only appear in contestation of Turkish State's rhetoric. But how should one treat the intergenerational conflicts in the family which at least maintain connections to state denialism, problematic conditions for facing the past and personal acts, and of course generational questions?

In addition, within the context of the family the search for ancestors' identities is in fact created by the perpetration of another ancestor; and is nourished by personal (socio-political) activities (ibid.). Indeed, Biner's article (2010) portrays the same issue from another perspective: the family that forced the grandfather to talk was not able to eliminate the gap in their past anymore. The children who forced their (grand)father to talk gained power from the existence of the Islamised Armenian (grand)mother and her silence. In these terms, there is a (family) conflict which is not transmitted to next generations, perhaps, but which is revealed by them.

Even if Biner critically reflects the Kurdish political discourse of "mutual victimhoodness" briefly – as a rhetoric of politics, that emphasises coevally the continuity of violence, this sort of politicisation of the issue finds representation in the literary works as well. In other words, ordinary people's arguments could (perhaps) flourish from such patterns. Or these could be entangled into the denialist habitus, when, for example, muting or masking the past is performed as a bypassing method among the peoples of Mardin – Arabs defining themselves as witnesses and Kurds embodying the next victims of the same perpetrator, the Turkish State (cf. Biner 2010, 88). Hence, it creates a new social context, perhaps against state denialism but through reconstructing the past together. And it correlates with silencing certain aspects.

Anachronic representations indwell such reconstructive spaces. When it comes upon naming the perpetrator, as mentioned before, the Ottoman State certainly appears as the main coordinator of political violence. And in the narrative, the bystander or local perpetrator role is applied either to local elites like aghas or the manipulated ones and profiteers – again illustrating a continuity with the Hamidiye Regiments (Çelik and Dinç 2015, 121–39). In their ethnographic study shedding light on the genocide memory of Diyarbakır region, Çelik and Dinç put this analogy in relation to *korucu*/the village guard system and disclose the oral accounts' perspective on "one of own kind", yet "embodying traitor-ness". This "other" from the own community had once performed the killings against Armenians and now, in the name of the state, they persecute their own kind: the Kurds. This analogy, however, disassembles the past and even the collective memory, I argue, since it somehow erases or mutes the Armenian subject from the narration through highlighting the Kurds and their experiences twice. In other words, Armenians appear to be not the remembered ones but the Kurds. Their agency is not considered.

This phenomenon of anachronism is also to be read in the stories regarding Armenian–Kurdish coexistence prior to Kurdish complicity. In the same study, Çelik and Dinç present one of the possible inter-family relationships between Christian and Muslim communities: *kirvelik* institution (pp. 53–85). It means that a family friend calms down the Muslim boy during the circumcision procedure which – based on these narratives – had to be performed by the Christian family friend. The authors claim that *kirvelik*, which they heard about repeatedly during their field research, should be marked as a mnemonic concerning the pre-genocide times and the coexistence. I would like to pose another question in order to reconstruct this feature in the present tense: what does this story tell us about the absence and far-away-existence of Armenians – and generally Christians – in today's Diyarbakır? What if this story does not aim to portray a past but rather present conditions, then how should we begin to discuss?

The *kirvelik* narrative is indeed fascinating because it subsumes several layers and elements: religion, inter-communal relations, local social structures, family traditions, et cetera. And because it is somehow generated from the past it can and should be considered first as a phenomenon of collective memory. Yet, in my viewpoint it also symbolises the current situation. It links the past to present just like the perpetrator constellation in the narratives. I assume, the subject of coexistence portrayed through *kirvelik* in these accounts points at, on the one hand, the absence of Armenians, Kurdish positionings towards recognition and the acknowledgement of persecution, reminding of the genocide victims. On the other hand, it supports the instrumentalisation argument while underscoring the peaceful life before the intrigue of Ottoman powerholders and fosters the "others" of the Kurdish society who profited from violent events together with the Turkish State, such as local elites, brutal landowners and (un)organised murderers. So, the victims of the genocide that embody the cohabited past in the narrative appear to be the Armenians as well as the Kurds because Kurds, so to speak, lost their friends, the *kirves*.

Nevertheless, it brings another noticeable aspect into discussion: the life in Western-Armenia and Northern-Kurdistan. It is still unclear to me if this (sort of) argument only dispossesses the non-actorship of a rigid victim category or blurs the victim category and victims' subjectivity further. Concerning the first option, it retells the existence of a social structure and an Armenian life in the past together with the Kurds and respects the actorship of Armenians, for example as *kirve* or neighbours. Yet the question is if the actorship in "coexistence" does make the Armenian subjectivity fuzzy since it gives the Armenians the only agency in peaceful times. Nonetheless, these two possibilities or frames – the erasure of non-actorship and overlooking the victims' subjectivity – are not opposites to each other. I suggest they are more or less different layers or compartments of the same narrative flows that can be constructed together.

Similar to the narratives concerning the actions emphasising the state's hegemonic role during the genocide, the property question which was "regulated" by the post-CUP Istanbul government and then by the Ankara-based Turkish Republic also appears in oral history accounts from Diyarbakır in such a contextualisation (Çelik and Dinç 2015, 258–72). The state structures had appointed first of all the collaborating Kurdish local elites as new owners of forsaken properties – buildings as well as premises, according to the accounts in the study. This sort of narrative subsumes the continuing perpetration on Armenians through confiscation, liquidation, and transformation – ruining, rebuilding, remapping – of immovable wealth, and blocking victims' ways back home. Moreover, it points at the ongoing cooperation of the elite and landowner caste, so to speak, with the state structure(s), for their own sake. Of course, the narrative itself also highlights the awareness of ordinary Kurds that this collaboration remapped the region. Furthermore, it sketches the frame of actions and possible participation forms in a similar scheme – the state and the elites utilising ordinary Kurds – as mentioned before. In this respect, without regarding if it truly happened in this way, I assume this storytelling is closely connected to the Kurdish collective narrative concerning violence and socio-political questioning. The crucial question is if it could be one of the triggers of the instrumentalisation thesis.

The ruination of forsaken Armenian cultural goods took place not only through plundering the immovable properties but also via ignoring the treasure hunting which wrecks the forsaken premises with the goal to become rich or live in prosperity. It is one of the post-extermination acts that seeks people's attendance. In her article, anthropologist Alice von Bieberstein (2017) discusses the social and political weight of "hidden Armenian treasures" in the Kurdish society of Muş. The present society's relation to the past further involves treasure hunting, material connotations, and "annotations". The act of digging lands and properties (churches or houses) is carried out by men, while in the paper, the women criticise this very action. The fetishism towards Armenian objects alongside the economic dreams appear to be the empowering ensemble of treasure hunting, according to von Bieberstein.

In Çelik and Dinç's book (2015, especially Ch. 13; 313–332), we again encounter the Islamised Armenians as the carriers of sorrow and memory in the local Kurdish societies, as well as in studies on Kurdish novels (Çelik and Öpengin 2016; Galip 2016), alongside the places of the mass murder that embody the genocidal violence as well as the collective memory of local people of the town next to such places. Connected to locality, the authors struggle with the naming of the Armenian Genocide and present a distinguished repertoire among Kurds in the region of Diyarbakır. Over ten different namings of that particular time period depict a struggle with the question of whether the emphasis has to be put on the action itself such as in *firxune Armeniyan* (extermination of Armenians) or *qirkina filehan* (massacre on Christians) or whether the perpetrators should be underscored such as in *ferman* (decree) and *fermana filehan* (decree for Christians) (pp. 88–94). Apart from variations and how they are formulated, the very fact of such a repertoire shows that the relation between locality and memory is one of the deciding points of the act of narrating. Be it in a collective or individual sense, memory is based on local circumstances and cannot be thought without this very premise.

Based on the discussions presented above, we can assume Kurdish memory politics and its generated discourse – and perhaps knowledge – draw a line of victimhood and suffering starting with the Armenian Genocide. The story of the annihilation of Armenians stimulates, so to speak, the persecution of Kurds in the structure of the storytelling. And with its help, it aims to oppose and deconstruct the dominant narrative: the Turkish State's official historiography and its produced memory. In other words, this memory regime aims to stabilise the position of Kurds in acknowledging the genocide under the denialist habitus (cf. Suciyan 2016) and, at the same time, to fight for own rights and recognise the repression and violence performed against Kurds. There is a multi-layered composition of the memory that provides possible narrators with cross-connections among past violent and repressive events and the contemporary state of violence in the region. Yet, as you will see in the next chapter, which tackles the autobiographical narratives, a significant question appears overtly: what would people tell if they could choose the subject?

5.5   Concluding Remarks

In sum, in the western part of Turkey, especially in Istanbul, the memory zone in general contains a reciprocal exchange and contestation between different discourses. They are established in dissimilar ways and distributed with various motives. As memory is about today, denialism is as well because it attacks peoples' memory. It does not target to alter the archival document.

Again Nichanian reminds us of the difference between history and the subjectivity of the witness. He (2011, 87) sees the novelists as the only possible historians of the *Aghet*, the catastrophe, while the term genocide undergoes the operation of historiography. Denialism mostly shows a "holistic, big picture" and creates a master narrative that belittles the way of individual remembering. In this way, for example in Turkey biographical narratives become masked. Concerning professionals' revisionism, Nichanian (1998, 262) argues: "It attacks the significance of the facts… it is undermining the reality of the event. The reason for this is simple, albeit infinitely profound: there is reality only where there is meaning." The "newly" produced trivialisation of the *Just Memory* tackles the meaning as well: the meaning of memory.

All three types of denialist manifestation drafted by Cohen (2001) can be observed regarding the Armenian Genocide. In a nutshell: a literal denial while telling "this story is not true, it is a lie of diaspora"; the *Just Memory* discourse itself is an interpretative denial, alongside the most distributed *tehcir*/deportation argument; which can also be described as a justificatory denial with regard to the "need of security". Continuing Cohen's discussion on simultaneous conduction of denialist arguments, the case of *Just Memory* shows that this sort of taxonomical separation does not indicate any strict boundaries (p. 103). These approaches are very much correlated, combined, and interwoven. Hence, they cannot function singularly, they need each other to generate knowledge and memory regimes for the collectivities.

Categorising this knowledge avoids the possibility to see fluid details such as the political commitment, its perpetual positioning courses, participatory ways of "ordinary" people or the afore-mentioned aspect of the multi-layered feature of denialism (cf. Charny 2000; 2001; Hovannisian 1998a). I argue instead of categories we need to focus on the process and amorphous patterns and trace contradictions in the process of making the social and political. Contradictions occur all the time even in a master narrative, for instance employing old discourses in community events – as portrayed in this chapter. In this process of knowledge and memory production, *Just Memory* conducts a "renewed" code using and reconstructing old euphemisms and cover-ups. Yet, this reconstruction does not subsume and change all former rigid patterns. Rather it aims to acquire them. Concerning reconstructing experiences in asymmetrical power relations, Obradovic (2017, 209) points out "Processes of remembering are thus not mere retrievals of existing information, but a negotiation, construction and at times, manipulation, of what is assumed to have occurred in the past."

Beyond that, this trivialisation leads to a further question: who can take part and how? In Nichanian's words the "master interpreters", e.g. professional historians, should find their proper places in the new field, for example with the symposium *Turkish-Armenian Relations 100 years after Tehcir: Just Memory and Normalization* that was organised in May 2015 at the Marmara University. (*Haberler.com* 2015; "'Tehcir'in 100.Yılında Türk-Ermeni İlişkilerinin Yarını: Adil Hafıza ve Normalleşme" Sempozyumu Daveti' 2015) At the same time, the inflated events and social media activism mark that ordinary people have become new memory agents (Nichanian 1998, 252)."As Havel shows, lies don't have to be believed as long as you participate in public rituals that affirm their acceptance of lies", postulates Cohen (2001, 138). In other words, the rule of acceptance of denialism is switched to active participation, from living under it.

Scholars' attempts through publications and speeches had built, perhaps, a quasi-foundation for *Just Memory*, however, the new activists' scene of denialism belongs mostly to the non-scholars. The civil participation increased in numbers since denialism does not take place in conference halls anymore but on the streets and in social media. The new "master interpreters" are the memory agents. These memory agents are not like the far-right racists even if they walk together, as we saw in the case of rallies. Today the users of denialist arguments are not the professional historians or state agencies in the majority of cases. It is rather the ordinary people.

Nevertheless, there is no rigid homogenous collective memory since there are different autobiographical elements that refer, for instance, to family experiences and flourish as artistic or academic works. Moreover, disobedience happens in these terms. It fosters the contested memory landscape further. I borrow the term *epistemic disobedience* from the scholar Walter Mignolo (2009; 2012; 2013); the term fits to a case which seeks bypasses, reorientations, and opposing voices under and against hegemonic denialist repression. Epistemic disobedience signifies an alternative knowledge production of the subaltern against the repression via produced knowledge by the powerholders.

On previous pages, I discussed some of the exhibitions launched in Istanbul in order to draft the situation on the other side of the coin, or in other words the attempts of epistemic disobedience. And even among these exhibitions there were some contradictive points to be traced, such as the approach of curators. The question if the exhibition objects should refer to the scholarly debates and archives in order to persuade visitors or if the originality of materials would be enough was to be answered. While criticising strict archival research tendencies, for example, *Bizzat Hallediniz* exhibition fell into the same hands of archival–effort–asking beholder. It could not escape the rooms of archives, even for an exhibit practice. Thus, I would like to pose a question whose form I borrow from Howard S. Becker. He uses it, based on Wittgenstein's discussions in *Philosophical Investigations*, in order to surface the core of a social phenomenon. Becker (1998, 138–41) calls it *The Wittgenstein Trick*. My question inspired by this trick would be: When we cut out the artistic touch and aesthetics from exhibition, what else remains as central?

On the other hand, the exhibition *Left Over* that was launched in *Depo* Istanbul was showing images of forsaken scenery in order to tell the story of present conditions and the blurry Armenian presence in the periphery. Hence, it sketched the dim relation between the past and the present through tangible carriers. It worked through aesthetics and making people and their stories talk. Even in the exhibition scene, the conflict of what to tell and how to transmit was lively, which I suppose was the core of the artistic touch.

Of course, disobedience occurs not only in scholarly composed manuscripts or exhibition halls, it occupies places and spaces, such as through commemoration events. Not to forget, this sort of occupation or sit-in disobedience has already been performed, for example, by *Cumartesi Anneleri*/Saturday Mothers. Inspired by Mothers of Plaza de Mayo, they have been gathering for more than 700 weeks and seek justice for their unreported missing relatives (Ahiska 2014). It inevitably provides a ground for learning and being in contact with the country's past as well as individual accounts. Therefore, it reshapes the place into a space of commemoration demanding reconciliation or coming to terms with personal and official pasts. Similarly, the 1915 commemorations held in Taksim Square, Istanbul, pursue the commemoration (and eventually transitional justice) and create a new layer for the space itself. In this sense, the commemoration activities attempt to relocate the question mark concerning the past onto the present. It is not about the archival knowledge (anymore).

The memory space in Van may not involve events, yet it subsumes bypassing strategies to protect personal and collective memory on violence exercised in the region. In these terms, the question would be whether we can speak of memory agents resisting the denialist hegemony. At every niche, what we are talking about are the "ordinary people", not the state institutions or foreign office strategies anymore. Both denialism as well as efforts targeting recognition and reconciliation are dressed with social engagement. Therefore, these contain in considerable size conflict zones. And this is also why we experience such debates in the social arena. Protecting the discursive boundaries came to be a part of public engagement.

Contrary to genocide scholar Mihran Dabag's argument (2002, 46) that negation is shared by the society through denying Islamised Armenian family members or silencing the stories of Armenian properties, the very same social phenomenon of Islamised family members has fostered various possibilities to communicate this past – as we have seen in different studies (Altınay and Çetin 2009; Biner 2010; Çelik and Dinç 2015; Çelik and Öpengin 2016; Galip 2016). The questions are (roughly) what is remembered; in which collective context is it remembered; and how is it narrated. In the next chapters, I discuss these questions and the social process of remembering considering the "biographical point of view" (Rustin 2003, 46) of different cases – or the perspectives "looking upon the collective memory" (Halbwachs 1991, 31 f).

6 Life Stories. Reconstructing Biographical Experiences and Memories

This chapter focuses on three biographical interviews provided by artisans of their own life stories. While two of the interview partners are from Van, I recorded the interview with Delal in Istanbul. Delal is also the informant whose biography has no ties to this respective border region. She was a gate-keeper for this present study first and later turned up as an interview partner. Alongside these three biographies, I analysed seven further interviews for this research. The three interviews and their analysis echo a proper scope of other life stories. Further life stories, or better said certain aspects out of them, are considered in the next chapter for comparison.

In comparison to the extensive analysis of the first two interviews, the last one, Zal's life story, provides a more compact portrayal. Every case reconstruction starts with a short contextualising introduction concerning the interview setting and the person talking. Thus, the reader would catch a glimpse of the "negotiation phase" with the interview partner (Schütze 2008b, 6) which is in my opinion pretty much important to understand the situation of talking about violence whilst living under violence. I have comparted the case analyses in two subchapters as *Biographical Synopsis*, in order to reconstruct the biography briefly, and *Elements of Violence in Narration*, to discuss the impacts of experienced or told violence in the biography. My target also is exploring the reconstructions my informants employed, and hence the relation of biography to society, and particular collectivities as well as their memories. Hence, biographical projects are understood with all their trajectories, agency, power to change flows, and decisions for their own or others' sake. On the one hand, they develop within certain embeddedness to social realms, yet on the other, they impose changes in these worlds. This reciprocal relation mirrors in remembrance regimes as well.

6.1 Mehmed

My gate-keeper in Van arranged an appointment with Mehmed which took place after Emin's interview, a linguist and language teacher from Van. Having meetings with two Kurdish intellectuals and language teachers who have had different biographies and careers – one (Emin) *medrese* educated and with university graduation from another country and another (Mehmed) with university graduation in Turkey – in the very same day was an exciting opportunity. Mehmed sought a café for our talk, and it was empty when we arrived. He told a story when we sat down and ordered our tea. The story was about his home village. He repeated it adding some further details when I started recording. At the end, he provided a two hours long account with a lot of argumentative and descriptive segments.

Mehmed, a teacher of social sciences in his mid-50s having worked in different parts of Turkey, grew up in the provincial side of Van. During the reforms about the Kurdish language and cultural practice in the 2000s, he was working in Istanbul. With his fellows, he had been engaged in the founding of one of the first Kurdish courses in Turkey. Since then he has been voluntarily part of the Kurdish language struggle as an instructor.

6.1.1 Analytical Abstraction

6.1.1.1 Biographical Synopsis

Mehmed spent his early childhood in the same village where he was born, S.. In the late 1960s, his family moved to the centre of the province T. (sequence 9). From his narration, we learn that his father served as a sergeant at his military service (sequence 8) and later in T. he worked as a carpenter perhaps producing goods for the military (sequence 45). He, therefore, was called *Sergeant Ahmet*. Nevertheless, Mehmed does not clarify what, for instance, his father was doing for a living back in the village.

The neighbourhood of T., where he lived, was a place for the newcomers mostly. The locals perceived these newcomers like Mehmed and his family as Kurds and treated them as their "other" (sequence 9). The scenes Mehmed talks about in this regard reflect the social circumstances and relations in this topography. For instance, he and children like him were treated as Kurds, foreigners, or rural "others" by the locals of T., and these elements emerge as bits of information regarding the time he spent in the centre:

> ... aaa we cannot play with other kids for the reason that we are Kurds, well the neighbourhood was Kurdish however because we came from the village we became the Kurds now, at that time there was an ongoing serious assimilation process. The locals of the town, which means those who came and settled in the town earlier, had been treated as Turkish, really such a time. (sequence 9: 162–165)

Once his uncle told him that he had to struggle with similar problems in the provincial centre. During his visit, having some people do the groceries for them was a way to avoid conflicts, "we ordered at the shop owner ... he got paid for his efforts. We couldn't enter another shop, when we were in another shop we had been treated like dogs, we were kicked out, swore 'you filthy Kurds'" (sequence 44: 697–700). His narratives on such experiences picture the dimension of othering and identity figurations based on a centre versus periphery relationship (for the political dimension of periphery notion and in respect of institutionalisation in Turkey, please see, Mardin 1973). In Mehmed's narrative, the definition of the periphery was socially constructed by the centre (or in other words, by the protagonists that are located in the centre) (cf. Kabalek 2014).[1]

The experience he had as a "foreigner" remained in his remembrance and has apparently influenced his biographical project. Being labelled as Kurdish by local Kurds – in a predominantly Kurdish environment – has become a biographical marking point for interpreting the setting of the town and the region – with which he deals retrospectively. Similar social interactions are reported by other informants as well, such as Delal about the centre of Diyarbakır in her childhood, Zal in descriptive terms about the migration to the urban areas, and Mamoş revealing the hardships that disabled members of the Kurdish society experience. They all point out apparent socio-political differences between centre and periphery – and how these influence the given community. Without a doubt, those moments bolstered the premises of turning points in personal trajectories (cf. Riemann and Schütze 1991), where people affected at some point began to raise questions backed by their agencies. In the case of Mehmed, his experience being labelled as "the other" coming from the periphery, that exclusion nourished by and nourishing further the social dynamics on the ground, came to be a significant background construction powering up his future success in school, university, and his career. He tells about the othering as an experience throughout his lifetime – from childhood onwards – that he had to make reiterating. Although parties involved changed, the core of the notion remained. Hence, in Riemann and Schütze's term (ibid.), he found the dominant process mechanism in being at a position of success.

As a child, Mehmed had also improved a defensive position in order to protect himself. It included using violence and beating other children who threatened him: "Well I, like you go there and wait for playing together, it made me furious I started a fight and beat em. Of course, after a while, we became friends, played together, they did speak Kurdish too." (sequence 9: 166 f). In

---

[1]   In his paper on the two social concepts, periphery and memory, and their possible connection to each other, Kobi Kabalek (p. 17) states "the transgressive capacity of peripheral perspectives to blur boundaries, break silences, destabilize centers and question common analytic categories in the study of memory…. [and] some aspects of peripherality that contributed to the creation and validation of centers and their versions of the past." Deriving from these points, we may consider Mehmed's illustration of his life in the provincial centre as well.

such an environment, it was not only an act of defence but also, for a rural immigrant, a shield to justify and make his existence visible.[2]

The polarized political and social circumstances in the 1970s further influenced his biography. In high school, he was politically socialised in a left-wing environment that was mainly formed by the Turkish socialist movement(s). As a footnote, Emin also comments on being part of the Turkish left-wing and criticises such political movements' approach to the Turkish–Kurdish conflict(s) that a future socialist revolution would be the first step to solve every problem, mean even a salvation for Kurds. Both, Emin and Mehmed have raised questions upon that approach which does not consider Kurds' rights. Their act was performative changing features in their political understanding. Recounting these times, beyond that, fosters and triggers Mehmed's narratives about different topics such as his encounters with the (conservative) Islamised Armenians:

... these Armenians had become such Muslims. I now think about it, well most probably it was for cloaking themselves. We were left-wing, talking about democracy, supposedly we were the Muslim side, we were left and the side talking about democracy, but they were trying to teach us religion.. Well from my point of view this shows, for example what it shows is they were afraid terribly, I call it hugging one's own hangman. With such a great fear they hugged their own hangman, and became the executioner, their own executioner, well it was a serious try out to fulfil the place of their own executioners. (sequence 4: 62–67)

He, furthermore, describes T. of the 1970s as a place politically divided and polarized for which he uses the term "fifty-fifty" town: "in this period aaa the awareness was raised step by step in the left cadres, and we had reached an important level of awareness as T. was a so-called fifty-fifty city" (sequence 46: 720 f). This story concerning the political environment of the town prompts him to emphasise the past of the region. Narratives concerning the intersections of personal and local past, however, are brief fragmented pieces rather than a detailed description:

---

[2] Additionally, the accounts about the atrocities and violence committed against his tribe/family, which he heard from the elder members of his family, (have) played a developmental role in his life. Concerning such family memories and the experience as a "foreigner" in the centre, I assume Mehmed faced and reconciled with peripherical memory even in his early ages. Perhaps, it was not actively treated in those years. The stories he tells are mainly forged by violence, impunity in favour of victimiser/ perpetrator and injustice with which he connects to his childhood.

There were also such big conflicts, some shops were burned down and so on. Aaa imagine there was the police, and there two grey wolfs set fire to a shop, burned down tailor's workshop … The son of the same tailor was murdered, or someone else maybe, I don't know he was called tailor's son.. There was a canal and vineyards at the upper side of T., vineyards aaa, it was said the vineyards were left by the Armenians, vineyards, a wide canal flowing through, that guy died in that canal, they hit his head with a shovel. He was a left-wing, and the right-wing killed him. (sequence 46: 721–730)

He talks in-depth about the time after the development of his political understanding, perhaps because he could not remember the very details of his childhood or because Mehmed's politicization dominates (his approach to) his narration. Even though that is an open question accompanying his entire talk, the background pictures – like violence and othering based on periphery versus centre conflict – triggering his trajectory remains.

Mehmed highlights the hardworking characteristics that defined his highschool years (sequence 10). Reportedly, these years resulted in success at the university and his graduation from a social sciences department in Ankara (sequence 10; 13; 14). Similarly, Delal speaks about dedicating her time to learn the Turkish language and receive good notes – resembling the dynamics of "double consciousness" (Du Bois 2007), yet, simultaneously revealing perhaps the only dominant structures that were left to be employed under regimes of violence.

Mehmed started his studies in the early 1980s (sequence 29) when the Turkish junta regime consolidated its power for the coming decades by passing a new constitution in Turkey. His hardworking character came to be the epicentre and thus he finished his studies in four years without any delay. His diligent studentship ensured a graduation in time. Moreover, Mehmed collocates this aspect with episodic memories such as how well his two professors had treated him or that he had been invited later by the same two for assistantship positions in different universities (sequence 13; 14). Alongside his studentship, he experienced police brutality in those years at the university too because of his activism in left-wing groups, "well, of course we got taken into custody, they battered us" (sequence 30: 467). Although generations passed, the seizures of armed forces in the universities has not changed, as the university years of Azim, a young informant of mine, portray. The only difference is that Azim states police attacks against Kurdish students' organisations instead of left-wing groupings.[3]

---

[3]   While editing these lines for the publication, we see the last steps of the regime consolidation in the academia in Turkey with the assigned rector to the Bosporus

In the university, the discrimination and (implicit) labelling as "the other", which Mehmed experienced in his youth, prevailed again. For instance, Mehmed was ignored by another professor because he did not identify himself as a Turk in the ethnic sense:

...he was a professor and gave the lecture, once he approached to me and said "son can you please come here", I went, "yes", he asked "are you Turkish". My answer was "No I am not", we had lots of internationals, for example people from Kenya, his goal with this question was, "are you from Iran or Pakistan", because physically speaking I look like I am an Iranian or a Pakistani, "are you Iranian or Pakistani?" he asked "are you Turkish?", I said "no", he asked "well where are you from", I repeated "I am not, I'm from Van", "well my son where did you come from to Van?", I said "I can go back for 11 fathers, 11 generations, and they were only from Van, it comes out they were from Van". Then he stopped "aaa my dear please, we all live under the same flag we all are Turkish" I replied "you are a professor, and I really like you, have respect for you, you could not put me in a category and I told you the truth, would you like to hear a lie from me". He turned his back and went like I wasn't talking to him ... (sequence 11: 186–194)

This is his first memory that appears about his university years in our talk. Highlighting the (insulting) meaning of this encounter, he concludes it with the words "even that [identity] was a problem for me" (sequence 11: 195 f). Perhaps, these experiences reminded him of his childhood and of how people in the centre made themselves non-Kurd via defining the other.

Additionally, the narrative about his university years subsumes the dimension of his political activism, which also applies to the biographies of four young participants of this project – even though some already made their first political experiences in high school. In Ankara, he met the organised left-wing. Despite the terror performed by the post-coup regime, Mehmed and his fellow students established a students' association that achieved a country-wide impact and motivated students of other universities to establish similar organisations (sequence 29). Discussions concerning the organisation's

University Istanbul by the presidential decree – following the years long violence against students, bureaucratic chicaneries of the Council for Higher Education and university administrations, and dismissal of thousands of scholars from various universities with statutory decrees after 2015. The students and academics of the Bosporus University Istanbul protest against the anti-democratic process against the rules of their university.

objective(s) involved, however, distinctive directions and opinions among its members. The discussions were, generally speaking, heterogeneous. While some were targeting a path for "revolution", for Mehmed, it was about becoming the voice of the repressed student scene and finding solutions for their issues in everyday life (sequence 30). Perhaps, his proposal could be described as basic claims in a path dependency, yet concomitant, claims to erode enough the dictated mind prison established by the generals in power. The student association arranged nonetheless meetings and events that were successful even beyond their imagination (sequence 31). This notion accords with his self-assumption of his hardworking character as well as the need among students.

Following his graduation, Mehmed first attended the military service and meanwhile weighed his options: becoming a school teacher or considering exams for assistantship positions (sequence 14). However, after his military service, he started his internship for teaching (sequence 15). Almost at the end of his internship, probably a year later, he applied for reassignment to the province of Van because he decided to live closer to his mother after his father passed away (sequence 15). Consequently, the relocation followed his formal request at the National Ministry of Education, and he was reassigned to a school in Van. When he arrived there, he faced arrest and interrogation (sequence 30) due to his political activities in the university. One of the police chiefs in Van ran the questioning during which Mehmed felt as if he was being held at gunpoint. Thus, his interrogator articulated Mehmed's Ankara years as if he was personally involved in the same political agenda at the same time with him and his fellow students together and described Mehmed's attitudes as moderate in comparison to others. As an asset work-ing for the police or the secret service, his interrogator, in fact, followed the group all the time, "well I sat always nearby, and observed you, you were the most rational one" (sequence 30: 473 f). In these terms, Mehmed's custody revealed the aspect that he and his fellow students had worked under strict state surveillance without noticing it. However, what rational one means remains open. Was Mehmed rational in the eyes of this officer because he decelerated the temper that would end brutally against such a regime or because he proposed one of the possible ways to raise the voice of studentship?

But it was not just that. Years later, the *Susurluk* accident on 3 November 1996 clarified Mehmed's hindsight: " ... it happened in N1, that truck accident [*Susur-luk*], as I was in N1, there was a guy at this accident, seemed not so unknown for me, after a long time I recognized yah he was my interrogator Mehmet Özbek [Özbay], Abdullah Çatlı" (sequence 30: 488–490). His interrogator who was a paramilitary assassin instructed by the state died in that car crash (Üngör 2020,

64 f).[4] Moreover, it gave Mehmed some clues to reveal some shadowed aspects of his life story, like who his interrogator was. Without a doubt, this arrest in Van had already become a crucial occasion for his biography, even without knowing his interrogator's identity. For he created a motive based on this arrest for not applying for the university position(s) in order to prevent his professors from being threatened due to Mehmed's political standing (sequence 32).[5] That decision he made changed his whole professional and, perhaps, political trajectory.

As mentioned before, he tells he was taken into custody in Ankara because of the political activities, although he does not reveal what the exact experience

---

[4] In his recent study, based on various international examples and with a historical lens, historian Uğur Ümit Üngör explores and discusses the concept of paramilitarism thoroughly. Instead of defining it as a separate criminal notion, Üngör problematises the state mechanisms that generate and support paramilitary groups – pointing out that "para-institutional structures emerged in a set of overlapping and competing networks that had armed groups under their command" (p. 184) or "[s]eeing paramilitaries as merely criminals de-politicizes them, as 'narcos,' 'bosses,' and 'dons' often want to be part of ruling capitalist elites and wield influence over both electoral democratic politics and authoritarian orders" (p. 189). Working on the concept – he structures in his book – the "plausible deniability" (for a description of deniability with examples, including from Turkey, please see pp. 159–76), he says "paramilitarism can be an act of commission as much as it can constitute an act of omission" (p. 192).

[5] Since he talks about his custody after the graduation in details – which happened in Van, I argue, that he does not avoid speaking about such experiences. Nevertheless, with time, this arrest (sequence 30; 32) became a dominant narrative in his memory vernacular. The experience with the state authorities might make his prior experiences irrelevant, or the interrogation in Van masters the reconstructions in this very area. This narrative suppresses, so to speak, other equal or similar experiences and creates domination. Other stories concerning police may not substitute or overcome this memory. Even though he had troubles with police in university years, he only mentions that period briefly. In a manner of speaking, arrest in Van was one of the most important occasions for a politically active life because its remembrance has been triggered with a noteworthy moment in the contemporary Turkish history: The *Susurluk* accident. From that moment on, his biography has involved on one more tie-point, a link to the country's history. Hence, it empowers him to locate his "self" in the historical and political context of Turkey.

In addition, the identity of the police chief hosts a noteworthy episodic memory which intermingles Mehmed's political commitment during his university years and his professional life as a teacher. At this moment, when he realised his interrogator was the well-known state sponsored militia Çatlı himself, on the one hand, he probably embraced relief because he did not become a target of an unsolved murder which was an "intervention method" of the Turkish State in those years. On the other, he became able to clarify memories connecting different aspects of his life story, for instance, the link between his university years and his first job as a teacher that he took up because he rejected assistantship positions.

was (sequence 30). While what he and his fellows went through remains vague, he tells the story of his arrest in Van in details. It has probably generated a motive for his further life story so that for example, he declined job offers for (research and/or teaching) assistantship positions made by his professors. Nonetheless, he projects these decisions onto another incident that one of his fellows experienced:

> that surveillance bothered me. Therefore, even if I wanted to make an academic career, given up this idea. There was a friend in our organization who got taken into custody, NN was his name, that fellow was under arrest so many times. He entered the university, lost his job there, he was a successful research assistant you know, entered yet, he was an example for all of us, we had seen, well the best would be staying home. (sequence 32: 513–518)

Perhaps, his interrogation was not the main reason, but it generated a significant motive in this regard. This turning point – rejecting to work in the academy – redefined his professional trajectory even if he attended exams of two different universities for master's programmes to become an academic. Based on this premise, he defines the university as a state-affiliated institution and links the problems to the very fundaments of the administrative bureaucracy, when for instance he articulates that in such a context he could not work on the subjects for which he would crave.

From his childhood to his teaching career – including his political activism – his biographical narration occupies two essential dimensions: the accurate success as marginalised one; and his resistant and disobedient standing. Both points are very well entangled with each other. While others were afraid of starting initiatives, he and his fellow students established an organisation that became a success story in a short period of time. For his disobedience, the same organisation – the students' association – is an example as well. This notion, e.g. disobedience, (has) influenced different trajectories in his life history many times. He stood against stigmatization in T. or he refused to work in a university context – probably, contrary to his desires. What these constituted are brief instances illustrating the influences of disobedience in his moves in various settings. Both patterns appear in the stories he further tells.[6]

---

[6] Resisting and disobeying occur to be vital in Delal's life as well. Furthermore, how such actions are performed should be asked, too, because except for one informant's earlier life story, Mamoş', resistance possesses no arms, but flourish from an intellectual capacity – by teaching language, publishing books, discussing socially constructed roles. Nevertheless, Mamoş' act of storytelling has this quality as well because he writes a diary and thinks through what he lived.

After his reassignment to the Van region – following his arrest – he worked in a stress-free environment thanks to the moderate *kaymakam* of town. That unusual time he spent as a teacher with a political background in public service came to an end when the *kaymakam* of the district, who realised or quasi supported that environment, had been reassigned. The position was substituted with a new governor closer to the government's mind. Troubled times had begun. The relocation of the local governor resulted in reassignment (or exile) for some oppositional teachers, including my informant. Mehmed's new address was now a provincial town in central Anatolia (sequence 15). Even if he probably and supposedly aimed to stay in his hometown – since he had arranged this position there, the state institutions led his ideals to a dead end.

His relocation brought him not as a teacher with a reputation but as a delinquent, "I moved to N1 as a person sent to exile, I was looked at suspiciously, of course, in general, the deputy principals were grey wolfs" (sequence 16; 270 f).[7] In this respect, the principal kept his distance from Mehmed as well. However, as the new psychology teacher of the school, he developed excellent relations with students so that they shared their secrets with him and sought his advice at different occasions (sequence 16).

After he and his wife separated, his wife moved out. Following this development, he applied for relocation to Istanbul. Their divorce, as he narrates, was followed then by his moving to the metropolitan city (sequence 17).

Moreover, he resumed his teaching position at a school on the Anatolian side of the city and worked in addition in two further secondary schools as a substitute teacher. In other words, in Istanbul, he started to work more than fulltime. This aspect implies that he struggled to surmount the emotions of divorce that most probably ignited a difficult period for him. Hence, he tried to live by a rigid schedule and dealt with the changes in his personal life.

Meanwhile, on a regular day in the school, he received a visit by police officers. This experience exposed the ongoing surveillance. Mehmed was still seen as a threat by the state institutions:

principal called me, summoned me to his room, I looked, they were there, "these gentlemen want to talk to you, please", "we are from the public order department, learned that you were relocated to this school,

7 Unfortunately, it is not an "exotic" case that the ultranationalist teachers and administrators have positions in state schools in Turkey. Being members of organizations like *Ülkü Ocakları*, known as grey wolves outside of Turkey, or having organic relations to ultranationalist party MHP has not been a discrediting notion for people seeking a post in the state structures, but more an advantage.

we are assigned to watch you", so open ... I said "Ok then, do your job, I am here and by the way, if there is something that I can help with, let me know, perhaps something that you want to ask, I am here." (sequence 18; 292–297)

Mehmed's response that the surveillance would not disturb him refers to his success path and his conviction that he did nothing wrong in my view. This attitude of him resulted in the favourable attention of his principals. Furthermore, he started to volunteer in the photography association(s) and opened a photography studio with his colleagues from the school. Thus, the disclosed surveillance changed trajectories in his life – and not as expected. I suggest, in his narration, the central part of his life starts with his voluntary activism in such organisations, but not with his childhood or youth "cleared off politics". The core dwells upon the political agency.

In Istanbul, after talking about overwhelming conditions – which happened due to his own decision of taking extra jobs as a substitute teacher – he met people who were active in the scene of the Kurdish language struggle (sequence 19). The issue of language rights has always been perceived and acknowledged as a question of freedom and a crucial part of the Kurdish political movements (Hassanpour 1992). Nevertheless, back then in Turkey, highlighting such questions in connection to an institutional context with a certain political demand was a new phenomenon. In other words, establishing a Kurdish course was new, an unknown territory which was discovered by Mehmed and his fellows. In this respect, his commitment made him one of the pioneers in this field. This role in the scene has led him to the professionalisation in language teaching and language rights. He took part in commissions that were established for developing language teaching rules, homogenisation of grammatical rules for teaching purposes and teachers' handbooks (sequence 19; 20; 21). He, moreover, has been assigned to teach Kurdish to students as well as teacher candidates.

In this context, he participated in establishing new language institutions rather than staying out of such administrative processes and resuming his role only as a teacher in the organisation(s). Meanwhile, he came to experience the attitude by the state apparatus against such efforts for institutionalisation in the legal sphere, "we establish the Kurdish language learning centre, we gave such efforts, they [bureaucracy] resisted six months long" (sequence 20: 324). Those language institutions co-established by Mehmed and his fellow teachers had to face yet new obligations that created zones to find new methods and ways of dealing at their every step:

... working further on establishing, aaa, our friends rented a building, building for 3750 dollars, if I am not wrong, they had to pay monthly

3750 dollars rent, and they paid it too. Thus they applied, municipality come- aa district education department officers, "the doors of these classes open inwards, it cannot happen." "Well, what should we do?" "they should open outwards. In case of earthquake kids will be stuck", all right they had a point, it took a month, reinstalling the doors, then well they came back and this time. "You don't have a fire escape." It again retook a month, our colleagues asked if they could tell us the issues not one by one. Let us please know what else we need, so that we can finish the work at once, well we pay the rent here, "nope, first handle it, then come further things". We were detained until everything was done, you know what happened later, lastly, the classes, furniture were prepared, well you know everything. And this time it was about the teacher, well there was no teacher. (sequence 25: 388–396)

Such struggles became part of the job. Seeing this feature overlapping with the demands of the Kurdish struggle, this newly learned, invented, or copied dimension of resistance contains not just questioning obligations and such chicaneries, but exposing their illogical nature and bypassing them through new tactics.

Until revealing that memory, Mehmed mentions these kinds of struggles only concerning his job and its circumstances. In other words, he was involved in such "hardships" as an actor inside the state apparatus – for instance, as a teacher appointed by the ministry. However, as his activist dedication was, in a manner of speaking, reanimated or reframed (by) another layer – here the Kurdish language – he began learning how to walk around the fortified problems and continue the political fight in the legal sphere as an actor from outside. He occupied two roles, one as a teacher (civil servant), another as a language activist and teacher in the civil society. In addition, he has now started to act and react in an outsider role concerning the bureaucratic mechanisms. After the Directorate of Education rejected the idea that the Kurdish institute might employ personnel with a foreign passport for the courses – for instance, from Iraqi Kurdistan (cf. Skutnabb-Kangas and Fernandes 2008), they had to find an alternative way for (volunteer) Kurdish teachers. Their response was then assigning – experienced but not certificated – people as "master educators" when the future employee could prove their experience. This act of bypassing came out at a meeting with the journalist Hrant Dink, when Mehmed and his colleagues visited him to hear his suggestions as an active person from a legally recognised minority (sequence 25).[8]

---

[8]   This passage refers to the Treaty of Lausanne (1923) signed between the Ankara government of Turkey and the opposite parties of World War I and the Greco-Turkish

Reportedly the institution, in whose establishment Mehmed was involved, has then been closed by an "internal order by the movement" (sequence 20). However, this did not mean that he had to quit fighting for language rights and teaching. He essentially led the founding of new organisations in different towns. His act has ensured spreading the institutionalisation in provincial areas since his students moved to towns in the periphery and started such initiatives as certificated teachers:

> I was asked for certifying the teachers for two years, about 60 people, I guess it was 64 people, we trained the teachers, certified them. We provided the certificate, those documents, maybe they still have em and, we were the ones who triggered the centres in the close distance, in Gever, Tatvan, well in Patnos, these colleagues that we certified established those institutions. (sequence 22: 351–354)

Because he believed in this cause, he was fighting for it voluntarily without any extra payrolls, notwithstanding that it replaced his substitute teaching positions in other schools, I assume. Such volunteer jobs may cause another sort of overworking of course. At the time of our interview, Mehmed was still working as a Kurdish language teacher in two different institutions alongside curricular teaching.[9]

In addition, he was involved in founding a publishing house in Van. He, again voluntarily, (has) worked as an editor for the publisher (sequence 23). This also is the publisher where he released his study on a massacre against Kurds performed by the Turkish military in the early republican period

war. The treaty is to be read as the legal and internationally ratified foundation of the Republic of Turkey, including protocols on borders, forsaken and appropriated properties in Greece and Turkey, population exchange between the two countries, and minority rights. The language rights of Armenians, Jews, and Greeks remaining in Turkey are protected, and these three groups are officially and legally acknowledged as minorities. However, the same treaty includes an "amnesty" to the perpetrators of genocides against Ottoman Armenians, Assyrians, and Greeks. In his thorough Talaat Pasha biography, historian Hans-Lukas Kieser (2018, 34) points out, "[c]oncluded by European victors of World War I and Turkish victors of the war for Asia Minor, not by all main groups involved, the Peace of Lausanne endorsed authoritarian rule and the 'unmixing of population' according to religion. It seemed to have opened a new chapter for the post-Ottoman world, but instead it perpetuated patterns and principles of Talaat's governance, even making them part of an attractive paradigm for law-breaking radical 'solutions' far beyond Turkey."

[9]   However, both organisations were shut down during the state of emergency after the coup attempt in July 2016. This happened a few months after our meeting.

(sequence 24; 40–43). He defines his research as his life-work, first because he worked for approximately two decades on the same subject that compounds his family background as people affected, his childhood as a person who lived in the region, his sociology graduation, his activism and his professional life with each other. In order to warn him because of his political activities back then, his father told him "son, I lost my father in front of my eyes, they killed my father, my brother. Aaa please don't let them kill my son too" (sequence 41: 677 f). His father was referring to the massacre that Mehmed later on studied. Mehmed's belief in the Kurdish struggle emerges through different layers and occasions beyond classical definitions of activism. It also is possible to generalise for the entire context of Kurdish movements in Turkey. Therefore, the question is how could one shift the course when a massive restrictive regime occupies everyday life – or where to start in the personal trajectory.

6.1.1.2 Elements of Violence in Narration

Briefly, Mehmed's main narrative – in Schütze's term extempore narrative (2008a) – has a length of 14:53 minutes and involves various stories concerning his family and the background of the village. Alongside these aspects, the first part of our interview subsumes the pattern of violence on different levels. Thus I have segmented his main narrative into five sequences – or found five brief portrayals, layered with arguments (cf. Bartmann and Kunze 2008; Schütze 2008a; 2008b). These stories motivated me to discuss the impacts of violence, state repression, and stories of such events further.

Making the subject discussable

How and when Mehmed narrates about the Armenian Genocide and violence which was exercised against him, his family, and Kurds are significant points. The focus in this context lies on how the stories of violence are told, maybe compounded, and how they conclude each other – in a cumulative way. For instance, the Armenian Genocide as a subject sparks the start of our conversation. It also echoes his interpretation of and positioning to different events and acts based on his individual, family, and generational experiences.

Mehmed draws the picture of violence with different actors playing various roles in his stimulus narrative, in Khezo's story:

I was born in aaa, the S. village of T.. S. is an old Armenian village. S. is called the village of Khezo ... Even today Khezo is famous for his honesty [integrity].. (noise: tee) he is known for his honesty, he is remembered with gratitude for the help he lent to a Kurd. One runs away from the state and hides in his [Khezo's] house for 20 days, he keeps the fugitive, doesn't betray him to the state. Aaa they took him, pull his teeth, they torture him severely, but he never betrays him. (sequence 1: 4–10)

This picture includes protagonists such as – in a simplistic way of portrayal – an Armenian man, Khezo, who has been known to Kurds for his dignity; good and bad Kurds; actors in the context of violence; instrumentalised naïve people; power holders as instrumentalisers; and other Armenians with further positive characteristics. In the story, the Armenian man Khezo hides a Kurdish elder who had been chased by the Turkish armed forces. It was then revealed that he, Khezo, was helping the fugitive, and he was captured, interrogated, and tortured by Turks. Then this Kurdish elder decides to leave Khezo's place in order to save him. Khezo sacrifices himself to save a Kurd and never tells where he is. In the next hide, the man who first welcomed the Kurdish elder betrays him and rats him on the authorities. In short, other Kurds did not stand like Khezo, the Armenian man, and they betrayed their own kin. Generalisations of figurations through betrayal, honesty, and helper and bystander positions appear to be observed. The protagonists are described through their committed actions and characteristics. The ones who seek a benefit are portrayed as betrayers. Moreover, while the Armenian man in this story bears a name, the Kurds do not. Mehmed continues in his further narratives this attitude of silencing names of Kurds and underlining Armenians with their "names." For instance, in the second sequence, referring to his grandmother he highlights a term which was used for Armenian girls by the Kurdish society; in the next story (sequence 3) his relative's name who committed murder during the genocide is not exposed. In another part (sequence 25) Mehmed points out the help he and his fellows received from Hrant Dink for the establishment of language institute. However, he does not name any of his fellows in any of these stories. Concerning such historical accounts, I do not suppose that he knows all the names, but he leaves them out. However, naming the protagonists is an issue showing how he regards these people. In these terms, I argue he respects the Armenians – honouring the other – and meanwhile problematises the past and present of the Kurdish society – a critique on own group.

Hereby, Mehmed points to the non-unity of the Kurdish people, I suggest. He pictures, in fact, this issue through a story about the Armenian past and the genocide. The Kurds who betrayed their own people are the victimiser protagonists. Beyond the critique on past and present conditions, his narrative "unites times" (Vico 1948, 251). The temporal organisations are interconnected to each other. Khezo's story epitomises today's problems in a historical setting. Dividing the Kurdish society into two clear groups in order to explain certain social settings and anachronistic templates are widespread notions and can be observed in further interviews with other narrators (for an in-depth discussion on these two features, please see the Chapter 7). Simultaneously, it raises whether political positions crystallise in this way since being a Kurd or being an Armenian is mainly considered a political position – as a quasi-rain check.

Such features continue in Mehmed's story about his disabled relative who participated in the genocidal violence and murdered Armenians (see the next subchapter). The notion applies to his relative as well; he is spared a name. Welzer and his team (2002) describe a similar situation with their theory of "cumulative heroisation" – concerning the motive of protecting own family and, at the same time, recognising the past violence. However, in the setting of the present study, this concept does not serve properly. I suggest, in this case, not-naming the victimiser shows us another side of the coin: naming the victims is an act of emphasis. It may, furthermore, reveal the question of using analepsis (flashback) for proleptic (future vision) stories (cf. Brescó de Luna 2017). In other words, stories that Mehmed tells draw our attention: first with its emphasis on the victims before the phenomenon of violence appeared, then through victimisers' actions, and further with an attempt which is performed by Mehmed rather than his relative. Perhaps, we can define this attempt as a sort-of-coming to terms with the past in an individual remembrance context.

This quasi-disassembling of the story would lead to a simple question: what could be the motives of this discursive action? In this regard, I argue that Khezo's story is not only about Khezo, or his relative's story is not only about a historical period. This story implies a gatekeeper position to talk about violence and open a path to discuss (cf. Bar-On 1999). Moreover, based on Prager's argument (1998, 90), this memory is "an effort to reconcile self-understanding or self-consciousness with one's [Mehmed's and/or his community's, E.Y.] inner world of feeling." Looking at the issue this way discards the heroisation thesis for this particular context. For heroisation means bypassing the problematic field of discussion. However, Mehmed does not bypass it because, in his view, the discussion should be carried out and yet connected to the (ongoing) state violence – through anachronistic templates. Both stories, Khezo's and his relative's, help him talk about the level and composition of violence.

The first part of our interview involves several stories and layers with regard to the genocidal past. Perhaps, Mehmed did not live within and experience this period at first hand but certainly acquired stories from the elders of his family. He links the past to the present so that he contextualizes a time frame of 100 years and beyond. This anachronistic approach, on the one hand, eases and ensures the *discussability* as well as *describability* of violence (Bar-On 1999), and it, on the other, supports building quasi determinative patterns (or clusters) for rendering experiences and narratives (cf. Young 1988).[10] His clusters are employed in defining violence. In this sense, the Armenian Genocide memory breaks the cycle of not-to-discuss and not-to-mention.

I argue that, for Mehmed, *narrating the stories on the Armenian Genocide sheds light on the violence performed against the Kurds*. It is the multidirectional quality of this particular memory (Rothberg 2009). Moreover, under these circumstances in Turkey, where the genocide has been a taboo theme, it becomes a functional oppositional instrument to intervene in the social scene and to stimulate further debates on silenced topics. In other words, talking about the Armenian Genocide opens further areas to discuss. It clears the pathway. From my point of view, this notion is a clear example for how memory allegorically represents the past and point at the present time. Furthermore, it also is about how stories are reconstructed thanks to particularities from different individual and collective experiences. In the case of Kurdish memory, we can include the political movement's perspective, deriving from what social scientist Molly Andrews puts forward "personal narratives are constructed within a wider social context; they both reproduce and are produced by dominant cultural meta-narratives" (Andrews et al. 2002, 78; cf. Zittoun 2017).

Halbwachs postulates that memory is a social construction, and it is not about the past, it is strongly related to the present (Halbwachs 1991). Or remembering Prager's terms, "[m]emory is embedded: that is, the rememberer remembers in a contemporary world, peopled by others who collectively contribute to the construction of memory and help determine the importance that the past holds for an individual in the present" (1998, 70 f). In this sense, the questions should be: What does the Kurdish collective memory point regarding the Armenian Genocide? How do discussions in Kurdish society conclude this memory regime? What does Mehmed's agency tell us? In Mehmed's case, the notion of violence pops up within the boundaries of the narrative reconstruction of his biographical project. His stories are his attempts to describe the violence in the region. First of all, talking about Armenians eases Mehmed to be discussing own experiences. Moreover, it helps him to rearrange the collective

---

[10] In his work on Holocaust narratives, James E. Young (pp. 95–98) discusses the violent events in the past – before the Shoah – as emerging comparative templates which are used in writing the Jewish history. He points out that the new experiences were considered by comparing them with the older ones. He calls this quality archetypal. Concerning the Holocaust, he underlines that it perhaps became "its own archetype" in which an event – with his example, the deportation of children – helps one to articulate the succeeding event of the Shoah, "[E]ven if the Holocaust itself would not become archetypal for other disasters until it was used afterwards to figure them, earlier parts of it did become archetypal for subsequent parts" (p. 100).

political discourse. Armenian Genocide as one of the most significant events in the history of Turkey and these very post-Ottoman regions represents the dimension and the grade of violence that could be achieved. Therefore, the genocide is perceived by Mehmed as a matter of narration on violence, I suggest. Telling his experiences, flagging up what Kurds have experienced, and employing reference points for associating with the Armenian Genocide is his choice.

Collective References concerning Violence

When Mehmed asked his relative questions about his disability, he started a process of facing performed violent actions and reflecting upon them. In this narrative about the participation in mass violence, some particular notions emerge, for instance, mosques' role and the so-called instrumentalisation of the Kurds:

> ... he said "in the beginning we were very gentle to each other," he told me the same thing. "At one point imams were changed. The imams in the mosques, well the newcomer imams in the mosques, gave a fatwa a speech you know told / gave a sermon, I was listening to that sermon, wherever you encounter an Armenian kill him, because killing an Armenian means the way to heaven, do you want to go to the heaven dear Muslims, dear fellow Muslims, yees, then don't give the Armenians a chance to survive." (sequence 3: 47–51)

Mehmed's relative talks about the sudden replacement of imams that had, so to speak, injected hate and prejudice against Armenians into the Kurdish society. The relation of Kurdish people to mosques had, reportedly, resulted in an instrumentalisation of civilians and their participation in killings. This story includes widespread narratives (collective references): the role of religion in the genocidal violence or how the Kurds were lured into it as perpetrators. Further four narrators employ similar approaches in describing past events; for instance, Murad builds a massive proportion of his storytelling on such a premise.[11] As discussed and pointed out in the historical chapter, the extermination campaigns took place within cumulative terms, and there occurs participants with different motives.

---

[11]   For a detailed discussion on the instrumentalisation thesis, please see the Chapters 5.4 Recognition Debate(s) among Kurds in Turkey and 7.1.3.2 Narrative of Instrumentalisation and Victimhood.

The pattern of instrumentalisation fades out and blurs the aspect of responsibility. There is indeed the exploitation by the government, yet, stressing a naïveté eases the hands of the narrator since this feature emphasises the orchestrators of the genocide and their power in managing different institutions – in this case, the religious authorities. Due to that, actors come forward in clearly framed structures, which reminds the listener/reader of who the powerholder was: The Ottoman State. The narrative quasi hierarchises the perpetrators: first the government, then the local institutions, then the landowners, and at the end perhaps the ordinary people. The question would be then if the form of the narrative hierarchises victimhood as well.

Mehmed's relative describes his disability as a curse of the Armenians he murdered in the past: "I am a murderer of 17 people, this is why my feet became like that, Armenians' curse took effect" (sequence 3: 57 f). The actorship which was taken from the Armenians earlier – in other words, Armenian agency was condemned to stem only from victimhood – is given back with the curse in their absence. The idea that before the violence there was coexistence is another string in this story. The post-violence curse creates a space where Armenians did not exist anymore, where there were no pockets for coexistence anymore, but a myth substituted their existence. This menace haunting perpetrators locates in the same framework with the Kurdish proverb "We are the dinner, you are the supper", which was reportedly said by the Armenians to the Kurds. It is a remarkable example for underscoring the substitution of existence through a mystification.

Beyond that, in the beginning of our interview Mehmed talks about the Hamidiye Cavalries (sequence 5; 6) that were established in 1891 under the rule of Abdülhamid II in order to foster state power over the influential Kurdish tribes, transform them into reliable state sponsored militias (Klein 2014, and please see the Chapter 4 of this present study), and to establish the imperial control in the periphery. The Hamidiye Cavalries were the main actors of the 1894–96 massacres of Armenians on the high plateau. Another controversial subject about these regiments is whether the militias (or the remaining state loyalist tribes since they were "reformed" or dissolved in 1913) participated in the events of the Armenian Genocide (Çelik and Dinç 2015; and for his presentation, Çelik 2015).[12] In this sense, the question I pose is not if Mehmed commingles the stories of the 1894–96 mass violence and the 1915 Genocide. For example, historians Ümit Kurt and Murad Uçaner (2015, 327) describe

---

[12] Based on their oral history investigation in Amed/Diyarbekir region, Adnan Çelik and Namık Kemal Dinç point at a new militia structure, *Cendermiyen Bejik*. Reportedly, it was founded regionally during the genocide and operated in the same territory.

this notion with which they were confronted in a similar case as "argument of continuation". Thus, the following two questions arise: Does Mehmed insists a clear linear path of violence against Armenians starting from 1894–96 hitting its uppermost level with the genocide – and, perhaps, continuing with the village guard (*korucu*) system until the present since Hamidiye Regiments are associated with that system because of their collaboration with the state power? Does this point suggest that Hamidiye Regiments bear a symbolic role for the Kurds, in the description of destruction and the notion of instrumentalisation? Where is the emphasis, on the continuation or instrumentalisation and victimisation?

I would like to take on with a further discussion point which would clarify some aspects of my argument concerning the issue of narrating on Hamidiye Cavalries. The sudden changes in the story of Mehmed's relative mark a coexistence before the violence, the devastation performed by power-holders and instrumentalised people – with their motivators, in this case, the imams. Genocide memory is narrated in a framework where the religious aspects are hegemonic instead of outlining some frames of social-Darwinist racism. How religion and its institutions were utilised for the massacres is the focus that this story puts forward. Regarding the aforementioned anachronistic nuances in historical stories, an assertion would be that the religious institutionalisation, especially the officially-controlled religion since the Kemalist rule, is the case thematised here in Mehmed's narrative. Mehmed also comes back to this issue in the later parts of our interview where he discusses – based on his observation and experience in his youth, and later as a sociologist and teacher as well – religion in the context of Islamised Armenians in Van (sequence 4); religion as an item in organising women in the 1980s (sequence 34); and its role in the life-world of young people in Van today (sequences 36–39; 54). In every case, religion is described as an instrument, not as faith or through the dimension of its practice:

> ... [in the 1980s] while three or four people were not allowed to meet, obviously, for example as we wanted to listen to Şivan's [Perwer] cassettes, we as three people came together, got a police investigation. Though 200 women could come together for a mevlit [religious ceremony], no one mentions what happens, sees or knows what happens. (sequence 34: 548–550)

Beyond framing religion as an instrument for depoliticising society, the role of women and youth in such a process is the point underlined by Mehmed. In this sense, he problematises the state handed interpretation of religion and its utilisation with political motives. In this regard, he discusses issues in a framework which is formed through collective references and nourishes his narrative from aspects of collective memory – highlighting questions relevant to present conditions (de Saint-Laurent 2017; Zittoun 2017). The term "collective reference" here indicates not just the content but the temporal hints, as well as possible motives. In bullet points, some of these aspects are the coexistence of Armenians and Kurds before the genocide – as it is the case with his grandmother's story (sequence 2); a will of reconciliation, yet mixing up the victimhood description – like with the subject of his relative's alleged curse; the continuity of structures such as the instrumentalisation with Hamidiye Regiments or division of the current Kurdish society; and the anachronistic construction of memories to highlight present injustice.

Others who perpetrated

Closely connected to, even embedded in the phenomenon of the collective references, Mehmed portrays the perpetration in the hands of "others". In some stories, "the other" is embodied by powerholders and in some by the "traitor Kurds". This "other" stresses an absolutistic total perpetrator role carried out by the Ottoman State – or by Turks. It pictures a centralised, "perfectly planned" process designed and performed by a totalitarian structure; filters out diverse motives of participation – profit, resentment, and government hailing – and assigns a hegemonic homogeny to the question of conduction.

Furthermore, the term "traitors" pinpoints an instrumentalisation concerning the relation of Kurdish society with powerholders; creates zones of participation for the so-called instrumentalised ones. Paradoxically, they are pictured as collaborators, yet at the same time as naïve people.

Due to these aspects regarding the phenomenon of "the other", we encounter in Mehmed's stories about the extermination campaigns no room for stories in the margin that of course existed like the resistance in Van (for instance please see, A-Do 2017). Although he portrays first the genocidal process in such frames, he grants contrary to his storytelling a non-conformity with "Armenians left the village before it started" (sequence 2–3). It clarifies his semi-open awareness about some incidents (cf. Glaser and Strauss 1965), yet also signs a total power controlling everything even the Kurds. It brings his narrative to the point of absolute victimhood, even the victimhood of Kurds (for victimhood works concerning the Armenian Genocide, please see, Türkyılmaz 2011). So, the possible agencies of actors become erased.

Beyond that, portraying the "other" as a total victimiser hands the narration the possibility to make reader/listener focus on it. This way of story-telling, however, does not reflect the participation of the regular people, I suggest. Indeed, the mass violence required orchestrators, in the case of the Armenian

Genocide first of all the CUP government, then the governors, and assets of state institutions such as the secret service, *Teşkilat-ı Mahsusa*. Nevertheless, without the participation in the perpetration of the regular people (or neighbours of the victims), it is not possible to gather thousands of people, deport and murder them at different places and reshape the process based on circumstances *in situ*. The extermination campaigns differed from region to region and were shaped in a cumulative process. The central government was aware of handing the responsibility to regional governors and rulers to maximise the effects of these campaigns. In these terms, the regional actors needed further assets like regular people, civilian Kurds, to perform violent campaigns. Therefore, the thesis of instrumentalisation and utilised people in the hands of powerholders blurs the very field of civilian participation in the genocidal events, in other words, the events that emerged alongside the total perpetrators, I suggest. This non-reflective pattern in stories, regarding the community, does deflect looking into various motives of involvement. Nevertheless, such a template is widespread, not just in the interviews with my informants, as articulated before (Aydınkaya 2015; Çelik and Dinç 2015; Çelik and Öpengin 2016; Galip 2016).

Historical Analogy and Anachronism

However, it also has to be asked why such stories were told, what this sort of narration means in the context of the Kurdish struggle. In this sense, another point of remembrance emerges, the interaction as the base of the narrative (Brockmeier 2015). Earlier I argued, in both stories, Khezo's and his relative's story, the emphasis is not on the extermination campaigns but on the violence targeting the Kurdish society. Some anachronistic descriptions are employed within this contextualisation. Furthermore, political cases like Armenian massacres and violence against Kurds are put in causal comparison. Historical analogies surface in this regard (Vico 1948, 251; Zerubavel 2003). The anachronistic attempt is very much connected to the question of how to discuss and describe.

Narrative vernacular regarding the Armenian Genocide subsumes descriptions of a catastrophic and tremendous size of violence. Beyond doubt, there is a sincere and significant moment of facing the past in such narrative. However, I assume the genocide is a "trauma-like memory" (cf. Prager 1998, 132) for Mehmed and further informants who declare their sorrow for what happened to Armenians, and, perhaps, a "chosen trauma" for the whole society (Volkan 2001). It sparks a moment of facing with the own experience of violence. From my point of view, the most explicit anachronism Mehmed employs is about naming the perpetrators, the "other Kurds." He projects the current problem to this very historical case or binds them to each other. This remark underlines the multidirectional nature of this particular memory in the Kurdish society (cf. Rothberg 2009).

In several stories, Mehmed lifts a concept of non-unity, one group collaborating with the Turkish State like Hamidiye Cavalries and another suffering like in Khezo's story. It can be seen in his critiques about the Kurds who took the side of the Turkish State and who fostered, therefore, non-unity. He uses the past in order to conceptualise his critiques in a narrative sense although he sees a start of unity today, thanks to the Kurdish political movement (sequence 39). Similarly, the relation between Kurds and Armenians, as two major ethnic groups of the region, is portrayed within the dimensions of ideal coexistence, until the outsider other – here, the government forces – or other Kurds appeared. The dichotomic representation is, in these terms, not based on an ethnic or national affiliation but other layers of activity and agency. This sort of case contextualisation paves the way to the links between the past and present.[13]

The continuity is, in fact, based on the governmental policies and actions. Once the Armenians suffered, then Kurdish "grandmothers lamented" for their loss at the massacres (sequence 40: 644 f). The descriptive fifth sequence of the interview, for instance, involves the Hamidiye Regiments – the non-unity and instrumentalisation; Christians of the region – coexistence as well as massacres; his study – individual links to the past; and the state of scholarship in Turkey – the institutional continuity of ignorance and denialism. Or in the sixth sequence, he pins down that his family was displaced, left its village and came to the empty Armenian village of S.. In the scope of continuity, the temporal agents in the narrative come to be freed of their temporal limits and establish anachronisms distinctively.

---

[13] Similarly, when he talks about the Islamised Armenians (sequence 4), he criticises them for becoming similar to their perpetrators. In this regard, he uses the traumatological term Stockholm Syndrome to describe the attitudes of Islamised Armenians and compounds it with the present conditions in Kurdish cities suffering from war, naming it Nusaybin Syndrome, in order to build a background for his argument. This historical analogy appears in a sequence in which the focus was set on his years in the provincial town of Van as a politically active young man. The critique he makes extends and involves the Kurds of today. It loops his biography with the place, history and current political circumstances (Zittoun 2017).

Place and Materiality

In Mehmed's life story, S. – the village, T. – the provincial centre, and Van, as well as Istanbul, appear to be significant to his biographical project. The first starts his family history; the second is the place of his childhood and youth; the latter connotes his adulthood. They prepare chronological steps for his narration. While S. contains the violence performed against Armenians as well as his family, T. and Van mean violence against Mehmed personally. Istanbul, furthermore, links his story to disclosing institutional injustice and ways of bypassing them. These places are anchors for his biographical narrative and describing the violence. He covers through these places not only different periods but various forms of struggle. Place, in this respect, has an anchor-role in opening and generating the narrative.

Moreover, these places are connected in some cases through materials like the grapes from his home village, "S. has a distinct quality, it is famous for its grapes" (sequence 2: 15) and the story of the tailor's son (sequence 46; for this story, please see the next chapter with the comparative discussion). The material culture, such as vineyards, are tied to these places and to events which characterise that particular space. These are loaded with symbolism (A. Assmann 2010). Another story that he recounts emerges around the rings worn by Armenian or Kurdish girls:

> she [grandmother] used to tell that they were neighbours with them …
> "We didn't marry them nevertheless we were together all day and we loved each other … they used to wear rings on their thumbs" she told, "it was their custom, we used to wear it on our middle fingers."
> (sequence 2: 22–28)

This symbolism refers to the differences between communities. At the same time, it emphasises the coexistence – with inter-ethnic boundaries.[14]

Another material symbolism from the same sequence refers to the awareness about who lived in S. before his family moved, "there are still their traces,

---

[14] Hence both aspects reach out the times after the extermination campaigns: through the stories told, even the treasure hunters. Digging the graves and ruins of Armenian properties constitute a profile of profiteer for the times after the genocidal violence. A benefit which would change the life course is chased. In comparison to the confiscation of the Armenian wealth during and after the extermination campaigns, digging the ground is an attempt to escape a "destiny". However, it still is a participative act in the violence. In most cases, ruining the Armenian remnants has been tolerated by the state institutions, which I discuss in the Chapters 5 and 7 in detail.

crucifixes everywhere, on rocks and mountains" (sequence 2: 20 f). The symbolism of Armenian gold and treasure hunters in the same part, "S. still has gold under its soil, villagers run into it and pick it, this is how several families got rich, this is Armenian gold"(sequence 2: 19 f), discloses the material remains of Armenians – the left behind existence, the ruination of this past and of course some sort of awareness about what happened in the region.

In sum, materiality and place locate in Mehmed's narratives as noteworthy scaffolds that provide an orientation. They also pinpoint aspects beyond the story itself, like the ruination of the Armenian past or peaceful living-together – which also is the case in two other cases, Kerem and Azim.

The Self in the Narration

Mehmed has learnt how to struggle with the Turkish State, like in the case of surveillance. Even if he had "staggered" in his earlier experiences of such situations like in his childhood in T., he showed his resistant nature, e.g. approach, in treating those issues. His years in T. as a young child who moved from the countryside mark a start for telling some unpleasant details about his biography. For instance, the violence other children exercised because of his background led him to use violence as well. For him it became a question of resistance:

> we could not play with other kids for the reason that we are Kurds ... After a long time of course, we raised up with such things, and I had to beat lots of people. Well I, like you go there and wait for playing together, it made me furious I started a fight and beat em. Of course after a while, we became friends, played together, they did speak Kurdish too. (sequence 9: 162–168)

His years in Ankara as a Kurdish student further fostered his way of dealing with such issues. Concerning his adult life, this notion emerges in the stories as disobedience vis-à-vis the authorities and bypassing the regulations. He was politicised in a Turkish left-wing environment. Being organised within the students' association introduced him a further dimension of political activities for his professional trajectory. He learned how to act and react in political space. He also learned how to create and chase collective goals. In such a description, his university years seem to be affected by positive experiences. The two individual layers – his childhood and the political experience in the university – overlap particularly in his biographical project, I argue, since he came to the point where he had to deflect from authorities' demands in order to reach the goals of the initiative he was involved in. Disobedience is the form that is performed against institutional injustice. It is the performative act of his "self" changing trajectories. First, he found out that he could defend himself against other children, then he discovered the meaning of dodging the institutional acts. His "self" draws the emphasis, not the setting or persons acting against his will. When it comes to violence, he is the main actor of the story because he resists.

In this context, I would like to consider Mehmed's research. His study pictures crossroads, a design of interconnections of various layers from Mehmed's life story. Furthermore, it is his way to articulate himself, not just through the content but also through how he had finished the manuscript – it took 20 years of work according to him. Reportedly, he carried out a research which he could not have done, for instance, as a scholar in a university context in Turkey because of its subject. In this sense, he performs, in Walter Mignolo's terms (2009; 2012), epistemic disobedience. He builds up a standing vis-à-vis knowledge production in the country. He, on the one hand, presents a sort of resistance via shedding light on this event since it became a covered, overlooked, and not-to-talk topic. His aim within this study is breaking another brick of this taboo while ensuring local people to talk, who experienced this mass violence at first hand. On the other, he emphasises how he was shocked when he found out that scholars did not study this event, "after my sociology graduation I would have regretted, why wouldn't I treat such a subject [in the university]. Why is this not discussed by anyone [else]" (sequence 40: 648 f). For Mehmed, it is not only pursuing a stubborn nature and revealing an untouched matter. It also is disobeying the scholarly world, the world that he already refused to enter. In short, his work is a form, an instrument and a proof of his resistance against authorities, here of course including academia.

In the end, he was successful in avoiding personal issues, maybe also thanks to the dominance of the subject matter, the violence and injustice. Mehmed's memories at the juncture of his village, family history, and stories concerning the Armenian Genocide prepare a quasi-ground on which his argumentative and descriptive frameworks emerge, as it applies to the further two informants of my study as well, Zal and Murad. They also employed many arguments in order to clarify their positionings. It shaped his political identity and professional trajectory significantly.

Contested Memories

The patterns and trajectories of remembrance discussed throughout Mehmed's narrative interview indicate a picture of contested memories. This contestation does include conflicts between the Turkish State's narrative and Kurdish recognitionesque perspectives regarding the Armenian Genocide as well as various attitudes among the Kurdish people. But how Mehmed looks upon the collective and collective remembrance, in Halbwachsian terms, constitutes the main frame of contestation in his narrative. So, he contests the general national narratives. Beyond the dimension of his research, his approach in contextualising different occasions, notions, and (violent) events such as the current social and political circumstances that are dominant in Kurdistan are rooted in his memories of his early ages. He tells his biographical first-hand experiences in an analogy to (regional) history. Not just his memories travelled, his memories are also encountered by others' narratives (Erll 2011). His biography stands in the centre and filters the stories that were listened to or that were spoken out. In other words, his biography renders collective stories and reconstructs own narratives.

There are several emphases that contest each other, yet build the memory together. A comparison with other biographies collected for this book would foster the analysis of the after-effects of violence. Instead of a "true" and "false" labelling of content, such a discussion should aim at the ambiguities, contradictions, and nuances in the terrain of contestation in Kurdish collective memory. The memory evolves, shapes, and surfaces in this interactionist sphere.

6.2   Delal

I received Delal's contact details prior to my Istanbul field research in November 2015. We made an appointment to talk about the project in-depth. At first, the idea was that she would take a gatekeeper role and arrange some contacts for the project. Over the course of time, it turned out that we would also record an interview about her life story. However, we had to postpone our interview-meeting because personal issues came up during my stay. Although we had already met several times, we could not arrange the meeting. Thus, our interview appointment ended up close to my departure back to Germany. We arranged the appointment without any time limit in an evening in her flat in Istanbul.

At the time of our interview, Delal was working for a non-governmental organisation located in Istanbul. Her work was concentrated on topics related to the Kurdish language and culture. She was born in Diyarbakır, but since her parents came from H., a provincial town of Diyarbakır, she identifies herself as a local of H. which pops up several times in the recording.

In her talk, Delal narrates some (short) stories that she already had told me as we met for other occasions. She needed a comfortable environment for our talk, perhaps in the light of the news from Diyarbakır – including Tahir Elçis murder, the chairperson of Diyarbakır bar whom she knew personally. The outcome of this meeting was a recording of three hours.

6.2.1 Analytical Abstraction

6.2.1.1 Biographical Synopsis

Born in the early 1980s in Sur, Diyarbakır, Delal spent her childhood and youth in the same district until she moved to K. for a few months in her mid-20s. After a time spent attending a master's programme at the university in K., she returned to her hometown, worked there for some years and then moved to Istanbul 2,5 years before we met. The feature of changing the roles for the study – from gatekeeper to informant – was to be noticed when I turned the recorder on and posed the stimulus question. Although she knew the concept, changing the role hampered her in the beginning. Perhaps, she was still bearing the role of a gatekeeper and could not occupy her newly tailored informant role.

The question was if Delal should start in a chronological way or design other frames for her narration. She laughs, for instance, several times which seems to provide her a moment to think (sequence 1). She seeks the track to starting her narration that she then finds with a disaster story, an earthquake in the 1970s. Following the disaster where her parents lost three children, they moved to downtown Diyarbakır. Delal and her siblings were born in this urban centre. She describes how her parents and family were affected by the disaster and associates their situation with being/feeling "like refugees" (sequence 1: 32). For the centre created a different social context. It hosted predominantly assimilated Kurds praising the Turkish State. She underlines the difference between her family coming from H. and the people of Diyarbakır through using a strong metaphor: being like refugees. She and her family felt like refugees in the centre. The intense power of her analogy is clear to her too perhaps since she replaces her laughing at this very moment with a cough. From this point forward, Delal is on a string for her further narration; she knows what to tell and how to tell her life story even though her narrative remains very fragmented like a patchwork.

Delal remembers only some incidents from her elementary school years such as the isolation that her father imposed; the wallop by her teacher; the following school change – based on her father's decision; and quasi being stuck in a completely different milieu because the new school was predominantly for civil servants' children:

> **however** there was this issue in this school, aaa it was a great school one of the best in Diyarbakır which was originally for the kids of army and police forces, it was located close to the lodging buildings of those departments, you know kids of attorneys aaa officers, soldiers and policemen, therefore there my. My psychology was upside down so

because I wasn't feeling anything, was learning Turkish learning swift
and really proper Turkish there wasn't any problem but I hated being a
Kurd. (sequence 2; 3: 44–50)

Delal commuted between different isolated zones daily: one at home, another
due to school. Two other young participants of this study, Kerem and Azim,
report language-based hardships in a similar contextualisation – school
meant Turkish and home Kurdish. Nevertheless, Delal additionally had to
struggle with the "unreal" social circumstances which the isolationist settings
produced. She furthermore adds that her brother was enrolled in the same
school. Probably her brother had experienced similar issues as well. Until she
met other children from a social circle identical to hers she was dealing with
the very setting of isolation, "I only remember two people with whom I felt
good when we were together ... they also enrolled him [one of the children
she speaks about] thanks to that teacher ... we became buddies and began
to run protests in the school, little/small scale (laugh)" (sequence 5: 85–90).
However, spending several hours in another milieu on a daily basis and experiencing a different kind of habitus brought the opportunity of coming out of
the actual isolation imposed by her father. The success path in her years of
elementary education was the way out even if it concurrently meant assimilation and adaptation to a foreign milieu, "I loved Turkish **very much** ...
I was reading permanently so that I could learn better ... Somehow trying to
prove yourself, I could not accept it for a while, that Kurdishness, I hated it"
(sequence 6: 93 f; 102 f). In comparison to Mehmed, we see in Delal's case
another form of utilisation of success.

Especially in secondary school, Delal composed cover-up stories for conditions ruling her life: she could not tell her peers that her father was a fugitive
or that she already, at this young age, experienced police raids. Although she
was in a school with local Kurdish children, it was not their shared reality at all:

there were kids like me at the secondary school, but it was like there
was a difference we / my family were too political those kids others
they were more aaa, it was the period close to the village deportations
there was nothing exactly like that so all of them were Diyarbakır kids,
so to speak they were locals, they had no political side neither did I for
also I was raised in such a place by family, there was only that difference I mean we were afraid of, there was that fear OK, you shouldn't
talk, you shouldn't talk about anything at school, don't tell that your
father is in custody, don't tell that your father isn't home (sigh) if anyone asks your father stayed with your uncles, in Istanbul, I used to see
that difference, they had no such concern. (sequence 8: 120–126)

The success path she started in elementary school remained in her secondary school years. The school authority, probably the principal, offered Delal to skip a year and to start in the 7th grade by reason of her success. Her father rejected this idea. It reveals the decision-making authority of her father again. She summarizes her recollections about those years around one specific feature, "I used to go to the school and return home, I was very hardworking, an excessive nerd" (sequence 7: 112 f). Additionally, she distinguishes the environment of this school from the previous one. It was a school with predominantly "Diyarbakır kids" (sequence 8: 122). So, she had to disguise her life at home further. In this manner, Delal defines her family as "too political" and comes to the point that she was covering up the facts dominating her household, like her father and uncle being away and on the run.

The school complex where Delal was studying included a high school which her sister was attending. It hosted, in Delal's words, a political environment, "it was a political school already, constantly witnessing activism, protests exercised by high school students" (sequence 7: 110 f). However, she did not engage in political protests during those years. She underscores the difference between studentship she had and the state of high school, but at the same time she quasi points at one of the possible paths of her future political socialisation.

Alongside her attending the school, secondary school years signed the moments of discovering her neighbourhood. Together with her peers, Delal strolled in the district, visited mosques and churches and the bastions of the walls (sequence 50). Some of these visits were accompanied by the fear of that "they [Christians] would strip us of our religion of Islam" (sequence 53: 1081). Yet, she became familiar with Sur and the city. She came to love the neighbourhood that she describes as chaotic and defines living there as "deficiency" (sequence 56). The neighbourhood even appears in her dreams. Delal underlines her relation to this particular place with the following comment: if she were to write a novel, a tale, then the story would take place in Sur (sequence 44). She probably became aware of the importance of this place in her life after she started to discover and see it from her perspective since she, for example, has vital childhood memories that help her to describe the circumstances of living in Sur, such as curfews and clashes. In other words, when she could change the lens through her friendship(s), she started to memorise and reorganise the neighbourhood with discoveries instead of the unpleasant, uncanny experiences she had – such as isolation, violence, and injustice. Just a reminder, she spent her childhood respecting the boundaries her father set. Deconstructing these by having friends yet provided her with the opportunity to remember Sur differently later. She reconstructed the neighbourhood in her particular biographical way.

In those years, she started mimicking other children's acts. Although she is not specific in explaining the time when she, her peers, and her brother took another path back home, where they cursed Armenians while passing Christian cemetery, I suppose it took place in the first years of secondary school. The nature of her relationship with her brother comes into narration when she talks about this particular time period. Their relationship was based on challenging each other and involving their mother in conflicts that erupted between the two of them when they needed a moral authority:

> once with my brother we said, like let's swear today, we discussed it like five minutes, a but we are not gonna tell mother (laugh), OK but we are not gonna tell mom or dad, we gonna keep it as our secret, my brother said let's swear for some minutes, three minutes or five minutes, we did it but of course during another discussion it was spoken out (laugh). My brother had bitched about it, or maybe I did it, you know when you have a discussion then you do it to get points, "**Moooom do you know**", she cursed (laugh), or I did it loudly my brother cursed but of course you forget it that you did it together and you with him-(laugh). (sequence 52: 1048–1056)

In secondary school, Delal could pursue the hardworking path further so that she could attend a better school with a foreign language programme. She describes this school as follows: "there were a lot of soldiers' or policemen' children, you know it was a super lycee" (sequence 39: 695 f). Then she got suspended because of a presentation she prepared together with her friends. That moment remarks another preliminary step in her confrontation with the social environment and reality of dominant structures.

For the presentation, students were assigned to pick up an artist they liked and to prepare a clipboard in English. The persons Delal and her friends chose were, however, Kurdish singers – Ciwan Haco and Şivan Perwer. First disciplinary hearings and then their suspension followed. Using Kurdish in public space, in their case in school, had simple and mostly non-political motives. Although it seems to be an act of disobedience, the motives of students were entirely different: "every one of them [from her peer group in high school] has a scar because of Kurdish language culture, but this group was totally, aaa let say posh, like it was not a group of people who would take stones in their hands and fight against police" (sequence 38: 670–672). After all, she and her friends loved these two artists. The school led a foreign language concept and therefore speaking Turkish was prohibited, yet they did not associate this rule with an alleged prohibition of Kurdish. This rule was, in fact, for the improvement of English competency. Hence she describes another motive as "expressing yourself" – that we should consider in the context of the para-military war of the 1990s where people became victims of enforced disap-pearances. This experience of her holds an identity-building-property indeed for her later decisions concerning her activities in the political milieus of her generation and in her professional life. The "scar" she points at emerges as a background construction she acquires with this event in other terms. Until that moment, the scar was jammed in the interactions between Delal and her father -within the context of curricular education, of course. Now, however, with the rage of the system – perhaps, beyond her reckonings – she realised the whereabouts of that scar. Pointing that she discovered the margins of her political track.

After her temporary suspension, her father decided to change Delal's school. She landed then in the high school section of her former secondary school. This school truly fostered her political activist path. Although her father tried to keep her away from possible political motives, for instance, through the isolation, he also enrolled her in such a school. Perhaps, he had no other choice for his suspended daughter. Not only calculated decisions change personal trajectories but lacking alternatives. Delal's childhood memories show simple examples in this sense.

In the same years, Delal found her future goal: university education. She was observing her elder brother and sister having their freedom as university students. This objective connotes her seeking a space free of her father's deci-sions, I argue. However, getting into this space required succeeding on another path with hardships. After she made enough points to enrol in a good university in Istanbul, her father objected to her moving out with the pretext of financial reasons. Her father's actual reason was, however, that she would engage in the movement if she found such freedom. Her mother disclosed it after her father passed away, "afterwards my mother told me he hadn't trusted me, well 'she will move and join the movement' he was afraid of it" (sequence 10: 164). Even if she would have accepted not to move to Istanbul, this prohibition by her father sparked her resistance. Now it was her turn. Delal could choose another university, yet, she relinquished filling the forms and repeated the exam the year after. On her third attempt to pass the university exams, she agreed to study in her hometown, Diyarbakır. Defending her agency has formed the trajectory unquestionably even though she decided to stay in her hometown after all. She suffered from the blockade of her father, yet, she had the chance to explore her selfhood in the puzzle of who-makes-the-decision. What she next reports clarifies what she learned from that fight.

Her father's anxious objection was pointless, nonetheless. She started being active in the students' association of the university in her hometown, which came to be the fundamental experience of her political activism (sequence 40–42).[15] That was a platform for expressing the Kurdish identity. In her first year, the association had the aim to represent the general needs of students (sequence 40), yet that had changed in time into a political struggle (sequence 41; 42). After disagreements with the newly formed authority figures in the student's movement, that Delal and some of her fellows disagreed and were therefore dismissed. Nevertheless, their leaving offered her another path to take: becoming a member of the political party. From her suspension in secondary school to that very moment, she clearly reports on a trajectory and how it advanced in the fact of objective impacts and her oppositional standing related to her biographical experiences.

Her narratives concerning her university years disclose three focal aspects regarding her biography: a) her father's efforts to prevent political activism were impractical; b) Delal's everyday life was dedicated to politics, not to her studies and she gave up the success path she (had) followed to that moment – eventually for a period of time, and it was her decision; and c) she could finally perform her Kurdish identity which is constituted as a political one.[16] After several years, Delal realised that she had spent extensive time doing political work. Thus, she came to decide focusing on her studies right after so that she would graduate with only one additional year, "I was not going to the university so well somehow in my last year … I was using all my off days for the class … so I graduated from university in my last year" (sequence 11: 176–178).

After her university graduation, she first worked as a teacher with a service contract – an hourly paid job, concept merged by the National Ministry of Education to smooth the need in the system pushing enormous precarity, mesmerising people with a fake dream of a future secure teaching position which, in fact, would never come true in the vast majority of cases. She briefly points out what her first job was, yet she gives no further details (sequence 12). In the meantime, she pursued volunteering in some NGOs active in Diyarbakır. Following that, she moved to K. for a master's programme. One of the motives

[15]   This part of her life story resembles the politicisation of Mehmed and Azim. They also were active in their university years.

[16]   Moreover, Delal reveals some details concerning the Kurdish movement's institutionalisation after the call of Öcalan, at the beginning of the 2000s. She mentions, for instance, a hierarchy that does not allow (and reorganise) emotional relationships emerging in its structure, "if there is a relationship then the last call is in the hands of leaders, not last call but they have to know, let's say so, but you as the person in a relationship you are obliged to keep it covered" (sequence 41: 756–758). Nevertheless, she had a boyfriend from the same structure. In these terms, she and her boyfriend had to inform the "superiors". Furthermore, they were not allowed to be active in the same organisation or to reveal their relationship in public, such as at the association events.

was breaking up with her boyfriend, who was also politically active like Delal. Via moving out, she sought time off from this relationship as well as politics. She emphasises that she wanted to distance herself from activism and K. appeared as a considerable option because she had an apolitical friend there, "if she were a political activist, I wouldn't have contacted her because I decided to keep my distance from political people, I broke up with my boyfriend, was in the doldrums" (sequence 64: 1349–1351).

However, these desires sank traumatically. From the beginning on, Delal was threatened by right-extremist groups of the town. Probably for the first time, she faced the real threat targeting her person. It pushed her back to the political milieu, this time in K., she found the student's movement and moved into a protected flat. The threats stopped right after. In the meantime, journalist Hrant Dink was murdered in Istanbul.[17] The assassins were affiliated to the Black Sea region where the town K. is located.

However, what she experienced after Dink's murder made her decide to leave K.. She witnessed how the perpetrator, the murderer, was praised and hailed by the locals in the public space. The perpetrator's beanie was publicly sold, new racist writings and graffiti targeting Kurds and Armenians occupied the walls, and impunity terrorised the everyday life of people like Delal. Racism on the streets rendered her helpless and caused fear and hate. That helplessness led her to the point of leaving her study behind:

they are threatening you with death you can answer then go ahead, kill me, it's really ok but against that wall writing you have nothing to do, it hurts **a lot**, you have nothing to do against that beanie, you just die like you know, this is exactly a reason to leave that city, aaa they force you but you haven't left, you don't leave but they sent you back through this way, well endure this beanie too, you can still resist if they beat you up, but what are you gonna do to that, it's too harsh these beanies too harsh. (sequence 65: 1398–1402)

When she returned to Diyarbakır, she further volunteered in NGOs, and at one point she assumed a position. It took some years to be employed by the NGO2. In both non-governmental and not-for-profit organisations in Diyarbakır, Delal organised events, attended conferences on Kurdish women struggle and conducted projects (sequence 20; 67). Experiences and decision thereupon she made earlier have formed her identity and equably paved her way towards civil

---

[17]   I have deliberately discussed Hrant Dink's murder in term of collective memory in Turkey. Please see Chapter 5 of this study.

society work. We will see next how she had to face a sort of repetition of her experience with racism and right wing terror.

She had to travel to the region of K. again, this time for one of her projects, and together with volunteers. She was already questioning her emotions concerning this city and the personal experiences she made. Yet, Delal wanted to confront her emotions, such as anger and hate. However, what expected her was again racism and willingness for impunity. Local newspapers threatened the project group, and the police were not interested in any extra measures to protect the team (sequence 67). She repeatedly underlines that she wanted to face and deconstruct her "hate", "I don't want to tell my children hateful stories after thirty years, it's a city" (sequence 67: 1420 f). However, her wish not-to-hate was on an impossible track because of the acts and events she faced in town.

Her job in the NGOs and activism involve several parallel components and goals that make it difficult for her to distinguish the political sphere from everyday life.[18] Both flourish from her idealism and enthusiasm. This notion, the overlap of activism and profession, was one of the crucial and ongoing problems that Delal highlights concerning her biography and everyday life.[19]

[18]   Another point she describes and reveals concerning her jobs is that her professional trajectory has changed remarkably since the employment after her graduation. First, she was an hourly paid teacher. When the first NGO employed her, she came out of the total precarity. However, the precarity was not gone since the NGOs work(ed) with project-based budgets. It shows us, perhaps, that she dedicated herself to realising her ideals instead of, for instance, becoming a teacher or a civil servant.

[19]   The first part of Delal's life story includes 14 sequences and lasts 20:40 minutes. In this part, she wraps up her last eight years very fast so that she does not give any detail with what I could expose the path for further information. I had to pose my questions due to our prior talks first and the rough outline she provided, like "since 2,5 years [in Istanbul] ... [coda]" (sequence 14). Back to the point I highlighted at the beginning of this analysis, during the interview she required, perhaps, an orientation or felt uncomfortable with having the full right to decide on the format of her narrative. In further sequences, Delal forces me, in a way, to change the subject. She is so clear when she does not want to stay on the topic anymore: "I don't how deep they should dig for the gas pipeline. Well that's it.." (sequence 57: 1183) or in another case, "It is also why it's so precious ... I don't disturb you with the cigarette, right" (sequence 59: 1220–1222). The first example is a coda in her answer to my question concerning her memories and life in Sur which starts in sequence 50. In these terms, I suppose she looks after a possible finish for her short stories and ends up with an argumentative part about the infrastructure of Sur which allows her to finish her narration. In the other occasion, she deals with my question concerning H.. After two short sequences, she cuts her biographical narrative with a brief argumentative part and underlines her coda with her question about the cigarette smoke. During the interview, both approaches made me change the subject.

Family

There are of course some unclarities in Delal's narrative collage. For instance, the "we" construction that she uses regarding her family emerges as a nuclear family in some stories, but in others it includes ancestors as well. This fogginess remains during the whole talk and comes to be a subject several times.

At the same time, she depicts her father, who died just a few years ago, in very much detail. Her father, who grew up in H. with two older brothers, was raised with a Kurdish consciousness that evolved in time into the Kurdish nationalism. Nevertheless, his nationalism did not emphasise political demands but cultural-political norms. For him, the Kurdish language had the priority to be protected and fostered. Under these terms, he opposed PKK's approach in armed struggle and pointed out that the armed political movement did not give enough attention to the preservation of the culture and language (sequence 60). In this respect, we should not forget that he helped his older brother escape in the 1970s; his older brother was also a Kurdish nationalist, engaged in the same movement and criminally charged because of his published works. This help had several political consequences, and long-lasting impacts on Delal's family, e.g. having a fugitive father and the beginning of fatherless years; experiencing state terror through police raids; material loss – father's business collapsed; protecting mnemonics and materials of gone family members; and having generated a ritual for the family:

> At home, we had such a story of [cousin's] anniversary of death, every year the preparations start a month before, you know what I mean with the preparation, preparation for my father, and my mother, when my father wasn't home, another thing was like, "uncle will come" "uncle will come" but uncle is not there, like, after three years, five years and six and seven years, you know, and after ten years, it was like, my father knew it then, he knew that my uncle won't come, my mother too but we didn't, I was like from my child- childhood on "my uncle will come", on the anniversary day we were sitting at the table and the door was knocked, I ran "yuppi, uncle is there", but it became a kind of game you know and my father didn't tell us anything, like "he won't come, sit down" and so, we were like on this very day uncle should come by. (sigh) (sequence 33: 574–581)

According to Delal, her father had very rigid political opinions that no one could change (sequences 1; 61; 63). In the talk he held to Delal about being Kurdish, we see that he hoped for a sort of regime change, "'we are Kurd- we are Kurds and Kurds are not bad but we don't have a flag, yet look we have a language and we are gonna have an anthem too, our leader's poster will be there too'" (sequence 3: 61 f). His opinion on religion was also unequivocal: He was an atheist raised by a *mala* father, yet married to a believer, Delal's mother. Although her parents reached an agreement right after the marriage that no one would influence children, her father insisted on raising them within his atheist world (sequence 62). She portrays in this sense a politically sectarian person who tried to dominate the majority of terrains in the family life. Based on his rigid political standing, he imposed isolation to his children. They were not allowed to play on the streets because the local children of Diyarbakır were assimilated and spoke Turkish instead of Kurdish (sequence 2; 25; 26). They were also not allowed to have an interest in religion (sequence 62). Visiting members of the maternal family was also prohibited (sequence 28).[20] A similar attitude can be seen in Merve's family biography, and especially at her paternal uncle – he forbade the whole family to have contact with Merve's maternal family because they were Kurds in his view.

As the authority figure at home, Delal's father "spoke out" his opinion concerning marriage as well. He opposed marrying a Turkish person, arguing that a Turk would assimilate his children in marriage even if they were a nice person. When her brother married a Turkish woman, to him "it was like dying" (sequence 16: 262).

From her childhood forwards Delal challenged this authority figure, her father, several times. She dared him by acting in prohibited zones in secret. She even found covers and support, such as when she attended a Quran course thanks to the silent support of her mother (sequence 62). She did not fill the university forms after her wish to move to Istanbul had been opposed by her father (sequence 10); and become active in the movement in the university (sequence 40; 41). The trajectory she followed was collided repeatedly with her father's interests.

Delal does apply this sort of comprehensive portrayal neither to her mother nor to her siblings but slightly to her uncle, who was the closest companion of her father. In this respect, perhaps she wants to understand her father's actions, arguments, and, of course, his person overall. This is why she looks into his biography:

---

[20] Delal's father was a cultural nationalist whose political standing influenced his relationship with his children and the way he raised them. Alongside the cultural and social isolation, in Delal's early childhood he even decided whom to meet from the family and whom not. While for instance her siblings and Delal were allowed to meet their paternal uncle in Diyarbakır, the maternal family in H., like uncles and aunts, were put in prohibited zone. The maternal family represents the conservative and assimilated side in the family biography. Therefore, her father did not tolerate a relation with this side of the family.

after the 1975 earthquake they left H., but my father you know because he read and was active in political field, he knew the structure a bit, but they lost their children they lost their three children at once, aaa one was nine, another seven and another six years old three kids died, so he couldn't go back, go back to H., yet he also didn't know how to protect himself out there, you know since they had done it [protection] successfully in Diyarbakır. (sequence 25: 406–410)

Delal portrays her father with his very characteristics and his actions vis-à-vis her, the family and mainstream society adding both sides of the coin in her narration: decisions affecting her life in both a positive and negative sense. In this respect, she offers an objective picture of her father as much as she can. This sort of unbiased picture helps her to remember, reorganise, and understand the past. Thus, her narrative on her father subsumes a lot of descriptive frameworks that biographical stories and encounters support, but it is not entirely dependent upon Delal's life story. In other words, her narratives concerning her father are not only concentrated on their relationship, but also on his actions before she was born that, yet, impacted her life in-depth, e.g. fugitive life.

Contrary to the latter aspect concerning the father figuration in her storytelling, Delal portrays her mother based on her individual experiences. Although her mother does not emerge in the interview frequently, she occupies the figure of moral authority in the family.[21] Thanks to her silent support, Delal spalled the isolation long ago while corroding its boundaries through her secret actions, such as taking other paths in the district with other children (sequence 53) or further learning the Quran despite her father's objection (sequence 62). Delal also lets us know that her mother is religious (sequence 62) and comes from a strict conservative family and, therefore, Delal and her siblings were not allowed to get in touch with them, "my maternal uncle had a house there [in H.], but of course we didn't visit him, it was forbidden to us, something my father forbade, my mother could but without us" (sequence 58: 1189 f).

Her mother was not able to get a (proper) education. She cannot read and write, which Delal discloses in a comparative and argumentative framework regarding the Kurdish woman since the republican reforms of the education

---

[21] As aforementioned, per contra to her father her mother generally appears as a moral anchor in the family, such as while explaining to children why not to spit on Armenian cemetery (sequence 54). In this respect, she has fostered moral foundations in the family. Her mother appears to be the bonding figure in the family. This moral figure has embodied a safe-haven for the whole family when they wanted to keep something in secret or when they wanted to discover new realms.

system (cf. Bartmann and Kunze 2008). According to her, Kurdish women have been discriminated through such modern policies of the republic:

> my grandma had fertility problems, very onerous like after five miscarriages, you know to one she could give birth. So in this period, he was totally against it, "I won't send my children to Atatürk's schools" aaa, because like you know that too aaa, I aaa I guess it was 2011 I visited south Kurdistan, went to Iraq, to a conference … My grandma had owned a gorgeous library for example, and still, we have some of these books and some in my uncle's place, my other grandmother [maternal side, E.Y.] could also read and write (caught) it means the elders could but for example my mother and her generation don't, my mother for example she cannot like Quran– she cannot, **neither Arabic script** nor Turkish alphabet, long time ago I also researched this topic, not a scientific research it was personally motivated, entirely, I read this and that like Kurdish aaa literature Kurdish art, Kurdish politics, like I looked into where Kurdish woman stands throughout politics literature arts what does she do (sigh), it was stopped with the republic, until the republican era … (sequence 20: 300–316)

With this story on schooling, Delal highlights her interest in the topic of how the Kurdish women were affected in multi-layered terms by certain policies. They were not allowed to attend mixed-gender classes by the father figures at home. Alongside this feature, the amendment of the alphabet change (has) impacted the lives of the Kurdish intellectual milieu in general and Kurdish women in particular. She emphasises a clear cut of the education for women – including her mother – due to the modernist policies of the republic (cf. Kandiyoti 2009).[22] While Delal's grandmother could read and write Kurdish in Arabic script, her mother's generation has faced a blockade. Thus, in her opinion and based on her research, the non-educative tendency upon women arose within the republican era.

Delal has five siblings (sequence 29). Nevertheless, in her interview, they only occupy a pint-sized space. Because of the insufficient information, proper reconstruction of Delal's relation with her siblings is not easy. Hence, three of

---

[22] Deniz Kandiyoti compares the "state-led modernisation" in the (post-)Soviet Central Asia and Afghanistan, considering the role of Islam. The question she asks is which gender politics were conducted in these countries and how such policies (have) echoed in lives. Inspired by Delal's narrative and Kandiyoti's paper, I find a comparative rereading of such political manoeuvres and their effects on certain communities – with their illegalised social qualities – thought-provoking.

her siblings – oldest brother, a sister, and the youngest one – are not a subject at all. Her older sister appears when Delal narrates on her secondary school years. Although she mentions once that her sister was her role model, she does not explain why. Her older sister occurs furthermore in a religion-related conflict in the family. Delal's sister wore headscarf – out of belief, not in order to protest – and that was harshly criticised by her father. It resulted in a year of break off in the father-daughter relation (sequence 63).

Delal rather talks about her one-year older brother, together with whom she grew up and attended secondary school. In those years, they tried to adapt in the Kurdish milieu of Diyarbakır. It, yet, was denied by their father because of the ruling assimilation which was welcomed by Diyarbakır Kurds back then. During these try-outs of adaptation, they mimicked other children and created a new domain for themselves where they actually came out of two isolated living zones: one created by their father and another dominating the urban life, namely the assimilation (sequence 53; 54). This newly achieved domain was offering challenges. When other children cursed (at Christians, for instance), which was not tolerated in Delal's household, she and her brother mimicked it, too, yet only with a bonding agreement "signed" by both. The challenging part started yet right after that moment because it was about ratting on one another to their mother, the moral figure at home, "when you get in a tight spot, you inform your mother, therefore you have to keep your cards up your sleeve (laugh)" (sequence 54: 1121). She highlights that they did not pull their father into this game because they were afraid of his reactions (sequence 52–54). Such habits like cursing an imagined other, like the Christians, was a no-go to him.[23] I suggest that it is essential to underline that even her mimicking was a reaction vis-à-vis her father's decisions whilst advancing her own pathway. In other words, such actions were based on the very idea of disobeying her father's attitudes towards her.

---

[23] Delal mentions briefly that her brother was almost gone when her parents did not interfere before it was too late (sequence 56). After her brother was suspended from school, he started to spend his time in the neighbourhood. She does not disclose the whole story; however, she gives some clues, such as dismissal and drugs. She underscores with this story the situation of the district and her father's opinion on the very neighbourhood. Another detail that she does pinpoint very vaguely is her relationship to her brother in those years. She corrects herself after telling "we saved him" and emphasises that her parents "saved him" (sequence 56). From my point of view, it raises the question if the siblings had a relation with errors, perhaps, because she still was on her success path and her brother was dismissed. However, again, she does not reveal the details in this regard.

6.2.1.2 Elements of Violence in Narration

Delal mentions that being in a family with strong political influences covered everyday conditions, "of course we were poor since my father had been totally engaged with the politics we could not see how poor" (sequence 1: 36). Father's political commitment as a Kurdish nationalist and his authority figure strongly impacted her life. In this sense, he enforced isolation on his children. When she started elementary school, she could not speak Turkish at all, she was not even familiar with the very existence of this language although it was the predominantly used language in centre of Diyarbakır. Hence, it clarifies the power of her father's influence and how it filled the niches of her life; on the other, how she "came along" with that experiencing her own agency.

The language question plays a crucial role in Delal's life. For instance, it produces the temporal norms: before school, she was living without Turkish, and once school started she overplayed Turkish in her life, which represents a success story. In these terms, the language issue draws clear lines between times. For instance, she got a wallop from her teacher because she could not speak Turkish (sequence 2). It caused her father (in her narration, it was not her parents) to seek a like-minded teacher, in another school and to reenrol Delal. In this sense, a violent act reasoned due to language issues marked a new period in her life. Meanwhile, she was experiencing her father's absence. He was a runaway and came back home occasionally; however, his authority was still to be sensed in the family. In other words, the father figure occupied the active family control despite his absence.

Under circumstances of isolation, she figured out a success path that accompanies her life story – until she could not distinguish between political activism and her graduation anymore (sequence 40–42). After the change of school, she has been learning Turkish very fast and adequately; reading Turkish poems on special occasions and events (sequence 6; 7). She spent her years in elementary and secondary schools in such a state. Perhaps, the success story provided her with the justification to pose her father critical questions:

> When I ran to him and cried again 'why are we no Turks', well he didn't beat me but he was **very harsh in words.** I cried then somewhere else, in the night I went to him again he calmed me down, (sigh) I asked him since when we were Kurdish. Well he said "I know seven generations of my ancestors they all were Kurds, we were Kurdish", "aa dad isn't that enough let us be Turkish." (laugh) (sequence 4: 70–75)

Delal explains the conditions under repression, prohibition, and violence impacting Kurdish identities. She reports on – personal and collective – political experiences instead of for instance cultural elements. In correlation with being a Kurdish woman (sequence 20), she points at such socio-cultural notions.

Throughout Places and Objects

Perhaps, focusing on the phenomenon of place would be a proper approach to scrutinise the state of violence in Delal's life. The four places where she (has) lived or to which she feels affiliated are all associated with violence and traumatic memories to some degree. In this respect, the place of living is treated as an apparatus to reconstruct her biography and schemata of her reorganisation of biographical memories. In a chronological looking glass, these are H. – a provincial town of Diyarbakır and where her family came from, Sur – the central district and the historical city centre of Diyarbakır and Delal's childhood environment, K. – the place for the master's studies and the attempt of having distance to politics, and Istanbul – the place of living which she has chosen herself.

In her life story, H. embodies the place to be affiliated to – due to family background. It is a place made through family stories and her childhood memories as well, like the village where Mehmed's family has roots. That begins in her narrative with a traumatic incident – the earthquake – that forced them to seek another place to live: so they moved to Sur, Diyarbakır, where Delal was born. The earthquake connotes victimisation of catastrophe for her parents, prior to her birth.

For Delal, H. had another meaning yet: enjoying the freedom. She was allowed to play on the streets with other children since her father's isolationist codex was not applied to this town. In other words, children of this town were not assimilated. Nevertheless, some restrictions were ruling there too, such as they were not allowed to visit the maternal family as mentioned before (sequence 58). Despite good memories, this very place also contains alongside the earthquake several traumatic memories that shaped her relation to H.:

> I don't miss, I don't do like, of course my beloved H. but, it was nice with these people. Two of my cousins died there, both in natural ways, one not natural but had an accident, another had epilepsy you know... Once when one of my cousins had a seizure, was in the water and got drowned, and was young, you know an aunt I loved a lot, my mother's. aaa relative like sibling, she died in her early ages, it was like that in H. aaa H. like old H. it's gone, but of course like childhood and identity, it is still the place you belong. (sequence 59: 1216–1220)

Additionally, the first clashes she witnessed took place in H.. She also gives brief examples of clashes in downtown Diyarbakır. Yet, she sees these early experiences of violence as the reason for a physical illness from which she suffers still. She mentions that every single time she gets under such stress – correlated to violence, her stomach aches begin (sequence 58) (on embodied memories, please see Tumarkin 2013). It symbolises the violence and victimisation in her realm of freedom – in H.. So, it is pretty much rooted in her childhood.

Furthermore, H. is remembered by Delal because of the violent acts of state forces in the 1990s when heavy arms were used against civilians. The curfew that lasted several days was declared in the downtown of the provincial town, and civilians were forcibly moved. The pretext used by the contemporary government was that PKK had killed a Turkish Army commander.

She narrates the situation at home during the raids in H., using powerful symbolic elements. Once when she came back home from school, she saw that everyone in her family was crying. Revealing the reason of why they were crying took some time. When her brother told her that "H. was burned down", her eyes were filled with tears remembering about "mulberry tree" and "castles" she built there with other children. Delal and her brother started to ask each other what would have happened to all these (sequence 47). They, in fact, tried to understand what would happen with their memories when the reality is demolished. Were these shattered too just like H.? They felt that they were being harassed and started to think about missing objects. In this sense, another question was perhaps: was also their freedom taken from their hands since H. was the only place where they had been free of isolation? Here, we have to keep in mind that Delal and her brother were too young at time of this incident to realise its impacts on their life-world. Still, via remembering and reconstructing what they experienced and with what they associate the place they resisted against the erasure of even memories.

Beyond that, they asked themselves why PKK did not intervene (sequence 48). They were familiar with PKK when it came to downtown H. to recruit. Moreover, regarding the brutal curfew, she could not forget the "green telephone" that symbolised the first-ever contact with the place under state terror and even with a perpetrator (about the relation of place and material in narrating, please see Woolfson 2013). Her father called his relatives repeatedly using the (green) telephone. At the end, the call was answered by a soldier who swore and told uncanny stories, causing disturbance. The green telephone, as a powerful symbol, triggers the following biographical memory:

And I can't forget the thing, we had a green telephone. Aaa H. was very exceptional for us, I mean for the family … And like my father had the telephone in his hand trying to reach them but their telephone was off, and then he reached, my father said, aaa Kurdish, this, in Turkish "you motherfucker you bastard and so", after like who answered my uncle's phone was a soldier, told "they are now in the barn we gonna rape everyone" to my father, (sigh) well it happened truly, not raped but they were in the barn like all of them, so, for three days five days we haven't heard anything … Really in this this this house that green phone and that moment I can't forget it, like I came back home in the evening and that scene in that flat I can't forget, that scene in a big room, can't forget that green phone, my father had in his hand and was trying to call them and everybody crying and my brother like "they burned H.". (sequence 46: 919–938; sequence 48: 972–975)

Alongside triggering the story, the "green telephone" that captures the whole string of narration symbolises a traumatic event, the perpetration and victimisation, descending a pleasant, for children enjoyable place into darkness. When H. is the topic, she could not stop herself associating that very place with violence.

Delal points out that families from H. arrived in Diyarbakır some days later and the people from downtown hosted them for approximately half a year until they could return. She even emphasises **not one person stayed,** nobody that we know stayed in Diyarbakır" (sequence 47: 959). She, perhaps, wanted to underscore that point in order to stress the strong connection of the people from H. to their land, and concomitant her and her family bond as well.[24]

Concerning the family background and place, Delal tells stories about her grandfather who rejected as a *mala* the centralisation of the education system in the early republican era, in the 1920s or 1930s. He did not allow his children to attend these schools, "in this period he [grandpa] was totally against it, 'I won't send my children to Atatürk's schools'" (sequence 20: 301). He organised an uprising and clashes followed. The family connection to H. has such historical and political roots as well.

She mentions that she did not visit the town for some years. The losses she had and the indirect experience of state terror in H. pushed her to keep her distance, I argue, even if she admits several times that H. has a special meaning to her. In this manner, she also uses a moment of silence and an unexpected

---

[24]   While they hosted families, the flat had become of course more crowded than ever. Although she felt discontent with this very fact earlier – six siblings and two parents living under the same roof, she embraced her relatives. She and her siblings asked, for instance, what the displaced children from H. experienced during the curfew and clashes even though they were warned by their parents not to talk about it. Nevertheless, it had a sort of therapy effect for children, as Delal figured out later: "I visit H., met these friends, they told us well 'it was totally good, how good that you asked us, that we told you, that we did not cage it in'" (sequence 48: line 968 f).

coda forcing me to change the subject, after she spoke about H. very briefly on another occasion, "H. it's gone, but of course like childhood and identity, it is still the place you belong, It is also why it's so precious... I don't disturb you with the cigarette, right" (sequence 59: 1220–1222).

Another influential place playing a role in her life story is Sur, the historic downtown of Diyarbakır. A clear distinction to other parts of the city remains in her life story: "... I still dream of Sur, only of Sur, where I belong is Sur, not any other flat of my mother" (sequence 43: 870 f). Delal discards eventually the flats in which her mother lived after her father died and recognises those at most that were memorised with her father.

Even if Sur embodied in her early childhood a physical and mental chaos – due to the crowdedness at home, changing flats repeatedly because of the police raids, the fatherless times and Delal as child seeking her father, it also brings about positive childhood memories like discovering different corners and enjoying freedom that was achieved through bypassing the isolation.[25] So, it was on the one hand about exploring the environment and on the other possible identity markers, like the act of bypassing. The reason for the isolation, as she points out, was to protect her from assimilation and violence, i.e. shielding her away from the wrong paths of downtown. In other words, the reason for isolation was the neighbourhood itself.

Sur is the place to live that she would pick first if it were possible – under the same conditions as in Istanbul, I suppose, for instance, with the job and so on. She experienced the attitudes of people of Sur earlier first from a political family perspective and then from a personal one based on her politicisation. She never left the district until she moved to K. for her master's studies (sequence 64). These almost 25 years involve various experiences of violence, from witnessed clashes to individually experienced curfews and raids. It is significant to remember that when we met for our interview, the very same neighbourhood was suffering under clashes and the curfew that was declared in Autumn 2015. The reports published by non-governmental organisations and committees show that a large proportion of the district was destroyed entirely or partially, and tens of thousands of people became displaced due to "collateral consequences" (Amnesty International 2016). In these terms, Sur was sort of living in her memories just like H.. Delal was emotionally affected by the clashes taking place in Sur and the news about the destroyed parts of the town where she had lived and that she had loved for many years. It influenced not

---

[25]   Delal mentions that Sur inhabitants, and Diyarbakır, in general, were assimilated Kurds back then – up to the arrival of the persons who were displaced because of the war in the 1990s from various towns and rural areas (sequence 1; 8).

only the conversation with her friends but also her dreams. She dreamed of Sur in its old "chaotic" shape, just like in her childhood. That quasi nostalgia accompanies her still.

She again uses strong symbolism in order to point at the struggles and particular events (A. Assmann 2010). They are deeply embedded and entangled in her biography, i.e. she does not borrow symbolisms from collective references, even if hers match with them. Her memories concerning violence in Sur host first of all the curfews and the times when she and her family were not allowed to leave their home. During the curfews and the state of emergency in the 1990s, she witnessed how soldiers beat her uncle:

> we couldn't get out of the house for days, like that, you know curfews, my aunts or my uncles house was so outside of Sur, they used to come to the gates of Sur, only to the corner and we see them getting beaten, the cops beating them they try to get in, they say our families are hungry we have to bring food, they beat them, we watch, they can't get in you are really hungry so to speak there remains nothing at home, there is the curfew that lasts for days. They continuously 'rake' the streets with machine-gun fire. (sequence 45: 896–900)

Her family had a so-called safe room that had no windows. The fact that everyone had a safe room, how she reveals, tells a lot concerning the circumstances. During the clashes and curfew, the whole family had to sleep in that very room so that no one would be harmed by bullets shot. In her biography, the safe room implies something more:

> In our building many people died or got wounded … therefore we were always in the safe room where you know the bullet couldn't hit … It was a summer I fell asleep in the living room, the large room and they forgot me there. Then a clash erupted, and I was like I woke up and walked, went to the windows, I was watching, they killed that boy there, that boy who lived upstairs, whom I thought I was in love with they killed him there I saw it openly a white Taurus car came, it hit him and went, then he was a – that flat was armed, so to say they were aiming at that floor from below, so think about it the fourth floor, we were at the third floor he the fourth floor. (sequence 45: 906–912)

Delal remembers that she was left alone or forgotten by her family. At midnight she woke up and witnessed that a white car (1990s Renault model, the so-called Taurus car has become the symbol of paramilitary violence) hit and killed the man living upstairs. It ignited clashes between the PKK cell upstairs and state forces – it is not clear in the narration if it was the police or paramilitaries (Üngör 2020).[26] The clashes ended with the death of the cell members living upstairs. Another point that both of these symbols – safe room and "Taurus car" – reveal is that the perpetrator did not have a uniform anymore, in comparison to H.. In her town of freedom, the violence organised by the army adopted the sign of the state: the uniform. The clashes that took place in Diyarbakır were in another form, in the form of brutal paramilitary activities. Furthermore, the victimisers were very close to her home, just like at the police raids. Similar to Delal, Zal points out a change of perpetrator in temporal terms. Furthermore, for instance, Mamoş as a former guerrilla experienced different perpetrator figures, not just in the soldier uniform but also members of paramilitary groups or even medical doctors (please see the Chapter 7).

As highlighted before, her purpose in moving to K. possessed a precise distance to Diyarbakır. The city meant to her back then a long-lasting yet finished relationship with her ex-boyfriend; an active political world; and, perhaps, the restrictions by her father that, for instance, stopped her from moving to Istanbul for the university some years ago. This is why she sought another city than Diyarbakır for her master's degree, where she had only one friend who was not interested in politics. However, frequent threats made her contact the students' movement of the city in order to protect herself.

After spending winter break in Diyarbakır, she came back to K., with the hope that she would not have to face further problems. Nevertheless, the reality was the opposite:

> … Well it was terrible as we came back you know there were these stands everywhere which sold the white beanies everybody wearing white beanies, (sigh) that was so painful.. Nobody was like hey he is one of my people and what he had done, is embarrassing nobody on the contrary, I can't forget these things with the white beanies… (sigh) … I was trying to take a picture they ran after- but of course I did it. Besides there were lots of other wall writings like Kurds Armenians… Fucks and bastards. (sequence 64: line 1381–1384; sequence 65: 1388 f)

It came to be clarified that she would not be allowed to graduate from the programme because her professors would block it. She then decided to return to Diyarbakır. The time she spent in K. was less than a year. However, it marked such a violent period in her life story that she could not forget. For the first

---

[26]   The white "Taurus" car is a widely known phenomenon that symbolises the paramilitary terror during the war in the 1990s.

time, she was victimised personally because of her identity. Furthermore, for the first time, she was not at gunpoint together with her affiliated group but severely as an individual, as Delal.

After leaving K., she spent some years in Diyarbakır working for different NGOs, until she found the position in Istanbul that she still has. When she moved to Istanbul, she first shared flats with some colleagues in X. – a district of Istanbul, thereafter she found the flat where we met. For the first time in her life, a neighbourhood corresponds to her needs, like being away from the chaos and enjoying safety. After spending such a time in K., she could not imagine living in an environment inhabited by Turkish nationalist groups. She would also not live in a predominantly Kurdish district:

> let's put Kurdish question aside, perhaps it would be solved or not, who knows, but in everyday life. Aaa I would not prefer to live with Kurds together so much. Because, you know, Kurds have this conservative side, conservative Muslim Kurds, and deliberately the socio- aaa economic state is determinative there, you said W., E. or T., when the economic conditions are bad then the conservative notions raise too. (sequence 74: 1601–1604)

This was the reason why she sought living in this very district because Christians and Jews predominantly inhabit its very space. Another informant of mine, Merve, found such a freedom (or its feeling) first abroad when she started to study for her master's degree.

Nevertheless, Delal's experiences shortly before the election of November 2015, after AKP lost the majority in parliament in the June election same year and reignited the war in Kurdistan, appear contradictive to her expectations. Once, when she was home during the brutal operations of the Turkish armed forces in Kurdistan, she heard crowds chanting "X will be grave to Armenians, Cizre [a Kurdish town, which has been demolished during these clashes] to Kurds" (sequence 69: line 1483). At this point, she distinguishes the parts of the district and argues where such rallies would take place. She defends the district, but deep down there is this question or fear of losing X too, just like H. faded away in her memories, and her beloved Sur facing urban destruction contemporarily. Although she escaped violence in K. and survived the violent acts in Sur, it followed her to Istanbul, to the life she built all by herself. The trajectory of suffering (Riemann and Schütze 1991) is to be identified at every single place that Delal reported on. She formed her own path leading her to a life in Istanbul in the face of threads.

Delal embraces symbolic gestures at different moments. These symbolisms represent not just the acts that she encountered but the places, neighbourhoods and towns as well. In several cases, she uses symbolisms employing objects, materials, and even places, such as H. embodying space without isolation and then devastation; or green telephone contextualising a particular time and violence. A symbol contains different layers from her biography and make the traumatic subject – in fact, the social setting – easy to describe (cf. Bar-On 1999).

How Delal discusses the past

Mostly Delal looks into her biography to unearth some subjects, as in the case of the state terror in the 1990s when she recounts her own experiences (sequence 27). In such instances, she does not embrace collective references or employ analogies and anachronisms, but focuses on her background.

In this regard, I want to look into another symbolic element Delal pinpoints: the balcony (sequence 49; 55). It emerges in her dreams, descriptions, and arguments. Her dream on Sur in which she takes a walk with her friend in the narrow streets of the district ends at the balcony of her mother's place watching the city walls:

> ... I said OK the balcony of my mother's place looks at, you know, the ancient city walls, we were watching the city walls, so but how happy I woke up, such a hope I had (ironic laugh), it makes so much, like it devastates me, all of them are devastating but there in Sur there is something personal. (sequence 49: 1000–1003)

While the clashes took place and these affected Sur brutally, Delal had this dream that gave her hope. However, she encounters it with an ironic laugh. It shows, I suppose, that she sees the situation as hopeless. With her twisted reaction, Delal underscores that she should accept the situation, but something prevents her from coming to that conclusion.

Her first visit to the city walls took place when she was a secondary school student, together with her class, guided by an author from Diyarbakır (sequence 55). She was astonished. At this point, she associates the city walls again with the balcony: "I was talking to my sister once, like 'it is a thing [city walls] you see from your balcony, why didn't we climb up there?'" (sequence 55: 1146 f). Looking from a balcony implies watching the happenings, crowds, and objects from a certain distance, just like living in Istanbul, having a physical distance to the violence in Sur. In these terms, she associates the city walls – the symbol of Sur – with her home or its boundaries, and the balcony with her contemporary physical distance to the socio-political conditions back home. She adds that the ongoing state violence in Sur makes her feel "like a burglar broke into my house" (sequence 49: 1005 f). The place speaks through Delal's memories.

In this sense, the balcony is a composition incorporating several layers for her narrative: experiences, opinions, and arguments. It contains (or stresses) her distance and, at the same time, points out her close relation. She should watch but could intervene the happenings. The balcony leads, perhaps, to brightness or possible visions of the future (cf. Brescó de Luna 2017) yet due to its mandatory placement it cages her in the present reality and to view what happens.[27]

Collective References

Delal does not reproduce circulated stories and employ such templates in a vast quantity. Once, she picks from the family biography a story that resembles such a concept. It constitutes the coda segment of her life story. Her maternal ancestors in H. had saved from genocidal violence an Armenian child who grew up then as an Islamised member of the family (sequence 80). The children and grandchildren stayed in contact with the Armenian members of the family. One of the grandchildren then converted back to Christianity.

Nevertheless, her maternal family did not welcome this news. She compares the reaction of the families – the maternal side and her nuclear family – at this juncture. Her parents were happy for the converted family member, while the maternal side was critical about it:

> Well I, or my dad were happy for him, in our small family it was never seen as a problem, on the opposite, we were happy for him but in my mother's family, well it was regarded as an issue, a burning issue, and you know he is a relative from the maternal side, so it was a problem. It still is. Well no one says anything of course, but for them, that question how come, after being such a good Muslim, and so on. His father was a good Muslim too, how come. You know ... (sequence 81: 1720–1725)

I suggest that Delal reemploys the sort of framework which her father had outlined and applied before when he forbade Delal and her siblings to visit the maternal side: because they are conservative. She adds that the Islamised

---

[27] Beyond that, my interpretation of the state of violence in Turkey and especially in Kurdistan, including my project's theme, motivated her to tell her experiences. She found in my approach a mutual understanding. Nevertheless, she also silences some elements concerning her family biography and life story, such as some details from K. that she told me earlier, but did not convey when the recorder went on. This act of muting also applies to some particular features concerning her oldest uncle. I suggest, the reason is she wants to protect people. That she puts her cell phone away when she talks about some aspects – because these might be used as pretexts – leads me to this assumption as well.

family members were called Armenians when it was about positively pinpointing their skills, "their Armenian roots were referred to, not in negative way, but as a positive aspect, not as discrimination. In positive ways mostly" (sequence 80: 1701 f). This label, she emphasises, was not used pejoratively. Nevertheless, being Armenian remained a quasi-birthmark.

Beyond the fact that it is a first-hand experienced family story, it matches some foundations of collective references, such as saving an Armenian child – without questioning the purpose; and exposing roots and conversion (cf. Altınay and Çetin 2009). Moreover, we see a comparative schema concerning the reactions of the family side – the maternal vis-à-vis nuclear family. Delal does face the reaction of the family, yet she does not look into the possible goals of adoption and conversion back in the years following the extermination campaigns (cf. Akçam 2014).

Naming "Others"

Delal mentions briefly that the assimilated Kurds were collaborating with the governmental forces in her childhood and assumes that they probably also collaborated with the Turkish State during the extermination campaigns:

> I don't know how Diyarbakır was in the times of the genocide, 1915 and so, you have to take a look into it but aaa when the Kurds did the genocide, the ones in Diyarbakır it means they had a collaboration with the state. And of course if you have a good relation with the state then you would hang the Turkish flag too. (sequence 27: 442–444)

She builds her argument regarding the genocidal perpetration through her own experiences. Hence, she comes to the point of anachronism. She talks about collaboration but only under a contextualisation of assimilated or corrupt Kurds. This inevitably forms a "we" contrary to the illustrated "other" in the own group. In this sense, her narrative on "other Kurds" resembles the portrayal of perpetrators by Mehmed, as well as by other four informants (please see the next chapter). I suggest, Delal's victimiser draft blossoms in some way from the circulated story forms. In addition to that, in the story with her maternal family's reaction to conversion, the maternal side occurs as "the other." Just a reminder, according to her father that side of the family also was assimilated. As a footnote, her comment attempts to give reasons for mass political violence through reconstructing the long-gone setting with an anachronistic reading, and arresting the extermination in the Turkish flag, i.e. nationalism (cf. Türkyılmaz 2011, and for an enquiry about the historiographical readings focusing on nationalism, please see the historical chapter of this present study).

Historical Analogy and Anachronism

In addition to the anachronism underscored above, Delal focuses on women's stories from Kurdistan and on the question of how Kurdish women's lives were deteriorated by the reforms introduced as a part of the Turkish republican modernisation. She tells this story in a part that is constructed on a mixture-premise of argumentation and biographical narration (cf. Bartmann and Kunze 2008). In these terms, she compares the systems of Kurdish Mahabad Republic and the Kurdish political movement in Turkey. It becomes highlighted that the co-chair concept, which the Kurdish rooted left-wing political party HDP in Turkey operates, was performed first in the Mahabad Republic in 1946 (sequence 20). She bridges the past through such idea(l)s to today's actors. Hence, a political tradition flourishes in her narrative. In this manner, she employs an analogy not in a negative sense (Zerubavel 2003) but in a positive concept like emancipation.

However, most of her comparisons are not anachronistic and simplistic since she binds them to her own biographical experiences that she made in her political and professional trajectory. For instance, another informant of mine, Merve, also remains within her biography (or family biography) when she narrates such times. Concepts from public discourse do not dominate Delal's act of storytelling. Yet, the (political) continuity such anecdotes imply produces the antagonist mirror image. In other words, when there is a struggle in continuum, then there should be an opponent as well. It is the injustice in Kurdistan.

Delal's self in her narration

In addition to the idea of having the "self" as the focal point of narrative (Bruner 2004; Ochs and Capps 1996; cf. Andrews et al. 2002), traumatic experiences establish the foundation of Delal's biographical memory as we can see in stories on H., Sur, the father figure and her family. At this juncture, I want to focus on her memories of her family.

Her uncle's biography and her father's involvement would underline the start of different harrowing experiences even if Delal was not born yet. It implies fatherless times, police raids, state repression targeting the family and her waiting for her uncle years and years. In the early 1970s, her cousin (her uncle's son) was kidnapped and murdered in a politically motivated assassination. In the meantime, her uncle was already under threat because of his publications (sequence 30; 31). After her uncle was arrested, her father intervenes and helps her uncle. He hides him underground and arranges the way out of the country together with his family (sequence 30; 32). Hence, her uncle could not attend the funeral of his son (sequence 32); her father also became a fugitive and could not even be at Delal's birth. Their home was then raided several times.

> my mother and father they had close friends, of course, they accompany her, they came by and moved the furniture, in hiding they moved our flat, after two mo- when our flat got recognised, then in the next two months the other flat, like that.. after years. After the lawsuit dropped, actually it wasn't dropped after it became calm, of course first the coup and so, for example at my birth my father was a fugitive. (sequence 32: 559–562)

When Delal was born, she was given to another woman to be cared because her mother was hospitalised due to an illness. It took two years before her mother could get Delal back. Later, every two months, her parents, actually her mother, had to move because of police raids. While they were repeatedly moving, her mother had kept and protected materials that once belonged to the murdered cousin and Delal's uncle who was on the run. These became the first objects to evacuate:

> his son's [her cousin] pen, last watch, you know his pen that he used everything that was at his table, at his table, paper notebook rubber and so on lots of things, and my mother kept them, can you imagine for so many years she was struggling to keep them while, while police raids occurred, these were the first things to rescue, like police surrounded our home, that chest was brought to neighbours immediately … you grow up in such a thing you hate it. (sequence 36: 631–635)

On the one hand, these items came to be mnemonics to hold the family memories, opposing the erasure by the oppressive regime, yet on the other, these were reminders of the hated raids. Most importantly, her father was not there when she needed him. I argue, this is why she treated topics concerning the identity question – being Kurdish vis-à-vis becoming Turkish – since she deeply struggled with such issues, and she somehow knew it was a key to keep her parents' attention which was concentrated on the items.

In addition, her uncle has become a role model for Delal; his image has influenced her and raised her interest in literature. This image of the uncle had compounded and strengthened the family back then. Her uncle promised to come back on his son's anniversary, yet could not fulfil his promise. However, Delal's parents initiated the tradition out of this promise to wait for the uncle on that specific day every year and continued to perform it, even when they realised that he would not come back (sequence 33).

The strong uncle image was not only based on this tradition but also the stories told by Delal's father and the way in which he described the uncle with fascination. This tragic memory, having lost someone because of his exile, piggybacked such an influential figure. Delal was the receiver of all the traumatic actions, from the police raid to "waiting for the uncle." She locates herself in these stories as the one who was not cared for by her father as well as by her mother. Perhaps she, therefore, overcompensated the demands with being the best in her environment. In other words, this background construction of her identity resulted in her working so hard that she would then ask for assimilation.

Her political socialisation is another subject of her life that has maintained its importance until today. It was influenced, first of all, by her father in a contra-productive way. He forbade, for instance, learning Quran and also criticised her sympathies for PKK. However, Delal pursued and even joined the political movement(s). Another indicator for her political activities was the state of violence. Even if she wanted to get out of the realm of politics, she was pushed again into it through violent events, like in K.. Again and again, her decisions to change the tracks of the trajectory was blocked by other parties.

Together with her brother, she mimicked other children. After a while, she confronted her own family story – that they have Armenian relatives (sequence 54). That she refused Easter bread from the Christians living around the church was a part of the days of discovering the district like Tom Sawyer:

> ... they used to give us sweet yeast bread. Aaa but there is such a problem, we had no issue of religion at all at home, but the religion was a big question outside, in our school on the streets, everywhere that was prevalent, so we were also influenced, therefore the kids used to do, the kids used to not to eat the bread they gave us, they used to throw it away, so did we naturally too, but of course outside, not there ... (sequence 53: 1075–1080)

Hence, the children kept "the other" awake and active. In her narrative, she reveals that rejecting the bread was a quasi-religiously motivated act. Even if religion was not a topic at home, it was dominant in the outside world. She was commuting through mimicking.

Contested Memories

Wartime circumstances "clarify" the sides by making people accept new norm systems. Delal refused that very setting and joined the political groups that was organised in her university. Her participation alone provides memories contesting, on the one hand, governmental stories concerning the Kurdish political thought. She reveals the niches that overcome such propagated emblems concerning the movement. On the other, her family stories discomfort the alleged homogeneous picture regarding Kurds.

Delal's narrative shows us the environment of Diyarbakır in the early 1990s. According to Delal, the majority of the locals took the side of the government. This picture has indeed changed due to the (enforced) migration from the rural side and political endeavours of various parties. In such fluid settings, Delal's memories that evolved in time and through interaction contradict the state proposed picture of war, and the movement proposed portrayal of Kurdish (politicised) society. Yet, how the violence was performed (and by whom) maintains its clarity in her memories. Her biographical narrative contests various collective and common references concerning the Kurdish past in Turkey. Blossomed through her agency at every single step on her political trajectory, her identity has formed over the course of incidents and family depended experiences – in which she played active roles. The mechanisms considered here, from third party threads targeting the family and place called home or even targeting herself to her power of decision-making on facing family past in the very context of this land, contests the structures and widely acknowledged or even propagated narratives. The selfhood of Delal discloses the contestation.

6.3 Zal

Zal is a lawyer in his 30s, coming from a provincial town of a neighbouring province of Van. When I arrived at his office, he first asked me some questions about the research project and then some personal questions, for example, about life in Germany. Because he had another appointment, we had to call off our interview after approximately 70 minutes but agreed to meet again. His bureau had a warm atmosphere for a lawyer's office, without shelves full of folders, documents, and trial records which generally belong to such working places. Instead, he had some family photos and pictures from his travels.

6.3.1 Analytical Abstraction

6.3.1.1 Biographical Synopsis

Born under the junta regime of the 1980s in the small provincial town T. south of Van,[28] Zal attended the school in his hometown and had not left there until

---

[28]   The town where Zal was born is not the same where Mehmed grew up, although both are anonymised with T.

he moved out for his university studies. He graduated from law school in the occupied side of Cyprus during the period of dialogue and then moved to Van in the mid-2000s to practice his profession (sequence 34). On the one hand, he views Cyprus as an expansion of Turkey due to the militarised zones and the occupation, yet on the other, the island provided him with a certain freedom, an impartial position concerning the conflict there – since it is not his conflict, not the conflict in Kurdistan; and with distance from the ongoing turmoil in Kurdish regions. As a footnote, the impacts of this time is also to be noticed in his analytical positioning concerning the younger generations' attitude vis-à-vis conflict in Turkey. Even if he attributes his standing – open to discussion, critical to extreme mindsets which he sees in today's youth – to his upbringing and to his generation's ideas, it is rather nourished by the time away from the region, and of course the everyday political violence, I suggest.

His retired father and mother still live in his hometown. Since there is no chance to work as a lawyer in T. and since he sought to stay close to his parents, Van became an option. He is married and a father of one. Nevertheless, Zal does not give any further information about his family. He reveals that he has five siblings, two of whom are teachers, (just) like their father (sequence 37). One of his brothers lived in a small town close to T. until the Turkish military operations severely damaged the place during the curfews. Then he moved to T. as well.

Zal grew up witnessing the armed conflict of the 1990s. The scenes of violence occupy his personal memory in massive amounts, like the Turkish military howitzer's bombing that he and his friends watched from the rooftop (sequence 5), or detained friends and neighbours (sequence 3). He also was personally affected by the oppressive regime, in institutional and individual terms. He grew up under the state of emergency, as whole generations had to, and since then has been visiting prisoners he knew from his childhood – nowadays with a professional identity. His profession enabled him having straight contact with different parties of the conflict (sequence 22). His (professional) trajectory thus rests upon his childhood experiences. Growing up under circumstances of war, at times watching from a certain distance and at times living in the midst of it, (has) affected him particularly. The impacts can be marked in his decision to move to Van, reforming his contact with the prisoners in professional terms, or even his choice to study law in Cyprus – in being away from his own conflict. On the one hand, he can support people in need with his professional identity; this is why he became a lawyer, not in the line of a careerist ideal. He has already been a part of the conflict – or made of it – so what other option could he have had, on the other hand, when he sought a corresponding distance. Now, he knows what would surprise him and what not; and it is not a professional cynicism until he made generational experiences.

He throws a glance in the history and sees a linearity in time which is undeniable to him. Violence blurs the time elapse so that the notion of continuity occurs framing his narrative. Nonetheless, there are some time markers in his narrative, such as his recollections on the collapse of the Soviet Union (sequence 2) or the so-called dialogue period in Cyprus. However, the conflict in Kurdistan crosses these with its dominant temporal dimensions, building a comprehensive social time (Sorokin and Merton 1937). These markers provide comparative orientation points in social time. Additionally, his observations and experiences in Cyprus concerning the unfinished longitude political problems on the island made him aware of the basis of both conflicts. It is more about the regime of Turkey than about Kurds and peoples of Cyprus. So, the underlying structure of this temporal understanding consists of experiences with the oppressive regime. It clarifies him how to interpret what he went through and how he has positioned himself in various occasions based on his selfhood.

Alongside violence in the region, nature occupies a significant part of Zal's life story. He renders scenes of nature surrounding his hometown and integrates them in his narrative construction. Yet, even though such stories vary, he basically cannot distinguish violence from landscape (sequence 5; 25). Nature also means the destruction and abnormal change due to the clashes and forced migration from villages into the provincial towns (sequence 9). Hassanpour, Sheyholislami, and Skutnabb-Kangas describe these times as follows: "During these armed conflicts, Turkey destroyed no less than 1300 villages and hamlets ... The rural population moved into cities in Turkey and was transferred into concentration camps on major highways. These 'forced urbanization' projects have diminished the rural bases of the language, and changed the dialect mosaic, a situation that remains to be studied" (2012, 12). Zal furthermore points out the irreversible consequences of this "forced urbanization" in case of Van based on his everyday experiences.

One of the main issues he treats in his life story is the generational disputes (cf. Erikson 1978). The continuing violence impacts the generational setting(s) and reshapes their interactions. It deprives people of his age of the chance to teach and accompany the next generations on their path. The consequence of violence's blurring effect is, on the one hand, the enhanced youth violence or the tendency among youngsters to engage in political violence; and, on the other, the erasure of the role of adults that could exist under stabilised conditions. It disturbs him a lot as a father, influencing his biographical project, social contacts, and his family relations enormously. Perhaps, such experiences have not the effect of the first shock anymore, yet, it makes him busy. Bridging to the discussion on his trajectory and identity, the essential distance he built up is now questioned by incidences of generational disputes.

6.3.1.2 Elements of Violence in Narration

Zal's narrative treats the subject violence questioning two vital aspects: time and generation. He deducts an argument of continuity of violence considering these two aspects. In this regard, he utilises contrasting narrative constructions, such as the mind-blowing nature to watch – but just to watch, not to enjoy it, vis-à-vis canons firing in the very same scene, "we climbed up there [the rooftop] and watched the clashes out there. Watched and had our tea, so that, there was a scene" (sequence 5: 32 f).

In a similar way, he puts an anecdote forward concerning his school years. At the same time that Zal and his fellows had off from school because of a military base visit under the supervision of their national security teacher (a class which is established by the 1980 junta regime and which still is taught by military personnel *in situ*) – coded as fun in view of teenager students, the very fact of practising with guns that had been far away earlier came into their lives, "then the target practice … of course back then we were kids, you know we need some fun, and we coded it as fun" (sequence 6: 52 f). Zal reports from a situation where the pupils had become a target group to be thought of "patriotism, love for fatherland and its military". Yet, they and their relatives also were a target group to be stopped by the same security personnel through repressive actions like gun violence, arrests, and imprisonment. Thus, we encounter a colonial position into which they were forced. We can call these cycles of examples that compete with each other, yet complement each other as well, the *contrasting juxtaposition*. Such notions are significant elements for comparisons that he employs every now and then. So, he reconstructs his life story. His narrative requires somehow such antagonistic, yet experience-based templates to build itself up further, "[p]ersonal narrative simultaneously is born out of experience and gives shape to experience. In this sense, narrative and self are inseparable" (Ochs and Capps 1996, 20). Zal applies this narrative technique, such juxtapositions, in addressing violence. That technique is not just about his way of narrating the past but for coming to terms with the notions that formed his trajectory. Finding ways to approach those notions is the key issue here. His professional identity requires that very ability, or better said, he had to practice that skill.

Starting with the time issue Zal problematises, it subsumes the following points: justice system, transition of social structure, eradication of conventional production processes, and of course nature. All of these are related to changed forms of violence and destruction, yet reconstructing a certain continuum. In order to point at that continuity, he utilises both abstractions and palpable phenomena, for instance, when he describes the distorted social participation in production. Furthermore, the composition of the continuity draws nourishment from changes that locate in Zal's story building. And the Armenian Genocide is an object to exemplify that continuity or, better said, to predate it since the social landscape of the region changed massively due to the extermination. Thus, his life story remains as a part of this continuing history. This also is why he excavates the notion of linear time that collides with (or becomes a part of) the Kurdish social time.

Although the generational issue appears to be the other facet of time and continuity question, in Zal's perspective it is based on an indispensable "change" in society: the inevitable incompetence of adults (due to the violence) in taking the role to influence, teach, and lead the youth. This discrepancy is followed by increased violence among young people. Zal distinguishes this new form of youth violence from the one in former generations. He points out an increasing ethnic resentment instead of ideological justifications, as it was the case in his generation. According to Zal, the adults' non-effective role has become a feature in the Kurdish society, raising the stagnation question (Erikson 1978, 240 f). Comparing his storytelling from an adult perspective with a narrative of a young member of the society would provide us with another viewpoint, I assume. For instance, in the interview with Azim, there is no clue for any role-modelling of an older member from his family or environment. His narrative sort of matches with Zal's descriptions of the social settings (for a detailed discussion, please see Chapter 7).

As mentioned, Zal shapes his narrative framework on two fundamental assumptions: time and generation (which I discuss in details in the next subchapters and Chapter 7 in comparison to other informants). These two underlined phenomena work like magnets in the structure of his story dragging personal experiences, elements from collective memory, and political understanding – in individual as well as collective ways, and drafting, i.e. reconstructing, his life story (Bruner 2004; Zittoun 2017). Since his biographical project comprises the past, present, and of course the trajectory for the future (Brescó de Luna 2017; de Saint-Laurent 2017), his biographical narrative plays with those temporalities as well (Brockmeier 2015). However, it displays a somewhat fragmented story due to the continuity of violence. It is another question whether or not the continuity exists. But in his perception and interpretation of happenings, that continuum occurs as a vital part of life in Kurdistan. Therefore, it inevitably impacts the fashion of his narrative, as it has impacted his biographical project immensely.

How Zal narrates

Some features are fundamental for Zal telling his life story, like the above-mentioned comparative structures, contrasting juxtapositions, highlighting extremes. The fragmented form of his narration is based on the violence he (has) experienced. Descriptions and explanations or what he argues feed the fragmented fashion further. Hence the arguments connote that he has an issue to talk about and that he thought in-depth. Perhaps, these arguments provide an orientation for his talk as well (cf. Bartmann and Kunze 2008; Schütze 2008b). In his main biographical narrative, Zal generally provides me with stories from his childhood sketching the conditions he had gone through. He finds himself in his narration, so to speak; structures the form of storytelling he seeks; and clarifies thematic cores such as generational issues (that I treat in-depth under the next subchapter about violence). In doing so, he mainly uses descriptive narratives and arguments touching the past and current circumstances to compare these two time periods and bridge them to each other. Most of the biographical information he discloses belongs to further segments that are stimulated by my questions. In other words, the first 32 sequences, the main narrative, can be considered as an analysis of arguments – entangled in biographical aspects. The partial distance he sought and achieved (due to the generational issues) provides him with argumentative and descriptive ways of telling his life story. I would argue that his biography is entangled in specific interpretative frameworks because he still deals with his past and identity. The contradictions in a life pop up in his narrative in juxtaposed forms.

He starts with contours of a usual life narrative, where he was born or what he does for a living (sequence 1). It prepares him for contrasts from his own life, "it would seem to be so without problems, but it wasn't the case" (sequence 2: 13). That signals other conditions that have ruled his life story. In this regard, he utilises contrasting juxtapositions. These constructions tell not only what he experienced, but also depict the complexities in telling a biography which the given circumstances impacted. It even raises the question of how to approach a life story from Kurdistan or similar conflict regions. While the beautiful nature stands before, you cannot enjoy it, you can only experience how it is destroyed. While high school pupils bunk off school and thus could have fun, having school off implies military training to improving the "love for the fatherland" (sequence 6: 46). Zal points out the paradoxes a life (in the periphery) would have. The structure of his narration stems from such contradictive elements. It resembles the balcony anecdotes of Delal, which designates the distance to the realm of violence, yet the oppression itself at the same time. Furthermore, they have been the forging features for his identity. When the military training experience as a schoolchild, his encounter with the soldiers on his way to picnic, and the argument of hating the uniform vis-à-vis contemporary ethnic prejudices are put side-by-side, we see the strings of how he forms an argument based on biographical experiences. So, he renders the biographical processes.

The comparison he conducts is not only based on his personal experiences. These are nourished by his social and socio-political observations as well. In contrast to individual episodic memories, such analogies prepare the path for wider time spans:

> Someone who doesn't live in Turkey or maybe living in Turkey, but has a proper understanding, that kind of person would be shocked, from the things I told you because there is no change, to be honest, after 30 years, today for example in that place I was born children experience the same, or something similar to that what I went through. (sequence 7: 65–68)

Based on this interpretation, he problematises issues of permanence. So, the comparisons emerge concerning his own experiences of socio-political conditions:

> my father, is a retired teacher. His first service place was a village in our province, back then there were 500 households. Now no one lives there ... Imagine, 500 households, multiply by three people, 1500, now there are only two or three houses, not more ... like in the 1960s, under normal circumstances this village with 500 households had to grow, but instead of that the number got reduced, it is not the only example. (sequence 23: 212–216)

Such comparisons, as aforementioned, draw the picture starting with the corners, the "extremities", like in the village example where his father served as a teacher. Nevertheless, these are only examples, the point he wants to stress – or his argument – is the continuity of austerity and discrepancy. Zal first fills the corners of the puzzle, then comes to the mid. He keeps the mid for his own and family biography.

While arguments blur the path of his talk, personal memories such as the impressionist scenes act as anchors. After Zal portrays nature in a very romantic way, "that would be unfair if we don't mention, for instance ... that nature, nature aa, its fantastic nature, couldn't skip that, such a terrific beautiful nature exists" (sequence 13: 128), he comes to describe the beekeeping, how it was performed earlier without any additional material, and where both sexes were pivotal to the production process. He highlights the details of producing, its social dynamics in Kurdistan, and how it all vanished because of the curfews and destruction of nature. This question is, in Zal's story, a consequence of the continuity of violence which is to be seen in embodiments or analogies of nature and its destruction; court and legal system change; clashes and curfew; and again, the youth violence that seems to be a newly formed social aspect in his perspective. Although poetic emblems occupy the storytelling of nature (sequence 13), nature also implies destruction. Moreover, the demolishment of this picture does include a massive change in the social contract and production processes of the rural population. Due to the curfew and used warfare, the people in the Kurdish rural side had to change their life. According to Zal, bee-keepers cannot work; women do not participate in the production; people have become unable to earn their food from the fields anymore (sequence 14; 15). In this regard, the damage is irreversibly done. He employs the argument that inequality robbed the place of equality in social participation since the military approaches have become standards of life (sequence 14 f).

The anchor of a personal memory leads him first to describe the notion and circumstances; then to compare it with current conditions; at the end, conclude with an argument (Schütze 1983; 2008a). Perhaps, Zal is aware of his narrative's fragmented quality, and this is why he uses such anchors. These stabilise the narrative flow that would be shaky otherwise due to the violence.

Time Issue and Continuity of Violence

The scene of youth violence has changed in Zal's perspective. He points out a growing resentment against another nation, ethnicity based on the identification of (the) powerholders – politicians, governors, and armed forces – who (have) performed large scale violence. He admires his generation for being interested in discussing the issues instead of radicalising conflicts. He also salutes the ideological commitment of his generation (sequence 24), which, according to Zal, lacks in the youth today. That observation is a shock experience to him in his adulthood so that he still remains questioning the circumstances and the role of adult in such a society. Being a father, experiencing violence, and now raising such questions have shaped the category of being an adult in the Kurdish society. His time construction looks over these phenomena.

Based on his professional life and expertise, Zal provides his narrative with a further comparison. He emphasises that the legal system in Turkey has become horrifying, even worse than under the junta regime of 1980. His father was once, back in the 1980s, criminally charged by the infamous State Security Courts (DGM) and yet acquitted by the same. After decades, Zal read the verdict:

> it fits the general principles of law, when I study it with my attorney identity, it is really in line with the general principles of law and it seems that the DGM made us of these [principles] and decided for his acquittal ... But now really, I swear, even when you have hundreds of thousands of pieces of evidence supporting your acquittal. Aaa but only and only a doubt supporting the penalty, let the fundamental principle of

that any doubt benefits the suspect or the accused, they would approach it with, with the logic that aaa any doubt shall be to the benefit of the state, with the upper limit of imprisonment term, and imposes the penalty ... back then there was this thing really, if the person is innocent then acquitted, or "if there is no offence, they'll be free" meant something. Back then. Now, it's gone. Right, back then, there were the acid pits and so on, and so forth, yet it had this tiny teeny side too, let me express this way. Well, now they are combined, on one side killings in the basements, don't allow em to live, when one's allowed then put behind the bars, torture, well I don't mean in a physical way (teaspoon clangs).. Therefore, these issues are hard issues. Tough issues. (drinks tea) (sequence 30: 283–296)

There is no doubt that these notorious courts had other very problematic verdicts ruining lives. The point which is significant for this study is the way how Zal utilises a past experience (and even a narrative) as a tool for evaluating times. His conclusion from another sequence, that circumstances have shifted from bad to the worst (sequence 22), conveys a framework for his comparisons. The continuity of violence has impacted the setting of bad circumstances and lifted it to worst, so to speak. It occurs to be that only these two settings had been the possible options for the ones who live in this region. The above quoted part from his interview should be read in these terms as well. Utilising a personal experience, he points out such a shift in the legal system. It is another brick of the framework he requires to evaluate times and express an argument.

Christians of the region, Armenians and Assyrians, who were the victims of the genocide, appear as a type for such a comparative structure (Schütz and Luckmann 2003, 313–28).[29] Zal designs a victim type or a victimhood category for this context. Thus, Armenians, Assyrians, and Kurds fell under this same category, "if one looks at this problem through the lens of the victims, it

---

[29] In his fundamental work, Alfred Schütz notes down: „Neue Erfahrungen werden vermittels eines in früheren Erfahrungen konstituierten Typs bestimmt. In vielen Situationen des täglichen Lebens genügt der Typ zur Bewältigung der aktuellen Situation ... Jeder Typ des lebensweltlichen Wissensvorrats ist ein in lebensweltlichen Erfahrungen ‚gestifteter' Sinnzusammenhang. Anders ausgedrückt, der Typ ist eine in vorangegangenen Erfahrungen sedimentierte, einheitliche Bestimmungsrelation ... Eine weitere Implikation der vorangegangenen Analyse ist es, dass es keine ‚endgültigen' Typen im lebensweltlichen Wissensvorrat geben kann. Jeder Typ, in einer ‚ursprünglichen Problemlage' gebildet, wird in weiteren Routinesituation und Problemlagen angewandt." (313–316)

doesn't matter, Muslim or not or someone else, everyone got affected and had the same result" (sequence 4: 28 f). Despite this argument, Zal considers the Armenians and Assyrians from his home region "not beaten" but protected by the Kurds, "at least we didn't let them get beaten in our province, but generally in Kurdistan we let Armenian and Assyrian get beaten, and others, now it's the turn for Kurds" (sequence 24: 225 f). However, this equal victimhood seems to be contradictive to his own descriptions about the little number of remained Assyrian villages in the region. Nevertheless, these victims help him describe and illustrate the questions regarding time:

> Like coming to terms with the past or like aaa we can maybe talk about, tell. (sighs) in the year 1915 there were more than 20 or 30 Assyrian villages in our province, now only one. And it is not really. Aaa... Like when someone who is 80 90 years old would tell you the stories of that time, people would think 'wow, that happened this happened', you know. But today, when I talk with the new generation, aaa in their view-point there is no change, what you experienced in your childhood they did or still doin too, not very much aaa changed you know. (sequence 8: 78–82)

Remembering his broad victim category, Assyrians give voice to current issues by which Kurds are affected. In this sense, the genocide fits into the corresponding setting in order to predate the violence and explain Zal's point(s). Furthermore, the "typification" of acts reaches a sort of anonymity due to the broad temporal spectrum, I suggest. It is not anymore about the events of extermination targeting a specific group, here the Assyrians. The victim becomes anonymised because of such temporal organisations. Hence, Zal's remodified equal victimhood disregards certain victim correlations and nuances. The question in these terms should be what happens to a fragmented collective memory when a universal type of victimhood or matter of being affected becomes neutralised. Who is the perpetrator of this universal victim figure?

Naming "Others"

In this setting influenced by the victimhood category which Zal proposes, the others are embodied in the uniform of soldiers first of all, "It is because when you see this uniform you get, changed it feels weird because that uniform was the sign of violence, this is why, violence. Aaa it was, the uniform was the point where the violence meets" (sequence 5: 40 f). Nonetheless, the perception of victimhood had also changed with the resentment of the new generation:

but now they hate literally. "They did it to me, I'll do it in return" they say, I mean, don't view it as a political problem, regards it as an eye for an eye situation, says "if they do it, they will get it in return." (sequence 12: 118–120)

The topic of "the others", where it finds a subjectivity in the minds of affected people, brings him to the comparison of generations. How different generations describe the "other" and position themselves vis-à-vis that "other" is the question here. Through that "other" and the phenomenon of violence, he could compare and describe what (has) happened. Although the army uniform signals something clear, in some other life stories people with a certain academic background, for instance scholars and physicians, occupy the place of the perpetrating subjects (for a detailed discussion, please see the Chapter 7). Zal's narrative hosts such a figure as well, a nationalist scholar. So "the other" varies based on personal experiences.

Zal's self in his narration

Beyond individual memories, Zal's person is to be found in arguments and descriptions as well. He describes non-changing circumstances in Kurdistan utilising his own experiences. Of course, every argument is a crystallisation of experiences. In Zal's case, he embeds the biographical details into the argumentative segments. When we look into the biographical segments, then we reencounter the contrasting juxtapositions. The story is, so to speak, not ripe without such competing notions. There is this peculiar nature that he could enjoy viewing on the rooftop, yet there is a clash going on in the middle of this impressionist scene (sequence 5). People were on their way to a picnic, yet, they were stopped and interrogated by the army officers (sequence 25). These are elements that are somehow paradoxical, yet, in Zal's perspective, integrant parts of region's story. He is not only the one who observed and experienced such antagonist scenes back then, but he also is the one who narrates further in order to question these times. He bared witness to the magnificent nature and its destruction, to the deterioration of the intergenerational contact, and to cycling state political violence targeting people. In this realm, he grounded his positioning and has, for instance, changed his professional trajectory in moving to Van.

Once, Zal had an encounter, better said a dispute, with a professor in Cyprus who came from Turkey as many of lecturers in the occupied part of the island do. The professor was not fond the answer Zal gave upon the question on state of emergency in his lecture since Zal exemplified with his biographical experiences instead of staying in the sterile language of constitutional law.

The professor cut the conversation short without exchanging arguments and stressing the nationalist "love it or leave it". This naïve disobedience and the experience Zal made was pivotal to his professional trajectory, I argue, in moving back to Kurdistan as he underlines that even in Cyprus, outside of Turkish borders in legal terms, there is no peace. So, the selfhood exists in contested areas that he conveys in narrative forms.

Contested Memories

Zal's life story shows the contestations in terms of memory of violence in Kurdistan, such as the victim type he provides. Let us remember, he mentions that the Assyrians had been the victims of the same perpetrator. He, in fact, considers the "dichotomous victim narrative" (Türkyılmaz 2011, 336), Turkish State versus Christians or Turkish State versus Kurds. In doing so, he compares several features in a broader time span. At the same time, his life story depicts how circumstantial the victimhood narrative is. A radical example emerges with the book that the former governor of his hometown has published:

> In fact, he wrote down the illegal, unlawful things he had done, everything. And tells these stories with such a pride, of course it is not such a country for justice. I mean he says as *kaymakam* what he has done, that thing, this and that, like joined the interrogation, left the interrogation, and the book is there, he wrote it, well when there exists such a civil servant, then you get scared. (sequence 39: 407–410)

How the power relations impact the remembrance can be read in these lines. At this juncture, while Zal is losing contact with the younger generations, another person of the same age or a bit older than him – yet from the proxy of perpetratorship – could still impose his mindset.

6.4 Concluding Remarks

Based on the reconstruction and analysis of biographical narrative interviews, the portrayed three biographies consist of different spatial properties, various familial, personal, group-based, and professional experiences, and individual political socialisation orders. However, some intersections crystallise in all three life stories and exhibit similarities: in biographical processes that the interviewees went through; trajectories that they developed in the face of certain conditions; and dominating structures that they could not change alone or with their fellows.

The centre-versus-periphery question occurs to be one of such substantial features. Mehmed, Delal, and Zal report on discrepancies in the centre and obstacles not-expected yet not to be bypassed for people moving from the peripheries. While Mehmed and Delal recall their childhood experiences – in the former, facing labelling as Kurd and enmity, and Delal seeking ways in a different society and the "feeling like refugees" among assimilated people – Zal narrates contemporary circumstances concerning these very phenomena in detail. His portrayal includes his analytical perspective considering the issue in synchronic and diachronic ways. Even though he was not challenged by the hardships of moving – forced or not – in his childhood, he has lived in the same territory, which is targeted by state violence for enough time so that he cannot disassociate his person from the political reality in Kurdistan. Zal's narrative also shows the results of years-long repression and violence, the destruction of villages in the 1990s and small towns in the mid-2000s, and their perpetual effects on urban and rural life. Generally for the Kurds in Turkey, this very question, centre-versus-periphery issue, is not about choice but about being constrained by the violent acts of the state.

Yet, the accounts do point at a further pattern: the experiences of othering in the centre. Mehmed points out that he and his father were personally targeted by the fellow civilian Kurds living in the centre. Later he experienced othering repeatedly in the university, his professional life as a teacher, and political life. Hence, he fostered his selfhood around identification with the hardworking character and exercised disobedience. The latter notion is to be observed later in his commitment to language struggle and studying a massacre performed by the military against Kurds in the early 1930s – which he calls his "life work". Delal tells that the conditions of assimilation made and/or accepted by the fellow citizens of Diyarbakır in the late 1980s, and early 1990s affected her and her family tremendously. On the one side, she had a rising interest in learning Turkish in his childhood to find a way into the assimilated society of Diyarbakır centre. Her father drafted and conducted terms of isolation on the other, from his perspective, to protect his children from the urban assimilative turn. Finding and generating methods to bypass the isolation, with or without accompanying friends, taught her ways of individual resistance. She was a target of political violence several times, as a child indirectly and later as a university student personally. She resisted in different forms adding pieces to and changing processes. Her later years in political practice and her professional trajectory (in non-governmental language, cultural, and socio-political work) are embodied by notions flourishing from her childhood experiences in disobeying her father and learning from him parallelly. Based on his narrative, Zal made experiences of othering more with the state institutions in his childhood than with people. Like other Kurdish youngsters, he was a subject to be taught the "proper ways" of loving the country and being persecuted by the same. The state's relationship with the young Kurdish people, where the state institutions count on an "other" and which subsumes colonial patterns, pretty much appears to be the core subject in Zal's life story. He stood against it several times. Nevertheless, observing the continuity of state violence, its effects on youth and adulthood and their deteriorated connection concerns him tremendously.

Thus, the biographers in these case studies give an account of the trajectories and biographical processes that have been formed by the intersection of spatial question (centre-versus-periphery), othering experiences, and state violence. These three accounts include significant examples of epistemic disobedience powered up through own agency and selfhood against a violent structure. Each of the biographers experienced biographical processes on the areal of such intersections.

Additionally, some narrative patterns in the biographers' memories of the Armenian and Kurdish past resemble each other by their construct. Memory of the Armenians makes the violence exercised against Kurds *describable and discussable*. It is the main reason for the resemblance. But we also can count several differences on various layers, such as when it is about the who-question pointed at the perpetrators, the role of the grandfathers, or own experiences with the victimisers entangled to the Turkish State structures.

7 Violence and Genocide in Memory. A Comparative Discussion

In addition to the case studies portrayed in the previous chapter, the focus here is set on the comparisons of certain narrative elements from the sample of this study (the ten biographical interviews). Herewith I regard the memory structures related to the genocide, family stories, and violence that affected the given person. In these terms, this chapter is organised under four subchapters, echoing the theoretical discussion on memory issues in Chapter 3. With a focus on the narrative, it first questions forms of meaning-making; then it pinpoints the temporal layers of remembering and talking about past violence; and sheds light on the contestation of stories that circulate in communities and stories stemming from individual and family experiences. In this latter manner, the "self" of the person surfaces as a significant layer in the area of contested memories, I suggest. The "self" stands as the renderer and the rendered component of stories, in reciprocal and simultaneous terms. Beyond that, the "self" changes trajectories powered by its own agency in certain social processes.

Based on my key findings, the main argument is that the Armenian Genocide memory provides a premise for the Kurdish narratives. Considering this premise, the social setting and one's own life become reconstructed. Stories on Armenians help the narrator to bring further examples of violence into the discussion (cf. Bar-On 1999); the violence that has been performed by the Turkish State structures. Moreover, it fosters temporal dimensions such as when the narrator seeks to articulate continuity of injustice and repression. Thus, the setting expands itself when the genocide, as conjunction so to speak, bridges the past to current conditions. Even though anachronistic features – projections of current problems on the portrayal of the past – ease the hand of the narrator in describing the current state and its interpretation (cf. Rothberg 2009, especially Part 5), these create (inevitable) novel temporal pockets as well – while "uniting" or dividing times (Vico 1948, 251). For instance, in ongoing violence, the narration occurs not just on a past-today-axis but anticipates future visions as well (Brescó de Luna 2017; de Saint-Laurent 2017; cf. Fischer 2018). In sum, the Armenian Genocide as a memory template stimulates descriptions of violence (or descriptive patterns) – relying on a continuity thesis and/or positively connotated envisioned futures, whilst opening the space to discuss Kurdish experiences (Bar-On 1999). I argue this is the multidirectional nature of this particular memory regime (Rothberg 2009).

Without a doubt, collective and individual memory reside in transition since political perimeters change, social needs are redefined, and the relation of the individual with the collective (and vice-versa) finds a new shape. The narratives about the past come to be open to the impact of transition – as it was sketched based on the exhibitions' analysis previously (please see Chapter 5). Thus, the memory redesigns (and is redesigned) through new power relations – it applies to denialism as well if we agree that the particular case of Turkish denialism has sort-of-left its historicist compound. Perhaps, recalling Bartlett's points and rephrasing Brockmeier's description on Bartlett that memories have a role to "fulfil a social function" would clarify my point concerning such social relations further (Brockmeier 2015, 57; cf. Bartlett 1995, 294–98; Gergen 1994, 95; Prager 1998, 167; Wertsch 2004).[1] The social reality changes throughout generations and every individual who is entangled to the given collective remodifies their memory in order to be a part of the new circumstances (cf. Welzer, Moller, and Tschuggnall 2002).[2] In this scope, we should not misrecognise the interwovenness of personal and collective memories, and less their relation to socio-political settings.

Following the theoretical discussion in Chapter 3, I argue that the contestation between memories should be regarded as a standard, so to speak, instead of an exception. The contestation I do talk about is a part of negotiation. Perhaps, it can be seen as an earlier stage of an emerging relation between memories – which would be followed, for instance, by a possible memory alliance at the endpoint. In such a context of interlinked memories and the impacts of social interactions, the correlation between collective memories (Halbwachs 1991) would also involve "disputes."[3] Where does the contestation start, in the personal elaboration of stories or social debates? Can we define the contestation as a part of this meaning-making attempt? If yes, it would mean that the contested interaction of memories begins in the individual processing of past experiences. So, the contestation and disputes are not equal to competition since the former does not cause or is nourished by a "zero-sum game" understanding of collective memories (cf. Rothberg 2009).

[1] Prager's remark with "sociobiography" fits at this juncture to the discussion of the function of memories as well, that the biography finds its form based on that particular social premise indicates memory's "(in)direct contact" – through biography – with the social conditions.

[2] What Welzer and his team underscore is a crucial point to discuss the relation of the individual with the society, that the younger generations pull out and reconfigure the experiences of their perpetrator grandparents, to avoid becoming an outsider of the changing times.

[3] The following questions occur in these terms: is the transformation on the social premise the only indicator of contestation? Are there any other triggers and "agents" that are involved in the transition of a certain national or communal memory? The narratives I gathered provide a glimpse on memory change in the context of Kurdistan.

7.1 Semantics of Violence. How to Describe, What to Discuss

In the biographical interviews, the phenomenon of violence frequently appears in various forms. The narrators did not – or perhaps could not – skip, mute, or fade out this part from their life story. Frequently, the violence is narrated based on individual experiences, for instance, when Delal speaks about the curfew in H. and the paramilitary operations in the downtown of Diyarbakır in the early 1990s, or when Zal had watched the clashes from the rooftop. In other words, the reconstruction of violence was built on the biographical property. Moreover, there is a significant proportion of family stories concerning the Armenian past as well as political violence exercised against Kurds. The informants recount such narratives after several decades, without having any individual experiences concerning these moments (Hirsch 2012).[4] These involve not just information about the event but also projections such as anachronisms (please see the next subchapter on temporalities). At this juncture, the violence phenomenon emerges in the storytelling in the form of arguments that contain personal and family experiences as well as collective references (cf. Pohn-Lauggas 2019).[5]

Explaining the violence, that (has) impacted one's life personally or a grouping in collective sense whatsoever, is part of the narrational meaning-making process. It also possesses a performative quality (cf. Austin 1972; Brockmeier 2015; Gergen 1994; Searle 2011; 2013). The questions of how to start a narrative and how to design – what elements it should include – require in my judgement an in-depth discussion that considers the spectrum of narrative elements critically. For instance, the injustice in legal form, impunity, denial of truth about the past – such as the genocide, and belittling the present conditions, or the politics towards Kurdish linguicide (Fernandes 2012; Hassanpour 1992;

---

[4]   In her distinguished work on the concept *post-memory*, Marianne Hirsch (p. 4) asks: "Why could I recall particular moments from my parents' wartime lives in great detail and have only very few specific memories of my own childhood, I began to wonder? Why could I describe the streets, residences, and schools of pre-World War I Czernowitz and interwar Cernăuți, where they grew up, the corner where they evaded deportation, the knock on the door in the middle of the night, the house in the ghetto where they waited for deportation waivers …?"

[5]   Sociologist Maria Pohn-Lauggas uses the term "collective reference" to describe the intergenerational memories in the Austrian context and point at the influence of national discourses. She underscores, "[t]he significance of collective references for individual memory is uncontested in the field of memory studies" (p.1). I do tend to consider the concept of collective references somehow separate than nation state rhetoric (and historiographies), but more generated and "graced" by various actors.

Hassanpour, Sheyholislami, and Skutnabb-Kangas 2012) stimulate personal stories in almost all the cases of this present study. Not any fond memories but such experiences build the fundament of storytelling. Beyond that, the place acts a significant part in the formation of stories. It even plays a triggering role to narrate further, to reconstruct a framework, for instance, Mehmed's and Azim's home villages and their past. This applies to materials as well; they bare a forming power for the narrative, for instance, the rings Armenian girls wore or the gold which is searched. Such items travel as remembered notions with people and influence their projections – or, perhaps better formulated, their post-memories (cf. Hirsch 2012).

Beyond such mnemonics, different protagonists – with their role, characteristics, and action schemes – are cast in the interviews. In the story of Delal's relative, her way of narrating (re-)confirms the role of her grandfather as saviour because he had adopted an Armenian child. However, the question arises: what is the influence of the narrator's agency and perspective into such narratives? The question of agency changes the meaning of the narrative elements, I suggest, because the contextualisation of a specific event derives from the perspective of the storyteller. Therefore, I prefer to scrutinise the meaning of certain elements – or their semantics, borrowing the term from linguistics and philosophy of language. The semantical investigation aims to shift the focus from the face values of memories onto the questions of what is behind; what does it want to tell.

Beyond a judicial issue of truth (Danziger 2008, Chapter 7),[6] the questioning is about reconstructing the motives and forms of remembering nourished by multiple pasts and current realities. The main argument is that the Armenian Genocide has become one of the epicentres[7] for narrating the victimhood of

---

[6]   In the given chapter, Kurt Danziger presents the history of the term "memory" in the context of psychology and psychoanalysis. He quasi-summarizes and problematises this history with the following question: "Are there indeed two entirely different systems covered by the term 'memory', one a system for reconstructing the past to suit the present, the other a recording system that preserves the true past?" (p. 213). Concluding the same chapter, Danziger points out "The distinction between 'true' and 'false' memories is not a psychological distinction. Psychology, as I showed earlier in this chapter, found its terrain in the vast gap that separates truth-telling from lying. In a psychological context the distinction between 'recovered' and 'false' memory of trauma (or of anything else for that matter) is indeed artificial, but it may be crucial in other contexts, where everything hinges on a sharp division between what is considered true and what false" (p. 215).

[7]   I use this oxymoron on purpose and in order to underscore the various possibilities in narrating individual experiences, yet also to stress their interwovenness.

Kurds in Turkey (cf. Türkyılmaz 2011).[8] In saying this, I merely insist that the topic Armenian Genocide is not only about the past when Kurds start to describe and discuss what happened, as the memory is about today (Halbwachs 1991; 2012; cf. Zittoun 2017).[9]

7.1.1 Mnemonics: Space and Material

Three of the narrators – Azim, Mehmed, and Ali, who is a descendant of a converted Nestorian – started our interview by telling some personal or family stories concerning the genocide. Moreover, seven of them recounted that notion during their narration – alongside Azim and Mehmed, Murad, Zal, Delal, Merve, and Kerem. Only one person, Mamoş, whose life story I scrutinise on these pages, did not mention any word about that particular past but concentrated his talk on his personal experiences of violence as a former guerrilla. His village was destroyed in the 1990s, and a bombed village and its "evacuated" people was the last picture ever about his home, perhaps, this is why he told me his story with anchor points to prison and Van.

Mehmed starts to talk about the Armenian past of his home village. He describes what the Armenians had accomplished, left behind – the vineyards for instance – and how people, Kurds and Armenians, lived together in peace referring to his grandmother's account. He narrates a family member's story on how this person perpetrated during the extermination campaigns. After five

---

[8]   In his study on the trajectory of the genocidal violence in Van, Türkyilmaz (pp. 4 f) suggests: "Victimhood claims do not operate merely as an expression of identity status, but also produce those very identities. For instance, most Armenians, Turks and Kurds are by now at least five or six generations removed from the bloody early 20th century turmoil in eastern Anatolia. And yet, they often believe that they – as unique collectivities – are still victims of those events. Victimhood discourses, after all, are not uniform and stagnant; they can wax, wane, or take new forms across the decades. This dissertation suggests that one major determinant of the formation, circulation, and popularization of discourses of victimhood is perceived political, social, and cultural uncertainty."

[9]   Zittoun (p. 297) points out "individual remembering demands certain semiotic loops, oriented toward what is culturally consider as the past, enabled by personal past experiences ... or by cultural elements in the present ..., interactions with others, as well as social representations (de Saint-Laurent & Zittoun, in press). Remembering a collective past can be in contrast conceived as remembering something about a configuration of events in the past, which affected many lives in an interrelated manner, a collectively designated as such ... These preliminary considerations highlight two basic principles of collective remembering: one is its inherent developmental nature; the other is the necessary tension that the notion presupposes between individual and collective acts of memory." From my point of view, this echoes as a theoretical conception what in the Kurdish society happens concerning the Armenian Genocide memory.

sequences – or 14:53 minutes, he ends his main narrative putting a coda with an argument of that after Armenians the violence has targeted Kurds. His argument also involves a description of how Kurds were involved in the extermination campaigns as perpetrators – predating the conflict to Hamidiye Regiments. After this main narrative, corresponding my question, he recounts about his youth. In order to make it understandable for me, he describes the topography and circumstances of his home region. The "circumstances" indicate here not just his lifetime but the time before, responding to his family biography and the past of this very place.

Azim,[10] who grew up in a village close to Van and continued his studies in the city when we met, also began to talk about the genocide before I started recording. After the machine was on, he first highlights his biographical experiences concerning language restrictions, racism, and discrimination that he (has) experienced as a young Kurdish man. His main narrative, which lasts for nine sequences, subsumes occasions and events from his childhood and studentship. Then for the next ten sequences, he provides further details about the experiences he made in various towns of Turkey as a student. In the 19th sequence, he first clarifies the mental impact of the events following the June 2015 election, the war in urban areas, and then asks if we could talk about the Armenians. He probably needs to change the subject and the other topic, e.g. Armenians, was the one that fits our meeting. After that moment, he narrates the points from the beginning of our unrecorded talk: at the book fair of Van, he had seen a book about the Armenian Genocide which motivated him to question his home village's history because the book starts with this very place. Finding that book was a shocking experience to him even though he knew that Armenians lived there back then or that there is a Christian cemetery in the village without Christians who should have still been alive. His narrative is, from that point on, tangential to two features: a) the coexistence of peoples before 1915; b) the willingness to confront the past crimes. The latter binds the past to his trajectory. His discovery reveals his selfhood in the context of remembrance.

In both interviews, the place, specifically hometown, plays a crucial role to articulate the past violence. The stories include different mnemonic subjects, for instance, the information about the Armenian properties that Azim found out in the book or the gold and crucifixes Mehmed pinpoints. These locate the village (and their biography in fact) in the temporal and geographical sense, while the place subsumes stories of violence. Hence, it correlates with the victimisation of the Kurds, and due to that highlights the Turkish State's role as powerholder.

---

[10]   Author interview with Azim, Van, 24.04.2016

Drawing her own biographical project into the epicentre of her narrative, Delal recalls a green telephone (sequence 46) that she associates with the brutal curfew of her father's hometown H. When she was a child, she comes back home from school and sees everyone crying. When she asks her brother what happened, he replies that H. had been burned down. Her father tries to reach his family in H., calling them with the "green telephone" they had. At one point, a soldier answers the call, according to Delal. He curses at Delal's father and tells uncanny stories about what he would do with the family. The "green telephone" is such a powerful mnemonic which helps Delal to recall her memories of H. (cf. A. Assmann 2010). It also binds Delal's childhood memories between two places, H. and Sur, the downtown of Diyarbakır. In Sur, she spent her years in isolation exercised by her father because he was afraid of his children being assimilated just like the people of downtown. She was not allowed to play outside because other children were speaking Turkish. In H., however, she did not have to face such restrictions. She was free to go out, find playmates, and speak Kurdish in public without being labelled. The symbolic quality of "green telephone" not just connects these two towns, Sur and H., but binds these two different realities to each other as well, and emphasises a possible end to an era. The era of spending time without isolation, the time of splendid childhood memories could have continued if H. was not "burned down".

Another material that she recalls is the yeast bread which the Christians of Diyarbakır gave her when she was a child. Like other children, she threw it away because it came from Christians. She and her brother mimicked other children cursing Christians. When they talked to their mother about such occasions, she criticised them. In these very paragraphs (sequence 53; 54), she mentions briefly that she has an Islamised Armenian relative. In these terms, the mnemonic of bread does not just draw the picture of social relations (and the power relations) between Christians and Muslims in downtown but discloses a family story. At the end of our talk, she provides the very details of this family question.

One of the common (discursive) mnemonics that some of my narrators, such as Murad, Mehmed, Kerem, and Merve, utilise is the notion of profit. Murad,[11] who moved to Van from his provincial hometown decades ago, emphasises the plunder phenomenon, *talan*, when he talks about the genocide and Kurdish complicity. He bridges this element (related to profit) to the present conflicts, and points indirectly at gravediggers (cf. von Bieberstein 2017; Cheterian 2015). Hence, benefiting from the mass violence leaves the chambers of expropriation – a time-specified act which occurred during the extermination

---

[11] Author interview with Murad, Van, 19.04.2016

campaigns and in the first years of the aftermath – and surfaces as treasure hunting and ruination of the "forsaken" Armenian properties. For Mehmed, it has perhaps become a sort-of-normality of everyday life. He (sequence 2: 19 f) points out that his home village "still has gold under its soil, villagers run into it and pick, this is how several families got rich, these are Armenian gold, everyone knows that." However, Kerem,[12] a local of another Kurdish town who moved to Van to study and took up a job some years ago, has a more critical viewpoint when it is about the alleged forsaken wealth, "our folks have destroyed all those canals, to find gold or something like that, they ruined all of their properties."

Merve,[13] who was born and raised in Van until she moved to Istanbul as a teenager with her family, narrates how plunder achieved another level. She mentions that her uncle used to work as a constructor. Hence, in one of his yards in Van, he found Armenian gold and had to deliver this treasure to the governmental institutions. In the same sequence, she tells that her grandfather's brother had owned an Armenian house, "from the landings, you know under the doors, they kept telling they found gold every single time. Is it an urban legend, don't think so. You know, adult people told these stories, it can't be an urban legend." Her trust is based on that person's years of age although she has already confronted her father concerning his patronizing thoughts on Kurds and Armenians, and the age was not even a topic. When it comes to wealth, the link to Armenians occurs to be unavoidable. This link is not just a simple emblem but represents a reconstructive power as well. It binds, for instance in Merve's case, the family biography to the past and to a place; the perpetration in 1915 to the patterns of bystanders' actions after decades; at the same time, the feature of Armenian wealth locates the family (or a family member) in the political context of Van – a constructor with connections to the administration.

Another point that reminds my narrators of what they had seen and experienced was the necropolitics of the Turkish State (cf. Mmembe 2003). An informant of mine whom I met in Van, Emin, speaks briefly about the unsolved crime that took the life of his compatriot in the 1990s. For Azim, the image of a PKK guerrilla whose dead body was dragged by special corps in the 2015–16 war was crucial in describing the brutality. This picture was circulated in the (social) media. Beyond that, he points out that Kurdish bodies were, PKK or not, exhibited regularly by the Turkish State forces *in situ*, such as the army or paramilitary special ops units. Just like him, Kerem is disturbed by the

---

[12]   Author interview with Kerem, Van, 25.04.2016
[13]   Author interview with Merve, Istanbul, 02.05.2016

exposure of death in the media, "even when you are killed you get labelled, even when you don't have any connection to the issue, to the [Kurdish armed] movement, when you are killed, then the label is already there 'terrorist' and then it'll be broadcasted to the west." The commodification of death, with the purpose of propaganda, is the theme here. A Kurdish body is not even handled and respected as a human's body – due to the ruling biopolitics (cf. Agamben 1998). At the same time, the remembrance of Armenians is fashioned through emblems of materials, such as canals, vineyards, or gold. Both determine the region's spacetime.

Mehmed highlights, for instance, that the Turkish State had destroyed (or removed, it is not very clear in the narrative) a commemorative plaque for the Kurdish victims of a massacre which was launched and operated by the military in the early republican period. Hence, it is not just the body that is not tolerated to remain human but also the posthumous abstraction and memorialisation (in spatial order). Under such circumstances, another informant, Ali, emphasises "death becomes ordinary because in front of you 20 young bodies lie." All of these remarks on the politics of war and concerning death (and others', the Armenians' deaths) localise the region in history. This remodification of the natural "time arrow" (cf. Subrt 2014, 245 ff)[14] "transmogrify" the death into an object – through being dragged, exposed, or ignored. Hence, it reminds the informants of what they as a society, as a "we", have experienced in the spacetime of Kurdistan. Despite (or thanks to) their travelling nature (Erll 2011), these memories stay put in a specified geography and frame it in terms of violence. The narrators pin their experiences and stories on the maps of that particular geography. So, they provide a context and deepen it through their act.

---

[14]   In his discussion on the relation between time, and society and Elias' and Durkheim's points concerning this very issue, Subrt (p. 245) claims: "Durkheim takes just rhythmic recurrence into consideration. Moreover, by conceiving time as a category or orientation tool, Durkheim and then Elias largely reduce the question of time to a problem of measurement; left aside is the whole matter of the temporal aspect of human existence, or Martin Heidegger's concept of 'being in time' (*Dasein*) (1996). The final, and evidently the most important, concept claiming that time is a human construct ignores the fact that progression toward an end represented by time's arrow exists very objectively in various forms and is definitely not a human invention or fabrication." In some terms, I agree with the author's argument; however, due to the necropolitics, the question arises how politics impact this "objective" notion. How people perceive the left quality of this "time arrow" is a further question as well.

7.1.2 Protagonists

As sketched in Çelik and Dinç's book on Diyarbakır region and collective memory (2015, 88–94), the Armenian Genocide has been named differently – dependent on the region and deriving from the form of victimisation or the act.[15] The protagonists in stories unsurprisingly vary as well, both in survivor and rememberer narratives. Just as a reminder, in historical reports and oral history accounts by survivors of the genocide, we encounter an undifferentiated image of the Kurd. The Kurdish groupings are described as (religious) fanatics, irregulars (*çete*), or plunderer – subordinate to the figure of the Turk, the head of massacres and slaveholders (cf. A-Do 2017; *Aghasi Ivazian – Zoryan Institute Oral History Archive* 1987; Sasuni 1992).[16] Some sort of generalisation occurs in the Kurdish works as well, for instance in Dersimi's account (2014) about the Armenians – where he claims mutual killings occurred on both sides. However, instead of such simplifying approaches to describe the victimisers, I would like to pose the following question: who remembers the Kurdish rememberer today and how? This enquiry, however, should subsume not only the perpetrating and victimising figures but the victimised one as well. In other words, the questions are: How is the act (of being persecuted or being violent) embodied in protagonists of different narratives? What do the protagonists of stories tell us with their characteristics, positionings, and affiliations? What does the narrator tell us with their figures?

Mehmed starts his main narrative with a short historical story to describe where he comes from. This short story tells how the Armenian man *Khezo* was abused and tortured because he helps a Kurdish elder who sought to hide from Turkish armed forces. Mehmed "empowers" his protagonist, Khezo, with favourable characteristics like integrity and loyalty, "he keeps the fugitive, doesn't betray him to the state. Aaa they took him, pull his teeth, they torture him severely, but he never betrays him" (sequence 1: 9 f). Afterwards, the Kurdish elder moves to a Kurdish village to stop Khezo's pain. However, in his next hiding, the local Kurds betray the Kurdish elder and hand him to the Turks. In doing so, Mehmed locates features antagonist to Khezo's attitudes to the proximity of Kurds from that village. In composing the story so, Mehmed describes the figures based on their actions. Hence, this story blossoms and forms an anachronistic template putting today's problems in a historical schema, or based on Vico's work (1948, 251) he "unites times".

---

[15] For a discussion on naming the events, please see Chapter 5.4.2 of this book.
[16] For an outlining discussion, please see Chapter 4.3.1 of this book.

Protagonists' agencies include clues about how Mehmed perceives the genocide and the Kurdish past. He views the case through groupings, such as Kurds that had been loyal to their Armenian neighbours vis-à-vis Kurds that had been collaborating with the powerholder and betraying their own kin. In his looking glass, ethics keep the higher ground. He applies this to the past as well as the present situation. In different spots, he points at the non-unity of the Kurdish society and the attempts to unite Kurds by the Kurdish political movement. The portrayal of the politically divided Kurdish society, and in particular of Kurds who position themselves proximal to the Turkish State, for instance, through being engaged in the village guard system, is transferred into a historical setting and Khezo's world.[17] As mentioned before in the case studies, in this story as well as on other occasions in Mehmed's narrative, the protagonists with negative constructions have no names. For instance, the Kurdish betrayers' names or the name of his relative who participated in the massacres remain silenced, yet these are drafted in the particular grouping(s). Contrarily, the Armenian man who teaches integrity bears a name.

In Azim's life story the Turkish State comes forward as the victimiser. This notion is based on his personal experiences; for instance, police brutality during the student protests. In this manner and due to the novel shocking experience of finding his village in a book about Armenians, Azim's protagonists who are connected to violence are much more based on his individual experiences, and are not lent from any family narrative.

Zal, for instance, emphasises that there was no violence against Christians in his hometown, "at least we didn't let them get beaten in our province, but generally in Kurdistan, we let Armenian and Assyrian get beaten" (sequence 24: 225 f). Nevertheless, he also talks about the dozens of Assyrian villages that are wiped out, "there were more than 20 or 30 Assyrian villages in our province, now only one" (sequence 8: 78 f). The victims somehow had left their home. Furthermore, in this particular province, if we stay in the frames of Zal's narration, we cannot find any perpetrator or victimiser. However, in his life story, the victimiser that has targeted his life pops up on different spots of continuing violence. It is the Turkish State.

The narrative on the village of Mehmed's grandmother discloses something similar, "she says they left later, they fled, our village didn't see much conflict, surrounding villages did, ours went, they left the village before a fight"

---

[17] Comparable to Mehmed's point, another narrator, Azim, points out in an argumentative line on his relation to the Turkish society and the state that "among Kurds, there is a lot of betrayers, vile too." This comment remains yet as a footnote since he does not describe this feature further.

(sequence 2: 32 f). After a massacre that was performed by the Turkish State, his grandparents were relocated to another empty village where earlier Armenians lived – people carried their memories of injustice to their new village (cf. Erll 2011). This village then became Mehmed's place of birth. Nevertheless, the actions resemble each other. In both villages, violence is absent even though there are no more Armenians. The place determines not just the protagonists but the time as well, for instance, after the Armenians Kurds inhabited that place. He also underlines the violence and who the victimised ones were because Armenians left and the state had forced his family to leave after another persecution (cf. Dinç 2016; Portelli 1988).[18] The term "fight", of course, raises further questions concerning the agency of the victimised protagonist(s) and how the victimhood is generated. It occurs to be the interlinked elements are not just place and people in such narratives but temporal organisations and the forms of violence as well.

In this respect, Emin,[19] a teacher and linguist of Kurdish language, born in a provincial town south of Van but living in the centre since decades, chooses Armenians as protagonists of his narrative on the times after the extermination and the present. He claims that Islamised Armenians of Van became "economically very powerful" because they worked together with the state assets and supported Turkish nationalism. Similarly, Mehmed (sequence 4: 62–66) recalls that "[Islamised] Armenians had become such Muslims ... supposedly we were the Muslim side ... but they were trying to teach us the religion ... with such a great fear they hugged their own hangman, and became executioner." In other words, the past victim became the victimiser and the past victimised became the victim. Emin further states that the governor offered his grandfather properties. According to him, Emin's grandfather rejected, and they landed in the hands of Armenians. He marks this offer as a chance to become wealthy – and powerful, yet it also means convergence towards cooperation with the government. He sketches the protagonists of his stories within a framework of collaborators versus loyalists-to-the-cause – similar to Khezo's story. The difference in Emin's narrative is that it refers to the years after 1915. And the non-loyal protagonist is embodied in the enforced converted Christians.

---

[18]   Remembering the title journalist Namık Kemal Dinç used for his interview collection, "They left, and we lost the peace", some narratives that summarize the genocidal trajectory disclose no violent actions, so to speak, allegedly some people left without any confrontation and conflict, and some other resettled at this empty spot. There is a genuine resemblance with Portelli's no-when event description, I suggest.

[19]   Author interview with Emin, Van, 21.04.2016

There are two further figures in the narratives which appear as assimilated-Christians: Ali's late grandmother and Delal's Armenian relative(s). Ali,[20] a novelist from a provincial town located south of Van, had a Nestorian grandmother who survived the extermination campaigns. When she was a teenager, she was dragged from the periphery and then was forcibly married to his grandfather. Ali heard rumours in the family and curses targeting his late grandmother. However, the woman he remembers was a kind, ideal grandmother. His explanations include neither any idealisation of Nestorians – because of their victimhood, nor any generalised group figurations. Yet, it is an idealisation of the specific person, his grandmother (cf. Bar-On and Chaitin 2001, 42–46).[21] Through this (narrative) act, he works on a certain figuration of family and social conditions questioning the subjects on conversion, victimhood, and victimisation in times of post-extermination campaigns. He reveals hints on what components his identity includes.

Delal also talks about an assimilated Christian relative who escaped the death toll in the province thanks to being adopted by her maternal grandfather who was a gendarme back then. This adoptee became a member of the family, yet with a label for him and his family, "that they are Armenian was well known … their Armenian roots were referred to, not in a negative way, but as a positive aspect, not as discrimination" (sequence 80: 1,700 ff). Delal does not problematise the adoption and conversion of this Armenian child or this very mark. However, she clarifies another present issue in this regard. The assimilated Armenian person had started a family and became a conservative Muslim. When some of the descendants converted back to Christianity after

---

[20] Author interview with Ali, Van, 25.04.2016

[21] In their qualitative study, which includes archival testimony recordings as well, "Parenthood and the Holocaust", Bar-On and Chaitin underscore the feature of "idealization of parents" in the interviews "to prevent negative emotions from surfacing" (p. 43). I am not sure if it is transferable in direct terms, first of all, since we do not talk about a parent-child relationship, but on remembering grandparents in particular contexts. Nevertheless, following point by the authors would be significant in the discussion on grandparent idealization: "We must now ask whether an idealization of parenthood or alienation from one's parents hampered the child's psychological well-being. Many Holocaust survivors were not as successful as Anat [an informant] when it came to holding on to such positive feelings of parenthood. However, it does appear that, for many of them, idealization of their parents served as a defense mechanism that, protect them from the horrors that they had to endure during the Holocaust. One cannot decontextualize the question of normalcy or psychological well-being. This brings us back to the necessity of a historically contextualized psychodynamic approach that takes into account the specific historical and social circumstances when discussing psychodynamic individual or family processes" (p.46).

decades, her maternal family became very critical, while Delal's father and family were happy and supportive.

In both narratives we encounter a similar template that shapes the protagonists: an assimilated survivor of the genocide (or descendants) who was stigmatised and criticised by the (conservative) Kurds. The only agency that the survivor still bares is then the willing silence and adaptation. These protagonists concur with the template of "we versus other Kurds" that I scrutinise later again. They offer a premise to justify the argument: the collaborator Kurd carried out violence that was contracted by the Turkish State (cf. Aydınkaya 2015; Balancar 2015).

When it comes to the violence in Kurdistan, we encounter further actor formations. In the life story of Mamoş,[22] a former guerrilla who has become paralysed during a clash in the early 1990s and has lived disabled since, the perpetrator image occurs as the Turkish State – particularly the bureaucrats. Following the clash, he was hospitalised and then delivered to the prison to serve his sentence. Although he could not live without his wheelchair, the doctor who was appointed to report on Mamoş' health conditions reported that he could handle his daily needs by himself. Mamoş' request to be relocated to another prison or to a handicapped-accessible floor was not even considered. The ones who held power affecting his life and body and who put him in such horrifying conditions surface as victimisers. Perhaps, even the soldiers of the opposite side, the Turkish military, are not levelled to such a power.

In Delal's narration, the persecutor of violence against the Kurds in the 1990s has two forms, one in army uniforms such as during the brutal curfew in H. and another as paramilitary in the downtown area. In Zal's case, the uniform epitomises the victimiser in some stories. He also explicitly tells that the army uniform embodied the injustice in his youth. This sentiment, however, has changed in the perception of the new generation, he adds. For the youngsters of today hate their "other", the Turks. Furthermore, in one segment, he emphasises an academic image. He states how nationalist the views of one of his professors were. Once, in a lecture, the question was about the state of emergency, and Zal answered, on the request of his professor. His answer was critical on how the state of emergency is scripted officially and how it is performed *de facto* since he expected "an intellectual. Worst case scenario, he would think as I do. Like, he's a professor specialised in constitution issues (sighs), well brother I swear, he had glasses with such a beard. He said 'Love it or leave it'" (sequence 40: 446–450).

[22] Author interview with Mamoş, Van, 19.04.2016

Being an academic or having intellectual capacity does not improve the cards for critical thinking on what happens in Kurdistan. This sort of protagonist construction reveals itself in two further life stories, Mehmed's and Kerem's, both experienced similar conflicts with academic figures, Mehmed in the university and Kerem during his military service.[23] In this sense, the type of academic figure embodies a system critique in itself that reconciles with victimiser concepts from other narratives: uniformed, armed, or medical – as in Mamoş' life story.

7.1.3 Collective References: Outlines and Frames

As highlighted in the case studies, the autobiographers utilise, stumble, and/ or pass by some circulated narrative structures. These reconstructions that are embraced in collective sense would influence the personal narratives – since according to the psychologist and memory scholar Qi Wang (2016, 297) the autobiographical memory "is thoroughly contextual." For the cases of this book, in particular, the social premise comes to be the family and the political premise reflects in the Kurdish movement – and mostly localised in related places like home towns and certain temporalities. In such a context, how does the narrator outline a story on enforced marriage and adoption when the person has (had) a relative who lived under such circumstances? Should a family story always contain links to specific collective references? Or is there any other way to describe the life of an ancestor?

Delal points out that her grandfather adopted an Armenian child in order to save him from atrocities. Thus, the (further) possible motives of grandfather, for instance, the wealth transfer or arranging new labour force (cf. Akçam 2014; Gasparyan 2014, 63 f; 90 ff),[24] become quasi exculpated. When she does not question what else would be behind the adoption, she mutes the social conditions that had perchance paved the way to adopting a child affected by the

---

[23] Kerem happened to be honest to one of the fellow soldiers, who was, in fact, a scholar, about how he feels regarding the military. Kerem openly criticised the ways the army treats people, degrading their individuality. Despite his expectations that a scholar would be more open and critical, Kerem faced a pure nationalistic outburst.

[24] In the booklet on the stories of genocide survivors, edited and published by Gasparyan, there are, for instance, two stories which expose the labour trajectories of adoptees. Lusine Mardeyan tells her grandfather's story who had worked for the house of his saviour for ten years (pp. 63 f). In another example to child labourers, Sargis Suvaryan's father had been picked up alongside other four or five Armenian children by a middle-class Turkish man to make them work for his household – at a certain moment, when they were waiting for death. According to Suvaryan, a few weeks later, these children escaped the house and ran towards Syria (pp. 90 ff).

massacres. On the other side, the stories on assimilated Armenians that Emin and Mehmed recount disclose a powerful Islamised Armenian image which occurs as collaborator against progressive forces (cf. Altınay and Çetin 2009).[25] The locality emerges at this very point building the connection to the temporal context. Both narrative forms involve some sort of reference to the collective perception of the genocide, I suggest.

In the case of collective references, the person associates own biography with a commonly used narrative or borrows suitable elements from these – and likewise changing both, the own story and the narrative that has been in circulation (cf. Hirst et al. 2009).[26] I also want to (slightly) differentiate my point from the hegemonic national narrative that would be propagated by state institutions (cf. Hobsbawm and Ranger 2012). This form of memory misrecognises not just some social groups' demands or their stories but also the possible ways of reciprocal connections. Here, such references on the contrary emerge in a bottom-up process and remain open for change and potential interlinking to various social groups, as Rothberg (2009) describes his concept of multidirectional memory as a two-way street.

On the following pages, I treat two exemplary structures that concur with the concept of collective references: portraying an ideal past and stressing an instrumentalisation of Kurds. Both are widespread patterns in Kurdish society. We see these concepts in literature (Çelik and Öpengin 2016; Galip 2016), writings of Kurdish intellectuals, and political speeches (for an in-depth discussion, please see, Chapter 5). We also encounter these constructions in the form of personal or family stories of three narrators (Azim, Mehmed, and Murad) and as arguments in seven interviews (in addition to the latter three, Zal, Delal, Merve, and Kerem). Some of such narratives involve the compartmentation of Kurds in "we" and the "others" in order to describe the perpetrator or the bystander. Beyond that, some of them struggle with subjectivities of victims, or better said the question: Who is the victim of this past?

---

[25]   In the introduction to their work on the descendants of Armenians who were adopted or forcibly married, Ayşe Gül Altınay and Fethiye Çetin point out that several descendants talked about "villages, neighbourhoods that are inhabited completely by Muslimised Armenians". "Intra-community marriages" and "radical Islamist or ultra-nationalist" tendencies belong(ed) to such communal spaces, according to their interview partners (p. 13). Ritter and Sivaslian (2013) underscore similar marriage practices in their work on the converted Armenians as well.

[26]   There is a resembling and often used terminology for such cases of collective reference: the flashbulb memory. However, these refer to indirect remembrance formations of singular events such as 9/11 or assassination of JFK, which the person did not witness individually but recalls thanks to different media as significant or even trajectory changing moment and locates themselves in this context.

7.1.3.1 Idealising the Past and Victims

Khezo's story, narrated by Mehmed, can be considered incipient for the idealised framing of the past. In this compelling story, the Armenian figure depicts positive, inspirational and humane aspects as discussed. Nonetheless, such an agency is not enough to correct circumstances for the sake of society. Whether or not this accentuation the protagonist receives masks collective notions of violence is a point of discussion. In further stories of Mehmed, we encounter peaceful social conditions in his home village – and within a somehow superior position of Armenians, "S. [his home village] has a distinct quality, it is famous for its grapes. There is this claim that the S. grapes came from Bourgogne or the Bourgogne grapes arrived there from S. Because the two grapes are the same" (sequence 2: 15–18). He continues this framework pinpointing the buried Armenian gold and beauty of Armenian girls, "we [Mehmed retells his grandmother's account] knocked on their door when we needed something, they never turned us down" (sequence 2: 28 f). Through the Armenian girls' beauty, the idealisation of the victims expands from "working man collective", that takes care of vineyards, to the Armenian collective, including women. Beyond that, the grape and Armenian gold also expand the temporal boundaries of idealisation because their rumours are still alive, triggering interest of gravediggers. Thus, an idealised victim flourishes from the violent past. For a comparison, concerning the Armenian stories on Van, Türkyilmaz (2011, 332) points out: "the fact that the Armenian suffering caused by Russian soldiers, Armenian militia and the new government itself [the governorship in Van] rarely, if at all, appears in Armenian victimhood narratives is a striking example of power relations and ideological nature of 'victimhood work'."

Such an idealisation of the Armenian other and the alleged coexistence is to be found in other interviews as well. For instance, in case of his biographical narrative, Kerem recounts the Armenian past of his hometown B. Similar to Mehmed, he mentions the vineyards there, and portrays hardworking people building and cultivating mountainous territories with orchards. In the same sequence, he puts Kurds among the parties who destroyed such remnants. Kerem further utilises this comparison in the next passages when he points out that after Armenians, Kurds did not add anything to the city.

We stumble upon similar features in Azim's narrative when he points to handcraft performed by Armenians in general or the long-gone mills of his home village that were reportedly built by the then Christian community. Murad also talks about coexistence before the genocide as well as an idealised victim, yet here specifically the Assyrians due to the region where he grew up. He idealises this victim image based on its success in cultivating rough lands perfectly, conducting scientific methods in these terms. Furthermore, he underscores organised Assyrian communities seeking political rights. Thus, the abilities for work become supported by socio-political aspects in his storytelling. According to Murad, Assyrians had organised councils for their well-being which had not been a case in Kurdish society in those years. Hence, he stipulates a framework involving his motion about coming-to-terms-with-the-past: the Kurds today have learned from their mistakes and adopt political approaches the Assyrians once exercised.

Four interview partners (Azim, Mehmed, Murad, and Zal) emphasise the coexistence in direct manners. Other three interview partners (Delal, Kerem, and Emin) mention mostly a life together with Armenians in indirect forms. Such a narrative intervention with the coexistence concept in recalling memories can also be observed in Kurdish oral history accounts from other regions, for instance, as the *kirvelik* institution (please see Chapter 5.4.2, and Çelik and Dinç 2015, 53–84).

Furthermore, the story of Mehmed's relative who participated in killings reveals another aspect concomitant with the outline of some collective references. In Mehmed's referring, his relative mentions a serene environment among Kurds and Armenians in the village. When Mehmed (sequence 3: 47–50) asks him why he murdered people, he starts with a background construction to his answer "in the beginning we were very peaceful to each other". In the same lines, Mehmed recounts how the situation flipped, "the newcomer imams in the mosques, gave a fatwa, a speech ... 'wherever you encounter an Armenian kill him because killing an Armenian means the way to heaven'." In other words, the peaceful living of Armenians and Kurds had changed its course because of outsiders' intervention. The naïve feelings of Kurds towards exercising the needs of religions were abused, so to speak, and people were lured into the conspiracy of the Turkish State in homogenising the country through mass killings.

As a footnote, there is another significant aspect which discloses the interpretational setting of idealisation. The first-ever question Mehmed poses was why his relative was disabled. The answer to that is related to the Armenians as well. According to his relative, the Armenians he killed cursed him and made his feet dysfunctional. The Armenian figure embodies a sort of superiority in its absence, not just because of the coexistence or the farming techniques but also based on its metaphysical powers. In other words, the persecuted people carry the responsibility for his relative's disability.

Returning to my point on the thesis of naïve ordinary people, the instrumentalised Kurds had changed the trajectory of this ideal past, or the coexistence, yet this very thesis stresses at the same time that not all Kurds can be marked as such. We encounter the instrumentalisation thesis generating a binary of betrayers vis-à-vis loyalists to their neighbours in the very coexistence descriptions (cf. Dinç 2016).

7.1.3.2. Narrative of Instrumentalisation and Victimhood

Similar to Mehmed's point, according to Kerem and Murad, the violence had occurred with the impact of outsiders' religious motion – or when imams started to take part in deceiving Kurds for killings. Murad associates this historicised religious aspect of the Armenian Genocide with the Yazidi Genocide of ISIS, using an anachronism and reasoning the situation with religion's misconduct. When we met in Van in Spring 2016, the news from Yazidi towns of Iraq, Sinjar among others, were floating into agencies. People were fleeing from jihadist militias or being captured and murdered by the same. In these terms, Murad relates the religious layers of the genocidal violence in 1915 to current events and comes to the conclusion that the dominance of belief triggering violence has not vanished at all. In doing so, he qualifies the Kurdish political movement (and society around it) as the enlightened one which has been able to face its own participation in extermination campaigns. Hence, according to him, it had evolved to not-to-be lured in again – despite the circumstances of injustice. The political positioning of the movement counteracts possible future crimes, so to speak. Yet, Murad also disqualifies further aspects of participation and concentrates the problem on the axis of religion and state institutions regulating religion (Çelik and Dinç 2015, 154–59).[27]

Even though the instrumentalisation argument Kerem employs involves the same contours, that Kurds were played through the religion, his narrative has a slight difference, "did Armenians kill too, well perhaps Armenians did too. But as not much as Kurds murdered, you know they're not powerful enough." He pictures killings on both sides, perhaps not mutual, but still, the violent event appears to have been carried out by both peoples. His argument, that Armenians were "not powerful enough", reorganises the victimhood indeed. On one side, it grades the victimhood on a scale of power, and on the other side, his point frames Kurds' authority in the region based on power relations. So, ambiguity surfaces: while powerholders instrumentalised the Kurds, they still kept a relative power in their hands that had made Kurds superior in conflicts, in comparison to Armenians. Thus, the superiority that we witness in Murad's narrative, occupying a relative distance to violence through coming to terms with the past – thanks to the organised community, for instance, dresses in Kerem's storytelling the notion of (physical) power.

---

[27]   The authors collected similar narratives from regions of Diyarbakır, pointing at the role of jihadism and religious institutions during the extermination campaigns. The motives some of which I have treated in the historical chapter of the present study, however, vary and cannot be narrowed down to two possibilities.

Let us remember at this point the stories on the opposite side: Emin mentioning Islamised Armenians with social power, or Mehmed underscoring converted Armenians backing powerholders of his youth, the 1970s. What else does the feature of superiority tell us? Is it perhaps a mark of an attempt in composing and figuring a community in the world of language? I do not have a definitive answer, yet this notion seems to be underscored hosting various elements (or motives) in order to generate a we-group. Likewise, it appears to connect periods, put a reasonable chronology forward, and clarify the context for the we-group in the realms determined by power relation. Perhaps, further narratives would be helpful in this manner.

In somehow contrary to such instrumentalisation compositions, Azim mentions that the "time after Armenians" has worsened everything, "for the Kurds it became much worse. They made a pact with the state, and later it was our turn…" His argument pins it down that there was a mutual understanding, a pact between the state and Kurds as a – generalised, homogenous – group which ended up with Kurds suffering under violence operated by their allies of this bygone pact (cf. Çelik and Dinç 2015, especially Chapter 6 on reasoning the massacres in Diyarbakir). In a later sequence, he says, "after they [Armenians] were deported from Kurdistan, Kurdistan became poorer and poorer because the jewellers in Midyat, carpenters in Diyarbakır … were all Armenians." The gone richness of this geography will haunt the Kurds but not the Armenians, perhaps, because Kurds lost them and now they have to live in their absence. Thus, the victim of the whole story appears to be the Kurds. He, for instance, continues his narrative describing the backlashes of being organised, comparing Armenians and Kurds in an anachronistic template – that Armenians had been attacked by Kurds who did not understand the Armenians' goals (being organised, having political claims, et cetera). Now Kurds are attacked due to the same reasons. It resembles very much Murad's articulation, as well as politicians' speeches from the Kurdish movement (*Agos* 2014; cf. Dinç 2016).

In our interview, Delal points to assimilated Kurds of her childhood who (have) sided with the Turkish State. When it comes to 1915, she presupposes that it would have been not much different in this period of time, "[a]nd of course if you have a good relation with the state then you would hang the Turkish flag too, and other things too, actually the thing shows itself totally different in village, in the provinces there happened, (cough)" (sequence 27: 443–445). In fact, she pursues her comparisons between Kurds from downtown, the assimilated ones, vis-à-vis Kurds from the province like her, the not-assimilated-ones. Her argument is empowered by the act of referencing her own childhood experiences, that downtown children were not able to speak Kurdish like her; and that Kemalism was to be seen clearly in the streets. She employs her interpretation of Kurds and comparting them into "we" and "others" in order to talk about the

Armenian Genocide. The instrumentalisation thesis comes in this sense into play, in schemata of the collaboration of the "other" Kurds.

As it is argued in the historical chapter and exemplified with the situation in Van in 1915, the organisation of extermination campaigns did not occur in sudden terms but in a process that had been tuned by local actors (A-Do 2017; Kévorkian 2015; Türkyılmaz 2011). Hence, these local protagonists, such as governors, required people willing to act on their flank. Thus, there was a social relation between perpetrator groups, be it organic (to "save" the empire, religion, community, or family) or lucrative (to benefit from the genocide) (cf. Kurt 2018; Üngör 2011; Üngör and Polatel 2013). In such a relation, being active in frames of violence cannot be ignored because the person should consider possible options in partaking. However, when the narrative highlights the end of a nostalgic, idealised coexistence due to people being played, it ignores (even covers and exculpates, perhaps) the agency of perpetrators and makes them inevitably naïve victims of the story. It rewrites the agency of the subject. It reformulates the past and enables access to history at the same time. Regarding anachronisms – which I treat in the next subchapter in-depth, Rothberg (2009, 136 f) points out, "although these forms of anachronism constitute different types of 'error' when perceived from a historicist perspective, they can also serve as powerful subversive and demystifying means of exposing the ideological assumptions of historicist categorization ..." In my view, the instrumentalisation thesis has the same effect.

The narrative elements that are provided by the informants of this study help them to make meaning of past events and most importantly of their present conditions. They are not just some protagonists or materials they recall. In the case of place, for instance, it determines the spacetime first: if the event took place in the periphery or in the centre; and when it happened. The question of whether it is about the genocide, the aftermath, or political violence on Kurds also influences the temporal organisation of the story. Likewise, the materials appear to me as a carrier of narration, the mnemonics for specific events as well as circumstances. For example, they are connected to the times when the Kurds and the Armenians shared a space or to the times after the Armenians were "gone". Even at the same time, they can pave the temporal road until today, such as through treasure hunters.

Similarly, protagonists act as indicators to "decipher" the narrator's motives, for instance, through the emphasised characteristics of certain protagonists. If they point to historical or present circumstances or even both at the same time can be questioned. In these terms, these narrative elements give us clues with which we can outline this very memory landscape and, likewise, the trajectories of remembrance (de Saint-Laurent 2017).

At times, the narrators tend to use collective references, such as about a long-gone coexistence and/or instrumentalisation thesis (also in artistic works, we encounter these forms, for a discussion please see, Çelik and Öpengin 2016; Galip 2016). Thinking that these theses are static would be a misrecognition of the quality of such references. They are constructions open to variables and new components – stemming from personal, family, or collective experiences, and aspects related to the political movement (cf. Brockmeier 2015; de Saint-Laurent 2017; Zittoun 2017). References have to concur with the changing conditions. In this transitional process, the selective argument of instrumentalisation has generated a new shape for the Kurdish victimhood narrative (Türkyılmaz 2011, 335):[28] setting the focus on Kurds as deceived ones and conjugating it with the political violence performed by the "other Kurds" and the same powerholder of the genocide, the Turkish State. The point Laura Jeffery and Matei Candea (2006, 289) underscore would be helpful to locate the property of this narrative: "… victimhood establishes a space for a specific kind of politics; but it clears the ground, it poses itself as the neutral or indisputable starting point from which discussion, debates and action – in a word, politics – can and must proceed."

What is the effect of narratives of instrumentalisation? Do they de-historicise the violent past through redesigning the "perpetrators" (cf. Pohn-Lauggas 2019; Welzer, Moller, and Tschuggnall 2002)?[29] I would argue to some degree, these overlook or even retune historical facts. The resistance in Van, and due to that the agency of Armenians, does not pop up. The reorganisation of the narrative occurs around the trajectory of the Kurdish history. In this design, 1915 provides the premise for recounting certain social constellations, for instance,

---

[28] Deriving from Sartre's arguments on antisemitism and Jewish life in Europe, Türkyılmaz (p. 351) points out "the Kurd was a person whom only others considered to be a Kurd. The idea of Kurd, in its current connotation, was only a nascent form in a handful of elite political imaginations." Other researches portray a similar picture of the Kurdish past as well (please see, Bozarslan 2015; Klein 2014). Then he (ibid.) adds, "This renders Kurdish 'victimhood work' focal to the construction of the Kurdish national identity, which like the Armenian and Turkish versions also entailed a collective self image of unique victimhood at its center. This dissertation illustrates that public victimhood narratives are contextual and often (re)shaped to suit elite political agendas." Concerning the aspect of political agendas, I do not deem that it applies to every aspect of the current state of Kurdish memory, as this present study argues. Collective memory is much more dynamic, fluid, and amorph than an "elite political agenda."

[29] In her study on an Austrian family biography that involves narratives of resistance, Pohn-Lauggas questions the depoliticisation and dehistoricisation attempts of Austrian master narrative on the Nazi era. In terms of victimhood narrative, the Kurdish storytelling provides us with a picture that resembles the Austrian one, I suggest.

we-and-others within the Kurdish puzzle (in Delal's, Kerem's and, Mehmed's narrations) or clear groupings in socio-economic terms (as Azim indirectly and Emin directly suggest). In other words, the Armenian Genocide puts the fundament for the victimhood narrative of the Kurds: alongside the violence in the region, victims of the instrumentalisation and bygone coexistence come to be (in the long run) the Kurds.

7.2 Continuity of Violence and Temporal Questions

All of these features that are highlighted in order to question the meaning-making efforts through narratives put content boundaries, so to speak, so that the story expands enough to point at the focal issue, the violence. These content boundaries blossom from social interactions of the narrator without a doubt (Bruner 2004; Schütz and Luckmann 2003). In such content loaded frames, the narrator utilises figures, places, and materials interlinked to personally and collectively determined (and depicted) stories, and links them to each other, with or without having such a purpose. In doing so, they become an actor in changing the flow of a particular story – acting their part in meaning-making and benefiting from the multidirectional nature of collective memories (cf. Rothberg 2009).

Beyond (and thanks to) content-dependent-brackets, the story marks a temporal dimension as well. Protagonists, items, and/or events that are interlinked determine the time organisation, not only the topic. In other words, these temporal brackets derive from the socially (and culturally) moderated notions (Wang 2016; cf. Wertsch 2004) that the given person points out in their narration. The temporal dimension of stories – due to their motives – should be considered fluid and interwoven, in Norbert Elias' words (1984, 50) "the separating line between past, present, and future is in constant movement since people who experience events as past, present, and future alter or change" [translated by E.Y.] – and as is it the case with memory issues (cf. Schütz and Luckmann 2003, 286–312).[30]

---

[30] Schütz points to "casual coherence" that appear for instance in constructions of "in order to" – pointing to causal framing for future – or "because" – reconstruction of the past within personal motives – and the "interwovenness of structures of relevancy" that "an experience constitutes itself when one utilises personal awareness unto described topic of the current situation" (p. 305) [translated by E.Y.]. This mechanism emerges based on experiences pulled into interpretation and sedimented in the biographical organisation (p. 279).

It is perhaps unclear in terms of their limits, what they could subsume or what not. An investigation of temporal elements will clarify the time question – and in particular the *social time* (Sorokin and Merton 1937).[31] The time reconstruction in the narratives on the Armenian Genocide and individual experiences of violence occur to be non-uniform – in contrast to objective astronomical time – but qualitatively determinant for the narrator's (causal) interpretation as well as biographical organisation (cf. p. 621). The Kurdish collective memory emerges in a specific organisation of temporal dimensions – and even generates them, for which I borrow the term social time. In the case of the present research, for instance, when time provides the narrators with an orientation "a kind of relative compass" (Subrt 2014, 240; Elias 1984), the concept of social time – pointing to epistemological time constructed by social indicators such as interactions – appears to be adequate to describe the temporal form emerging between temporal brackets (Fischer 2018, 464; Nassehi 2008).

In the interviews with Zal, Mehmed, and Azim, the temporal dimension includes the genocide deriving from collective references as well as the present situation based on personal experiences – the retrospective conduct. Hence, the biographical narrative designates the widening of time scope. It includes in this manner arguments and descriptions about the political movement and regime of violence in the region. All of these three informants provide in this sense a story of the last 100 years (at least) that is nourished with family and personal experiences; supported by their acquired knowledge on the history of war, Kurds, and/or Armenians; and reconstructed through interpretational and transformative patterns formed in intersubjective space (cf. de Saint-Laurent 2017; Wertsch 2004). In these terms, the semantical approach on stories highlights not just unique elements to interpret such as the place or protagonists but grants the path to clarify temporal layers. The contextualisation of a particular time the narrator adopts in their talk includes various features, as pointed out, in a certain spacetime, such as the national or socio-politically determined one – or the stateless form (cf. Hirsch 2019). Thus, the social time ruling in the lives of people echoes in the narrative.

A specific example concerning the interwovenness of subject matter(s) – blurring and rebinding time dimensions – belongs to the life story of Mehmed. When he gives details about his youth years in the 1970s and under what

---

[31] Pitirim A. Sorokin and Robert K. Merton describe the term *social time,* which they investigate and propose in their paper, "… that social time, in contrast to the time of astronomy, is qualitative and not purely quantitative; that these qualities derive from the beliefs and customs common to the group and that they serve further to reveal the rhythms, pulsations, and beats of the societies in which they are found" (p. 623).

circumstances he politicised, he describes the political polarisation in town, "imagine there was the police, and there two grey wolves [ultra-nationalists] set fire a shop, burned down tailor's workshop … all the people, they watched, and the policemen protected them, staying at a safe distance" (sequence 46: 722 ff). Then, he exposes another aspect to conclude the tailor's story strengthening the connections to the situation in town and its past:

> the son of the same tailor was murdered, or someone else maybe, I don't know he was called "tailor's son".. There was a canal and vineyards at the upper side of T., vineyards aaa, it was said the vineyards were left by the Armenians, vineyards, a wide canal flow through, that guy died in that canal, they hit his head with a shovel. He was a leftwing, and the right-wings killed him. (sequence 46: 727–730)

The Armenian past comes into light in the absence of Armenians. This background construction contours the frame in which the town narrative settles: the violence (has) continued in different ways, through further figures, but still governed by state assets. The past violence was to be seen in remnants – the canal or vineyards, even to be lived with when the new events took place. The notion of oppression reaches a supratemporal quality, due to the actors that perform it – state assets and right-wing militants – and the place where it occurs. In Mehmed's narration, Armenians (and their fate) appear to be unclear, even perhaps concurring the quality of a *nowhen event* (Portelli 1988). For when it comes to Armenians in this particular narrative, it has an open-ended structure: the Armenians had left.

Azim also looks into the history of his village with which he was not familiar until he discovered that oral history collection of genocide survivors from different regions. After narrating his biography for 19 sequences without any word on the genocide memory, he puts a coda asking me to talk about the Armenians. Thus, he returns to the "actual topic" he pointed out just before our interview. This discovery has motivated Azim to pose critical questions concerning the past of his village:

> it was always told that Armenians lived there, but for the very first time I've seen it in that book and aaa was shocked, started to read, there had been twelve mills, one church, one school, yesterday night I asked my dad, how many ch/ aaa mills there were [in his childhood], he counted six.

With the medium of oral history accounts, he began to bridge the past to his present, involving his family in his endeavour. His confrontation with this particular knowledge triggered an emotional encounter as well, so that he could not view his village with his "old lenses" any longer. He has been feeling as "an invader" since, says Azim.

The notion of violence surfaces as a forced change in a certain locus: the ruination of the Armenian properties. Nevertheless, set in connection to previous segments in which he tells stories of violence concerning his biography, he uses the phenomenon of social time in reconstructing his biography, I suggest. Changing the subject from his life story (and in the collective sense, Kurdish society) to Armenians is not just a move for relief. It also is an attempt to localise his experiences in a widened temporal framework of injustice as well, or "biographies provide ... social and individual time structures and arrange for future orientation" (Fischer 2018, 466).[32]

According to Mamoş, his life story splits into two parts. The first is framed by the years before he became paralysed during the clash. His life as a man in a wheelchair shapes the second part. The latter has been longer than the first part. However, this separation also underscores the moment when his life changed through being politicised and joining the guerrilla. Moreover, these two parts can be differentiated from each other concerning the injustice and violence he experienced. For after he was shot and caught, he was delivered to the hospital that started the systematic unjust treatment. He also associates his experiences of injustice with the experiences that the Kurdish collective has made. Due to this fact, Mamoş builds with his narration an argument of continuity of violence and exemplifies it with his own life story. He tries to find a place for his life story in the broad setting, in the concept of Kurdish collective – and its social time.[33]

---

[32] Regarding the contextualisation of time and biographies' relation with time, Wolfram Fischer (ibid.) points out: "In der Gesellschaft der Gegenwarten entwickeln sich auch biographische Formulare. Sie sind in der Lage, Synchronisationsprobleme von Funktionssystemen und solche der einzelnen Indviduen zu bearbeiten. Nassehi spricht hier systemtheoretisch von der ,Form der Biographie' (Nassehi 1994), die Anschlussprobleme bearbeitbar macht, die durch inkonsistente Zeitstrukturen entstehen. Indem in Konstruktionen von Biographie das, was dazu gehört ... von dem unterschieden wird, was zwar vorkommen kann, aber nicht genannt wird ... bringt die Form der Biographie einen Differenzierungsgewinn. Das macht Biographien als Temporalisierungen moderner Identitäten, d. h. anschlussfähig für Weiteres."

[33] The political impacts on the Kurdish social world do surface through his biography. Hence, his struggle aims to confront the injustice and to say it out loud, for instance, in such an interview. It is furthermore vital to point out that Mamoş does tell explicitly his biography (or highlight moments that are life-changing to him); not any pieces related to collective memory (such as how the Armenians had lived and been murdered or what Kurdish movement has been through). His biography, in other words, embodies the last decades of the continuity of violence. One of the reasons is, I suggest, he writes an autobiography. He already had collected some experiences in facing what happened in his personal life story.

Beyond protagonists and incidents carrying temporal loops, the issue of language rights plays a crucial role in forming biographical projects, as it is the case in the (family) biographies of Mehmed, Azim, and Delal. Azim reports how the state institutions and their environments – the school or university in western Turkey – had treated him in his childhood and youth. He puts these in relation, reconstructs his experiences, and aims to highlight the systematics of oppression on language use. Thus, it comes not to be graded as some personal attitudes of others but as a structural concept. Mehmed points out the resistance of bureaucratic structures against accepting Kurdish as a teaching language, even in language courses, not in school curricula. In these terms, how the veteran Kurdish initiative dealt with the blockade and ignorance of state institutions comes into narrative. He portrays a political premise on which the actors consider their options to bypass oppressive rules performed on the Kurdish language (cf. Hassanpour 1992; Skutnabb-Kangas and Bucak 1995). In Delal's narrative, the issue of language turns out to be the fight for rights in multiple generations – her grandfather rebelling against Kemalist school reforms; her father protecting the language in the family; and Delal using the language as a tool for her job. Due to that, this point expands its spectrum in content (it is not just about the use of language) as well as in time (covering decades), marking the structural aspects of deformation.

The language issue surfaces as a pivotal element for the content as well as temporal brackets. Alternatively said, the law-related question mark hanging on the Kurdish language – the oppression and repression – (Skutnabb-Kangas and Fernandes 2008; Zeydanlıoğlu 2012) occurs to be a supratemporal and supraregional element, it reminds of the personally experienced injustice, and the repression conducted on the collective in the past and at present. Four of the participants of this study, Azim, Delal, Mamoş, and Mehmed, have recounted stories about this particular issue. In addition to the above mentioned three cases, in Mamoş' life language is very much related to his disobedient disposition. He helped an old Kurdish woman in the army hospital who was mistreated by the medical personnel because she could not talk Turkish. At the same time, Mamoş was a prisoner and enemy in this particular building.

As pointed out above, the notion of gravedigging echoes the casual element of profit in describing the past and violence. Nevertheless, it also has a temporal pattern stretching the injustice against Armenians from 1915 to the ruination of Armenian remnants today. In Merve's narrative on her family, the properties "forsaken" by Armenians occur in frames of benefiting from the past by non-Armenian figures at present. Similar to that, the idea Mehmed briefly touches upon, that several families had become wealthy through Armenian gold allegedly, points to the same structure concerning this very act, reconfiguring the spacetime of the place.

One of the latest occasions in these terms – that found nationwide critiques – had happened in the Black Sea region when the locals drained a 12,000-year-old crater lake with the permission of the provincial governor. The reason for this human-made-disaster was rumours that there were treasures left by Christians (bianet 2019). This simple and recent example shows how structured and systematised the ruination runs and that a single person could only carry one of the possible roles in such a setting.

At this juncture, these narratives point out a social time of Kurds. This social time is yet narratively framed through a sort of linear continuum of violence anchoring the beginning to 1915 – even before when we consider the coexistence arguments; connecting it to different protagonist types; and underscoring, for instance, an instrumentalisation. This fierce linear motion clashes with the circular time perception of humans nonetheless, which is shaped by "the basic cycles" like "day, then the week, month, year, seasons, a whole life, generations" (Bertaux and Bertaux-Wiame 1980, 114). It even masquerades the circular understanding in narratives. Therefore, the following questions arise: which facets can we count in terms of the continuity narrative? Would such elements entirely point to institutional – systemic and structural – notions, as in the case of language issues? Is there a relation of reconstructed groupings of "we" and "the others" in this state shaped by the continuum of violence? Where can we find the realm of the "self"?

7.2.1 Anachronisms and Analogies

Close to the end of our interview, Azim puts forward an argument, which occurs to be the most apparent anachronism of the interviews I conducted for this research. He says that "in fact what we [Kurds] go through is the same with what Armenians lived. Like Tahir Elçi, that scene of him falling [after being assassinated] resembles Hrant Dink's, what Armenians live[d] we live, at least our end could have been like theirs, with a state" and adds then other possible "if-outcomes", if not a state then at least a status or autonomy for the Kurds. Beyond the analogy of Elçi and Dink (cf. Zerubavel 2003, 48–52), the alleged outcome for the Armenians, having established a state, is taken to be the initial point to depart. Since the "results" become so highlighted, the history of the genocide and the fact of mass organised violence fade out.[34] At the same time,

---

[34] Here, I do see a listing unnecessary, in terms of what else comes to be suppressed with such a narrative formation, for instance, the Soviet-Armenian struggle under circumstances of Cold War and the post-Soviet Armenian state's struggles in finding its place in times of transition, for which I recommend Gerard Libaridian's work *Modern Armenia* (Libaridian 2004). Similarly, I do not seek to specify the events in which

that he sort-of-disintegrates the happenings from the last 100 years' history, he brings the periods closer to each other (cf. Vico 1948, 251).[35] In my view, such anachronistic structures would execute that masking effect on various topics inevitably. Nonetheless, this particular argument points clearly to the continuity of things, for example, violence, but also the fight against that.

Azim compares the Armenian past with the Kurdish present. He contextualizes Kurds' socio-political demands vis-à-vis non-understanding of other ethnic groups that can be clustered as Turkish nationalists. He mentions that Armenians had claimed rights and were not understood by Kurds back then which would, according to him, resemble the relation of Kurds – the ones who demand rights – and some other ethnic groups in Turkey – the ones who position themselves with the Turkish State. In a blatant formulation, he argues the Kurds are the new Armenians. What he underscores is not the past or remembrance; it is today's problems. For anachronism employs projection on the past having the focus on the present, or as Zerubavel (2003, 50) articulates "[l]ike any other symbol, historical analogies clearly transcend their historical specificity."

Such constructions should need not have to be so precise while "[r]eflecting on anachronism and anatopism can refine our understanding of time and space" (Aravamudan 2001, 343). Different mnemonic elements can subsume anachronistic comparisons that occur to be slightly a political argument referring to history. Continuing Azim's narrative, similar to Murad he blends the Yazidi Genocide by ISIS in 2015 with his experience of watching Fatih Akin's movie The Cut, "it was 2015, the Yazidi massacres in Sinjar happened, Armenians', well it was the 100th year of the genocide, perhaps it was a historical manifest after 100 years, the same happened to the Kurds." He reads history through his loupe loaded with current conflict(s). The Armenian genocide has the function of a bridge in a temporal sense. Nonetheless, Azim starts to build this bridge from his present. It also embodies a pillar for his arguments.[36] In this sense, 1915 plays the role indicating loops of different temporalities and events (cf. Zittoun 2017), through its semiotic quality in social time.

Kurds of different regions were victimised and how – Iran, Iraq, Turkey, and Syria, and particular regions where violent events took place, for instance, Dersim or Halabja.

[35] He performs both parallelly, emptying the content and uniting the times.

[36] Similarly, Murad points to brutal ISIS campaigns against Kurds in Syria and Iraq and compares them with unjust and violent AKP-politics targeting Kurdish society. The vantage point in his narrative is the "Muslimhood" – and imams in the historical sense – that he sees critical and responsible for crimes. In these terms, he fractures the Kurdish society into "we-and-others", the ones that follow(ed) the path to violence and the ones that reject(ed) – his projection on the past bases on this given framework.

Let us consider another case. After explaining the assimilated environment of downtown Diyarbakır in comparison to her provincial hometown, Delal argues that probably during the extermination campaigns it was not much different, "when the Kurds did the genocide, the ones in Diyarbakır it means they had a collaboration with the state" (sequence 27: 442 f). Similar to the temporal expansion mentioned before, her argument bridges two temporal scopes, only this time it stems from her contemporary experiences instead of linearity starting from the past. Nevertheless, the positioning of her late father (and even the isolation he imposed) (have) influenced those experiences pretty much.[37] The effect she yields from that time – her childhood, before her father passed away – is decisive in shaping the temporal organisation of the continuity argument since she blurs the division of periods and highlights the collaboration. Her father's point of view mirrors in her argument, when she distinguishes two Kurdish groupings.[38]

---

[37]   Delal struggles with stories circulated in collective sense and bridges personal and family connections to them. The father figure who was dominant in her household and performed restrictions to "protect" his children and identity issue is decisive in forming her narration. These have even been pivotal in making decisions and experiences in her social world. Her father, who passed away some years ago still holds the strings, when she wants to locate herself and her family biography in the context of Kurdish history and struggle. In other words, this dominant figure is the epicentre of her narration that also determines the temporal and casual dimensions. Her late father impacted her politicisation contractively; the start of her studying is related to her father; how her grandfather's story pops up is correlated to her father as well; and what she informs about her maternal family is very well linked to her father's arguments about this part of the family.

[38]   In another occasion, she emphasises that her father "was at least not an Islamist. This is a relief" (sequence 63: 1342). She compares her own biographical experiences with these two indexical types, a hegemonic nationalist (from her past) and an Islamist (a prevalent figure from her present). Not to forget is that while our interview, she was struggling with the very fact that her home, Sur, was facing devastation because of the clashes and curfews. The time was already an amorph question for her, I assume.
A similar question dwells in Merve's biographical narration. She struggled for a long time to "unshackle" herself from her uncle's influence that was strong in the whole family. She was not allowed to visit her maternal family because it was stigmatised as Kurds by the paternal side. Her father, according to Merve, decided to move to Istanbul; his intention was leaving the uncle's sphere of influence. At this time being, she was preparing for secondary school. When her uncle died, she was relieved to not being forced to revisit Van. She does not want to return to the city because she sees her uncle everywhere. Her arguments with her father, concerning human rights issues in Turkey or Kurdish movement, for instance, are very much influenced by this influential uncle figure a lot. She tells stories first and foremost related to her father, then mother and then comes her uncle even though she has not lived in the same city or shared a

The anachronism and such historicised comparisons substantiate the continuity narrative. For "good versus bad Kurds" anecdote find discursive pockets to exist, and when we consider the village guard system in Turkey, the narrator becomes able to exemplify the division and continuity in practice. The feature of "we" contemplates the non-violence and a coexistence. The feature of "other Kurds" regards collaboration with the orchestrator of violence. Even though it is possibly not the intention, the responsibility question would be brushed aside – or transferred, when this image of "others" occurs in their current "uniforms" in a historical setting and bears the entire responsibility.

It is significant to highlight that the deniers, nationalists, and victimisers of today employ anachronisms concerning the Armenian Genocide as well. Although the point to drive off is altered, the arguments of such groupings involve a series of attempts in explaining the present and history through projections. In Chapter 5, I have discussed how such patterns are made use of in historiography and political arguments by public agents and deniers, for instance, in reconstructing PKK as the chronological follower in the category of "traitor" to ASALA. After Dink's assassination, Delal for instance saw wall writings and graffiti popping up in the city of K., hailing the murderer's actions, "there were lots of other wall writings like Kurds Armenians … Fucks and bastards, stuff like that … well Hrant was murdered, but it, linked to the Kurds I have no idea how, why Kurds now" (sequence 65: 1388–1390). Without question, for racists, there would be no apparent difference between "other" groups, that are generalised in cultural terms (cf. Balibar and Wallerstein 1991). However, what I want to point out is that in this racist rhetoric, there are traces of denialist anachronistic arguments to find.

On another occasion, after the war was reignited in 2015, Delal again experienced a nationalist rally in Istanbul, "meanwhile Cizre [a Kurdish town, which suffered weeks-long curfews and witnessed demolishment of town's locus] was under siege, and 'X. [a district in Istanbul, predominantly inhabited by Armenians] will become a grave to Armenians, Cizre to Kurds'." This nationalist analogy shows us that the resulting point of historical facts, such as the genocide, is far from being ignored or denied; such historical events are well accepted and find therefore pockets in "anachronistic aesthetics" (cf. Rothberg 2009, 135–74). It is even their envisioned future (Brescó de Luna

busy social world with him for more than a decade. Just to compare, the stories about her siblings are the least ones in the quantitative sense.

Furthermore, lots of points that she raises about her parents are also related to her uncle's attitudes. This protagonist, her uncle carries the temporal dimension: from the family's past until the moment of our interview, I suggest. He is the vital polar in arguing and narrating. He has the forming power of what to talk and how to talk.

2017; de Saint-Laurent 2017; cf. Ochs and Capps 1996). This motto remodifies denialist arguments about the genocide – that Armenians had allegedly rebelled and were therefore "deported" – and projects onto the conflict in Kurdistan. Perhaps, we need to question the level of trivialisation in denialist arguments (Cohen 2001) and start seeing the ascribed superiority that is given by the perpetrator role.

7.2.2 Generational Questions

In most of the narrators' lives, being politicised plays a vital role. Especially experiences in their childhood and youth in this regard come to be very formative, for their perspective concerning the present issues as well as past ones. Some of them look into and try to understand differences between generations and some come to generalised descriptions. Their point of departure for both consists of personal experiences that they made in their early years. Furthermore, in discussing generational aspects, it would be crucial to keep in mind that the aspect of childhood years means the family interaction (or dialogue) on specific topics that maybe they did not experienced personally – a sort of post-memory on oppression in early republican years for instance (Hirsch 2012; cf. Rosenthal 1997; Pohn-Lauggas 2019).

The fragmented area of memories in generational framework does appear beyond the family setting, e.g. in the social venue that is (in our case, the Kurdish society) shaped by various political demands and trajectories of politicisation. In these terms, different generations represent different manners obviously (for instance, concerning the Armenian past). Based on the narratives I gathered, the generational questions have not only been concentrated in the frames of the family institution but are also considered in broad terms referring to generations of the society, so to speak. One of the examples, which is already treated in different manners, would be the Kurds who were deceived into killing Armenians for further benefits. This phenomenon determines a generational framework. Hence, it organises the time structure in collective memory, when the victimiser Kurd appears as the played ancestor. It is, yet, not the only example concerning meaning-making attempts via generational narratives.

As a teacher, Mehmed sees a generalised discrepancy in today's youth. Answering my questions concerning his university years (sequence 33; 34; 35), he reconstructs first his own experiences related to social change from the 1980s onwards and then comes to his points on how this new generation acts. According to him, society has been put on a successful track of depoliticisation – starting with the military coup in 1980. He claims this was a calculated political manoeuvre by the junta regime and successive governments. His argument stemming from social sciences graduation and his observations as a teacher includes critiques on not just the policy but the youngsters as well, "There is no analytic thinking no questioning, questioning is, taken for granted, forbidden" (sequence 37: 587 f). In this regard, he sees only some crumbs of a political youth in Kurdistan which he localises around the Kurdish movements. The way how Mehmed describes the issue sounds that this group, however, has a destiny to be condemned by the armed measures of the Turkish State.[39] The two forms of youth positioning he talks about surface as either being apolitical or being at gunpoint. It appears to be a mirroring of the "we" and "other Kurds" composition in the context of youth.

Mehmed's interpretation of things seems to be engraved by his adult perspective, nonetheless. The question, therefore, should be: what would a young member of the society tell us? To the question about his childhood years, Azim replies, quoting an Iraqi Kurdish director, "I was born as an adult, we Kurds had no childhood." He specifies this point by bringing up his past. Learning Turkish had (or even has) meant power abuse to Kurdish children, including him. He reads the generational issues putting the state repression into the focal point. In his conclusion, probably nothing has changed since, for instance, the language policies of the country were not redesigned fundamentally.

Furthermore, from my point of view, the development of Azim's awareness would deliberately show what a young member of the society (experiences and) perceives in his childhood and teenage years. He became familiar with the issues surrounding the Kurdish society through different media and personal encounters. In the elementary school, he once thematised a (Kurdish) song he listened to and was harshly criticised by his teacher because of the language (cf. Skutnabb-Kangas and Bucak 1995, 347 ff).[40] The only-Turkish-context of the school and the only-Kurdish-context back home had clashed in his life

---

[39] Thus, while Mehmed points to the polarised political situation in the Kurdish society, religious depoliticised people on one side and the movement on the other, he reconstructs his argument of "we-and-other" Kurds further for the setting of the younger generation. In the following passages, he points out that the Kurdish politics started to deconstruct this gap between those two groupings embracing religious figures. Thus, in short, the continuity of state handed social engineering that affects Kurdish generations was criticised and even stopped by the Kurdish movement itself.

[40] Kangas and Bucak's paper starts with the Kurdish journalist Eşref Okumuş' testimony that he gave in spring 1990 to the Conference on Minority Rights, Policies and Practice in South-East Europe: "… When you, seven years old, go to school, you won't be able to communicate with your teachers. At least if you, just like me, have parents who do not speak Turkish. It will take 4 or 5 years before you at all can speak with your teachers…" (ibid.) Although the situation of "post-junta" 1980s was different, as one can argue, the experiences Kurdish children make still have some similarities with regard to perception by the authorities.

several times, from his childhood onwards to his university years. Furthermore, he experienced stigmatisation because of his skin colour; student protests, disobedience actions, and subsequent police seizures in the universities, in the western as well as the eastern part of the country. His friends had joined the guerrilla, and their dead bodies had been brought back. Thus, he had not only been through the absence of his friends but the consequences of the unjust regime as well.

At this juncture, he treats the theme of him becoming familiar with the Kurdish conflict in one segment of our talk in particular. He portrays the process of his awareness' improvement, starting with two other pupils from the school who read books on the equality issues concerning the Kurdish society. Azim also visited and borrowed books from the city library but mostly Turkish literature. Following that, he read newspapers and watched prohibited Kurdish TV channels. Due to this contextualisation, Azim's remark – "Kurds have no childhood" – gains importance because it indicates the social challenges that a young Kurd has to go through – in order to become an aware member of the society and community. Furthermore, he personifies the Kurdish collective of his generation in his "self" (cf. Hinrichsen, Rosenthal, and Worm 2013).[41] In these terms, the generation before him could not offer him an orientation, yet the systematic repression negatively guided him. So, he discovered his agency. The elders have no place in his narrative, except his questioning his father about the Armenians of the village.

As mentioned in the section of the case studies, what preoccupies Zal most is his lost role for the next generations because of the impacts of violence. The violence in the region surfaces in his narratives as a two-edged dagger. It fosters radicalisation among young people and at the same time mutes adults' voices so that they could not establish any connection with the following/new generations anymore. According to him, the generations have started to lose contact with each other. His biographical project, now as a father, struggles with the issue of not being able to keep up the adult role (cf. Erikson 1978). When there is no younger generation which is ready to listen, there is no sense in having elders that show the wise path. The adulthood's need of the contact

---

[41] In the cited paper, the authors discuss the Palestinian "we-image" and its representation by the youngsters in life story interviews. They speak of a homogenous collective standing vis-à-vis an opposite side. The argumentative domination in the interviews the authors underscore are then bounded with personal experiences of the informant. And in this process, the person becomes the discursive representative of the "we-group" (pp. 179 ff). In another part of our interview, after describing the fate of his friends (who joined the guerrilla and died), Azim for instance argues that he was the only figure who did not leave the town, yet nothing else could differ him from his friends.

to younger generations has become damaged severely (cf. ibid.). According to Zal, continuing violence is the reason why it has come to this point. Parallelly, he incorporates his years in Cyprus that he spent in considerable distance to the conflict in Kurdistan, even indirectly, as a quasi-culminating point in viewing happenings from a different perspective. It, perhaps, also was the tool helping him to set such a distance to generational conflicts. No matter what, for him the impact of this permanency is so significant that he reconstructs his narrative on this very premise: the detachment of generations.

Why has this issue of generations any importance in discussing collective memory at all? If we consider memory as a fluid feature that roots into the social world and blossoms from interaction (cf. Gergen 1994; Halbwachs 1991; 2012; de Saint-Laurent 2017; Wang 2016; Wertsch 2004), then – under circumstances of "stagnation" (Erikson 1978, 240 f) – we would eventually encounter a gap of interaction between living realities of different age groups. Nevertheless, they (have) experience(d) the very same or similar events and grades of violence. Perhaps, in time the (collective) memory would mirror this deficiency in the social framework as well. Nevertheless, for now, the generational aspect turns out to be a noteworthy aspect in illustrating the impure political landscape (Bar-On 1999). Its effects can be described eventually as two separated (relative) social times, the first employed by the older generations and the other shaped by the youngsters in their struggle. Although these two have similar shapes, their subjects stay arrested in their very own temporal organisations.

7.2.3 Envisioned Futures

Remembering that the trajectory of remembrance encapsulates past, present, and (possible or sought) future endeavours (de Saint-Laurent 2017; cf. Fischer 2018), the bridge between (a positive) past and the future appears to be an essential subject matter in this enquiry. The past narrated by my interview partners, be it a family story or personal encounters, involves in several ways imagining-attempts of the coming future. Ochs and Capps (1996, 24) underline that "[p]redominantly, narratives of personal experiences focus on past events ... However, such narratives link the past to present and future life worlds." In case of the interviews presented in this book, it is the will to come back to good old times, the period of coexistence, or the years when Kurds could make a living in their hometowns. For instance, the coexistence was not lived by the very persons who participated in this very study. It is the hope that designs the envisioned future. A future vision in the context of memory implies a connection between the past bright experience – reserving the possibility that it is not experienced one-to-one, or is even a uchronia (Portelli 1988) – and the hope to repeat it in the future.

In this sense, Azim pinpoints books and movies which raised his interest in the questions concerning the Armenian past. His encounter with the information about the Armenian past of his village, which he recounts before I started recording, seems to be a prolepsis (Brescó de Luna 2017). He begins his narrative, giving such details. Moreover, based on his readings, he plays with the template of coexistence, "I really would like to see that Armenians would come back and live here, well I [have] loved heterogeneity, always." However, he also identifies racism (of Turks) as the counterpart to this reconstruction – of his will, "but Turks, I don't know, they are too conservative for such diversity, and there is this terrible lynch culture." In such a way, he provides a template for his wish that is yet affected by the conflictual situation. Even though he projects the problem onto the "other", who would principally not allow his wish coming true according to Azim, he underscores a grey zone for a possible future of coexistence as well.

In contrast, it is hard to encounter a sort-of-prolepsis in Zal's narration, perhaps, since his everyday life is troubled by the questions of his role as an adult in the society and obstacles that hinder him from being proactive in this very role. While the ongoing deterioration of circumstances, which is connected to the continuity of violence, he does not talk about a possible bright future. For he has seen the degraded quality of life in Kurdistan during the war. In this worsened scenario of reality, he could not find a path that would bring him to dream of or to hope for improvement. Perhaps, being a lawyer has allowed him to see the hardest living conditions. He knew some of his clients from his childhood. They were arrested back then, and they have continued their life imprisoned since then. Hence, he sticks to the reality of that very present, which depicts the continuity.

Zal craves giving meaning to the present, yet he has been not able to do it. His narrative concerning his father who was charged by the notorious State Security Courts (DGM) in the 1990s and yet acquitted by the same (please see the case study on Zal's biography) provides some clues in these terms. According to him, when he compares the court ruling back then that found his father not guilty with the present verdicts, he comes to the conclusion that the circumstances have worsened over time. Zal argues, even such infamous courts had been able to give a verdict based on the principles of law, which the courts today ignore. Deriving from the ruling about his father, he tries to describe the worsening of the situation and the continuity of injustice.

Remembering De Luna's point (2017, 283), that collective memory is "aimed at giving meaning to the past in order to meet present demands and attain different future goals", the question appears: does the wish for regeneration of the long-gone coexistence fulfil this empty spot of "the future goals"? However, there is another question. It stands opposite to and yet inspired by the discussion on generations and continuity of violence: Is a future involving no-violence thinkable for narratives from Kurdistan when injustice occupies pictures of past? I believe all my informants try to find an answer to these questions with their life story reconstructions.

The topic which the narrator recounts occurs in a specific temporal organisation. It is very much related to (or even embedded in) the social time (Sorokin and Merton 1937) of the Kurdish society. This organisation takes references to collectively circulated stories – as in the case of vineyards – as well as individual experiences – for instance, how Mamoş was treated in prison. In stories of the Armenian Genocide, two particular time-related constructions appear to be in conduct: the continuity argument and the anachronisms. While the argument of continuity of violence has an involving quality concerning periods – for instance, in narration predating the violence to 1915 and expanding it until the present, the anachronistic structures and historical analogies are carried out in order to stress a comparison (cf. Zerubavel 2003, 48–52) between the fate of the Armenians and the Kurds – in other words, a similarity of the destinies of these two peoples. Indeed an anachronism discloses the framework of continuity in the narrative as well. However, in some cases, continuity is emphasised without any such "time uniting" structure (Vico 1948, 251), for instance when Zal describes an ongoing injustice yet in a worsening continuum since his childhood. Beyond that, the anachronism could also be the argument itself, like in Azim's storytelling when he puts these two peoples in direct comparison. Hence, the social time's scope becomes then determined by the narrator's capacity for recounting the Armenian Genocide and/or certain events concerning the Kurds. By means of recruiting anachronisms or reshaping the social time – including the Armenian past, the unjust regime in Turkey becomes highlighted. With the help of such a comparative setting, the informant obtains the chance (or becomes able) to describe and discuss what has happened in the Kurdish cities. Nonetheless, the generational issues pose a challenge at this juncture because a generational "dispute" which Zal recounts would intervene in the transfer of memory – concerning the Kurdish experience as well as the stories on Armenians.

7.3   The Contested Area and the Self

The contestation of narratives in a memory landscape (or even in the individual reconstructions) is from my point of view, not an "abnormal" feature. The change in memory issues over time, be it collective, cultural, or personal memory or transition in politics of memory, would occur through new active parties in the interactional setting. However, this sort-of-change would not provide a final stroke for the "old" or "older" narratives and erase them from the given memory pattern (cf. Connerton 2008). In most cases yet, the power of transition tends to include, transform, and utilise these non-novel, "established" narratives, as in cases of alliances of memorialisation or even denialism. It also applies to the techniques (the methods) of how stories are conveyed, as the exhibitions launched in Istanbul 2015–16 shed light on this specific pattern (for a detailed discussion, please see, Chapter 5). We could observe the contestation between progressive and well-established narratives in these exhibitions, as well as competitive and inclusion-seeking methods – remembering the points from Chapter 5, *Bizzat Hallediniz'* fashion competing denialism with its his-toriographic tools and *Left Over* proposes new compendiums. The question of contestation is tangent to approaches inasmuch as the narratives (in a similar way we can read the development of trivialisation of the genocide as well, cf. Göçek 2016; Turan and Öztan 2018).

But again, as articulated in the theoretical chapter of the present book, the contestation happens not only between two parties – in a constellation dom-inated by a master narrative produced by state institutions vis-à-vis resisting minority voice(s). Due to the fluid nature of memories, there are several master and minority narratives. They remain in exchange with each other reproducing collective references. In the interwoven context of memory in the collective (cf. Bartlett 1995), the persons who narrate obtain the chance integrating further experiential points that they have collected in their, for instance, professional trajectory. In these terms, memory builds up itself in a cumulative process that interlinks various points of biographical and social experiences as well as different perceptions and ways of treating those experiences. Memory even becomes that process itself (cf. Brockmeier 2015; Erll 2011). In such a proces-sual design, I see contrastive and contested elements as central subject-matters of debate. The question should be if improvement into new memories can be possible without such notions triggering rereading, negotiation, and perhaps even harmonisation, or new conflicts (Purdeková 2018).

In my gathered interviews, the clearest example of such narrative frame-works, which I call *contrasting juxtapositions*, belongs to Zal. When he tells stories from his childhood about the terrific nature of his hometown, this story subsequently contains features of violence, for instance, scenes of clashes and howitzer fires. However, neither of them, nature or violence, loses its impor-tance in the narrative. Both of them are just as significant for his biography as they are for his narrative flow. Based on his life story, this appears to be the pattern that helps Zal to locate himself in the social time of the Kurdish society, which is deteriorated by the ongoing violence.

Furthermore, his narratives possess the modifying power of this spacetime. Hence, his juxtapositions occur in the reciprocal process of reconfiguring the narrative of self and the narrative of society. Similarly, for instance, while he narrates his high-school years, he comes to the part how his class was taken to the army base for target practice in order to increase the "love for the fatherland" (sequence 6: 46). Having school off was fun. Nonetheless, at the same time, students met guns, for the first time personally, that have been in use in this continuous violent space. Zal portrays this occasion through, at least, two perspectives: one as a former student and another as an adult and, of course, lawyer. These two perspectives locate in contrastive ways: student standing for fun and lawyer condemning this action. Yet, his narrative requires both to be told and in order to contextualize the situation.

That very moment in the army base counts to the process of change in his identity structure – as his encounter with the nationalist professor for his (professional) trajectory is. Cyprus provided him obviously with a certain distance to the conflict and a non-party perspective for another political issue – occupation of the island. So, that distance was already connected to the terrain of his experiences he made in Kurdistan and with the institutions of the Turkish Republic. Zal built up his identity construction through such contrastive moments in his trajectory. When he came to tell his story he referred to such antagonisms in his biographical project.

Such juxtapositions help us eventually to clarify the picture of contestation between memories since they reflect the biographical and professional trajectories. They provide sketches concerning different ways of reconstruction of past events and their connection to and clashes with each other. What we encounter is hence a contestation of reconstruction in one biographical talk, not in a collective debate. The narrational approach conducted here utilises two radically different frames in order to draw a picture of the past properly. The self of back then and the self of today render the experience together. Either because of his openness or because he wants to depict the ambiguities, Zal does not fade out any of them. Via such contrastive juxtapositions, he evaluates what he made through and how he acted; he elaborates his agency back then and in present; and he considers his choices vis-à-vis individually experienced incidents and *long durée* of violence.

Moreover, individual and family stories in the interviews disclose various forms of relation to collective references. Some narratives reveal the contestation, for instance, Delal's childhood stories concerning the churches of the town, children's attitude and her mother's criticism. We should consider Delal's years long reflexive positioning on the history of Kurds and Turks – including the genocide – as an affirmative response or consideration of her mother's critique. It was indeed a turning point for young Delal. Its crumbles are pretty much present in her biography and that milestone is to be traced in her identity construction. Yet, some narratives can be located around the collective references, apprehending their face value, such as Delal's instrumentalisation argument in the very same interview. She has sought a balance between collective writings (or perception) and her own experiences.

In the case of anachronisms, as argued – inspired by Rothberg's discussion – that these were mostly utilised for making the narrative easy to follow and provide a "comprehensible" argument. They conjugate with the present to the notions from the past (via anchoring collective references). We can, of course, persuade ourselves that these people do not know what happened because they did not live in this specific period of time or that they are not proficient in historiographic scholarship. Nonetheless, the question should be: how do such stories emerge even when these people are not historians? In these terms, I come to the conclusion that at times the attempts in forming a narrative need anachronism so that the listener and the narrator would find common ground for mutual understanding. That common ground should be stable enough to carry Kurdish collective experiences on ongoing violence and happenings in biographical projects (choices, decisions, and acts in identity fostering trajectories). It also provides the opportunity to inquire time and personal ways of its reconstruction where the contestation between general time recording and individual state occurs.

There is no need to answer to whether the narrators believe in such comparisons of "what back then happened to Armenians is now in the run against us." Their analogies yet show us something else. These contest first of all the perimeters of official denialist positioning and the produced denialist stories concerning the Armenian Genocide. Then they open the path to discuss what has happened in Kurdistan following the extermination campaigns. In this sense, the episodic memory (such as the murder of Hrant Dink or state repression and oppression on Kurds) would correlate with the family biography (armed forces brutality in the 1980s and even in the 1930s, as such in Mehmed's case) and the collectively experienced, interpreted, and determined patterns – regime of injustice, instrumentalisation, and impunity. Perhaps, the narrative reaches a new design again on another occasion since the self of the individual locates in social time (Fischer 2018).

In his research paper on the descendants of Nazi perpetrators, psychoanalyst Werner Bohleber (1998, 259) underscores that these children were "made the bearer of a secret" of their parents so that they "adopt it [the secret emerging from silence] in its identifying measures" [translated by E.Y.]. In this context, the Nazi parents abuse their children with their ideological background idealising their past. He, then, adds that there occurs the danger of "the de-realization of the past" – the psychoanalyst needs to be critical and reflexive to such forms in order to treat the patient properly (1998, 271; cf. Bar-On 1993; Rosenthal 1997). In the case of the biographies I gathered, it is of course not about the first descendent generation of the perpetrators, neither is any real contact with such grandparents spoken out – except for Mehmed. The informants of this present work are freed from such a relation, a social and familiar constellation with ancestors who took part in and benefited from persecution. However, they personally and in their families were target of state political violence. And based on this very feature – no contact to perpetrators back then and being in the mid of war, they tinkered their identity constructions after experiencing trajectory changing events. So, they disclose the political and societal disputes on remembering.

Beyond that, narratives and narrative frameworks that are mostly circulated in society (collective references) have a rapid influence in matters of storytelling. One's narrative is nourished in the web of (socially dependent) memories (cf. Prager 1998, 89–94), mediating temporal and cultural structures that probably stay in contestation. Precisely therefore, disassembling the self from such a web becomes a rough issue because this space is a conglomerate of contradictive memory elements, the ones in the process of reconfiguration – with or without purpose. The traumatic memories of experienced violence, the non-critical treatment of performed violence by ancestors, and political memory discourse that posit remembrance – and perhaps even reconciliation and memory alliance (cf. Heimo and Peltonen 2012; Hirsch 2019; Nijhawan, Winland, and Wüstenberg 2018; Rothberg and Yildiz 2011; Wegner 2018)[42] – define the contested landscape further.

---

[42]   An Armenian–Kurdish transcultural memory alliance – that Wegner elaborates in his research paper concerning Jewish and Black rappers' alliance in the USA; Nijhavan et al. focusing on the pluralistic society of Canada and demands to remember of different communities; Rothberg and Yıldız exploring migrant interventions and initiatives on the Holocaust memory in Germany; Heimo and Peltonen in case of Finnish Civil War memory and emerging image of "foreign power" in the 1990s' narrative – or such constellation possibilities are the questions here. Marianne Hirsch's paper *Stateless Memory* triggers further questions on the role of citizenship, national affiliation (or absence of it), and how the member of the given society perceives it – and of course how the scholars have sought an orientation in national boundaries to investigate memory issues. She describes possible carriers of the stateless memory as follows: "and so are these who have either lost their citizenship, or who have never been fully recognised as citizens by the states in which they live, and who are thus stateless 'at home'" (p. 419). Perhaps, collective memory of Kurds requires to be discussed in these terms as well.

7.3.1 Memory in Transition

As sketched in Chapter 5, the perception of the Armenian Genocide by the Kurdish political movement(s), intellectuals, and society varies and has been a subject of change over the course of time. While a "mutual perpetration" – which, from my point of view, can be described as uchronia, "a nowhen event" (Portelli 1988, 46), was proposed and acknowledged by the Kurdish circles (Aydınkaya 2015; Dersimi 2014). However, in the meantime, there were genocide survivors in the same communities who were adopted or married and forcefully assimilated. Hence, this victim group was arrested in silence.

What Delal narrates concerning her Islamised Armenian relative who converted to Christianity shows that the genocide was already a part of everyday reality in her family due to this specific memory. With the conversion, being Armenian and the Armenian past came to be a topic that deliberately sparks controversies in the family setting. Until that moment, the Armenian roots were associated with positive connotations, according to Delal. From that moment on, the power relations in the society concerning Armenian survivors yet surface in this very family context. When the agency of the person takes a performative step such as conversion, then the discussions achieve another level. The why-question dominated the discursive area. Why has this person converted to Christianity although they come from such an orthodox Muslim family? What is the personal motive behind all of this story? However, the answer to why is sought not in the socially based power relations but the person. This aspect shows us that the very protagonists, in this case, the Armenian relative, possess the power to transform the trajectory. Furthermore, when the victim's wishes come to the fore, then it dwells a very different impact than a political party, it unleashes debates that would eventually become personal in such a family setting.

Nonetheless, this performative action of the family member would perhaps ignite a possible change in the memory. From another standpoint, it appears to be the contestation of memories: some remember the enforced conversion during the extermination campaigns in at least neutral means and defend their memory; and some, in this case the descendant(s), contradict this memory with their action, like through converting back. It happens in the very same space, in the family setting. This contestation plants seeds of change in the remembrance regime, perhaps not effective in the current generation(s), yet this act would have influences in the longer run, I suggest.

With the change of social circumstances and individuals' acts like my interview partners under circumstances of oppression, we encounter a slight alteration in the "mutual victimhood" portrayal. This new framing of victimhood refers to the years of injustice and violence in Kurdistan. Moreover, another point of reference occurs to be the so-called instrumentalisation of "ordinary" Kurds during the genocide. The construction of being a victim through being lured into the perpetratorship disregards, as illustrated before, the active participation of person(s). We see the transformation of collective memory in the Kurdish society with the help of such examples. However, such a change does not mean that there would not be any room for the "mutual perpetratorship" thesis anymore. Deriving from Cohen's points on denialism (2001; cf. Zerubavel 2006), I would suggest the pockets that were already created by and in the Kurdish discursive realm are still there and could offer refuge in discussions at times, or options for recodifications.

Zal brings up a regional perspective stressing that his people from the small provincial town southern of Van had not attacked but even protected Christians (Erll 2011; cf. Levy and Sznaider 2002; Welzer, Moller, and Tschuggnall 2002).[43] He compares his home region with other lands of Kurdistan, reviewing the clusters of reaction and participative motives of ordinary people. For Zal, not-to-victimise-anyone appears to be the unique property of his people. Thus, the region differs from other places. What his hometown occupies in this constellation is the positioning he welcomes, the positioning of resistance; disobeying the rules that claim superiority through instrumentalising people; and opposing the benefit of killings. This exceptional property of people can also be read in different segments of our interview, such as when it is about nature. He seeks a balance between his experiences and the collective references in composing his storytelling, just like Delal. In Zal's but also Delal's case, the regional aspect weighs in. Reflexive or not, both recall what they lived related to supraregional and regional references and find their ways to refer to their identity constructions.

What Zal tells contests the relativising arguments on the massacres and the mutual perpetratorship thesis *par excellence*. This notion points out a transition, a change in collective memory since he (and his thesis) pins down a contradiction in the framework of positions via stressing that his people did not "let them get beaten" (sequence 24). He however blurs the victimhood category at the same time and anonymises the victims, when he stretches the temporal dimension(s) of victimisation. In this context, the question appears

---

[43] Zal moves this special memory from the periphery to the centre of Van. Nevertheless, remembering Levy and Sznaider's points on cosmopolitan Holocaust memory and Welzer et al.'s remarks on alteration of perpetrators' experiences, there are further similar narrative constructions regarding different communities, as we have seen in Mehmed's recollection. Do these other constructions tell us, that there is a mutual social perception concerning the mass political crimes exercised in 1915 or that there is a pattern that is changing?

whether the regional perspective – perhaps without disbanding from collective references – and widening the time of violence reconcile with each other and hence could mark a transformation of the memory.

In Merve's narration, we encounter several layers in these terms: the generational conflict, the feature of gender, political disposition, and disputes in the family that have a massive impact in the (articulation) of these latter three features. Her maternal side, and especially her mother, had to face ethnic slanders by the paternal family because of their being Kurdish. These mostly involved Armenians too, connecting Kurds and Armenians as scapegoats (cf. Cheterian 2015; Turan and Öztan 2018; Holz 2000).[44] However, similar slurs came from the other side as well, targeting the paternal family, according to Merve. This notion, having "Armenian blood" as the paramount element for an assault, degrades the existence of a people through racist frames. Nevertheless, in this case, it happens in a family context. It was not only the slander and curse which disturbed her immensely: until she was 15, she was prohibited by her uncle to meet members of the maternal family. After her and her family left Van and moved to Istanbul in her teenage years, she came off such political fronts of the family and started to shape her individual positioning. It brought her to refusing such slurs or distancing herself from denialism. For Merve, moving to Istanbul definitely connotes change of events. The distance to slanders provided her with a self-reflexive space to consider what was happening in her family in Van. So, she could now take a stand. She reports a similar development in her mother's and sister's attitude.

She recounts another occasion concerning her father's patronising assumption that Merve "would not know" anything about Armenians. While watching the news – and particularly news on international affairs regarding the Armenian Genocide recognition, her father begins to tell her a negationist story involving her grandfather's life in Van and how he had witnessed and resisted to killings executed, this time, by the Armenians. Her father tries to link this question to the Kurds while her mother was in the room. Nevertheless, her

---

[44] At the latest, from the 1980s onward, with the rise of PKK, the analogies entangling Kurdish separatism with the Armenians have started to circulate in the Turkish public discourse. The Turkish nationalist protagonists propagated that Armenians were behind the Kurdish political movements (mostly PKK) so that an evil Armenian figure emerged as the one who allegedly pulled the strings. Hence, the Armenian was advanced to be the so-called figure of the third, or to fill the shoes of the Jew from antisemitic conspiracy theories since this figure had allegedly power to operate behind the closed curtains. The question of national affiliation concerning the "figure of the third" (see Holz' paper) also appears I suppose, due to the effects of national constellations of the cold war and Armenian diaspora communities in different western countries.

mother does stand against such allegations since perhaps "her children grew up", according to Merve. She retells the story first and then compares with what her maternal uncle told concerning the Armenians in Van. Although these differ at some measures, for instance, her uncle underscores genocidal violence against Armenians, they share the focal point: there were mutual killings. However, what Merve together with her siblings think concerning Kurds and Armenians represents another perspective in the family (cf. Nugin 2019).[45] The generational difference crystallises in political disposition again. How younger generations have acted and positioned themselves vis-à-vis stories of grandfathers and grandmothers or their own experiences of victimisation make thus the generational difference.

Merve is more open to discuss and acknowledge past crimes (or the delinquencies that are still going on). She stands for equal rights. Hence, she turns the question mark upside down when it is about family conflicts. What she points out is the projections on the woman in her patriarchally shaped family world – without a doubt, her past in the family has an impact on that standing. Issues concerning Kurds or Armenians were discussed in connection to the family conflicts, pulling her mother into the epicentre. Nevertheless, what she seeks for is her own freedom, having left all such experiences behind. That is also why she studied abroad and why she wants to live abroad again. Besides, this is why she only felt relieved when her uncle, who restricted her life immensely, died. Together with him, potential conflicts have vanished as well.

The transition of a (family or collective) memory could happen through a "newly" obtained information, as in Azim's case when he found the book, or new acts of some members of the very community, as in Delal's example. What the above portrayed biographical moments show is that the remembrance regime changes due to the change of trajectories and generational organisation. Trajectories of politicisation differ not only based on the region and family[46] but in time as well, as Merve's biography outstandingly discloses, and as is also the

---

[45] In his study on family narratives in Estonia, Raili Nugin (p. 1.) puts it that "[e]ach generation has their own agenda, and they creatively shape the narratives using the existing cultural codes and modes of interpretation. It is here that the intergenerational transmission of narratives becomes important."

[46] For instance, another interview partner of mine provides a contrary image. Zeki (whose biography I do not bring into the discussion in this study) comes from a village guard family, and he has also been a *korucu* for over 20 years. The interpretational and historical patterns he utilises are hugely different from my other informants, who position themselves in the proximity of the Kurdish movement. Zeki's viewpoint is very much shaped by his affiliation to the village guards so that he reads the history of Armenians from a more conservative perspective.

case with Delal and Kerem's biographies. This change, as pointed out before, does not erase the old somehow stabilised forms but challenges them in the very same (discursive) space, as in the case of Merve.

What we today witness concerning the Kurdish remembrance is a transitional period that includes narratives on Armenians. This period seems to be a process of modification, resembling the change from mourning to remembering. Cheterian (2015, 107) points out that in the first fifty years after the genocide the Armenian families remembered what they have been through and whom they had lost. According to Cheterian, "it [the remembrance day, 24 April] was a day of mourning" without political motives, "for half a century the generation that had survived was unable to talk openly about what it had gone through" (ibid.). The similarity is that there is no proactive socio-political debate about the years of violence against Kurds, embracing different corners of the society, and mainly focusing on the experiences of the Kurdish communities, except the discussions in the heated political arena, I suggest. There is indeed an enormous scholarly archive about the conflict(s) in Turkey now. Furthermore, different initiatives attempt to de- and reconstruct the settled narratives.[47] With the impact of public (political) discourses and the change over the course of last decades thanks to the individual acts in families and society, the closed space of mourning, so to speak, has started to open itself and to involve further narratives such as the extermination of Armenians. Connections are made. These find public resonance, and when they achieve to be heard, the contestation of memories also becomes present. The relation between memories then leaves the "conundrum" of their biographical organisation even though they pretty much flourish in personal life projects. Nevertheless, this is a process, and it has not ended, eventually will not end too since memory is an ever-evolving notion.

7.4 Concluding Remarks

When I was transcribing Azim's interview, I became preoccupied with the following question a lot: why did he stop narrating about the circumstances and his own life under these very conditions after about 20 sequences and ask me to talk about the Armenians? He sought a new line for his narrative. At least for

---

[47] For instance, the Istanbul based Hafiza Merkezi (Memory Centre) works on the violence and impunity in Kurdistan and especially on cases of enforced disappearance. The initiative has also established a data bank of enforced disappearances. https://hakikatadalethafiza.org/en/

five sequences, he then talks about his experiences with Armenians – or better formulated, about the Armenian past. Perhaps, he craved for a break, a breather thanks to which he would not have to talk about himself, his family and friends anymore. Yet, he pursued telling his story, looping back to the moment he found the book of Armenian oral history collection. After reading the sections on his village, he "felt like an invader." Nevertheless, he has already disclosed in previous sequences that in his village there are an Armenian cemetery and a fountain constructed by the Armenians. The past has hidden in plain sight. The shock this book gave him has changed the trajectory of his recollections. Furthermore, in these very same passages, he compares his wish for coexistence. Azim considers the linkages of the Kurdish and Armenian past in these five sequences, utilising the space of his village, "empowering" materials to remind him and his community (or society) of the past, and placing both victimhoods in a mirroring constellation. The injustice performed in Kurdistan echoes the impunity ruling in West-Armenia on the same premise, contesting older narratives such as "mutual killings" and blossoming future visions. Perhaps most importantly, he asks questions that the older generations from his village have not posed up to the present.

8 Conclusion

This study has had two main aims: to explore the forms of remembrance on the Armenian Genocide in the Kurdish society, in particular in the city of Van; and to examine the structures of narratives, analogies concerning political violence, and the landscape of collective memories. In order to accomplish these two tasks, the study has set a focus on the analysis of biographical narrative interviews. It first explores the history and historiographies related to the extermination campaigns and the region of Van specifically (please see Chapter 4) and then contextualizes the denialist trends and recognition debates in Turkey (please see Chapter 5). Based on this fundament, this study includes reconstructions of Kurdish life stories as in-depth case studies (please see Chapter 6) and further compares the narrative structures of talking about the genocide and unjust regime that has performed violence against Kurds in Turkey (please see Chapter 7).

Hence, giving a voice to life stories discloses different perspectives on the subject matter. The accounts of my narrators have revealed that the Kurdish collective memory on the genocide is about an unfinished past. This continuing history is very much related to the constantly changing topography: the ancient Western-Armenia, the political North-Kurdistan, and the nationalised East-Anatolia of the Republic of Turkey. The narratives point at the long-gone Armenian past and, at the same time, the ruling conditions in the present Kurdish socio-political world. Bridging the reconstructions of these two realities, collective memories depict a multidirectional quality (cf. Rothberg 2009).

The empirical data have painted an unanticipated picture for me. Recalling the hypotheses from the introduction of this book, the narratives that I gathered have first and foremost presented diverse possibilities of remembering located between the two polarities of the genocide memory: one as *a political tool* striking the denialism and disturbing established nationalist norms of the Turkish State; and another determining the memory as *a motion emptied of its political power*. In this sense, one of the core virtues of recounting stories on Armenians has occurred to be paving the path to *describe and discuss Kurdish experiences,* borrowing the terms from Dan Bar-On (1999). Viewing Armenian Genocide memory this way allows us to leave the preconceptions of remembering as a blatant political tool against the powerholder or as a naïve act. Collective memory, and in particular remembering the Armenian Genocide is indeed political (cf. Türkyılmaz 2011). Nevertheless, its political power is often employed in order to make the phenomena of violence and injustice describable in the personal sense, and discussable in the collective sense. Intersections of personal, family, and group dependent remembrance regimes inevitably occur at which we can find nuances.

Concerning the Holocaust memory and its multidirectional meaning for post-colonial reality, Michael Rothberg (2009, 6) suggests "there is probably no other single event that encapsulates the struggles for recognition that accompany collective memory in such a condensed and global form." The Armenian Genocide memory has a similar role when it comes to Kurds in Turkey. For at the same time it "encapsulates" the efforts of recognition of the violent events impacting lives in the region; the denialist ventures; the decades-long silence and political fights of both peoples; domestic and international debates; and, of course, the ongoing impunity concerning the war against Kurdish political movements and the reintegration of the genocide perpetrators into the post-Ottoman state structures of Turkey. The (present) social time of the Kurdish society and the Armenian past thus become "united" (Vico 1948, 251). In other words, the genocide and the Kurdish political struggle in Turkey are explained within the scope of chain of events. The determinant of this quasi linear continuum is the violence. The persecution has been quasi repeating in a circular form for decades targeting different groups. The composition of Kurdish social time functions as a frame by locating these events in temporal terms.

Due to its historical context, the genocide memory fulfils the function of analogy in the narratives. It is to be witnessed in the storytelling acts of my informants as well as public figures. Thus, in Kurdish collective memory, the genocide has become a model to compare and understand the recent Kurdish past and the present conditions. That form of remembrance contains patterns to make meaning of a broad spectrum of social and political experiences: from victimisation over the struggle for peace and recognition to the efforts to compose new memory regimes. In accounts, variations of actorship appear with their particular agencies – be it portrayed as perpetrator, victim, or instrumentalised one. Additionally, questions of space, place, and temporality play significant roles in defining this memory landscape.

By means of highlighting such an "archetype" (Young 1988), the political oppression in Kurdistan comes to be the subject matter. Hence, it helps the person to remember own experiences, compare them with the historical ones, and locate the self within the social time of this very region. May they be reconstruction of personal experiences or collective references, these possible memories appear to be interwoven. Yet, due to the nature of memories it is an intersection of fluid elements which are open for alteration.

Furthermore, this multidirectional remembering does not occur in a harmonised space. The interwovenness mentioned above subsumes diverse elements concerning remembering, forgetting, and belittling the extermination of the Armenians and oppression in Kurdistan. In this sense, we should speak of a contested landscape of memories with different actors, generations, and their changing motives in recounting. Nevertheless, it does not mean that there would not be any consolidation emerging rhetoric of remembrance. On the contrary, such memory interactions create pockets to remember different events at the same time (please see Chapter 3).

Looping back to the beginning of my conclusion, further examples apart from the narratives and ethnographic data I gathered point at an unfinished past and entanglements in this regard. In the first quarter of 2018, Turkish Armed Forces started an operation on the *de facto* Kurdish canton Afrin in Rojava, West-Kurdistan. The achievements of the Kurdish people and the Kurdish political movement in Syria hence came under a massive threat. Almost at the same time as the deployment of the Turkish units, *#stopAfrinGenocide* tags started to circulate on social media. The intention was to raise awareness of the military intervention. One-and-a-half years later, in autumn 2019, a similar reaction occurred when the Trump administration withdrew US soldiers and the Turkish Armed Forces, supported by Syrian militias, started another offensive against the *de facto* Kurdish cantons in North-Eastern Syria. This time, the *#stopKurdishGenocide* campaign was launched. Meanwhile, the government of Turkey was conducting a decree-law regime, in which elected Kurdish Members of the Parliament in Ankara from the HDP, among them the former leaders of the party Figen Yüksekdağ and Selahattin Demirtaş, and mayors of several Kurdish towns were (already) suspended, detained, and arrested. The mayors were replaced with the appointed trustees – in several cases with the district or provincial governors of the same town. Beyond the MPs, thousands of local politicians and political activists engaged in the Kurdish movement have been imprisoned.

The question of how people might perceive a specific event is usually related to their earlier experiences and acquired knowledge – by the family, milieu, and institutions. The situation in Turkey and its expansionist regime, which is clearly interested in more than occupying some regions of war-torn Syria, pushed me to follow the news keeping the notions of actorship, Turkish denialist politics, continuity of violence, impunity work and reintegration of perpetrators, anachronism, and its possible role in meaning-making attempts in mind. As discussed before, collective memories have profound connections to present societal and political circumstances and their meanings for different groups and people. Whilst fulfilling diverse functions in society, memories alter with regard to changing conditions. As formulated above, the perception of a specific event is complex in these terms, not to mention the effects of regional differences. Kurdish memories of the Armenian Genocide and, based on the question of locality again, of Assyrians depict such entanglements flourishing from various time dimensions, generational conflicts, own struggles with oppression, and the continuity of injustice.

The life stories show us that the points listed or, in other words, the very context in North-Kurdistan certainly affected the biographical processes and personal trajectories. The narrators came to talk about the genocide and violence reigning since then when they had the opportunity to reconstruct their biographies freely. However, we should not forget that facing the past has already begun in the Kurdish society when the interviews took place. It empowered lots of people to talk about family biographies. What the interview setting provided was that the interwovenness of various events came to be the relevant topic. The narrators stood in the centre of this reconstruction process and referred to their individual experiences with violence. Their storytelling crystallise linkages among and contestation of memories. At this junction, Kurdish collective and personal experiences become describable and discussable. Undoubtedly, further studies considering biographical materials and life stories with varied and wider samples conducted in different regions would help us analyse the situation better and raise new questions.

In sum, the Armenian past ignites the reassessment of different times in narrative: the past, present, and even the future scenarios. The public political discourses about remembrance, facing past crimes, and remodifications of trivialisation affect the meaning-making. In this regard, this book has aimed to serve the purpose of reconstructing the amorph landscape of Kurdish collective memories of violence in times of unfinished pasts.

References

Adanır, Fikret. 2015. '"Ermeni Meselesi"nin Doğuşu'. In *1915. Siyaset, Tehcir, Soykırım*, edited by Adanır, Fikret and Oktay Özel, 3–43. Istanbul: Tarih Vakfı Yurt Yayınları.

A-Do. 2017. *Van 1915: The Great Events of Vasbouragan*. Translated by Ara Sarafian. London: Gomidas Institute.

Agamben, Giorgio. 1998. *Sovereign Power and Bare Life*. Homo Sacer 1. Stanford, Calif: Stanford University Press.

Ahiska, Meltem. 2014. 'Counter-Movement, Space and Politics: How the Saturday Mothers of Turkey Make Enforced Disappearances Visible'. In *Space and the Memories of Violence*, by Estela Schindel and Pamela Colombo, 162–75. London: Palgrave Macmillan UK. https://doi.org/10.1057/9781137380913_12.

Akçam, Taner. 2007. *A Shameful Act: The Armenian Genocide and the Question of Turkish Responsibility*. London: Constable and Robinson.

———. 2012. *The Young Turks' Crime against Humanity: The Armenian Genocide and Ethnic Cleansing in the Ottoman Empire*. Human Rights and Crimes against Humanity. Princeton, N.J: Princeton University Press.

———. 2014. *Ermenilerin Zorla Müslümanlaştırılması: Sessizlik, İnkâr ve Asimilasyon*. 1. baskı. Araştırma-İnceleme Dizisi 350. İstanbul: İletişim.

———. 2016. *Naim Efendi'nin hatıratı ve Talat Paşa telgrafları: Krikor Gergeryan Arşivi*. 1. baskı. Araştırma-inceleme dizisi 394. İstanbul: İletişim.

Akçam, Taner, and Ümit Kurt. 2012. *Kanunların Ruhu: Emval-i Metruke Kanunlarında Soykırımın İzini Sürmek*. 1. Baskı. İletişim Yayınları 1815. Cağaloğlu, İstanbul: İletişim.

Aksel, Kevork. 2012. '1970 Sonrasında Türkiye'de "Ermeni" Temsilinin Üç Tarzı'. In *Toplum ve Kuram*, 243–70. 6/7. Istanbul: Toplum ve Kuram Yayınları.

Aktar, A. 2007. 'Debating the Armenian Massacres in the Last Ottoman Parliament, November December 1918'. *History Workshop Journal* 64 (1): 240–70. https://doi.org/10.1093/hwj/dbm046.

Altınay, Ayşe Gül, and Fethiye Çetin. 2009. *Torunlar*. 1. basım. Beyoğlu, İstanbul: Metis.

Amnesty International. 2016. 'Displaced and Dispossessed. Sur Residents' Right to Return Home'. EUR 44/5213/2016. London, UK: Amnesty International. https://www.amnesty.org/download/Documents/EUR4452132016ENGLISH.PDF.

Andonian, Aram. 2018. *The Memoirs of Naim Bey: Turkish Official Documents Relating to the Deportations and Massacres of Armenians*. Suzeteo Enterprises.

Apitzsch, Ursula. 2003. 'Biographieforschung. In: Orth, B. / Schwietring, T. / Weiß, J. (Ed.): Soziologische Forschung: Stand Und Perspektiven.' In *Soziologische Forschung: Stand Und Perspektiven*, edited by B. Orth, T. Schwietring, and J. Weiß, 95–110. Opladen: Leske + Budrich.

Apitzsch, Ursula, and Lena Inowlocki. 2003. 'Biographical Analysis: A "German" School?' In *The Turn to Biographical Methods in Social Science: Comparative Issues and Examples*, edited by Prue Chamberlayne, Joanna Bornat, and Tom Wengraf, 53–70. New York: Taylor and Francis.

Aravamudan, Srinivas. 2001. 'The Return of Anachronism'. *MLQ: Modern Language Quarterly* 62 (4): 331–53.

Assmann, Aleida. 2010. *Erinnerungsräume: Formen und Wandlungen des kulturellen Gedächtnisses*. Fünfte, Durchgesehene Auflage. München: Verlag C.H.Beck.

Assmann, Jan. 2013. *Das kulturelle Gedächtnis: Schrift, Erinnerung und politische Identität in frühen Hochkulturen*. 7. Auflage. Beck'sche Reihe 1307. München: Verlag H.C.Beck.

Astourian, Stephan. 1990. 'The Armenian Genocide: An Interpretation'. *The History Teacher* 23 (2): 111–60. https://doi.org/10.2307/494919.

———. 2011. 'The Silence of the Land. Agrarian Relations, Ethnicity, and Power'. In *A Question of Genocide. Armenians and Turks at the End of the Ottoman Empire*, edited by Ronald Grigor Suny, Fatma Müge Göçek, and Norman M. Naimark, 55–81. New York ; Oxford: Oxford University Press.

———. 2018. 'Türk-Ermeni Çatışmasının Jeneolojisi Üzerine: Sultan Abdülhamid ve Ermeni Katliamları'. In *Türkiye'de Tarih ve Tarihçilik. Kavramlar ve Pratikler*, edited by Ümit Kurt and Doğan Gürpınar, 57–112. Istanbul: Heretik Yayınları.

Austin, J. L. 1972. *Zur Theorie der Sprechakte: How to do things with words*. Stuttgart: P. Reclam.

Awad, Sarah H. 2017. 'Documenting a Contested Memory: Symbols in the Changing City Space of Cairo'. *Culture & Psychology* 23 (2): 234–54. https://doi.org/10.1177/1354067X17695760.

Aydınkaya, Fırat. 2015. 'Sıradan Kürtlerin Ermeni Soykırımı'na iştiraki meselesi'. *Birikim Dergisi*, no. 312 (April): 18–26.

Bakhtin, M. M. 1981. *The Dialogic Imagination: Four Essays*. Edited by Michael Holquist. University of Texas Press Slavic Series, no. 1. Austin: University of Texas Press.

Balakian, Grigoris. 2010. *Armenian Golgotha: A Memoir of the Armenian Genocide, 1915–1918*. 1. Vintage Books ed. New York: Vintage Books.

Bali, Rıfat N., ed. 2016. *Meçhul Yahudiler Ansiklopedisi*. 1. basım. History 164, 189. İstanbul: Libra Kitap.

———. 2017. *Türkiye'de Holokost Tüketimi (1989–2017)*. 1. basım. Tarih 203. Osmanbey, İstanbul: Libra Kitapçılık ve Yayıncılık, A.Ş.

Balibar, Étienne, and Immanuel Maurice Wallerstein. 1991. *Race, Nation, Class: Ambiguous Identities*. London ; New York: Verso.

Bardakçı, Murat. 2008. *Talât Paşa'nın Evrak-ı Metrûkesi: Sadrazam Talât Paşa'nın Özel Arşivinde Bulunan Ermeni Tehciri Konusundaki Belgeler ve Hususî Yazışmalar*. İnceleme, Araştırma, Tarih 16. Cağaloğlu, İstanbul: Everest Yayınları.

Bar-On, Dan. 1993. *Die Last des Schweigens: Gespräche mit Kindern von Nazi-Tätern*. Frankfurt: Campus-Verl.

———. 1999. *The Indescribable and the Undiscussable: Reconstructing Human Discourse after Trauma*. Budapest: Central European Univ. Press.

———. 2006. *Tell Your Life Story: Creating Dialogue among Jews and Germans, Israelis and Palestinians*. Budapest ; New York: Central European University Press.

Bar-On, Dan, and Julia Chaitin. 2001. *Parenthood and the Holocaust*. Search and Research 1. Jerusalem: Yad Vashem.

Bartlett, Frederic C. 1995. *Remembering: A Study in Experimental and Social Psychology*. Cambridge ; New York: Cambridge University Press.

Bartmann, Sylke, and Katharina Kunze. 2008. 'Biographisierungsleistungen in Form von Argumentationen als Zugang zur (Re-)Konstruktion von Erfahrungen'. In *Perspektiven erziehungswissenschaftlicher Biographieforschung*, 177–92. Wiesbaden: VS Verlag für Sozialwissenschaften. http://link.springer.com/10.1007/978-3-531-91036-9.

Bartov, Omer. 2018. *Anatomy of a Genocide: The Life and Death of a Town Called Buczacz*. New York ; London ; Toronto ; Sydney: Simon & Schuster.

Becker, Howard Saul. 1998. *Tricks of the Trade: How to Think about Your Research While You're Doing It*. Chicago Guides to Writing, Editing, and Publishing. Chicago, Ill: University of Chicago Press.

Ben Aharon, Eldad. 2015. 'A Unique Denial: Israel's Foreign Policy and the Armenian Genocide'. *British Journal of Middle Eastern Studies* 42 (4): 638–54. https://doi.org/10.1080/13530194.2015.1043514.

Bertaux, Daniel. 2018. *Die Lebenserzählung: ein ethnosoziologischer Ansatz zur Analyse sozialer Welten, sozialer Situationen und sozialer Abläufe*. Translated by Ingrid Harting. Qualitative Fall- und Prozessanalysen. Biographie – Interaktion – soziale Welten. Opladen Berlin Toronto: Verlag Barbara Budrich.

Bertaux, Daniel, and Isabelle Bertaux-Wiame. 1980. 'Autobiographische Erinnerungen Und Kollektives Gedächtnis'. In *Lebenserfahrung Und*

Kollektives Gedächtnis, edited by Lutz Niethammer, 108–22. Frankfurt (am Main): Syndikat.

Bertaux, Daniel, and Paul Thompson, eds. 2005. *Between Generations: Family Models, Myths & Memories*. Memory and Narrative Series. New Brunswick, NJ: Transaction Publishers.

Bieberstein, Alice von. 2017. 'Treasure/Fetish/Gift: Hunting for "Armenian Gold" in Post-Genocide Turkish Kurdistan'. *Subjectivity* 10 (2): 170–89. https://doi.org/10.1057/s41286-017-0026-x.

Biner. 2010. 'Acts of Defacement, Memories of Loss: Ghostly Effects of the "Armenian Crisis" in Mardin, Southeastern Turkey'. *History and Memory* 22 (2): 68. https://doi.org/10.2979/his.2010.22.2.68.

Bjørnlund, Matthias. 2008. 'The 1914 Cleansing of Aegean Greeks as a Case of Violent Turkification'. *Journal of Genocide Research* 10 (1): 41–58. https://doi.org/10.1080/14623520701850286.

Bloxham, Donald. 2005. *The Great Game of Genocide: Imperialism, Nationalism, and the Destruction of the Ottoman Armenians*. Oxford: Oxford University Press.

Bohleber, Werner. 1998. 'Transgenerationelles Trauma, Identifizierung Und Geschichtsbewusstsein'. In *Die Dunkle Spur Der Vergangenheit. Psychoanalytische Zugänge Zum Geschichtsbewußtsein. Erinnerung, Geshichte, Identität 2*, edited by Jörn Rüsen and Jürgen Straub, 256–74. Wissenschaft 1403. Frankfurt (am Main): Suhrkamp.

Bora, Tanil. 2003. *Türk Sağının Üç Hali. Milliyetçilik, Muhafazakarlik, Islamcilik*. Istanbul: Birikim Yayinlari.

Bozarslan, Hamit. 2015. 'Tehcir'den Lozan'a Türkler, Kürtler ve Ermeniler'. In *1915. Siyaset, Tehcir, Soykirim*, edited by Adanır Fikret and Oktay Özel, 471–87. Istanbul: Tarih Vakfi Yurt Yayınları.

Brescó de Luna, Ignacio. 2017. 'The End into the Beginning: Prolepsis and the Reconstruction of the Collective Past'. *Culture & Psychology* 23 (2): 280–94. https://doi.org/10.1177/1354067X17695761.

Brink, Cornelia. 1989. 'Visualiserite Geschichte: zu Ausstellungen an Orten nationalsozialistischer Konzentrationslager'. Magisterarbeit, Freiburg: Universität Freiburg/Brsg.

Brockmeier, Jens. 2015. *Beyond the Archive: Memory, Narrative, and the Autobiographical Process*. Explorations in Narrative Psychology. Oxford ; New York: Oxford University Press.

Bruinessen, Martin van. 1992. *Agha, Shaikh, and State: The Social and Political Structures of Kurdistan*. London ; Atlantic Highlands, N.J: Zed Books.

Bruner, Jerome. 2004. 'Life as Narrative'. *Social Research* 71 (3): 691–710.

Bryce, James and Arnold Toynbee. 2009. *Osmanlı İmparatorluğu'nda Erme-
nilere yapılan muamele, 1915–1916: Vikont Bryce'ın Fallodon Vikontu
Grey'e sunduğu belgeler*. London: Gomidas Institute.

Çelik, Adnan, and Namık Kemal Dinç. 2015. *Yüz Yıllık Ah! Toplumsal
Hafızanın İzinde 1915 Diyarbekir*. İstanbul: İsmail Beşikçi Vakfı.

Çelik, Adnan, and Ergin Öpengin. 2016. 'The Armenian Genocide in the Kurdish Novel: Restructuring Identity through Collective Memory'. *European
Journal of Turkish Studies*, 17.

Çetin, Fethiye. 2004. *Anneannem*. 1. basım. Metis Edebiyat. İstanbul: Metis
Yayınları.

Çetinkaya, Y. Doğan. 2015. *Osmanlı'yı Müslümanlaştırmak: kitle siyaseti,
toplumsal sınıflar, boykotlar ve milli iktisat (1909–1914)*. 1. baskı. İletişim
yayınları Araştırma-inceleme dizisi, 2120 355. İstanbul: İletişim.

Çetinoğlu, Sait. 2006. 'Sermayenin "Türk"leştirilmesi'. İn *Resmi Tarih
Tartışmaları*, edited by Fikret Başkaya, 79–152. İstanbul: Özgür Üniversite.

Chamberlayne, Prue, Joanna Bornat, and Tom Wengraf. 2003a. 'Introduction:
The Biographical Turn'. In *The Turn to Biographical Methods in Social
Science: Comparative Issues and Examples*, 1–30. New York: Taylor and
Francis.

———. 2003b. *The Turn to Biographical Methods in Social Science: Comparative Issues and Examples*. New York: Taylor and Francis.

Charny, Israel W. 2000. 'Innocent Denials of Known Genocides: A Further
Contribution to a Psychology of Denial of Genocide'. *Human Rights
Review* 1 (3): 15–39. https://doi.org/10.1007/s12142-000-1019-6.

———. 2001. 'The Psychological Satisfaction of Denials of the Holocaust
or Other Genocides by Non-Extremists or Bigots, and Even by Known
Scholars'. *IDEA* 6 (1): 30.

Cheterian, Vicken. 2015. *Open Wounds: Armenians, Turks and a Century of
Genocide*. First publ. London: Hurst.

Chorbajian, Levon. 2016. '"They Brought It on Themselves and It Never Happened": Denial to 1939'. In *The Armenian Genocide Legacy*, edited by
Alexis Demirdjian, 167–82. Palgrave Macmillan.

Cohen, Stanley. 2001. *States of Denial: Knowing about Atrocities and Suffering*. Cambridge, UK : Malden, MA: Polity ; Blackwell Publishers.

Connerton, Paul. 2008. 'Seven Types of Forgetting'. *Memory Studies* 1 (1):
59–71. https://doi.org/10.1177/1750698007083889.

Cora, Yasar Tolga. 2015. 'Doğu'da Kürt-Ermeni Çatışmasının Sosyoekono-
mik Arkaplanı'. In *1915. Siyaset, Tehcir, Soykirim*, 126–39. Istanbul: Tarih
Vakfı Yurt Yayınları.

Coward, Martin. 2008. *Urbicide. The Politics of Urban Destruction*. Routledge Advances in International Relations and Global Politics. London ; New York: Routledge.

Dabag, Mihran. 2002. 'Der Genozid an den Armeniern im Osmanischen Reich'. In *Verbrechen erinnern. Die Auseinandersetzung mit Holocaust und Völkermord*, edited by Volkhard Knigge and Norbert Frei, 1st ed., 33–55. C.H. Beck.

Dadrian, Vahakn N. 1999. 'The Determinants of the Armenian Genocide'. *Journal of Genocide Research* 1 (1): 65–80. https://doi.org/10.1080/14623529908413935.

———. 2003. *Warrant for Genocide: Key Elements of Turko-Armenian Conflict*. New Brunswick, N.J: Transaction Publishers.

———. 2004. *The History of the Armenian Genocide: Ethnic Conflict from the Balkans to Anatolia to the Caucasus*. 6., revised ed. New York: Berghahn Books.

Dadrian, Vahakn N., and Taner Akçam, eds. 2008. *Tehcir ve Taktil: Divan-ı Harb-i Örfî Zabıtları: İttihad ve Terakki'nin Yargılanması, 1919–1922*. 1. baskı. İstanbul Bilgi Üniversitesi Yayınları ; Tarih, Belge, 231. 2. Şişli, İstanbul: İstanbul Bilgi Üniversitesi.

Danziger, Kurt. 2008. *Marking the Mind: A History of Memory*. Leiden: Cambridge University Press. http://www.myilibrary.com?id=179127.

Davis, Fred. 1959. 'The Cabdriver and His Fare: Facets of a Fleeting Relationship'. *American Journal of Sociology* 65 (2): 158–65.

Davutoglu, Ahmet. 2014. 'Turkish-Armenian Relations in the Process of De-Ottomanization or "Dehistorization": Is a "Just Memory" Possible?' *Turkish Policy Quarterly* 13 (1): 21–30.

De Nogales, Rafael. 1925. *Vier Jahre unter dem Halbmond*. Berlin: Reimar Hobbing.

Der Matossian, Bedross. 2015. 'Explaining the Unexplainable: Recent Trends in the Armenian Genocide Historiography'. *Journal of Levantine Studies* 5 (2): 143–66.

———. 2016. *Parçalanan devrim düşleri: Osmanlı İmparatorluğu'nun son döneminde hürriyetten şiddete = Shattered dreams of revolution : from liberty to violence in the late Ottoman Empire*. İstanbul: İletişim.

Derderian, Dzovinar. 2016. 'Shaping Subjectivities and Contesting Power through the Image of Kurds, 1860s'. In *The Ottoman East in the Nineteenth Century: Societies, Identities and Politics*, by Yasar Tolga Cora, Dzovinar Derderian, and Ali Sipahi, 91–108. I.B.Tauris.

Dersimi, Nuri. 2014. *Hatıratım: Dersim'den Halep'e bir muhalifin yaşamı (1892–1973)*. 1. baskı. Dam yayınları Kültür: tarih, 4 3. İstanbul: Dam Yayınları.

Dinç, Namık Kemal, ed. 2016. *'Onlar Gittiler, Biz Barışı Yitirdik': Ermeni Soykırımı ve Kürtler: Söyleşiler.* 1. baskı. Bugünün Kitapları 200. İstanbul: İletişim.

Dost-Niyego, Pınar, and İlker Aytürk. 2016. 'Holocaust Education in Turkey: Past, Present, and Future'. *Contemporary Review of the Middle East* 3 (3): 250–65. https://doi.org/10.1177/2347798916654581.

Du Bois, W. E. B. 2007. *The Souls of Black Folk.* Edited by Brent Hayes Edwards. Oxford World's Classics. Oxford [England] ; New York: Oxford University Press.

Dündar, Fuat. 2013. *Kahir Ekseriyet: Ermeni Nüfus Meselesi (1878–1923).* Eminönü, İstanbul: Tarih Vakfı Yurt Yayınları.

———. 2015. '"Eski Rejim"de Ermeni Nüfus Meselesi, 1828–1908'. In *1915. Siyaset, Tehcir, Soykirim,* 109–25. Istanbul: Tarih Vakfı Yurt Yayınları.

Elias, Norbert. 1984. *Über Die Zeit.* Edited by Michael Schröter. 1st ed. Arbeiten Zur Wissenssoziologie 2. Frankfurt (am Main): Suhrkamp.

Erikson, Erik Homburger. 1978. *Childhood and Society.* Frogmore, St. Albans: Triad Paladin.

Yesayan, Zabel. 2014. *Yıkıntılar arasında: tanıklık.* Aras 143. İstanbul: Aras.

Estukyan, Vartan. 2015. 'Ermeni Soykırımı'nın izini Talat Paşa'nın telgraflarıyla sürmek'. *Agos,* 5 December 2015.

Farzana, Kazi Fahmida. 2017. *Memories of Burmese Rohingya Refugees.* New York: Palgrave Macmillan US. https://doi.org/10.1057/978-1-137-58360-4.

Felden, Heide von, ed. 2008. *Perspektiven erziehungswissenschaftlicher Biographieforschung.* Wiesbaden: VS Verlag für Sozialwissenschaften. https://doi.org/10.1007/978-3-531-91036-9.

Fernandes, Desmond. 2012. 'Modernity and the Linguistic Genocide of Kurds in Turkey'. *International Journal of the Sociology of Language* 2012 (217). https://doi.org/10.1515/ijsl-2012-0050.

Fischer, Wolfram. 2018. 'Zeit und Biographie'. In *Handbuch Biographieforschung,* edited by Helma Lutz, Martina Schiebel, and Elisabeth Tuider, 461–72. Wiesbaden: Springer Fachmedien Wiesbaden. https://doi.org/10.1007/978-3-658-18171-0_39.

Foss, Clive. 2016. '"Van'ın Zalim Ermenileri" Modern Türk Bakış Açısı'. In *Van,* by Richard G. Hovannisian, 273–88. Istanbul: Aras.

Foucault, Michel. 1984. *Language, Counter-Memory, Practice: Selected Essays and Interviews.* Edited by Donald F. Bouchard. 1. printing, Cornell paperbacks, [Nachdr.]. Cornell Paperbacks. Ithaca, NY: Cornell Univ. Press.

Galip, Özlem Belçim. 2016. 'The Politics of Remembering: Representation of the Armenian Genocide in Kurdish Novels'. *Holocaust and Genocide Studies* 30 (3): 458–87. https://doi.org/10.1093/hgs/dcw063.

Gasparyan, Lilit', ed. 2014. *Yüz Yıl ... Gerçek Hikâyeler: 1915–2015*. İstanbul: Ermeni Kültürü ve Dayanışma Derneği.

Gaunt, David. 2011. 'The Ottoman Treatment of the Assyrians'. In *A Question of Genocide. Armenians and Turks at the End of the Ottoman Empire*, edited by Suny, Ronald Grigor, Fatma Müge Göçek, and Naimark, Norman M., 244–59. Oxford ; New York: Oxford University Press.

Gerçek, Burçin. 2016. *Akıntıya Karşı: Ermeni soykırımında emirlere karşı gelenler, kurtaranlar, direnenler*. 1. baskı. Tarih dizisi 110. İstanbul: İletişim Yayıncılık.

Gergen, Kenneth J. 1994. 'Mind, Text, and Society: Self-Memory in Social Context'. In *The Rememberin Self. Construction and Accuracy in the Self-Narrative*, edited by Ulrich Neisser and Robyn Fivush, 78–104. Cambridge University Press.

Gerlach, Christian. 2010. *Extremely Violent Societies: Mass Violence in the Twentieth-Century World*. Cambridge ; New York: Cambridge University Press.

Glaser, Barney G., and Anselm L. Strauss. 1965. *Awareness of Dying*. Observations. Chicago: Aldine Pub. Co.

———. 2009. *The Discovery of Grounded Theory: Strategies for Qualitative Research*. 4. paperback printing. New Brunswick: Aldine.

Göçek, Fatma Müge. 2016. *Denial of Violence: Ottoman Past, Turkish Present, and Collective Violence against the Armenians, 1789–2009*.

Goffman, Erving. 1990. *The Presentation of Self in Everyday Life*. Nachdr. Anchor Books. New York, NY: Doubleday.

Gölbaşı, Edip. 2015. 'Hamidiye Alayları: Bir Değerlendirme'. In *1915. Siyaset, Tehcir, Soykırım*, 164–75. Istanbul: Tarih Vakfı Yurt Yayınları.

———. 2017. 'The Official Conceptualization of the Anti-Armenian Riots of 1895–1897'. *Études Arméniennes Contemporaines*, 31.

Güven, Dilek. 2005. *Cumhuriyet dönemi azınlık politikaları bağlamında: 6–7 Eylül olayları*. 1. basım. Tarih Vakfı yurt yayınları 149. Beşiktaş, İstanbul: Tarih Vakfı.

Halbwachs, Maurice. 1991. *Das kollektive Gedächtnis*. Ungekürzte Ausg., 4.-5. Tsd. Fischer Wissenschaft 7359. Frankfurt am Main: Fischer.

———. 2012. *Das Gedächtnis und seine sozialen Bedingungen*. [Nachdr.], Lizenzausg. Suhrkamp-Taschenbuch Wissenschaft 538. Frankfurt am Main: Suhrkamp.

Hartmann, Elke. 2017. 'Gülizars Geschichte Frauenraub in den armenischen Provinzen des Osmanischen Reiches in neuer Perspektive'. In *Jahrbuch für Antisemitismusforschung*, 184–208. 26. Berlin: Metropol.

Hassanpour, Amir. 1992. *Nationalism and Language in Kurdistan, 1918–1985*. San Francisco: Mellen Research University Press.

Hassanpour, Amir, Jaffer Sheyholislami, and Tove Skutnabb-Kangas. 2012. 'Introduction. Kurdish: Linguicide, Resistance and Hope'. *International Journal of the Sociology of Language* 2012 (217): 1–18. https://doi.org/10.1515/ijsl-2012-0047.

Havel, Václav. 2018. *The power of the powerless: citizens against the state in Central-Eastern Europe.*

Hegasy, Sonja. 2019. 'Archive Partisans: Forbidden Histories and the Promise of the Future'. *Memory Studies* 12 (3): 247–65. https://doi.org/10.1177/1750698019836187.

Heimo, Anne, and Ulla-Maija Peltonen. 2012. 'Memories and Histories, Public and Private: After the Finnish Civil War'. In *Contested Pasts. The Politics of Memory*, edited by Katharine Hodgkin and Susannah Radstone, 42–56. London ; New York: Routledge, Taylor & Francis Group.

Hewsen, Robert H. 2016. 'Dünyada Van, Ahirette Cennet'. In *Van*, edited by Richard G. Hovannisian, 21–52. Tarihi Kentler ve Ermeniler. Istanbul: Aras Yayıncılık.

Hilberg, Raul. 1992. *Täter, Opfer, Zuschauer: die Vernichtung der Juden 1933–1945.* 4. Aufl., 16.–17. Tsd. Frankfurt am Main: S. Fischer.

———. 2017. Die Vernichtung der europäischen Juden. Band 1. 13. Auflage. Frankfurt am Main: S. Fischer.

Hinrichsen, Hendrik, Gabriele Rosenthal, and Arne Worm. 2013. 'Biographische Fallrekonstruktionen. Zur Rekonstruktion der Verflechtung "individueller" Erfahrung, biographischer Verläufe, Selbstpräsentationen und "kollektiver" Diskurse. PalästinenserInnen als RepräsentantInnen ihrer Wir-Bilder'. *Sozialer Sinn* 14 (2): 157–84.

Hirsch, Marianne. 2012. *The Generation of Postmemory: Writing and Visual Culture after the Holocaust.* New York: Columbia University Press.

———. 2019. 'Stateless Memory'. *Critical Times* 2 (3): 416–34. https://doi.org/10.1215/26410478-7862541.

Hobsbawm, E. J., and T. O. Ranger, eds. 2012. *The Invention of Tradition.* Canto Classics. Cambridge [Cambridgeshire]: Cambridge University Press.

Hodgkin, Katharine, and Susannah Radstone. 2012. *Contested Pasts: The Politics of Memory.* London ; New York: Routledge.

Hovannisian, Richard G., ed. 1992. *The Armenian Genocide: History, Politics, Ethics.* New York: St. Martin's Press.

———. 1998a. 'Denial of the Armenian Genocide in Comparison with Holocaust Denial'. In *Remembrance and Denial: The Case of the Armenian Genocide*, 201–36. Detroit: Wayne State University Press.

———, ed. 1998b. *Remembrance and Denial: The Case of the Armenian Genocide.* Detroit: Wayne State University Press.

————. 2016. 'Ermeni Van/Vasburagan'. In *Van*, edited by Richard G. Hovannisian, 7–20. Tarihi Kentler ve Ermeniler. Istanbul: Aras.

Hayreni, Hovsep. 2015. *1915 Bağlamında Kürt-Ermeni Tarih Muhasebesi ve Güncel Tartışmalar.* Birinci baskı. Belge Yayınları ; Türkiye Incelemeleri Dizisi 781. Cağaloğlu, İstanbul: Belge Yayınları.

Holz, Klaus. 2000. 'Die Figur Des Dritten in Der Nationalen Ordnung Der Welt'. *Soziale Systeme* 6: 269–90.

Hroch, Miroslav. 1993. 'From National Movement to the Fully-Formed Nation'. *New Left Review*, no. 198 (April): 3–20.

Hutton, Patrick. 2000. 'Recent Scholarship on Memory and History'. *The History Teacher* 33 (4): 533. https://doi.org/10.2307/494950.

Huyssen, Andreas. 2000. 'Present Pasts: Media, Politics, Amnesia'. *Public Culture* 12 (1): 21–38.

Ihrig, Stefan. 2016. *Justifying Genocide: Germany and the Armenians from Bismarck to Hitler.* Cambridge, Massachusetts: Harvard University Press.

Jeffery, Laura, and Matei Candea. 2006. 'The Politics of Victimhood'. *History and Anthropology* 17 (4): 287–96. https://doi.org/10.1080/02757200600914037.

Kabalek, Kobi. 2014. 'Memory and Periphery: An Introduction'. *HAGAR Studies in Culture, Polity and Identities* 12: 7–22.

Kandiyoti, Deniz. 2009. 'Islam, Modernity and the Politics of Gender'. In *Islam and Modernity. Key Issues and Debates*, edited by Masud Masud Muhammad Khalid, Armando Salvatore, and Martin van Bruinessen, 91–124. Edinburgh: Edinburgh University Press.

Kapmaz, Cengiz. 2011. *Öcalan'ın Imralı Günleri.* 2. baskı. Tarih, Toplum, Kuram 126. İstanbul: İthaki Yayınları.

Karrouche, Norah. 2018. 'Memory as Protest: Mediating Memories of Violence and the Bread Riots in the Rif'. In *The Social Life of Memory. Violence, Trauma, and Testimony in Lebanon and Morocco*, edited by Norman Saadi Nikro and Sonja Hegasy, 219–38. Palgrave Studies in Cultural Heritage and Conflict. Switzerland: Palgrave Macmillan.

Kaymak, Özgür. 2017. *İstanbul'da Az(Inlık) Olmak: Gündelik Hayatta Rumlar, Yahudiler, Ermeniler.* 1. Basım. Tarih 186. İstanbul: Libra Kitapçılık ve Yayıncılık.

Kévorkian, Raymond H. 2011. *Soykirimin Ikinci Safhasi. Sürgüne Gönderilen Osmanli Ermenilerinin Suriye-Mezopotamya Toplama Kamplarinda Imha Edilmeleri (1915–1916).* Belge Yayınları.

————. 2015. *Ermeni soykırımı.* Translated by Ayşen Taşkent Ekmekci. İstanbul: İletişim.

Kévorkian, Raymond H., and Paul B. Paboudjian. 2012. *1915 öncesinde Osmanlı İmparatorluğu'nda Ermeniler.* Aras 132. İstanbul: Aras.

Kışanak, Gültan. 2020. 'Gerçekten 40 Yıl Oldu Mu?' In *40 Yıl 12 Eylül*, edited by Tanıl Bora, 121–44. Istanbul: İletişim.

Kieser, Hans-Lukas. 1997. 'Mehmet Nuri Dersimi, ein asylsuchender Kurde'. In Kurdistan und Europa. Beiträge zur kurdischen Geschichte des 19. und 20. Jahrhunders / Regards sur l'histoire kurde (19–20e siècles), edited by Hans-Lukas Kieser, 187–216. Zürich: Chronos.

———. 2007. *A Quest for Belonging: Anatolia beyond Empire and Nation (19th-21st Centuries)*. Analecta Isisiana 97. Istanbul: Isis Press.

———. 2018. *Talaat Pasha: Father of Modern Turkey, Architect of Genocide*. Princeton, New Jersey: Princeton University Press.

Kimenyi, Alexandre. 2001. 'Trivialization of Genocide: The Case of Rwanda'. In *Anatomy of Genocide: State-Sponsored Mass-Killings in the Twentieth Century*, edited by Alexandre Kimenyi and Otis L. Scott, 429 – 445. Lewiston, N.Y: E. Mellen Press.

Klein, Janet. 2014. *Hamidiye alayları: imparatorluğun sınır boyları ve kürt aşiretleri*.

———. 2015. 'Kürt Milliyetçileri ve Milliyetçi Olmayan Kürtçüler: Azınlık Milliyetçiliğini ve Osmanlı İmparatorluğu'nun Dağılışını Yeniden Düşünmek, 1908–1909'. In *Kıyam ve Kıtal. Osmanlı'dan Cumhuriyet'e Devletin İnşası ve Kolektif Şiddet*, edited by Ümit Kurt and Güney Çeğin, 277–95. İstanbul: Tarih Vakfı Yurt Yayınları.

Knoblauch, Hubert. 2001. 'Fokussierte Ethnographie: Soziologie, Ethnologie Und Die Neue Welle Der Ethnographie'. *Sozialer Sinn* 2 (1): 123–41.

———. 2004. 'Die Video-Interaktions-Analyse'. *Sozialer Sinn* 5 (1): 123–38.

———. 2005. 'Focused Ethnography'. *Forum Qualitative Sozialforschung / Forum: Qualitative Social Research* 6 (3). http://nbnresolving. de/ urn:nbn:de:0114-fqs0503440.

Knoblauch, Hubert, and Bernt Schnettler. 2012. 'Videography: Analysing Video Data as a "Focused" Ethnographic and Hermeneutical Exercise'. Edited by Hubert Knoblauch. *Qualitative Research* 12 (3): 334–56. https:// doi.org/10.1177/1468794111436147.

Kohli, Martin. 1981. 'Zur Theorie der biographischen Selbst- und Fremdthematisierung'. In *Lebenswelt und soziale Probleme: Verhandlungen des 20. Deutschen Soziologentages zu Bremen 1980*, edited by Matthes Joachim and Deutsche Gesellschaft für Soziologie, 502–20. Frankfurt/Main ; New York: Campus Verlag.

Köhr, Katja. 2012. *Die Vielen Gesichter Des Holocaust: Museale Repräsentationen Zwischen Individualisierung, Universalisierung Und Nationalisierung*. Eckert. Die Schriftenreihe, Bd. 128. Göttingen: V & R Unipress.

Korucu, Serdar, and Aris Nalci. 2014. *1965. 2015'ten 50 Yil Önce, 1965'ten 50 Yil Sonra*. Istanbul: Propaganda Yayinlari.

Kuhls, Heike. 1994. 'Konzeptionen und Praxisformen westdeutscher Gedenk-stättenspädagogik seit den 80er Jahren'. Staatsexam, Münster: Universität Münster.

Kurt, Ümit. 2018. *Antep 1915: Soykırım ve Failler*. 1. Baskı. Tarih Dizisi 135. Fatih, İstanbul: İletişim Yayınları.

Kurt, Ümit, and Murad Uçaner. 2015. 'Besnili Ermeni Yetimlerin Hikayesin-den Bir Kesit'. In , 319–32. Istanbul: Hrant Dink Vakfı Yayınları.

Lepsius, Johannes. 2011. *Bericht über die Lage des armenischen Volkes in der Türkei*. Unveränd. Neuaufl. mit Orig.-Text der Ausg. von 1916. Bad Schussenried: Hess.

Levy, Daniel, and Natan Sznaider. 2002. 'Memory Unbound. The Holocaust and the Formation of Cosmopolitan Memory'. *European Journal of Social Theory* 5 (1): 87–106.

Libaridian, Gerard J. 2004. *Modern Armenia: People, Nation, State*. New Brunswick, N.J: Transaction Publishers.

Lorenz, Chris. 2014. 'Blurred Lines – History, Memory and the Experience of Time'. *International Journal for History, Culture and Modernity* 2 (1): 43–63. https://doi.org/10.5117/HCM2014.1.LORE.

Mahçupyan, Etyen, Dilek Kurban, Pınar Önen Süren, and Tamer Aker. 2008. 'Guidelines for Persons and Organisations Providing Support For Victims of Forced Migration'. Istanbul: TESEV. https://www.tesev.org.tr/wp-content/uploads/report_Guidelines_For_Persons_And_Organizations_Providing_Support_For_Victims_Of_Forced_Migration.pdf.

Mardin, Şerif. 1973. 'Center-Periphery Relations: A Key to Turkish Politics?' *Daedalus* 102 (1,): 169–90.

Melson, Robert. 1996. *Revolution and Genocide: On the Origins of the Armenian Genocide and the Holocaust*. 1st pbk.ed. Chicago: University of Chicago Press.

Menin, Laura. 2018. 'A Life of Waiting: Political Violence, Personal Memories and Enforced Disappearances In Morocco'. In *The Social Life of Memory. Violence, Trauma, and Testimony in Lebanon and Morocco*, edited by Norman Saadi Nikro and Sonja Hegasy, 25–54. Palgrave Studies in Cultural Heritage and Conflict. Switzerland: Palgrave Macmillan.

Mignolo, Walter D. 2009. 'Epistemic Disobedience, Independent Thought and Decolonial Freedom'. *Theory, Culture & Society* 26 (7–8): 159–81. https://doi.org/10.1177/0263276409349275.

———. 2011. *The Darker Side of Western Modernity: Global Futures, Decolonial Options*. Durham: Duke University Press.

———. 2012. *Local Histories, Global Designs, Coloniality, Subaltern Knowledges, and Border Thinking*. Princeton University Press.

————. 2013. 'Geopolitics of Sensing and Knowing: On (de)Coloniality, Border Thinking, and Epistemic Disobedience'. *Confero Essays on Education Philosophy and Politics* 1 (1): 129–50. https://doi.org/10.3384/confero.2001-4562.13v1i1129.

Míguez Macho, Antonio. 2016. *The Genocidal Genealogy of Francoism: Violence, Memory and Impunity*. The Canada Blanch Centre for Contemporary Spanish Studies. Brighton ; Chicago ; Toronto: Sussex Academic Press.

Misztal, Barbara A. 2003. 'Durkheim on Collective Memory'. *Journal of Classical Sociology* 3 (2): 123–43. https://doi.org/10.1177/1468795X030032002.

————. 2010. 'Collective Memory in a Global Age: Learning How and What to Remember'. *Current Sociology* 58 (1): 24–44. https://doi.org/10.1177/0011392109348544.

Mmembe, Achille. 2003. 'Necropolitics'. *Public Culture*, Duke University Press, 15 (1): 11–40.

Morack, Ellinor. 2017. *The Dowry of the State? The Politics of Abandoned Property and the Population Exchange in Turkey, 1921–1945*. Bamberger Orientstudien, Band 9. Bamberg: University of Bamberg Press.

Morgenthau, Henry. 2012. *Ambassador Morgenthau's Story*. Forgotten Books.

Mouradian, Khatchig. 2018. 'Internment and Destruction: Concentration Camps during the Armenian Genocide, 1915–1916'. In *Internment during the First World War: A Mass Global Phenomenon*, edited by Stefan Manz, Panikos Panayi, and Matthew Stibbe, 1st ed., 145–61. Routledge Studies in First World War History. London: Routledge.

Nassehi, Armin. 2008. *Die Zeit der Gesellschaft: auf dem Weg zu einer soziologischen Theorie der Zeit*. 2. Aufl., Neuaufl. mit einem Beitrag "Gegenwarten". Wiesbaden: VS, Verl. für Sozialwiss.

Neyzi, Leyla, Hranush Kharatyan-Arak'elyan, and Samvel Simonyan, eds. 2010. *Speaking to One Another: Personal Memories of the Past in Armenia and Turkey: Wish They Hadn't Left*. Bonn, Germany: Dvv international.

Nichanian, Marc. 1998. 'The Truth of the Facts: About the New Revisionism'. In *Remembrance and Denial: The Case of the Armenian Genocide*, edited by Richard G. Hovannisian, 249–70. Detroit: Wayne State University Press.

————. 2011. *Edebiyat ve felaket*. Translated by Ayşegül Sönmezay. 1. baskı. İletişim yayınları Edebiyat eleştirisi dizisi, 1676 23. İstanbul: İletişim yayınları.

Nijhawan, Michael, Daphne Winland, and Jenny Wüstenberg. 2018. 'Introduction: Contesting Memory and Citizenship in Canada'. *Citizenship Studies* 22 (4): 345–57. https://doi.org/10.1080/13621025.2018.1462506.

Nugin, Raili. 2019. 'Rejecting, Re-Shaping, Rearranging: Ways of Negotiating the Past in Family Narratives'. *Memory Studies*, February, 175069801982986. https://doi.org/10.1177/1750698019829865.

Obradović, Sandra. 2017. 'Whose Memory and Why: A Commentary on Power and the Construction of Memory'. *Culture & Psychology* 23 (2): 208–16. https://doi.org/10.1177/1354067X17695765.

Ochs, Elinor, and Lisa Capps. 1996. 'NARRATING THE SELF'. *Annual Review of Anthropology* 25 (1): 19–43. https://doi.org/10.1146/annurev. anthro.25.1.19.

O'Connor, Paul. 2019. 'The Unanchored Past: Three Modes of Collective Memory'. *Memory Studies*, December, 175069801989469. https://doi. org/10.1177/1750698019894694.

Olick, Jeffrey K. 1999. 'Collective Memory: The Two Cultures'. *Sociological Theory* 17 (3): 333–48. https://doi.org/10.1111/0735-2751.00083.

———. 2009. 'Between Chaos and Diversity: Is Social Memory Studies a Field?' *International Journal of Politics, Culture, and Society*, May. https:// doi.org/10.1007/s10767-009-9059-7.

Olick, Jeffrey K., and Joyce Robbins. 1998. 'Social Memory Studies: From "Collective Memory" to the Historical Sociology of Mnemonic Practices'. *Annual Review of Sociology* 2: 105–40.

Onaran, Nevzat. 2013. *Emvâl-i Metrûkenin Tasfiyesi: Inceleme, Araştırma.* Birinci basım. İstanbul: Evrensel Basım Yayın.

Oshagan, Hagop. 2014. *The Way of the Womb*. 2. ed. Remnants, Hagop Oshagan. Transl. from the Armenian by G. M. Goshgarian; Book 1. London: Gomidas Institute.

Öcalan, Abdullah. 2016. Demokratik kurtuluş ve özgür yaşamı inşa: (İmralı notları). Neuss: Wesanen Mezopotamya.

Özyürek, Esra. 2006. *Nostalgia for the Modern: State Secularism and Everyday Politics in Turkey*. Politics, History, and Culture. Durham, NC: Duke University Press.

Passerini, Luisa. 2012. 'Memories between Silence and Oblivion'. In *Contested Pasts. The Politics of Memory*, edited by Katharine Hodgkin and Susannah Radstone, 238–54. London ; New York: Routledge, Taylor & Francis Group.

Pelt, Mogens. 2017. 'Remembering Home: Christians, Muslims and the Outside World in Late-Ottoman Cilicia and Cappadocia'. In *Contested Memories and the Demands of the Past. History Cultures in the Modern Muslim World*, edited by Catharina Raudvere, 81–106. Islam and Nationalism. Switzerland: Palgrave Macmillan.

Pohn-Lauggas, Maria. 2019. 'Memory in the Shadow of a Family History of Resistance: A Case Study of the Significance of Collective Memories for Intergenerational Memory in Austrian Families'. *Memory Studies*, May, 175069801984969. https://doi.org/10.1177/1750698019849698.

Portelli, Alessandro. 1988. 'Uchronic Dreams: Working Class Memory and Possible Worlds'. *Oral History* 16 (2): 46–56.

Prager, Jeffrey. 1998. *Presenting the Past: Psychoanalysis and the Sociology of Misremembering*. Cambridge, Mass: Harvard University Press.

Purdeková, Andrea. 2018. 'Itinerant Nationalisms and Fracturing Narratives: Incorporating Regional Dimensions of Memory into Peacebuilding'. *Memory Studies*, October, 175069801880074. https://doi.org/10.1177/1750698018800749.

Redlich, Shimon. 2002. *Together and Apart in Brzezany: Poles, Jews, and Ukrainians, 1919–1945*. Bloomington ; Indianapolis: Indiana University Press.

Riemann, Gerhard. 1987. *Das Fremdwerden der eigenen Biographie: narrative Interviews mit psychiatrischen Patienten*. Übergänge 19. München: Fink.

Riemann, Gerhard, and Fritz Schütze. 1991. '"Trajectory" as a Basic Theoretical Concept for Analyzing Suffering and Disorderly Social Processes'. In *Social Organization and Social Process. Essays in Honor of Anselm Strauss*, edited by Maines, David R., 333–58. New York: Aldine de Grumer.

Ritter, Laurence, and Max Sivaslian. 2013. *Kılıç artıkları: Türkiye'nin gizli ve müslümanlaşmış Ermenileri*. İstanbul: Hrant Dink Vakfı Yayınları.

Roberts, Jo. 2013. *Contested Land, Contested Memory: Israel's Jews and Arabs and the Ghosts of Catastrophe*. Toronto: Dundurn Press.

Rosenthal, Gabriele. 1995. *Erlebte Und Erzählte Lebensgeschichte: Gestalt Und Struktur Biographischer Selbstbeschreibungen*. Frankfurt/Main ; New York: Campus.

———, ed. 1997. *Der Holocaust Im Leben von Drei Generationen: Familien von Überlebenden Der Shoah Und von Nazi-Tätern*. 2. korr. Aufl. Reihe 'Edition Psychosozial'. Giessen: Psychosozial-Verlag.

Rothberg, Michael. 2009. *Multidirectional Memory: Remembering the Holocaust in the Age of Decolonization*. Cultural Memory in the Present. Stanford, Calif: Stanford University Press.

Rothberg, Michael, and Yasemin Yildiz. 2011. 'Migrant Archives of Holocaust Remembrance in Contemporary Germany'. *Parallax* 17 (4): 32–48.

Rustin, Michael. 2003. 'Reflections on Biographical Turn in Social Science'. In *The Turn to Biographical Methods in Social Science: Comparative Issues and Examples*, edited by Chamberlayne, Prue, Joanna Bornat, and Tom Wengraf, 33–52. New York: Taylor and Francis.

Ryan, Lorraine. 2011. 'Memory, Power and Resistance: The Anatomy of a Tripartite Relationship'. *Memory Studies* 4 (2): 154–69. https://doi.org/10.1177/1750698010366502.

Saint-Laurent, Constance de. 2017. 'Personal Trajectories, Collective Memories: Remembering and the Life-Course'. *Culture & Psychology* 23 (2): 263–79. https://doi.org/10.1177/1354067X17695758.

Saint-Laurent, Constance de, Ignacio Brescó de Luna, Sarah H Awad, and Brady Wagoner. 2017. 'Collective Memory and Social Sciences in the Post-Truth Era'. *Culture & Psychology* 23 (2): 147–55. https://doi.org/10.1177/1354067X17695769.

Sarafian, Ara. 2001. 'The Aborption of Armenian Women and Children into Muslim Households as a Structural Component of The Armenian Genocide'. In *In God's Name: Genocide and Religion in the Twentieth Century (War and Genocide)*, 209–21. War and Genocide 4. Berghahn Books.

Sarafian, Ara. 2011. *Talaat Pasha's Report on the Armenian Genocide*. Gomidas Institute Studies Series. London: Gomidas Institute.

Sasuni, Garo. 1992. *Kürt ulusal hareketleri ve 15. yüzyildan günümüze Ermeni Kürt Iliskileri*. Istanbul: Med Yayinevi.

Schütz, Alfred. 1932. *Der Sinnhafte Aufbau der Sozialen Welt*. Vienna: Springer Vienna. https://doi.org/10.1007/978-3-7091-3108-4.

Schütz, Alfred, and Thomas Luckmann. 2003. *Strukturen der Lebenswelt*. 1. Aufl. UTB 2412. Stuttgart: UVK Verl.-Ges.

Schütze, Fritz. 1981. 'Prozessstrukturen des Lebenslaufs'. In *Biographie in Handlungswissenschaftlicher Perspektive*, edited by Joachim Matthes, 67–156. Nürnberg: Sozialwissenschaftliches Forschungszentrum der Universität Erlangen-Nürnberg.

———. 1983. 'Biographieforschung und narratives Interview'. *neue praxis. Zeitschrift für Sozialarbeit, Sozialpädagogik und Sozialpolitik*, no. 3: 283–93.

———. 1984. 'Kognitive Figuren des autobiographischen Stegreiferzählens'. In *Biographie und soziale Wirklichkeit*, edited by Martin Kohli and Günther Robert, 78–117. Stuttgart: J.B. Metzler. https://doi.org/10.1007/978-3-476-03188-4_5.

———. 1995. 'Verlaufskurven Des Erleidens Als Forschungsgegenstand Der Interpretativen Soziologie'. In *Erziehungswissenschaftliche Biographieforschung*, by Heinz-Hermann Krüger, 116–57. Opladen: Leske + Budrich.

———. 2008a. 'Biography Analysis on the Empirical Base of Autobiographical Narratives: How to Analyse Autobiographical Narrative Interviews – Part I'. *European Studies On Inequality And Social Cohesion* 1 (2): 153–242.

———. 2008b. 'Biography Analysis on the Empirical Base of Autobiographical Narratives: How to Analyse Autobiographical Narrative Interviews – Part II'. *European Studies On Inequality And Social Cohesion* 3 (4): 5–77.

Searle, John R. 2011. *Making the Social World: The Structure of Human Civilization*. First publ. in paperback. Oxford: Oxford Univ. Press.

———. 2013. *Sprechakte: ein sprachphilosophischer Essay*. Translated by R. Wiggershaus. 12. Aufl. Suhrkamp-Taschenbuch Wissenschaft 458. Frankfurt am Main: Suhrkamp.

Şekeryan, Ari, ed. 2015. *1909 Adana Katliamı: Üç Rapor*. Beyoğlu, İstanbul: Aras Yayıncılık.

Seni, Nora. 2016. 'A Breakdown of Memorial Processes in Turkey'. In *Bystanders, Rescuers or Perpetrators? The Neutral Countries and the Shoah*, 289–300. IHRA Series 2. Berlin: Metropol.

Shirinian, George, ed. 2017. *Genocide in the Ottoman Empire: Armenians, Assyrians, and Greeks, 1913–1923*. First edition. New York ; Oxford: Berghahn.

Sivac-Bryant, Sebina. 2016. *Re-Making Kozarac: Agency, Reconciliation and Contested Return in Post-War Bosnia*. Palgrave Studies in Compromise after Conflict. London: Palgrave Macmillan.

Skutnabb-Kangas, Tove, and Sertaç Bucak. 1995. 'Killing a Mother Tongue – How the Kurds Are Deprived of Linguistic Human Rights'. In *Linguistic Human Rights*, edited by Tove Skutnabb-Kangas and Robert Phillipson. Berlin, New York: DE GRUYTER MOUTON. https://doi.org/10.1515/9783110866391.347.

Skutnabb-Kangas, Tove, and Desmond Fernandes. 2008. 'Kurds in Turkey and in (Iraqi) Kurdistan: A Comparison of Kurdish Educational Language Policy in Two Situations of Occupation'. *Genocide Studies and Prevention* 3 (1): 43–73. https://doi.org/10.3138/gsp.3.1.43.

Smart, Carol. 2011. 'Families, Secrets and Memories'. *Sociology* 45 (4): 539–53. https://doi.org/10.1177/0038038511406585.

Somay, Bülent, ed. 2015. *Tarih, Otobiyografi ve Hakikat: Yüzbaşı Torosyan Tartışması ve Türkiye'de Tarihyazımı*. 1. baskı. İstanbul Bilgi Üniversitesi Yayınları ; Tarih, 508. 55. Şişli, İstanbul: İstanbul Bilgi Üniversitesi Yayınları.

Sorokin, Pitirim A., and Robert K. Merton. 1937. 'Social Time: A Methodological and Functional Analysis'. *The American Journal of Sociology* XLII (5): 615–29.

Strauss, Anselm L., and Juliet M. Corbin. 1990. *Basics of Qualitative Research: m Procedures and Techniques*. Newbury Park, Calif: Sage Publications.

Subrt, Jiří. 2014. 'Norbert Elias and the Enigma of Time'. In *Norbert Elias & Empirical Research*, edited by Tatiana Savoia Landini and François Dépelteau, 239–52. New York: Palgrave Macmillan US.

Suciyan, Talin. 2016. *The Armenians in Modern Turkey: Post-Genocide Society, Politics and History*. Library of Ottoman Studies 48. London ; New York: I.B. Tauris.

Suny, Ronald Grigor. 2015. *'They Can Live in the Desert but Nowhere Else': A History of the Armenian Genocide*. Human Rights and Crimes against Humanity. Princeton: Princeton University Press.

Tatz, Colin Martin. 2003. *With Intent to Destroy: Reflecting on Genocide*. London ; New York, N.Y: VERSO.

Ter Minassıan, Anahide. 2016. '20. Yüzyılın Başında Van'. In *Van*, edited by Richard G. Hovannisian, 193–216. Tarihi Kentler ve Ermeniler. Istanbul: Aras Yayıncılık.

Ternon, Yves. 1998. 'Freedom and Responsibility of the Historian: The "Lewis Affair"'. In *Remembrance and Denial: The Case of the Armenian Genocide*, edited by Richard G. Hovannisian, 237–48. Detroit: Wayne State University Press.

Ternon, Yves. 2012. *Bir Soykirim Tarihi. 20 Yil Sonra 'Ermeni Tabusu' Davasi*. Edited by Ragip Zarakolu. Translated by Emirhan Oguz. Belge Yayınları.

Thompson, Paul. 2000. *The Voice of the Past: Oral History*. 3rd ed. Oxford [England] ; New York: Oxford University Press.

Torossian, Sarkis. 2012. *Çanakkale'den Filistin Cephesine*. Edited by Ayhan Aktar. Translated by Gizem Şakar. 1. baskı. Anı dizisi 59. Cağaloğlu, İstanbul: İletişim Yayınları.

Turan, Ömer, and Güven Gürkan Öztan. 2018. *Devlet aklı ve 1915: Türkiye'de 'Ermeni Meselesi' anlatısının inşası*. İletişim Yayınları Araştırma, inceleme dizisi, 2584 426. İstanbul: İletişim Yayınları.

Türker, Nurdan. 2015. *Vatanım Yok, Memleketim Var: İstanbul Rumları: Mekân, Bellek, Ritüel*. 1. baskı. Araştırma-İnceleme Dizisi 365. İstanbul: İletişim.

Türkiye'de Göç ve Yerinden Olmuş Nüfus Araştırması. 2006. Ankara: Hacettepe Üniversitesi Nüfus Etütleri Enstitüsü. http://www.hips.hacettepe.edu.tr/tgyona/TGYONA_rapor.pdf.

Türkyilmaz, Yektan. 2011. 'Rethinking Genocide: Violence and Victimhood in Eastern Anatolia, 1913–1915'. USA: Duke University.

———. 2015a. 'Devrim içinde Devrim: Ermeni Örgütleri ve İttihat-Terakki İlişkileri, 1908–1915'. In *1915. Siyaset, Tehcir, Soykırım*, 324–53. Istanbul: Tarih Vakfı Yurt Yayınları.

———. 2015b. 'Why Do We Need a Historiographic and Conceptual Re-Evaluation of the Armenian Genocide?' presented at the Critical Approaches to the Armenian Genocide. History, Politics and Aesthetics. Workshop Armenian-Turkish Scholarship 2015, Istanbul, October 2. https://www.youtube.

com/watch?v=BvdTrhu6m_I&list=PLrV5tKkl8-JixGpAYWNDmVKQr-LUYlQQGL&index=8.

Unger, Hella von. 2018. 'Forschungsethik, Digitale Archivierung Und Biographische Interviews'. In *Handbuch Biographieforschung*, edited by Helma Lutz, Martina Schiebel, and Elisabeth Tuider, 681–93. Wiesbaden: Springer VS.

Üngör, Uğur Ümit. 2011. *The Making of Modern Turkey: Nation and State in Eastern Anatolia, 1913–1950*. Oxford: Oxford University Press.

———. 2020. Paramilitarism: Mass Violence in the Shadow of the State.

Üngör, Uğur Ümit, and Mehmet Polatel. 2013. *Confiscation and Destruction: The Young Turk Seizure of Armenian Property*. London: Continuum.

Ünlü, Barış. 2014. 'Türklük Sözleşmesi'nin İmzalanışı (1915–1925). In: Mülkiye Dergisi 38(3). 47–81

———. 2018. *Türklük sözleşmesi: oluşumu, işleyişi ve krizi*. 1. baskı. Dipnot Yayınları 279. Ankara: Dipnot yayinlari.

Ussher, Clarence D. 1917. *An American Phsycian in Turkey*. Boston and New York: The Riverside Press Cambridge.

Van Ooijen, Iris, and Ilse Raaijmakers. 2012. 'Competitive or Multidirectional Memory? The Interaction between Postwar and Postcolonial Memory in the Netherlands'. *Journal of Genocide Research* 14 (3–4): 463–83. https://doi.org/10.1080/14623528.2012.719669.

Vico, Giambattista. 1948. *The New Science*. Translated by Thomas Goddard Bergin and Max Herold Fisch. Ithaca, N.Y: Cornell University Press.

Volkan, Vamik. 2001. 'Transgenerational Transmissions and Chosen Traumas: An Aspect of Large Group Identity'. *Group Analysis* 34 (1): 79–97. https://doi.org/10.1177/05333160122077730.

Wall, Sarah. 2015. 'Focused Ethnography: A Methodological Adaptation for Social Research in Emerging Contexts', 15.

Wallerstein, Immanuel. 1988. 'The Inventions of TimeSpace Realities: Towards an Understanding of Our Historical Systems'. *Geography* 73 (4): 289–97.

———. 1998. 'The Time of Space and the Space of Time: The Future of Social Science'. *Political Geography* 17 (1): 71–82. https://doi.org/10.1016/S0962-6298(96)00097-2.

Wang, Qi. 2016. 'Remembering the Self in Cultural Contexts: A Cultural Dynamic Theory of Autobiographical Memory'. *Memory Studies* 9 (3): 295–304. https://doi.org/10.1177/1750698016645238.

Wegner, Jarula MI. 2018. 'Rethinking Countermemory: Black-Jewish Negotiations in Rap Music'. *Memory Studies*, August, 175069801879480. https://doi.org/10.1177/1750698018794801.

Welzer, Harald, Sabine Moller, and Karoline Tschuggnall. 2002. *Opa War Kein Nazi: Nationalsozialismus Und Holocaust Im Familiengedächtnis*.

3. Aufl. Die Zeit Des Nationalsozialismus. Frankfurt am Main: Fischer Taschenbuch.

Wengraf, Tom. 2003. 'Uncovering the General from within the Particular: From Contingencies to Typologiess in the Understanding of Cases'. In *The Turn to Biographical Methods in Social Science: Comparative Issues and Examples*, edited by Prue Chamberlayne, Joanna Bornat, and Tom Wengraf, 140–64. New York: Taylor and Francis.

Wertsch, James V. 2004. *Voices of Collective Remembering*. UK: Cambridge University Press.

———. 2008. 'The Narrative Organization of Collective Memory'. *Ethos* 36 (1): 120–35. https://doi.org/10.1111/j.1548-1352.2008.00007.x.

Wetzel, Juliane. 2003. 'Die Auschwitzlüge'. In *Geschichtsmythen. Legenden über den Nationalsozialismus*, 27–41. Berlin.

Woermann, Niklas. 2018. 'Focusing Ethnography: Theory and Recommendations for Effectively Combining Video and Ethnographic Research'. *Journal of Marketing Management* 34 (5–6): 459–83. https://doi.org/10.1080/0267257X.2018.1441174.

Woolfson, Shivaun. 2013. 'Everything Speaks: A Multidimensional Approach to Researching the Lithuanian Jewish Past'. In *Documents of Life Revisited. Narrative and Biographical Methodology for a 21st Century Critical Humanism*, edited by Liz Stanley, 193–208. UK: Ashgate.

Yılmaz, Altuğ, ed. 2015. *Müslümanlaş(Tiril)Miş Ermeniler: Konferans Tebiğleri Kasım 2013*. İstanbul: Hrant Dink Vakfı Yayınları.

Young, James Edward. 1988. *Writing and Rewriting the Holocaust: Narrative and the Consequences of Interpretation*. Bloomington: Indiana University Press.

Zerubavel, Eviatar. 2003. *Time Maps: Collective Memory and the Social Shape of the Past*. Chicago, Ill: University of Chicago Press.

———. 2006. *The Elephant in the Room: Silence and Denial in Everyday Life*. Oxford ; New York: Oxford University Press.

Zeydanlıoğlu, Welat. 2012. 'Turkey's Kurdish Language Policy'. *International Journal of the Sociology of Language* 2012 (217). https://doi.org/10.1515/ijsl-2012-0051.

Zittoun, Tania. 2017. 'Dynamic Memories of the Collective Past'. *Culture & Psychology* 23 (2): 295–305. https://doi.org/10.1177/1354067X17695768.

Exhibition booklets, Newspaper Articles, Oral History Accounts and Websites

Aghasi Ivazian – Zoryan Institute Oral History Archive. 1987. Sacramento, California.

Agos. 2014. 'Ahmet Türk: Süryani, Ermeni ve Ezidilerden özür diliyorum', 16 December 2014. http://www.agos.com.tr/tr/yazi/9956/ahmet-turk-suryani-ermeni-ve-ezidilerden-ozur-diliyorum.

Agos. ———. 2016. 'Van Belediyesi eşbaşkanı Bekir Kaya tutuklandı', 18 November 2016. http://www.agos.com.tr/tr/yazi/17056/van-belediyesi-esbaskani-bekir-kaya-tutuklandi.

Agos. ———. 2019. 'Hrant Dink Vakfı'nın düzenlediği Kayseri konferansı yasaklandı', 17 October 2019. http://www.agos.com.tr/tr/yazi/23080/hrant-dink-vakfi-nin-duzenledigi-kayseri-konferansi-yasaklandi.

Babil Der, ed. 2015. *'Bizzat Hallediniz'. Telgraflarin Izinde 1915*. Istanbul: Tarih Vakfı.

Balancar, Ferda. 2015. 'Bir başka açıdan Kürtlerin Ermeni Soykırımı'ndaki rolü'. *Agos*, 27 April 2015. http://www.agos.com.tr/tr/yazi/11405/bir-baska-acidan-kurtlerin-ermeni-soykirimindaki-rolu.

bianet. 2019. 'Lake Wiped off the Map by Treasure Hunters to Be Declared Natural Protected Area', 19 November 2019. https://bianet.org/english/environment/216002-lake-wiped-off-the-map-by-treasure-hunters-to-be-declared-natural-protected-area.

Dağlıoğlu, Emre Can. 2016. '1915: Sorumluluk, "Kürtler", "Ermeniler"'. *Azad Alik* (blog). 27 April 2016. https://azadalik.com/2016/04/26/1915-sorumluluk-kurtler-ermeniler/.

Diler, Fatih Gökhan. 2016. '"Derdimiz tüm olayı 1915'e kilitlemeden, o dört yıllık zaman diliminde anlamak"'. *Agos*, 21 April 2016. http://www.agos.com.tr/tr/yazi/15087/derdimiz-tum-olayi-1915-e-kilitlemeden-o-dort-yillik-zaman-diliminde-anlamak.

Eleanor Baker-Ussher – Zoryan Institute Oral History Archive. 1983.

Gül, Mahsuni. 2021. 'Ordu Ermenileri: Müslüman oldular, fislenmekten kurtulamadilar'. *Agos*, 22 April 2021. http://www.agos.com.tr/tr/yazi/25585/ordu-ermenileri-musluman-oldular-fislenmekten-kurtulamadilar.

Gültekin, Uygar. 2016. 'Churches of Diyarbakir Also Expropriated'. *Agos*, 28 March 2016. http://www.agos.com.tr/en/article/14839/churches-of-diyarbakir-also-expropriated.

Haberler.com. 2015. 'Marmara Üniversitesi Rektörü Arat: "Soykırım İddiaları Zamanın Ruhuna Aykırıdır"', 15 May 2015. https://www.haberler.com/marmara-universitesi-rektoru-arat-soykirim-7310677-haberi/?utm_source=facebook&utm_campaign=tavsiye_et&utm_medium=detay.

Milliyet. 2016. 'Van'da çatışma: 1 polis şehit, 12 terörist öldürüldü', 10 January 2016. http://www.milliyet.com.tr/van-da-catisma-1-polis-sehit-12-gundem-2176676/.

Ozinian, Alin. 2014. '"Adil hafıza" ne kadar adil?' *Zaman*, 1 August 2014. http://www.yeniduzen.com/adil-hafiza-ne-kadar-adil-4458yy.htm.

Richard Ashton – Zoryan Institute Oral History Archive. 1986. Fresno, California.

T24. 2016. 'İşte Van'da OHAL kararnamesiyle kapatılan vakıf, dernek ve okullar', 23 July 2016. https://t24.com.tr/haber/ iste-vanda-ohal-kararnamesiyle-kapatilan-vakif-dernek-ve-okullar,351609.

'"Tehcir'in 100.Yılında Türk-Ermeni İlişkilerinin Yarını: Adil Hafıza ve Normalleşme" Sempozyumu Daveti'. Marmara University Invitatation Letter. 2015, May 2015. http://dosya.marmara.edu.tr/www/etkinlik/2015/mayis/ Ermeni_iliskileri_Davetiye_023.jpg.

Tert.Am. 2010. 'Van Times Published Also in Armenian', 18 September 2010. https://www.tert.am/en/news/2010/09/18/vantimes/186735.

Türkyilmaz, Yektan. 2016. 'Tarih vertigosu, hafıza hipnozu: Nar Niyetiyle Hatirlamak'. *Agos*, 21 April 2016. http://www.agos.com.tr/tr/yazi/15089/ tarih-vertigosu-hafiza-hipnozu-nar-niyetiyle-hatirlamak.

Van Sesi Gazetesi. 2014. 'Zeve Toplu Mezar Kazisi', 2 April 2014. http://www. vansesigazetesi.com/haber-van__zeve_toplu_mezar_kazisi-14588.html.

Van Sesi Gazetesi. 2016a. 'YYÜ'den Anlamlı Etekinlik: Van Zeve'ye Yürüyecek', 24 April 2016. http://www.vansesigazetesi.com/haber-_yyuden__ anlamli_etekinlik_van__zeveye_yuruyecek-31623.html.

Van Sesi Gazetesi. 2016b. 'Van Zeve'ye Yürüyor', 25 April 2016. http://www. vansesigazetesi.com/haber-van_zeve'ye_yuruyor-31680.html.

Index

Adana Massacre 69, 71, 76
agency
    agency of Armenians 241
    agency of perpetrators 240
    agency of the victimised 231
    Armenian agency 170
    cultural agency 129
    political agency 162
anachronism 59, 60, 145, 173, 202, 203, 238, 240, 247, 248, 250, 256, 259,
    269
anachronistic 60, 167, 171, 172, 173, 202, 203, 220, 229, 239, 248, 250, 256
ARF 69, 74, 76, 79, 80, 81, 82, 83, 86, 94
argumentative form (motive, passage, segment, and scheme as well) 34, 35,
    36, 52, 70, 85, 146, 159, 160, 163, 167, 182, 201, 233, 253, 261
    descriptive 34, 35, 38, 153, 154, 174, 177, 189, 211, 220
Berlin Congress 71, 92
biographical identity 31, 33, 34, 35, 41
biographical process 35
collective identity 18, 129
collective references 139, 169, 172, 197, 200, 202, 222, 234, 235, 237, 241,
    243, 257, 258, 259, 260, 262, 263, 268
commemoration 44, 83, 105, 108, 116, 127, 128, 132, 150
confiscation 64, 75, 146, 175. *See also* expropriation, plunder, and *talan*
Congress of Berlin 77
contestation (of memories and contested memories as well) 25, 44, 57, 59, 61,
    177, 220, 261, 265, 270
    contested landscape (of memories) 19, 260, 268
    non-contested memory 61
continuity argument 249, 256
continuity of violence 139, 141, 143, 144, 209, 210, 212, 214, 245, 255, 256, 269
contrasting juxtaposition 209
CUP 65, 66, 67, 68, 69, 70, 73, 74, 75, 76, 77, 79, 81, 83, 92, 93, 106, 136,
    138, 146, 173
curfew 20, 194, 195, 196, 197, 212, 213, 222, 226, 233
Dashnak 69, 73, 74, 83
denialism 19, 24, 88, 91, 96, 97, 100, 101, 102, 103, 104, 105, 106, 107, 109,
    114, 115, 116, 122, 127, 128, 129, 135, 137, 140, 143, 144, 148, 149, 150,
    174, 221, 257, 262, 263, 267

Dersim Genocide 19, 96, 105, 136
DGM 213, 255
disobedience 58, 101, 149, 150, 160, 176, 177, 182, 217, 218, 219, 253
    epistemic disobedience 58, 149, 177, 219
displaced people 89, 125
displacement 77, 125, 131, 132
epistemic disobedience 58, 149, 177, 219
exhibition 101, 109, 111, 112, 113, 116, 117, 118, 119, 120, 121, 149, 150
    Bizzat Hallediniz 116, 117, 118, 119, 120, 121, 150, 257
    Left Behind (or Left Over) 90, 121
    Nar Niyetiyle 101, 111, 112, 116, 121
expropriation 65, 71, 75, 226
forced adoptees 92
forced conversion 72, 77
framework 20, 39, 41, 45, 46, 54, 58, 67, 70, 99, 101, 102, 103, 109, 112, 114,
    122, 132, 138, 170, 171, 172, 189, 201, 210, 214, 223, 231, 236, 237, 245,
    248, 251, 254, 256, 262
Hamidian massacres 64, 68, 71, 79, 93, 97, 134
Hamidiye cavalries
    regiments 72, 73, 135, 170
idealisation 114, 143, 232, 236, 237
    idealised coexistence 110, 143, 240
    idealised Ottoman past 109
    idealised victim 236
identity figuration 76
impunity 65, 107, 113, 127, 139, 155, 185, 186, 222, 259, 265, 266, 268, 269
instrumentalisation 105, 133, 138, 139, 140, 141, 142, 143, 145, 146, 169,
    170, 171, 172, 173, 174, 235, 237, 238, 239, 240, 241, 242, 247, 259, 262
Islamised Armenians 143, 144, 147, 155, 171, 174, 231, 239
Just Memory 101, 109, 110, 111, 112, 114, 116, 137, 148, 149
Kirvelik 145, 237
Kurdish identity 128, 133, 138, 184
Kurdish language 153, 162, 163, 164, 178, 182, 187, 231, 246
language policies 252
Left Behind 90, 121
linguicide 222
multidirectional 19, 60, 61, 62, 131, 142, 168, 174, 220, 235, 242, 267, 268
mutual killings 93, 137, 229, 264, 266
national identity 75, 138, 241
PKK 16, 17, 20, 41, 122, 128, 140, 187, 194, 197, 205, 227, 250, 263
plunder 64, 65, 75, 76, 77, 85, 88, 92, 96, 117, 226, 227

post-extermination 63, 64, 93, 97, 146, 232
reactions 35, 39, 191, 202
reintegration 92, 268, 269
resistance in Van 84, 172, 241
resistance of Vanetsis 79, 130
social time 17, 19, 208, 210, 243, 245, 247, 248, 256, 257, 259, 268
Sur 179, 181, 186, 193, 196, 197, 199, 200, 203, 226, 249
Susurluk accident 158, 159
talan 85, 88, 226
trajectory 18, 20, 36, 41, 47, 49, 67, 100, 136, 156, 159, 160, 165, 176, 177,
    183, 184, 186, 188, 199, 203, 205, 206, 207, 208, 209, 210, 216, 217, 218,
    224, 225, 231, 235, 237, 241, 254, 257, 258, 260, 261, 266
urbicide 88, 98, 127
victimhood narrative 58, 128, 138, 139, 217, 241, 242

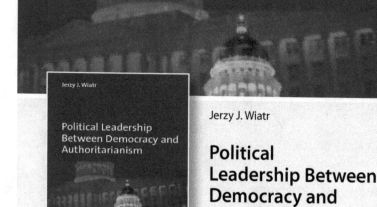

Jerzy J. Wiatr

Political Leadership Between Democracy and Authoritarianism

Comparative and Historical Perspectives

2022. 203 pp. • Hardcover • 42,00 € (D) • 43,20 € (A)
ISBN 978-3-8474-2538-0 • eISBN 978-3-8474-1693-7

This book sheds light on the theory of political leadership, which is still an under-researched field of political science. It is related to the philosophical argument about determinism versus activism and helps to understand the basic conflict of the 21st century between liberal democracy and new authoritarianism. The book looks at Max Weber's typology of political rule and his concept of the ethics of responsibility, which are key to the theory of leadership. The author shows that the unfinished contest between democracy and new authoritarianism in the 21st century confirms the importance of leadership in old and new democracies as well as in the neo-authoritarian regimes and calls for a new type of political leaders.

www.shop.budrich.de